Place
Names
in
Alabama

Virginia O. Foscue

Place Names in Alabama

The University of Alabama Press
Tuscaloosa and London

Copyright © 1989
The University of Alabama Press
Tuscaloosa, Alabama 35487–0380
All rights reserved
Manufactured in the
United States of America

Library of Congress
Cataloging-in-Publication Data
Foscue, Virginia O.
    Place names in Alabama / by Virginia O. Foscue.
       p.   cm.
    Bibliography: p.
    ISBN 0-8173-0410-X
    1. Names, Geographical—Alabama—Dictionaries. 2. Alabama—
History, Local. 3. English language—Etymology—Names. I. Title.
F324.F67 1989
917.61'003'21—dc19   88-828

British Library Cataloguing-in-Publication
Data available

3 4 5 6 7 8 9 • 07 06 05 04 03 02 01 00

Contents

Acknowledgments
vii

Introduction
1

Phonetic Symbols
4

**Dictionary of Place Names
in Alabama**
5

Sources
153

Appendix: Maps of Alabama, 1820–1903
169

Acknowledgments

For the grant-in-aid that enabled me to complete the research for this study and for the mini-grant I used to have the maps prepared I am grateful to the Research Grants Committee of The University of Alabama. For help in finding essential information I am indebted to the staff of The University of Alabama Library, particularly Joyce Lamont, Curator of Special Collections, and her assistant Gunetta Rich; Sarah Reeves, Documents Librarian; Frances Barton, Microtext Librarian; Alex Sartwell and Dorothy Brady of the Geological Survey of Alabama Library; and the staffs of the Birmingham Public Library and the Alabama Department of Archives and History.

I also wish to express my appreciation to the graduate research assistants who helped me, particularly Alan Holmes and Melissa Ridge; all my informants, who are named in the bibliography; James B. McMillan, who was an ever helpful source of information and criticism; and Malcolm M. MacDonald, Director of The University of Alabama Press, whose encouragement enabled me to complete this volume.

Place
Names
in
Alabama

Introduction

Because the geographic names in a region can reveal a wealth of information about the land and its inhabitants, they deserve careful study. I became interested in Alabama place names in 1957, after I. Willis Russell encouraged me to write my master's thesis at The University of Alabama about the names in my home county of Sumter.

The only book then available about names throughout the state was William A. Read's *Indian Place Names in Alabama*, first published in 1937. After that date, several studies of the names in one or two counties were completed, but no systematic statewide investigation was considered until 1973. At that time, graduate students in my English language classes at The University of Alabama in Tuscaloosa and colleagues like James B. McMillan who have long been interested in Alabama place names began assisting me with the project that was to be designated, five years later, the Place Name Survey of Alabama. This comprehensive study is to be a part of the Place Name Survey of the United States, now being conducted under the auspices of the American Name Society, a group of scholars organized in 1951 to do research in all areas of onomastics.

In 1982 W. Stuart Harris published *Alabama Place-Names*, an independent study of the names of well-known geographic features. Although the book contains interesting historical details, Harris relies upon the explanations given in secondary sources, not all of which are accurate; he omits important names like those of two current county seats without stating the reasons for his choices; and he ignores the linguistic aspects of most of the names he does include. Therefore, after closely examining his book, I continued writing this one, already begun in order to make available the preliminary findings of the Alabama survey.

Although the complete linguistic and statistical analysis of the state's names must await the completion of the survey, my assistants and I have collected enough data to reveal the significance of place-name study in Alabama. One observation is that the state has preserved a large number of American Indian forms in its geographic names. According to William A. Read in *Indian Place Names in Alabama* (xi), the native American tribes once inhabiting the land within the present state boundaries belong to the Muskhogean

1

family. Most of the names are derived from the languages of the Choctaw and the Creek or Muskogee tribes.

The etymological information contained in the entries for these names in the following dictionary was obtained from Read's book and from the appendix by James B. McMillan included in the revised edition of 1984. As Read observes in his introduction (xiii–xiv), the Indian names consist primarily of "designations of animals, birds, fish, soil, reptiles, water-courses, plants, trees, settlements, and prominent features of the landscape" and "personal and tribal names." Most of them are composed of more than one element: in names like *Tuscaloosa* an adjective follows a noun, in those like *Sucarnochee* the equivalent of the English *his*-genitive is used, and in others like *Alamuchee* and *Arbacoochee* a diminutive or locative suffix occurs. Other details about Alabama's Indian names can be found in their dictionary entries.

European colonists, as well, left evidence of their importance in Alabama place names. Between 1507 and 1699 Spanish adventurers, among them Hernando de Soto, explored much of the land later included within the state's boundaries and claimed it for their rulers. Between 1699 and 1763 the French, first under the command of Jean Baptiste Le Moyne, Sieur de Bienville, occupied the area around Mobile Bay. In 1763 the British gained possession of this land and held it until 1783 when the Spaniards, for the second time, occupied it. They, in turn, held the region bordered by the Gulf of Mexico until 1798 when the United States organized the Mississippi Territory, which then included Alabama, after obtaining the land by treaty. Between 1817 and 1819 Alabama was a separate territory, finally becoming a state on December 14, 1819. Such place names as *Bayou la Batre, St. Stephens*, and *Majors Creek* date back to the periods of European occupation of the land that is now Alabama.

From 1798 through the early 1900s people moving into the area from other states gave their new settlements the names of older towns to the north or east such as Society Hill in South Carolina. They also remembered the soldiers and statesmen from their homes, five counties receiving the names of early presidents of the country. These settlers preserved many of the names of local landowners and community leaders, *Huntsville*

and *Guntersville* being well-known examples. The many descriptive designations they chose provide information about the natural regions in the state, its abundant streams, and its varied flora and fauna. In addition, the settlers revealed their humor with names like *Lickskillet*, their ideals with those like *Christian Home*, and their love for their churches in their practice of naming towns for the building that was the nucleus of the community.

The following dictionary of 2,700 names of approximately two thousand geographic features, selected from the Place Name Survey of Alabama and listed alphabetically, includes entries for the names of all towns of over one hundred people and a sizable number of smaller settlements and communities with fewer inhabitants than that figure, as determined by the 1980 census, and all the incorporated municipalities in the state. From the most recent United States Geological Survey Base Maps of Alabama, I obtained all the names of the state's counties, cities, towns, communities, mountains, valleys, capes, islands, rivers, creeks, lakes, bays, lagoons, and sounds appearing on them. Because these maps were published in 1966, I updated my collection with the names of some 240 towns and communities and twenty lakes, these being the ones not on the U.S.G.S. Base Maps that are on the *1983–84 Official Alabama Highway Department Map*, the most recent edition when I completed my research. In addition, I include the 30 municipalities incorporated between 1968 and 1980 not on any of the maps. Because I name the former county seats as well as the current one in county entries, I also have separate entries for the 40 former county seats not on the maps, even though some of these are "dead" towns (see Harris 1977, vii). Finally, because I discuss earlier or alternative names of the geographic features, I also include most of these in the alphabetical list.

The only names not cross-referenced but discussed in entries for current towns or *communities* or for major streams are longer names of the features that consist of the current name plus a morpheme like *-ville* or one or more words like *city*; no-longer-used early spellings of Indian names; names of buildings such as stores, churches, schools, mills, and gins that were the focal points for settlements or communities; designations including the generic terms *cowpen, field, precinct* and *beat* (a *regional* word meaning 'voting precinct') of areas where settlements or communities later developed; and tributaries of large streams whose names begin with words such as *little* or *east* denoting size or direction. Information about these tributaries can be found under the names of the larger streams that they feed.

I am aware that there must be other names for many of these places than the small number I have included in this study. Also, I recognize that all readers familiar with Alabama will think of names of significant places I have excluded. The reason for such exclusions is that I could not treat all of the more than 52,000 place names in the state in a single volume. Local authorities in some counties have suggested additional names, but I was unable to find such people throughout the state. Because I did not wish to include a disproportionate number of names from only a few counties and because a word like *significant* has different connotations for different people, I decided to use only the objective criteria I have listed above to make my selections.

The following information, if it could be found, is included in the name entries

1. the current name and other names the place has had;
2. the pronunciation of the current name used by the majority of residents transcribed in phonetic symbols (see Phonetic Symbols), unless a transcription is already available in a biographical, geographical, or English language dictionary;
3. the identification of the feature, unless this is obvious from its name;
4. the location of the place in latitude and longitude to the nearest second (for streams, the coordinates for both the source and the point at which the river or creek empties into a larger stream or body of water), followed by the name of the county or counties;
5. the origin of each name of the feature and the circumstances of each naming;
6. the classification of the name according to type (personal, descriptive, inspirational, etc.) and the process by which the name was formed, unless such details are obvious;
7. the earliest date I have been able to find (for obsolete names, both the earliest and the latest discoverable dates);
8. the source or sources from which I obtained the information about the origin and/or the circumstances of the naming.

Although most studies of the place names in a state locate the places by merely naming the county in which each is located, and a few others contain statements of the approximate distance and direction of the place from a better-known one, I have chosen, instead, to include in most of the dictionary entries the more exact degrees of latitude and longitude. However, readers not familiar with computer-printed coordinates may find these difficult to understand. To locate the city of Birmingham in Jefferson County, for example, one interprets 333114NO864809W as 'Latitude 33 degrees, 31 minutes, 14 seconds north' and 'Longitude 86 degrees, 48 minutes, 9 seconds west' and uses these coordinates in the same way as the letters and numbers appearing to the right of the names of settlements in the indices on recent state maps like those of the Alabama Highway Department and Rand McNally Company.

Many of the sources for the origin of the name and circumstances of the naming given in the dictionary entries are secondary ones, though I did consult all available primary sources as well. To avoid needless repetition, I have not included the following references in every name entry. I obtained the geographic coordinates for the places from the *Alabama Geographic Names: Alphabetical Finding List*, prepared by the Office of Geographic and Cartographic Research of U.S.G.S., which I then verified with the Department of Agriculture Soil Maps of Alabama. The dates for the post offices are from microfilms of the "Record of Appointment of Postmasters." The dates of incorporation of municipalities are from the complete list sent to me by John F. Watkins, Executive Director of the Alabama League of Municipalities, which I then verified by consulting the published acts of the Alabama general assembly and legislature or local elected officials. These sources and every other book, article, manuscript, document, map, and individual from which or whom I obtained information is identified in the bibliography, listing some six hundred items, at the end of the book. Also included in this list are unpublished works cited by such authors as Bush, McMillan, Rich, Sockwell, and Tamarin that I was unable to consult myself.

Readers interested in the history of Alabama may expect more facts about each place than would be appropriate in a study in which the emphasis is upon the names of places rather than the places themselves. However, if, for example, these readers wish to learn the name of the county or counties in which an older settlement that was not a county seat was located before the creation of its present county, they can do so in two ways. The first is by finding the place on a recent map, using its latitude and longitude as explained above, and then comparing this recent map with the ones in the appendix that show in chronological order the changing names and boundaries of Alabama's counties. The other way is by consulting one or more of the historical sources listed in the bibliography.

It has not been possible for me to account fully for all the place names I selected nor have I been able to answer all questions likely to occur to readers of some of the more nearly complete name entries. However, I have included all the facts that I could find about each name and the circumstances of its naming. When I use undocumented information, I indicate that I am doing so. Each folk etymology contains either the phrase "traditional explanation" or "it is said." The most reasonable suppositions contain the word "probably." The less likely ones begin with "possibly" or "perhaps" or are phrased "may be."

Because some questions about the Alabama place names in this book remain unanswered despite my efforts and those of my assistants to find all the facts, I urge those readers who can supply information to complete or correct any of the dictionary entries to send it to me so that I may include it in the Place Name Survey of Alabama and in later editions of this book.

Phonetic Symbols

The phonetic symbols in the transcriptions of the names considered most likely to be mispronounced by persons not familiar with them are those of the International Phonetic Alphabet. The exceptions to conventional phonetic transcription are my uses of [ɜr] and [ər] to represent r-colored vowels; [ən], [əm], and [əl] for syllabics; single vowel symbols

like [e] rather than [eɪ] and [o] rather than [ou] for tense vowels; and no diacritics to show modification of the vowels.

International Phonetic Alphabet

Symbol	Key Word	Transcription
ɑ	cod	[kɑd]
æ	cad	[kæd]
ɛ	fed	[fɛd]
ɪ	kid	[kɪd]
ʌ	cud	[kʌd]
ɔ	caught	[kɔt]
e	fade	[fed]
i	feed	[fid]
u	food	[fud]
o	code	[kod]
ʊ	could	[kʊd]
aɪ, a	wide	[waɪd], [wad]
aʊ	loud	[laʊd]
ɔɪ	coil	[kɔɪl]
ɜr	curl	[kɜrl]
ə	away	[ə'we]
b	bait	[bet]
d	date	[det]
g	gate	[get]
h	hate	[het]
hw	white	[hwaɪt]
j	yoke	[jok]
f	fate	[fet]
s	safe	[sef]
θ	thin	[θɪn]
ð	then	[ðɛn]
ʋ	vane	[ʋen]
z	zone	[zon]
l	lane	[len]
m	main	[men]
n	name	[nem]
p	paid	[ped]
t	tame	[tem]
k	code	[kod]
r	rake	[rek]
w	wake	[wek]
ŋ	sing	[sɪŋ]
ʃ	shame	[ʃem]
tʃ	chain	[tʃen]
ʒ	rouge	[ruʒ]
dʒ	jail	[dʒel]

ˈ = primary stress   ˌ = secondary stress

4

Dictionary of Place Names in Alabama

ABANDA [əˈbændə] Settlement with discontinued PO at 330603NO853147W in Chambers Co. When the Atlanta, Birmingham and Atlantic RR (Atlantic Coast Line) was routed through this area, the town was founded and given for its name the acronym for the RR *A.B. and A*. PO est. in 1908 (Dugas [Chambers Co.] 56).

ABBEVILLE [ˈæbɪvəl] Inc. co. seat with PO at 313418NO851502W in Henry Co. Named for nearby ABBIE CREEK. Became co. seat in 1831 and acquired its PO in 1833. Inc. in 1872 (T. M. Owen 1:1).

ABBEVILLE JUNCTION See GRIMES in Dale Co.

ABBIE CREEK Stream rising at 314343NO851558W in Barbour Co. and joining Sandy Creek at 312442NO850448W in Henry Co. YATTAYABBA C. on La Tourette's 1844 map. Owen derives name from Creek *ataphalgi*, a compound of *atapha* 'dogwood' and *algi* 'grove,' but Read says that if the first element has been transposed from Creek *atapha*, then the second may be Creek *api* 'trunk of a tree' or 'tree.' The voiceless sound [p] of this second element then assimilated to the vowels surrounding it, becoming the voiced sound [b] in the current form of the name (T. M. Owen 1:1; Read 3).

ABEL Community with discontinued PO at 333255NO854245W in Cleburne Co. Probably a biblical name, for the son of Adam and Eve who was killed by his brother Cain. PO est. in 1889.

ABERFOIL Settlement with discontinued PO at 320413NO854116W in Bullock Co. Probably named for the village Aberfoyle, mentioned in *Rob Roy*, the novel by Sir Walter Scott. PO est. in 1837.

ABERNANT [ˈæbərˌnænt] Settlement with PO at 331725NO871153W in Tuscaloosa Co. Named for the local Abernanth family and the Abernant Coal Co., active during the early 1900s. Earliest form of the name was ABERNANTH CITY. PO est. in 1902 (Rand McNally, 1894 map; Rich 1979, 71).

ABERNANTH CITY See ABERNANT in Tuscaloosa Co.

ACKERVILLE Settlement with discontinued PO at 320146NO870359W in Wilcox Co. Named for the local Acker family. PO est. in 1892 (Harris 1982, 11).

ACMAR Settlement with PO at 333717NO862946W in St. Clair Co. Designation is a combination of the first syllable of *Acton*, name of a nearby mining community in Shelby Co., and the first syllable of *Margaret*, name of the wife of Charles F. DeBardeleben, a director of the coal mining operation here. PO est. in 1911 (Crow 85, 133; Rich).

ACORN   See AKRON in Hale Co.

ACTIVE   Settlement with discontinued PO at 325204NO865837W in Bibb Co. on the Mobile and Ohio RR. An inspirational or symbolic name. PO est. in 1899 (Ellison 192, 197).

ACTON   Settlement with discontinued PO at 332122NO864825W in Shelby Co. Probably named for William Acton, born in KY in 1805, who became one of the earliest coalmine operators in the area and who also served as a Presbyterian minister. PO est. in 1908 (Tamarin 1).

ADA   Settlement with discontinued PO at 320619NO861635W in Montgomery Co. Named for the wife of Willis V. Bell, the first postmaster, appointed in 1881 (Harris 1982, 11).

ADAMSBURG   Settlement with discontinued PO at 342356NO854020W in DeKalb Co. Named for Simon Russell Canfield Adams, a minister from Fort Payne, who donated land for a school here. PO est. in 1902 (Landmarks 79).

ADAMSVILLE   Inc. town with PO at 333603NO865722W in Jefferson Co. Named for William B. Adams, whose house served as a temporary depot for the Kansas City, Memphis and Birmingham RR (St. Louis and San Francisco). PO est. in 1890. Inc. in 1901 (Brown and Nabers 189; Hagood 20).

ADDISON   Inc. town with PO at 341208NO871053W in Winston Co. May have been named for a local family, or possibly for Addison Co., VT, because some of the settlers of Winston Co. came from New England. The Addison PO was est. in 1888 in Cobb's Store, the business of Martha W. Cobb, the first postmaster (Ford; Harris 1982, 11).

ADGER   Settlement with PO at 332302NO870513W in Jefferson Co. Named for Andrew Adger, from Charleston, SC, who was secretary and treasurer of the first mine operations here. PO est. in 1889 (Brown and Nabers 195; Hagood 31–32).

ADKINS GAP   See GOODWATER in Coosa Co.

ADKINSON HEAD   First name of the settlement in Barbour Co. moved in the 1880s approximately 1 mile west to its new location on the Central of Georgia RR and renamed CLIO. After the move, the settlement remaining at the original location became known as OLD CLIO. Its first name was probably for the first postmaster, William A. Adkinson, appointed in 1855, and for the town's location at the head of Little Judy Creek (Ellis 26).

AFFONEE CREEK   ['æfoni]   Stream rising at 325952NO872042W in Bibb Co. and flowing into the Cahaba River at 325206NO871105W. AFANEE C. on La Tourette's 1844 map. Choctaw *nafoni* 'bones' is the source of the name (Read 3).

AFRICA   See NATCHEZ in Monroe Co.

AIMWELL   Community with discontinued PO at 320717NO875422W in Marengo Co. An inspirational and symbolic name, for Aimwell Baptist Church, founded in 1860. PO est. in 1890 (W. Smith).

AIR PO   See ODEN RIDGE in Morgan Co.

AKRON   Inc. town with PO at 325235NO874433W in Hale Co. First given the environmental name ACORN, but after the Alabama Great Southern RR reached here, its officials changed the name to AKRON for the city in OH. PO est. in 1871. Inc. in 1918 (Holliman).

ALABAMA   Twenty-second state, admitted to the Union on Dec. 14, 1819. Bounded on the north by TN, on the east by GA, on the south by FL and the Gulf of Mexico, and on the west by MS. Part of the MS Territory, 1798–1817. In 1817 became a separate territory, named for the Alabama River, with its territorial capital at St. Stephens. Its state capitals have been Huntsville, a temporary one in 1819; Cahaba, 1819–26; Tuscaloosa, 1826–46; and Montgomery, the present one, since 1846 (V. V. Hamilton xviii, 10, 122; Matte 364; Read 4).

ALABAMA PORT   Settlement on Mobile Bay with discontinued PO at 302146NO880653W in Mobile Co. Named for the state. PO est. in 1905 (Boudousquie, 1889 map).

ALABAMA RIVER   Stream formed by the confluence of the Coosa and Tallapoosa rivers at 323021NO861558W between Elmore Co. and Montgomery Co. It flows southwest until it forms the boundary between Clarke Co. and Baldwin Co. and joins the Tombigbee River at 310809NO875636W east of Washington Co. It was called RIVIÈRE DES ALIBAMONS by the early French cartographers. The Alabama Indians were an Upper Creek tribe known to the French as early as 1702 as the "Alibamons." Read derives their name, which he translates as 'thicket clearers,' from Choctaw *alba* 'plants' and *amo* 'to cut, to gather.' Swanton believes *alba* is to be understood in a medicinal sense so that the name means something like 'herb gatherers' (Read 4; Swanton 1937, 212).

ALABASTER Inc. town with PO at 331439NO864859W in Shelby Co. Name refers to the large body of high-calcium limestone upon which the town is located. A lime plant was opened here in the early 1930s by George Scott, Sr. PO est. in 1951. Inc. in 1952 (Thompson High School 50).

ALAMUCHEE CREEK [ˌælə'mʌtʃ/i] Stream rising in MS and joining the Sucarnochee River at 322938NO881001W in Sumter Co. ALLIMUCHA C. on La Tourette's 1844 map. The name may mean 'a little hiding place,' from Choctaw *alumushi*, a compound of *aluma* 'hiding place' and the suffix *-ushi* 'little,' or it may mean 'hiding places are there' if the second element is Choctaw *asha* 'are there' (Read 4).

ALANTHUS See HALLTOWN in Franklin Co.

ALBERTA Settlement with PO at 321355NO872436W in Wilcox Co. on the Mobile and Birmingham RR (Southern). Named for the wife of Thomas G. Bush, president of the RR. PO, first called ALBERTA STATION, est. in 1888 (Harris 1982, 13).

ALBERTVILLE Inc. town with PO at 341603NO861232W in Marshall Co. Named for Thomas A. Albert, a native of GA who moved here before 1860 and was a town leader until his death in 1876. Inc. in 1891. PO est. in 1910 (Roden 52).

ALDRICH Settlement with PO at 330627NO865328W in Shelby Co. Named for the Aldrich brothers, William F. and Truman H., who came here from NY in 1874. That year Truman est. T. H. Aldrich & Co., an extensive coal-mining operation. In 1883 William was appointed first postmaster (Tamarin 1).

ALDRIDGE Settlement at 334225NO871431W in Walker Co. Also called STITH, possibly an abbreviation of *stithy* 'anvil' or 'smithy.' One of the oldest coal-mining towns in the co., it was named, c. 1870, for an early local family (Gant).

ALEXANDER CITY Inc. town with PO at 325638NO855714W in Tallapoosa Co. First building here was called *Georgia Trading Post* or *Store*, probably because the trader came from GA. In 1872 the settlement was inc. as YOUNGSVILLE. Named for the family of Harrison Young, father of Bird Young, the model for J. J. Hooper's fictional character Simon Suggs. By 1873 when the Savannah and Memphis RR (Central of Georgia) was being routed through Youngsville, the name was changed to honor E. P. Alexander, president of the RR. PO est. in 1873 (Dugas [Tallapoosa Co.] 86).

ALEXANDER CROSSROADS See UNDERWOOD CROSSROADS in Colbert Co.

ALEXANDRIA Settlement with PO at 334626NO855308W in Calhoun Co. In 1828 M. M. Houston, the Indian agent, operated Houston's Store here; after a battle of the Creek Indian War of 1813–14 was fought near here, area identified as *Battle Ground*. In 1834 town called COFFEEVILLE for John Coffee, commander of the TN troops at the Battle of Tallaseehatchee. Later that year the PO was est. and named for the Alexander family who had settled in the area in the early 1830s. Two years later the town was given the name of its PO (Jolly).

ALICEVILLE Inc. town with PO at 330746NO880905W in Pickens Co. Named for the wife of John T. Cochrane, president of the Tuscaloosa Belt Line (Alabama, Tennessee and Northern RR). PO est. in 1903. Inc. in 1907 (N. F. Brown 23; T. M. Owen 1:38).

ALICEVILLE LAKE Artificial lake made by the impoundment of the Tombigbee River with Aliceville Lock and Dam in 1981 at 331341NO881727W in Pickens Co. Named for the town. Also called PICKENSVILLE LAKE for another nearby town (N. F. Brown).

ALLEN Community with PO at 313547NO874340W in Clarke Co. In 1813 a defensive fort was founded in this area and named FORT MADISON for James Madison

(1751–1836), president of the U.S. (1809–17). After the Southern RR reached this point, the settlement was called SUGGSVILLE STATION for the town located 1 1/2 miles to the east. Now known as ALLEN in honor of Allen Coleman, an early settler. Allen PO est. in 1900 (Clarke Co. Historical Society 17).

ALLEN CREEK Stream rising at 325834NO852347W in Clarke Co. and joining Chatahospee Creek at 325835NO853354W. Probably honors a local family.

ALLENTON Settlement with discontinued PO at 315550NO870125W in Wilcox Co. Probably named for a local family. PO est. in 1832.

ALLGOOD Inc. town with PO at 335443NO863034W in Blount Co. By 1848 known as CHEPULTEPEC in honor of the location of an American victory in the Mexican War. Renamed for one of the founding families, probably that of William B. Allgood, the first postmaster of Allgood, appointed in 1912. Inc. in 1959 (Blount Co. Historical Society 31; T. M. Owen 1:156).

ALLSBORO Settlement with discontinued PO at 344139NO880637W in Colbert Co. Named for the family of Bradley Alsobrook ['ɔlz,bruk]. PO est. in 1851 (Sockwell).

ALMA Community with discontinued PO at 312750NO874514W in Clarke Co. Named for Alma Flinn from Barlow Bend, the community's first schoolteacher. PO est. in 1890 (Clarke Co. Historical Society 19).

ALMOND ['ɔlmənd] Community with discontinued PO at 330847NO853718W in Randolph Co. Probably named for first postmaster, Almond P. Hunter, appointed in 1852 ("Record of Appointment of Postmasters").

ALPINE Settlement with PO at 332055NO861419W in Talladega Co. Named for Alpine, plantation home of Nathaniel Welch near the Alabama and Tennessee Rivers RR (Southern), routed here during the 1850s. PO est. in 1858 (McMillan).

ALSTON See TEXASVILLE in Barbour Co.

ALTON Settlement with PO at 333445NO-863815W in Jefferson Co. Perhaps a descriptive name, a combination of *alt* 'high' and *-ton* 'town.' PO est. in 1908 (Sartwell).

ALTOONA Inc. town with PO at 340134NO861934W in Etowah Co. Founded in 1900 and named for the city in PA by W. T. Underwood of Birmingham, who owned coal

mines here. PO est. in 1900. Inc. in 1907 (Jolly; E. L. Watson 200).

ALVAREZ STATION See SARALAND in Mobile Co.

ANDALUSIA ['ændə,luʒə] Inc. co. seat with PO at 311715NO862810W in Covington Co. First called NEW SITE because John W. Robinson gave land here in 1844 for a new co. seat after the flooding of Montezuma, the original one. In 1847 given the same name as the PO, which had been est. in 1844 and called ANDALUSIA for the region in southwest Spain. Inc. in 1901 (T. M. Owen 1:48).

ANDERSON Inc. town with PO at 345542NO871559W in Lauderdale Co. Settled c. 1825 and first named ANDERSONS CREEK for the creek. Anderson PO est. in 1860. Inc. in 1973 (Sockwell).

ANDERSON CREEK Stream rising at 345650NO871659W in Lauderdale Co. and joining Elk River at 344848NO871323W. Named for Samuel Anderson, who built a gristmill, before 1820, by the creek (Sockwell).

ANDERTON PO First PO for nearby CLEVELAND in Blount Co. Est. in 1879 and named for John Anderton, Sr., an early settler (Blount Co. Historical Society 27; Weaver).

ANNEMANIE [,æni'meni] Settlement with PO at 320310NO873415W in Wilcox Co. Named for Anne, the daughter of A. M. Manie, the owner of a cotton gin here. PO est. in 1893 (Harris 1982, 15).

ANNISTON ['ænɪstən] Inc. co. seat with PO at 333935NO854954W in Calhoun Co. First called WOODSTOCK for the Woodstock Iron Co., but that name was soon changed to ANNIE'S TOWN, for Mrs. Annie Scott Tyler, wife of Alfred L. Tyler, president of the South Carolina RR and a founder of the city. Name shortened to ANNISTON a few days later, when the PO application was submitted. PO est. in 1873. Inc. in 1879 and made co. seat in 1899 (Jolly).

ANSLEY ['ænslɪ] Settlement with discontinued PO at 315310NO860657W in Pike Co. First named BERRYVILLE for a family who settled here c. 1869. After the Alabama Midland RR reached the town in 1889, the name was changed to honor Willie Whit Ansley, an employee of the RR. Ansley PO est. in 1890 (Farmer 1973, 109).

ANTIOCH Settlement at 312308NO-862259W in Covington Co. Possibly named

8

for a church. Many churches have this name because of the associations that the city in southern Turkey, once the capital of Syria, has with the beginning of Christianity (*Official 1959 Alabama Highway Map*).

APPLETON Community with discontinued PO at 311315NO870717W in Escambia Co. The name, a combination of *apple* and *-ton* 'town' for the apple orchard of Greene Shell, was suggested by Shell's son Andrew. PO est. in 1901 (Waters 178).

ARAB ['e,ræb] Inc. town with PO at 341905NO862945W in Marshall Co. Received its name when PO officials mistook the handwritten *d* for a *b* in the application for a PO to be named *Arad* for the son of the first postmaster, Stephen T. Thompson, appointed in 1888. Inc. in 1892 (Roden 52).

ARARAT Settlement with discontinued PO at 315805NO880848W in Choctaw Co. Probably named for the mountain in eastern Turkey where Noah's ark is said to have landed. Earlier MOUNT ARARAT. PO est. in 1878 (Burroughs, 1846 map).

ARBACOOCHEE [,abə'kutʃi] Community with discontinued PO at 333434NO-853102W in Cleburne Co. Founded after gold was discovered here in the 1840s. Named for an Upper Creek town in Talladega Co., Abihkuchi, whose name is Creek for 'little Abihka.' The Abihka were an ancient Muskhogean tribe, the meaning of whose name is uncertain. One proposed translation is 'pile at the base,' referring to their custom of heaping a pile of scalps at the foot of a war-pole; another explanation is that the name refers to the peculiar manner in which the Abihka answered questions or expressed approbation; a third interpretation is that *abihka* comes from Choctaw *aiabika* 'unhealthful place.' PO est. in 1842 (Read 5).

ARBACOOCHEE RIVER See COOSA RIVER.

ARCUS Community with discontinued PO at 313047NO855718W in Coffee Co. Although origin of name is unknown, the word is Latin for 'archery bow.' PO est. in 1901.

ARDILLA [,ar'dɪlə] Settlement with discontinued PO at 311032NO852137W in Houston Co. Named for the wife of Henry J. Wood, the first postmaster, appointed in 1898 (F. S. Watson 1972, 35).

ARDMORE Inc. town with PO at 345931NO865049W in Limestone Co. First called AUSTIN for Alex Austin, who selected the place as a site for a station for the Louisville and Nashville RR; then the name was changed by the RR to ARDMORE for the city in Pennsylvania. Inc. in 1922 (Wellden).

ARGO Settlement with discontinued PO at 334805NO870701W in Jefferson Co. Said to be the name of a local family, but it is also that of the ship in which Jason sailed to find the Golden Fleece. PO est. in 1869 (Hagood 22).

ARIOSTO Settlement on the Atlantic Coast Line in Dale Co. now part of ARITON. Possibly named for the Italian poet Lodovico Ariosto (1474–1533), author of *Orlando Furioso*. PO est. in 1890.

ARITON ['erətən] Inc. town with PO at 313600NO854308W in Dale Co. Named DEAN'S STATION, probably for a local family, when the Central of Georgia RR reached here in 1889. By 1891 renamed CHARLESTON for the city in SC. In 1890 after the Atlantic Coast Line reached nearby Ariosto, the two communities were combined and given a name that was a blend of their two names, *Ari-* and *-ton*. PO est. in 1903. Inc. in 1906 (F. S. Watson 1968, 47–50).

ARK See HALEYVILLE in Winston Co.

ARKADELPHIA Settlement with PO at 335418NO865745W in Cullman Co. One proposed explanation is that the name was that of the wife of John A. Donaldson, the first postmaster. However, it may be a combination of *Ark*, the name of an early nearby settlement and PO in Winston Co., and *-adelphia*, a pseudo-Greek combination, meaning 'brother-place,' probably taken from *Philadelphia*. PO est. in 1854 (Jones 1972, 67–69).

ARLEY Inc. town with PO at 340444NO-871244W in Winston Co. When PO was est. here in 1900, the town received the middle name of Robert Arley Gibson, the deceased child of George W. Gibson, a Baptist minister who served the area for many years. Inc. in 1965 (Harris 1982, 16).

ARLINGTON Settlement with PO at 320325NO873519W in Wilcox Co. Grew up around the Mobile and Birmingham RR (Southern) station and was named for the VA home of Robert E. Lee (1807–1870), commanding general of the Confederate army. PO est. in 1887 (Harris 1982, 16).

ARMSTEAD Settlement at 335255NO-863129W in Blount Co. Probably a local family name (U.S.G.S., 1966 Base Maps).

ARMSTRONG Settlement with PO at 321422NO853928W in Macon Co. Named for Samuel Armstrong, a Methodist bishop in the area during the 1830s. PO est. in 1891 (Nunn 94).

ARONA See ARONEY in DeKalb Co.

ARONEY [ˌeˈronɪ] Community with discontinued PO at 341318NO860455W in DeKalb Co. Incorrectly spelled ARONA on 1966 U.S.G.S. Base Maps. Origin of name unknown. PO est. in 1890 (Landmarks 91).

ASBERRY Community at 335340NO854441W in Calhoun Co. Named for first church here, a discontinued Methodist one organized before 1900 that honored Francis Asbury (1745–1816), America's first Methodist bishop. ASBERRY is now the approved form of the name (Jolly).

ASBURY Settlement at 342229NO860750W in Marshall Co. Named for the Methodist church that honored Francis Asbury (1745–1816), first Methodist bishop in America (*Official 1983–84 Alabama Highway Map*; Roden 52).

ASHBANK See CAMP HILL in Tallapoosa Co.

ASHBY Settlement with discontinued PO at 330115NO865510W in Bibb Co. A flag stop on the Selma, Rome and Dalton RR, it may have been named for Turner Ashby (1824–1862), a brigadier general of the Confederate army. PO est. in 1883 (Harris 1982, 16).

ASHFORD Inc. town with PO at 311058NO851411W in Houston Co. A station on the Atlantic Coast Line named for the family of the wife of John Davis, the first postmaster, appointed in 1889. Inc. in 1892 (T. M. Owen 1:61; F. S. Watson 1972, 37).

ASHLAND Inc. co. seat with PO at 331625NO855010W in Clay Co. Named for the home of the famous KY statesman Henry Clay. PO est. in 1866. Chosen co. seat in 1867. Inc. in 1871 (McMillan).

ASHRIDGE Settlement with discontinued PO at 341405NO872807 in Winston Co. Probably a descriptive and environmental compound of *ash* and *ridge*. PO est. in 1898.

ASHVILLE Inc. co. seat with PO at 335013NO861516W in St. Clair Co. First called ST. CLAIRSVILLE, then renamed in 1822 for John Ashe, a senator in the state's first general assembly who settled in the area in 1818 and served as one of the commissioners appointed to erect the courthouse

when the town was chosen to be the co. seat in 1821. Since 1907 it has been the seat of justice for the Northern Judicial District of the co. Inc. in 1822 and received its PO the same year (T. M. Owen 1:61).

ATHENS Inc. co. seat with PO at 344810NO865818W in Limestone Co. Founded in 1818 by John Coffee, Robert Beaty, John D. Carroll, and John Read and inc. that year. First called ATHENSON, this name was then shortened to ATHENS for the ancient city in Greece. Became co. seat and acquired its PO in 1819 (T. M. Owen 1:67).

ATHENS See RAMER in Montgomery Co.

ATHENSON See ATHENS in Limestone Co.

ATMORE Inc. town with PO at 310125NO872938W in Escambia Co. When the Louisville and Nashville RR reached this point c. 1867, William L. Williams, who lived a short distance away over the state line in FL, built a freight station called WILLIAMS STATION here. In 1895 when the PO was est. the name was changed, at the suggestion of William M. Carney, the first postmaster, to honor C. P. Atmore, general passenger agent for the RR. Inc. in 1907 (Waters 221, 225, 229–30).

ATTALLA [əˈtælə] Inc. town with PO at 340118NO860519W in Etowah Co. When first settled in 1830 called NEW TOWN. This was changed to NEWTON in 1832 by the Wills Valley RR promoters, who were from the MA town of that name. In 1870 officially designated ATTALLA for the earliest settlement here. *Atale*, the name of the Indian village, is derived from Cherokee *otali* 'mountain.' Briefly, during the 1860s, a small settlement on part of the town's site was called BAINESVILLE in honor of the co. then known as BAINE. PO est. in 1870. Inc. in 1872 (Jolly; T. M. Owen 1:72).

ATWOOD Settlement with discontinued PO at 342138NO875942W in Franklin Co. Named for Abner Atwood, who practiced medicine here. PO est. in 1898 (Knight 16).

AUBURN Inc. town with PO at 323635NO852851W in Lee Co. Lizzie Taylor, the fiancée of Thomas Harper, son of one of the town's founders, suggested the name after reading Oliver Goldsmith's poem "The Deserted Village." Inc. in 1839. PO est. the same year (Nunn 59–60; T. M. Owen 1:75).

AURORA Settlement with PO at

340700NO861133W in Etowah Co. Possibly a personal name, but the word is Latin for 'dawn' and 'goddess of dawn.' PO est. in 1837.

AUSTIN See ARDMORE in Limestone Co.

AUTAUGA COUNTY [ə'tɔgə] Created by the AL territorial legislature on Nov. 30, 1818, and formed from part of Montgomery Co. on Dec. 13, 1820. Now bordered on the north by Chilton Co., on the east by Elmore Co. and Montgomery Co., on the south by Lowndes Co., and on the west by Dallas Co. Named for Autauga Creek. Its co. seats have been Washington, 1820–30; Kingston, 1830–68; and Prattville, the present one, chosen in 1868 (McMillan in Read 100; T. M. Owen 1:77).

AUTAUGA CREEK Stream rising at 324416NO863629W in Chilton Co. and flowing into the Alabama River at 322425NO862722W on the border between Autauga Co. and Lowndes Co. AT-TAU-GEE in Benjamin Hawkins's "A Sketch of the Creek Country in 1798 and 1799" (36). Named for an Indian village situated below the point where it empties into the Alabama River. Probably derived from Creek *atigi* 'border' (T. M. Owen 1:77; Read 6).

AUTAUGAVILLE Inc. town with PO at 322602NO863917W in Autauga Co. First settler was William N. Thompson, Sr., who had sawmills and gristmills here in the 1820s. Named for the co. PO est. in 1857. Inc. in 1907 (Biggs 20; T. M. Owen 1:83).

AVON ['evan] Inc. town at 311121NO851710W in Houston Co. Name suggested by Edgar Forrester for a park in FL where he had worked as a young man. Inc. in 1957 (F. S. Watson 1972, 43, 45).

AWIN ['ewɪn] Settlement with discontinued PO at 315016NO865656W in Wilcox Co. The local explanation for the name is that the first postmaster, Jack M. Williams, after asking for suggestions for a name for the PO, wrote "A win" beside the one the majority of residents had favored, and PO officials took

his comment to be the chosen name. PO est. in 1881 (Harris 1982, 18).

AXIS Settlement with discontinued PO at 305547NO880138W in Mobile Co. It grew up around the large lumber mill founded by Charles M. Kirk and Charles Anderson. The name is said to have been chosen for the town's PO because it was short and easy to remember. PO est. in 1905 (Harris 1982, 18).

BABBIE Inc. town with discontinued PO at 311646NO861932W in Covington Co. Possibly the name of a local person, but it is also that of the heroine of the novel *The Little Minister* by Sir James M. Barrie. PO est. in 1902. Inc. in 1957.

BAHIA DEL ESPIRITU SANTO See MOBILE BAY.

BAILEYTON Inc. town with PO at 341544NO863646W in Cullman Co. Named for Robert Bailey, a farmer from GA who settled here in 1870. PO est. in 1883. Inc. in 1973 (Jones 1972, 46–49).

BAINE COUNTY See ETOWAH COUNTY.

BAINESVILLE See ATTALLA in Etowah Co.

BAKER COUNTY See CHILTON COUNTY.

BAKER HILL Settlement with PO at 314652NO851808W in Barbour Co. Partly situated on a hill, the town was named for the family of James Baker, a local resident. PO est. in 1876 (Ellis 17).

BALDWIN COUNTY Created by act of the MS territorial legislature in 1809. Its boundaries having shifted several times, it is now bordered on the northwest by Washington Co., on the north by Clarke Co. and Monroe Co., on the east by Escambia Co. and FL, on the south by the Gulf of Mexico, and on the west by Mobile Co. Named for Abraham Baldwin (1754–1807), clergyman and statesman, who was born in CT but spent much of his life in GA. A member of the U.S. House of Representatives and the U.S. Senate, he founded Franklin College, now the University of GA. The co. seats have been the temporary one at McIntosh Bluff, now in Washington Co., 1809–20; Blakely, 1820–68; Daphne, 1868–1901; and Bay Minette, the present one, chosen in 1901 (T. M. Owen 1:85).

BALLPLAY   Settlement with discontinued PO at 340331NO854829W in Etowah Co. Name is said to be a translation of the designation of a sport of Indians living here during prehistoric times. PO est. in 1840 (Jolly).

BALTIMORE   See FERNBANK in Lamar Co.

BANGOR   Settlement with discontinued PO at 335828NO864524W in Blount Co. Originally given the environmental name COPPER'S GAP or COPPERAS GAP, the latter being the designation of the PO est. in 1856. The name refers to the PO's location between mountains, near mineral springs. When the Louisville and Nashville RR reached here, the name of the settlement was changed because the tree-covered hills reminded the RR developers of their former home in Bangor, ME. Bangor PO est. in 1872 (Blount Co. Historical Society 32).

BANKHEAD LAKE   Artificial lake in Walker Co., Jefferson Co., and Tuscaloosa Co. formed by Bankhead Lock and Dam on the Black Warrior River at 332729NO-872124W in Tuscaloosa Co. Named in 1956 for John H. Bankhead (1842–1920), U.S. senator from AL (1907–20). Also known as LAKE BANKHEAD (Rich 1979, 83).

BANKS   Inc. town with discontinued PO at 314854NO855035W in Pike Co. Founded as a station on the Alabama Midland RR in 1890, it received its PO the same year. Named for the family living on the site when the RR reached the area. Inc. in 1897 (Farmer 1973, 413).

BANKSTON   Settlement with PO at 334017NO874017W in Fayette Co. The first settlement, c. 1831, was called BYLER for the road on which it was located built by John Byler. When a water tank for the Georgia RR (Southern) was erected here c. 1883, it was named *Bank's Tank* for one of the train's engineers. In 1887 when the PO was est., it and the town were both called BANKSTON, a combination of *Banks* and *-ton* 'town.' The settlement and its PO were identified with the environmental name BUCKSNORT, a compound of *buck* and *snort*, 1873–87 (Newell and Newell 12–13; Peoples 2).

BARBER'S CROSSROADS   See RUTLEDGE in Crenshaw Co.

BARBOUR COUNTY   Created by act of the state general assembly on Dec. 18, 1832, from portions of Pike Co. and land that had been ceded to the state by the Creek Indians. Now bordered on the north by Russell Co., on the east by GA, on the south by Henry Co. and Dale Co., and on the west by Pike Co. and Bullock Co. Named for James Barbour (1775–1842), governor of VA (1812–14). The co. seat was Louisville until 1834 when Clayton, the present one, was chosen (T. M. Owen 1:118).

BARBOUR CREEK   Stream rising at 315208NO852559W in Barbour Co. and flowing into the Chattahoochee River on the border between AL and GA. Probably named for the co. (U.S.G.S., 1966 Base Maps).

BARBOURSVILLE   See COOPER in Chilton Co.

BARBOURSVILLE   See CAMDEN in Wilcox Co.

BARFIELD   Settlement with discontinued PO at 332140NO854257W in Clay Co. Named for the Young C. Barfield family. PO est. in 1894 (McMillan).

BARLOW BEND   Community with discontinued PO on the bend of the Alabama River at 312716NO873805W in Clarke Co. Named for Thaddeus Barlow on whose plantation the PO was est. in 1877 (Clarke Co. Historical Society 44).

BARNETT CROSSROADS   Community at intersection of co. highways 17 and 40 at 311316NO871816W in Escambia Co. Named for a family living here in the early 1900s (Waters).

BARNEY   Abandoned settlement at 334258NO870931W in Walker Co. Possibly named for the manager of a local coal-mining operation (Gant; U.S.G.S., 1966 Base Maps).

BARNWELL   Settlement with discontinued PO at 302529NO875246W in Baldwin Co. Named for a local family. PO est. in 1903 (Harris 1982, 20).

BARREN POINT   Cape on Mon Louis Island on Mississippi Sound at 301902NO-881131W in Mobile Co. Probably a descriptive name. Approved by the U.S. Board on Geographic Names in 1960.

BARRYTOWN   Dead town at 315014NO-881510W in Choctaw Co. Originally called BARRYTON, a reduction of the compound *barrel* plus *town*, a descriptive name given because of the barrels of turpentine produced by the local still. PO est. in 1833. Name changed to BARRYTOWN in 1849. Co. seat of Washington Co., 1842–47, until Choctaw Co. was formed from parts of Washington Co. and Sumter Co. PO discontinued in 1914 (Choctaw Co. Bicentennial Commission 109).

BARTON   Settlement at 344419NO-875328W in Colbert Co. on Memphis and Charleston RR (Southern). Founded in 1906 and named for Armistead Barton, a businessman from Tuscumbia who owned land in the area. Earlier known as BARTON DEPOT or STATION (Sockwell).

BASHAM   ['bæʃəm]   Community with discontinued PO at 343053NO870105W in Morgan Co. Originally BASHAM'S GAP, named for James H. Basham, who settled here c. 1818, and for its location between mountains. PO est. in 1847 (Ackley 13).

BASHI   ['bæʃˌaɪ]   Settlement with discontinued PO at 315816NO875141W in Clarke Co. Probably named for the creek. PO est. in 1849.

BASHI CREEK   Stream rising at 315318NO874715W in Clarke Co. and flowing into the Alabama River at 315723NO-880422W. BASHAI C. on La Tourette's 1844 map. Name seems to be derived from Choctaw *backaya* 'line, row, course.' Thus "Line Creek" was an appropriate name for a stream that served as a boundary between Indian communities (T. M. Owen 1:124; Read 6).

BASS   See ROCK RUN in Cherokee Co.

BASS   Community with discontinued PO on the Louisville and Nashville RR at 345555NO855447W in Jackson Co. First called BASS STATION by Vernon King Stevenson in honor of his wife, whose maiden name was Maria Louisa Bass. PO est. in 1873 (Melancon).

BASSETT CREEK   Stream rising at 312638NO881909W in Clarke Co. and flowing into the Tombigbee River at 312430NO-875546W. Probably named for Thomas Bassett, an early settler (D. S. Akens 72; U.S.G.S., 1966 Base Maps).

BATES CREEK   Stream rising at 311128NO881622W in Washington Co. and flowing into the Tombigbee River at 311321NO875747W. Named for an early local family (Matte 13; U.S.G.S., 1966 Base Maps).

BATESVILLE   Community with discontinued PO at 320032NO851840W in Barbour Co. Named for the plantation of Wilson Michael Bates, who moved here from SC in 1845. PO est. in 1877 (A. K. Walker 1941, 326; Ellis 18).

BATTENS CROSSROADS   Settlement at intersection of state highways 27 and 134 at 311539NO855324W in Coffee Co. Named for the Batten family, who lived in the area (U.S.G.S., 1966 Base Maps; F. S. Watson 1970, 155).

BATTLES WHARF   Settlement with discontinued PO on Mobile Bay at 302939NO-875540W in Baldwin Co. Originally named YARBOROUGH, probably for a local family; next DADEVILLE for R. R. Dade; then BATTLES, probably to honor another local family. Because Battles PO, est. in 1875, was frequently confused with another PO in the state having a similar designation, in 1903 its name was changed, at the suggestion of Paul C. Boudousquie, to NARCISSUS, for the mythological Greek turned into a flower. The next year the PO was renamed BATTLES with the addition of the word *wharf* (Bush 30, 65).

BAY MINETTE   Inc. co. seat with PO at 305258NO874623W in Baldwin Co. Named for Minette Bay, itself having a diminutive form of *Minet*, the name of a Frenchman who was a surveyor associated with Jean Baptiste Le Moyne, Sieur de Bienville (1680–1765), the founder of Mobile and New Orleans. Settlement begun in 1861 when the Louisville and Nashville RR reached here. PO est. in 1868. Chosen to be the co. seat in 1901 and inc. in 1907 (Harder 36).

BAY MINETTE CREEK   Stream rising at 305144NO874734W in Baldwin Co. and flowing into Minette Bay at 304147NO875435W. Probably named for the town. Designation approved by the U.S. Board on Geographic Names in 1941.

BAYOU LA BATRE   [ˌbajələ'bætrɪ]   Inc. town with PO at 302411NO881454W in

Mobile Co. The stream near the site was known during the period of French occupation as *Rivière d'Erbane* for a man killed here; then as *Rivière la batterie* because of the French artillery battery located on its banks. Town's name consists of *bayou*, the Gallicized form of *bok*, the Choctaw word for 'creek,' and *la batre*, derived from *la batterie*. PO est. in 1860. Inc. in 1955 (P. J. Hamilton 1910, 171).

BAY OF ICHUSA See MOBILE BAY.

BAYOU SARA [,bajə'serə] Stream rising at 305839NO880739W in Mobile Co. and flowing into Mobile Bay at 304811NO-880052W. The creek or *bayou*, the French form of the Choctaw word for 'creek,' is named for Sara Alvarez, the wife of an early settler in the area (Harris 1982, 144; U.S.G.S., 1966 Base Maps).

BAZEMORE Settlement at 335340NO-874200W in Fayette Co. Perhaps named for a local family (*Official 1959 Alabama Highway Map*).

BEAR CREEK The following stream names are probably derived from Indian designations referring to encounters with bears.
1. Stream rising at 315213NO874126W in Clarke Co. and joining the Alabama River at 315227NO873144W in Wilcox Co. (U.S.G.S., 1966 Base Maps).
2. Stream also known as BIG BEAR CREEK rising in MS and flowing through Colbert Co. into the Tennessee River at 345334NO880553W. BEAR CREEK 'Just-like-a-river' appears in Gaines's survey of 1808. OAKOCHAPPA, an Indian name of unknown origin, was changed to BEAR RIVER in 1887 by the state legislature, but this action was repealed in 1899. Since then known as BEAR or BIG BEAR CREEK. Its tributary Little Bear Creek rises at 342157NO874226W in Franklin Co. and joins Bear Creek in MS (Sockwell).
3. Stream rising at 310708NO853457W in Geneva Co. and flowing into the Little Choctawhatchee River at 311511NO853242W on the northern boundary between Dale Co. and Houston Co. (U.S.G.S., 1966 Base Maps).
4. Stream also known as BIG BEAR CREEK rising at 342510NO873109W in Marion Co. and flowing northwest through Franklin Co. into MS (U.S.G.S., 1966 Base Maps).
5. Stream rising at 314420NO870229W in

Monroe Co. and joining Pine Barren Creek at 315853NO870104W in Wilcox Co. (U.S.G.S., 1966 Base Maps).
6. Stream rising at 322444NO872604W in Perry Co. and joining Boguechitto Creek at 321709NO871744W in Dallas Co. (U.S.G.S., 1966 Base Maps).
7. Stream rising at 332725NO875304W in Pickens Co. and joining Lubbub Creek at 331105NO880447W (U.S.G.S., 1966 Base Maps).
8. Stream rising at 332327NO863643W in Shelby Co. and joining Kelly Creek at 332901NO862602W (U.S.G.S., 1966 Base Maps).

BEAR CREEK Inc. town with PO on the Southern RR at the headwaters of Bear Creek at 341629NO874202W in Marion Co. Site of Allen's Factory, a cotton factory, 1857–61, operated by the family of the first postmaster, George C. Allen, appointed in 1857. Bear Creek PO est. in 1888. Inc. in 1907 (T. M. Owen 1:125).

BEATRICE [bi'ætrɪs] Inc. town with PO at 314400NO871217W in Monroe Co. While the Selma to Pensacola branch of the Louisville and Nashville RR was being built, the general superintendent of construction, a Col. Seymour of Nashville, TN, asked that the town growing up around the station here be named for his granddaughter Beatrice Seymour. PO est. in 1900 (Dugas [Monroe Co.] 94).

BEATY CROSSROADS ['bedɪ] Settlement at intersection of state highways 75 and 117 at 344144NO854010W in DeKalb Co. Probably named for Oliver Beaty, a teacher and founder of Beaty School, located near here (Raughton 18; U.S.G.S., 1966 Base Maps).

BEAUREGARD Community surrounding Beauregard School at 323257NO852224W in Lee Co. Name of the school was suggested in 1903 by Kate Grimmetts, one of the teachers, probably to honor Pierre Gustave Toutant Beauregard (1818–1893), Confederate general (Nunn 110).

BEAVER CREEK See TOWN CREEK.

BEAVER CREEK The following stream names are descriptive and environmental, some probably derived from Indian designations.
1. Stream rising at 315507NO874402W in

Clarke Co. and flowing into the Alabama River at 320012NO872830W in Wilcox Co. (U.S.G.S., 1966 Base Maps).
2. Stream rising at 321150NO874323W in Marengo Co. and flowing into the Tombigbee River at 321144NO880033W (U.S.G.S., 1966 Base Maps).
3. Stream rising at 340340NO875157W in Marion Co. and flowing into the Buttahatchee River at 335546NO880725W in Lamar Co. (U.S.G.S., 1966 Base Maps).
4. Stream rising at 334129NO862553W in St. Clair Co. and flowing into the Coosa River at 335021NO860407W on the boundary between St. Clair Co., Etowah Co., and Calhoun Co. (U.S.G.S., 1966 Base Maps).

BEAVER CREEK MOUNTAIN   Ridge at 334614NO861636W in St. Clair Co. Also called BEAVER MOUNTAIN. Named for the creek (Rich; U.S.G.S., 1966 Base Maps).

BEAVERDAM CREEK   Both stream names are probably descriptive and environmental.
1. Stream rising at 311426NO860233W in Coffee Co. and joining Whitewater Creek at 311152NO860043W (U.S.G.S., 1966 Base Maps).
2. Stream rising at 345656NO864214W in Marion Co. and joining Briar Fork of the Flint River at 345047NO863231W (U.S.G.S., 1966 Base Maps).

BEAVERTON   Inc. town with PO at 335552NO880113W in Lamar Co. Name is a combination of *beaver* and *-ton* 'town.' It and the creek where it is located received their names because of the many beavers in the area. PO est. in 1878. Inc. in 1910 (Acee 5, 23).

BECK   Settlement with discontinued PO at 311522NO863505W in Covington Co. Probably named for a local family. PO est. in 1898.

BEECHWOOD   Settlement at 320733NO863922W in Lowndes Co. Name is probably a descriptive and environmental compound of *beech* and *wood* (*Official 1983–84 Alabama Highway Map*).

BEHRMAN   See FULTON in Clarke Co.

BELFOREST   Settlement with discontinued PO at 303613NO875109W in Baldwin Co. Name is probably a subjectively descriptive compound consisting of the French masculine adjective *bel* 'beautiful' and *forest*. PO est. in 1900.

BELGREEN   Settlement with discontinued PO at 342829NO875159W in Franklin Co. Co. seat, 1878–81. Richard S. Watkins, later a probate judge of the co., suggested the name, a subjectively descriptive compound consisting of French masculine adjective *bel* 'beautiful' and *green*. PO est. in 1879 (Knight 17).

BELK   Settlement with PO at 333851NO875553W in Fayette Co. Named for a local family. PO est. in 1903 (Newell and Newell 13).

BELLAMY   Settlement with PO at 322656NO880801W in Sumter Co. that grew up around E. F. Allison's sawmill. When the PO was est. in 1901, Allison's brother Charles suggested that the usual procedure of naming a place for its most respected citizen be reversed; hence it received the name of Volney Bellamy, a Union veteran working in the area (Foscue 28).

BELLEFONTAINE   [ˌbɛl'fauntən]   Settlement at 302936NO880613W in Mobile Co. Name is probably a subjectively descriptive compound consisting of the French words *belle* 'beautiful' and *fontaine* 'fountain' (Boudousquie, 1889 map).

BELLEFONTAINE CREEK   Stream rising at 304221NO873311W in Baldwin Co. and flowing into the Styx River at 303525NO873045W. A subjectively descriptive compound consisting of the French words *belle* 'beautiful' and *fontaine* 'fountain' (U.S.G.S., Topographic Maps, 1941 Robertsdale Quad.).

BELLEFONTE   ['bɛlˌfant]   Dead town with discontinued PO in Jackson Co. near Hollywood. Co. seat, 1821–59. Name is a subjectively descriptive compound consisting of the French words *belle* 'beautiful' and *fonte* 'fount.' Inc. in 1821. PO, 1830–59 (Melancon).

BELLEFONTE STATION   See HOLLYWOOD in Jackson Co.

BELLE MINA   [ˌbɛl'maɪnə]   Settlement with PO on the Southern RR at 343924NO865245W in Limestone Co. Named for the plantation of Thomas Bibb (1783–1839), the second governor of the state (1820–21), where the RR station was located. The name of the plantation seems to consist of the French feminine adjective *belle* 'beautiful' plus *mina*, the designation of an ancient Greek silver coin, thus meaning 'beautiful rare coin.' PO est. in 1878 (T. M. Owen 1:126).

BELLEVILLE Settlement with discontinued PO at 312547NO870633W in Conecuh Co. The first permanent white settlement in the area, dating from the latter part of 1815. Originally given the environmental name THE PONDS, then the pseudo-French compound name of *belle* plus -*ville* in honor of an Irishman, a Mr. Bell, who drained the ponds. PO est. in 1828 (Conecuh Co. Historical Society 43).

BELLVIEW Community with discontinued PO at 315037NO872122W in Wilcox Co. Name is probably a subjectively descriptive combination of French *belle* 'beautiful' plus *view*. PO est. in 1907.

BELLWOOD Settlement with discontinued PO at 323331NO875633W in Geneva Co. Designation is a compound of *Bell*, the name of Jonas Bell, one of the commissioners who organized the co. in 1868, plus *wood*. PO est. in 1900 (T. M. Owen 1:127).

BELMONT Settlement with discontinued PO at 323331NO875633W in Sumter Co. Founded in 1832 by David Blacksher; Joseph Gillespie, Sr.; a M. Martiere, one of the French settlers of Demopolis; and the Rushing family. Originally spelled *Belmonte*, the name is a subjectively descriptive, pseudo-Italian compound of *bel* 'beautiful' plus *monte* 'mountain.' PO est. in 1835 (Foscue 20).

BENEVOLA [ˌbɛnə'volə] Settlement with discontinued PO at 330633NO875754W in Pickens Co. Name is probably the feminine singular form of the Spanish adjective meaning 'benevolent.' PO est. in 1835.

BENSON CREEK Stream rising at 325127NO864423W in Chilton Co. and joining Mulberry Creek at 324719NO864951W. Honors an early settler (B. D. Roberts; U.S.G.S., 1966 Base Maps).

BENTON Settlement with PO at 321824NO864904W in Lowndes Co. on the Alabama River. An important shipping point, it was named for Thomas Hart Benton (1782–1858) from SC, a colonel in the U.S. army who commanded the 39th Infantry Regiment in the Creek Indian War, 1813–14. PO est. in 1833. Inc. in 1964 (Brannon 1951, 134).

BENTON COUNTY See CALHOUN COUNTY.

BENTONVILLE See ELBA in Coffee Co.

BERLIN Settlement at 341053NO864432W in Cullman Co. While called HOBART, possibly for Garrett A. Hobart (1844–1899), NJ

16

legislator, later vice-president under William McKinley (1897–99), it had a PO, 1895–1903. The present name was suggested by J. S. Schultz c. 1914 to honor the capital of Germany, the former homeland of many of the town's residents (Jones 1975, 16).

BERMUDA [bər'mudə] Settlement with discontinued PO at 312914NO871118W in Conecuh Co. Named for a kind of grass being tested in the area. PO est. in 1877 (Harris 1982, 23).

BERRY Inc. town with PO at 333935NO873600W in Fayette Co. on the Georgia Pacific RR (Southern), which reached this point, 1882–83. Named for Thompson Berry, an early settler who came here in 1840. Inc. in 1883. PO est. as BERRY STATION in 1887, *station* being dropped in 1903 (Newell and Newell 14–16).

BERRYVILLE See ANSLEY in Pike Co.

BERTHA Settlement with discontinued PO at 313228NO852541W in Dale Co. Probably a personal name. PO est. in 1891.

BESSEMER Inc. town with PO at 332406NO865716W in Jefferson Co. Named in 1888 by Henry DeBardeleben for Sir Henry Bessemer (1813–1898), the Englishman who invented the iron smelting process that bears his name. PO est. in 1887. Inc. in 1888 (Hagood 28).

BEULAH Settlement with discontinued PO at 324240NO851056W in Lee Co. Named for Beulah Baptist Church, organized in 1851. PO est. in 1872 (Nunn 100).

BEXAR Settlement with discontinued PO at 341127NO880850W in Marion Co. Founded in the 1830s but named for Bexar Co., TX, where the Alamo is located. The TX co. bears the same designation as Bejar, Spain, *Bejar* being the name of a branch of the Spanish royal family. The name was brought back to Marion Co. by men who fought with Sam Houston in TX during the war with Mexico. PO est. in 1845 (*Alabama: A Guide*, 328; G. R. Stewart 1970, 46).

BIBB COUNTY Originally part of Monroe Co., created by the MS territorial legislature on June 29, 1815; part of Montgomery Co., MS Territory, in 1817; part of Montgomery Co., AL Territory, 1817–18; Cahawba Co., AL Territory, Feb. 7, 1818–Dec. 14, 1819; Cahawba Co., AL, Dec. 14, 1819–Dec. 4, 1820; then name changed to BIBB. Present boundaries est. in 1868. Now bordered on the north by Tuscaloosa Co. and Jefferson Co., on the east by Shelby Co. and Chilton Co., on the south by Perry Co., and on the west by Hale Co. Named CAHAWBA for the river that flows from north to south through the co. Renamed in 1820 to honor William Wyatt Bibb (1781–1820), territorial governor and first governor of the state, who had died the preceding summer. Its co. seats have been the temporary one, Falls of the Cahawba, 1819–22; Bibb Court House, later named BIBBVILLE, 1822–29; and the present one, first known as CENTREVILLE COURT HOUSE, now CENTREVILLE, chosen in 1829 (Ellison 41–43; T. M. Owen 1:128).

BIBB COURT HOUSE　See BIBBVILLE in Bibb Co.

BIBBVILLE　Community with discontinued PO at 331136NO871035 in Bibb Co. A sawmill town that served as first official co. seat under the name of BIBB COURT HOUSE Sept. 1822–May 1829. Bibb Court House PO est. in 1822. Name of PO changed to BIBBVILLE in 1872 (Ellison 41–43, 167).

BIGBEE　Community with PO at 313650NO880959W in Washington Co. Named for Tombigbee River. PO est. in 1880 (Read 7).

BIG BRUSH CREEK　Stream rising at 324434NO873120W in Perry Co. and flowing into the Black Warrior River at 324954NO-874857W. Probably a descriptive and environmental name for the dense vegetation in the area. Two of its tributaries—Brush Creek, which rises at 325149NO872251W in Perry Co. and joins Big Brush Creek at 324433NO-873120W in Hale Co., and Little Brush Creek, which rises at 324956NO872546W in Perry Co. and joins Big Brush Creek at 324956NO872546W in Hale Co.—share its designation, approved by U.S. Board on Geographic Names in 1964.

BIG CANOE CREEK　Stream rising at 334440NO863425W in St. Clair Co. and flowing into the Coosa River at 335158NO-860416W in Etowah Co. Its tributary Little Canoe Creek rises at 335801NO861648W in St. Clair Co. and joins Big Canoe Creek at

335352NO866817W in Etowah Co. Names probably refer to their relative lengths and depths that made the travel by canoe of Indians and later white explorers possible (U.S.G.S., 1966 Base Maps).

BIG COON CREEK　Stream rising at 345510NO860455W in Jackson Co. and flowing into the Tennessee River at 345138NO-855421W. Its tributary Little Coon Creek rises in TN and joins Big Coon Creek at 345138NO855421W. Descriptive and environmental name (U.S.G.S., 1966 Base Maps).

BIG COVE　Community in the gap between Monte Sano and Keel's mountains at 343446NO862820W in Madison Co. Area has had this descriptive name since the middle 1860s (Green).

BIG CREEK　Descriptive name for the following four streams.
1. Stream rising at 310905NO852856W in Houston Co. and crossing the state boundary into FL at 310039NO852020W (U.S.G.S., 1966 Base Maps).
2. Stream rising at 305907NO881911W in Mobile Co. and flowing into Big Creek Lake at 303121NO882605W. Designation approved by U.S. Board on Geographic Names in 1931.
3. Stream rising at 331943NO880614W in Pickens Co. and flowing into the Tombigbee River at 331120NO881615W (U.S.G.S., 1966 Base Maps).
4. Stream rising at 314729NO855804W in Pike Co. and joining Whitewater Creek at 312845NO860259W in Coffee Co. (U.S.G.S., 1966 Base Maps).

BIG CREEK　See COKER in Tuscaloosa Co.

BIG CREEK LAKE　Artificial lake at 304243NO882024W in Mobile Co. that serves as the reservoir for the city of Mobile. Also known as CONVERSE LAKE, because it was the J. B. Converse Co. that impounded the waters of Big Creek, the stream for which the lake was officially named in 1941 (Pipes).

BIG ESCAMBIA CREEK　See ESCAMBIA CREEK.

BIG FLAT CREEK　See FLAT CREEK in Monroe Co.

BIG NANCE CREEK　Stream rising at 343504NO871949W in Lawrence Co. and flowing into the Tennessee River at 344726NO872337W. Name refers to a natural rock formation in the shape of a big chair on the creek bank said to have been the judgment seat of a legendary Indian chief, Big

Nance (Gentry 36; U.S.G.S., 1966 Base Maps).

BIG PRAIRIE CREEK   Stream rising at 324136NO872433W in Perry Co. and flowing into the Black Warrior River at 323443NO874525W in Hale Co. Its tributary Little Prairie Creek rises at 323552NO873812W in Perry Co. and joins Big Prairie Creek at 323317NO874152W in Hale Co. Names are probably descriptive and environmental (U.S.G.S., 1966 Base Maps).

BIG SANDY CREEK   Stream rising at 330820NO871504W in Tuscaloosa Co. and flowing into the Black Warrior River at 330242NO873724W. Its tributary South Sandy Creek rises at 325524NO872322W in Bibb Co. and joins Big Sandy at 330118NO873108W in Tuscaloosa Co. The names, in John Coffee's 1820 survey, are descriptive and environmental (Rich 1979, 103–04, 517).

BIG SHOAL CREEK   Stream rising at 343516NO871016W in Lawrence Co. and joining West Flint Creek at 342900NO870811W. Probably a descriptive and environmental name (U.S.G.S., 1966 Base Maps).

BIG SHOALS CREEK   See CHOCCOLOCCO CREEK.

BIG SPRING   See TUSCUMBIA in Colbert Co.

BIG SPRING CREEK   Stream rising at 3340804NO863049W in Blount Co. and flowing into Guntersville Lake at 342148NO861650W. Descriptive phrase designation approved by U.S. Board on Geographic Names in 1895.

BIG SPRINGS   See SPRINGVILLE in St. Clair Co.

BIG SWAMP   See HAYNEVILLE in Lowndes Co.

BIG SWAMP CREEK   Stream rising at 320221NO863333W in Lowndes Co. and flowing into the Alabama River at 321826NO864845W. Probably a descriptive and environmental name (U.S.G.S., 1966 Base Maps).

BIG TALLAWAMPA CREEK   See TALLAWAMPA CREEK in Choctaw Co.

BIG WILLS CREEK   Stream rising at 343418NO853559W in DeKalb Co. and flowing through the valley between Lookout and Sand mountains into the Coosa River at 335908NO860002W in Etowah Co. Named for William Webber, a part-Cherokee Indian leader better known as "Chief Big Will" or "Red Headed Will." Stream received the

18

name soon after 1770 (E. L. Watson 8).

BILBO CREEK   Stream rising at 311736NO881533W in Washington Co. and flowing into the Tombigbee River at 311319NO875621W. Named for Matthew Bilbo, a pioneer settler who owned property beside the creek c. 1798–1800 (D. J. Brown).

BILLINGSLEY   Inc. town with PO at 323934NO864304W in Autauga Co. Named for a local family. PO est. in 1884. Inc. in 1901 (Biggs 22).

BINION CREEK   ['bɪnjən]   Stream rising at 333246NO874413W in Fayette Co. and flowing into North River at 332325NO873631W in Tuscaloosa Co. Named for William Binion, an early settler (Rich 1979, 106).

BIRMINGHAM   See PRINCETON in Jackson Co.

BIRMINGHAM   ['bɜrmɪŋ,hæm]   Inc. co. seat at 333114NO864809W in Jefferson Co. In 1870 Josiah Morris, a banker from Montgomery, and John T. Milner, a local engineer, chose this site for a new city because of its mineral resources and location where the Chattanooga and Alabama RR (Alabama Great Southern) crossed the South and North RR (Louisville and Nashville). James R. Powell, a land developer from Elyton, named it for England's iron and steel center in Warwickshire. PO est. in 1870. Inc. in 1871 and chosen to be co. seat in 1873 (Hagood 6; T. M. Owen 1:140–41).

BIRMINGHAM JUNCTION   See WILTON in Shelby Co.

BIRMINGPORT   Community with discontinued PO at 333359NO870624W in Jefferson Co., 18 miles west of Birmingham on Locust Fork of the Black Warrior River. The name, a blend of *Birmingham* and *port*, was given because the town was the freshwater port for the city of Birmingham. Also known as PORT BIRMINGHAM. PO est. in 1920 (Hagood 6).

BISMARCK   See WILTON in Shelby Co.

BLACK   Inc. town with PO at 310033NO854440W in Geneva Co. Name honors the Black family, its founders. PO est. in 1902. Inc. in 1905 (T. M. Owen 1:154).

BLACK BLUFF   See WHITFIELD in Sumter Co.

BLACK CREEK   Stream rising at 341246NO855018W in DeKalb Co. and flowing into the Coosa River at 335920NO860020W in Etowah Co. Descriptive name, said to be a translation of an Indian designation, refers to the dark color of the water. Mentioned in the 1844 *Acts of the General Assembly* (Jolly).

BLACK DIAMOND   Settlement with discontinued PO at 332041NO870512W in Jefferson Co. The name, for the Black Diamond Coal Co., is a metaphor for 'coal.' PO est. in 1947 (Sartwell).

BLACK GROUND MOUNTAIN   Mountain whose summit is at 343831NO872346W in Lawrence Co. Name is probably a descriptive one, referring to the dark stone of the mountain (U.S.G.S., 1966 Base Maps).

BLACK ROCK   Community with discontinued PO at 314639NO862513W in Crenshaw Co. Name is a descriptive and environmental one, probably referring to some kind of dark stone in the area. PO est. in 1898.

BLACKSHER   Community with discontinued PO at 311238NO874418W in Baldwin Co. Probably named for the family of the first postmaster, Jeptha Blacksher, appointed in 1889 ("Record of Appointment of Postmasters").

BLACK WARRIOR FALLS   See TUSCALOOSA in Tuscaloosa Co.

BLACK WARRIOR RIVER   Stream formed by the confluence of Locust and Mulberry forks at 333325NO871109W in Jefferson Co. It joins the Tombigbee River at 323155NO875111W between Greene Co. and Marengo Co. TASCALOUSSA R. on De Crenay's 1733 map. Modern name is a translation of Choctaw *tashka* 'warrior' and *lusa* 'black.' Another early name, PATAGAHATCHE R., from Choctaw *apotaka* 'side' or 'border' and *hacha* 'river,' used because the stream served as a boundary between the Choctaw and Creek territories, appears on Mitchell's 1755 map. Also known as WARRIOR RIVER, though BLACK WARRIOR, its official designation, was approved by the U.S. Board on Geographic Names in 1941 (McMillan in Read 86; Read 71–72).

BLACKWATER CREEK   Stream rising at 340506NO873614W in Winston Co. and flowing into the Mulberry Fork of the Black Warrior River at 334852NO870810W on the border between Winston Co. and Walker Co. Descriptive and environmental name, possibly referring to the dark stone of the creek bed. Designation approved by the U.S. Board on Geographic Names in 1961.

BLACKWATER RIVER   Stream rising at 303823NO874208W in Baldwin Co. and flowing into Perdido Bay at 302856NO872607W. Descriptive and environmental name, possibly referring to the appearance of the river bed (U.S.G.S., 1966 Base Maps).

BLACKWOOD CREEK   Stream rising at 312325NO851826W in Henry Co. and flowing into the East Fork of the Choctawhatchee River at 312236NO852800W in Dale Co. Possibly a descriptive and environmental name referring to trees with dark wood growing in the area (U.S.G.S., 1966 Base Maps).

BLACKWOODS   CROSSROADS   See CLEVELAND in Blount Co.

BLADON SPRINGS   Settlement with PO at 314350NO881151W in Choctaw Co. Named for the original owner of the land upon which the mineral springs were discovered. Its first PO, named WARRIOR BRIDGE in honor of the Indians who had once occupied the area, was est. in 1831. PO renamed BLADON SPRINGS in 1844 (T. M. Owen 1:155).

BLAKELY   Dead town with discontinued PO at 304431NO875527W in Baldwin Co. on the Tensaw River. Founded in 1813 by Josiah Blakely, for whom it was named. Co. seat, 1820–68. Gradually abandoned after a number of severe yellow fever epidemics. PO, 1818–66 (Nuzum 71–76).

BLANCHE   Settlement with discontinued PO at 342148NO853636W in Cherokee Co. Probably a personal name, though it may be descriptive and environmental, because the word is the French feminine adjective meaning 'white.' PO est. in 1891.

BLANTON   Settlement with discontinued PO at 324404NO850802W in Lee Co. Named for a family who operated a ferry on the Chattahoochee River. PO est. in 1900 (Nunn 100).

BLEEKER   Community with discontinued PO that grew up around the Central of Georgia RR depot at 323456NO850951W in Lee Co. c. 1901. After a short time the houses and stores were moved a short distance away to U.S. Highway 431. Probably named for a local resident or for an employee of the RR. PO est. in 1920 (Nunn 114).

BLEVINS   CREEK   Stream rising at 341822NO870055W in Cullman Co. and joining Rock Creek at 341122NO870848W in Winston Co. Probably a local family name (U.S.G.S., 1966 Base Maps).

BLOSSBURG   Settlement with discontinued PO at 333750NO865648W in Jefferson Co. Originally named PINKNEY CITY for the family who moved here from PA; renamed in 1889 for Blossburg, PA, when a PO was est. here (Hagood 8).

BLOUNT COUNTY   Created by the AL territorial legislature on Feb. 7, 1818. Reduced to present limits in 1824. Now bounded on the northeast and east by Marshall Co., Etowah Co., and St. Clair Co.; on the south by Jefferson Co.; and on the west and northwest by Walker Co. and Cullman Co. Named for William G. Blount (c. 1767–1835), governor of TN (1809–15), who had sent troops to aid the white residents of this area during the Creek Indian War of 1813–14. Its co. seats have been Blountsville, 1820–89, and the present one, Oneonta, chosen in 1889 (T. M. Owen 1:155).

BLOUNT MOUNTAIN   Ridge extending across Blount Co., Etowah Co., and St. Clair Co. whose summit is at 335253NO862054W in Blount Co. Probably named for the co. (U.S.G.S., 1966 Base Maps).

BLOUNT SPRINGS   Settlement with discontinued PO that grew up around sulphur springs at 335552NO864739W in Blount Co. Named for the co. PO est. in 1830 (Blount Co. Historical Society 27).

BLOUNTSVILLE   Inc. town with PO at 340453NO863528W in Blount Co. Named for the co. Co. seat, 1820–89. PO est. in 1820. Inc. in 1827 (Blount Co. Historical Society 8, 20).

BLUBBER CREEK   Stream rising at 331457NO880816W in Pickens Co. and flowing into the Tombigbee River at 330427NO-881049W. Possibly a humorous name descriptive of the sound made by the flowing water (U.S.G.S., 1966 Base Maps).

BLUE CREEK   Stream rising at 333428NO-872855W in Tuscaloosa Co. and flowing into the Black Warrior River at 332611NO-872251W. Name is descriptive of the mineral deposits in the water (U.S.G.S., Topographic Maps, 1893 Jasper Quad.; Rich 1979, 114).

BLUE GIRTH CREEK   Stream rising at 325512NO872201W in Bibb Co. and flowing into the Cahaba River at 324902NO871431W

in Perry Co. Name is probably descriptive of the mineral deposits under the widest part of the stream (U.S.G.S., 1966 Base Maps).

BLUE MOUNTAIN   Inc. town with PO on the Southern RR and the Louisville and Nashville RR at 334104NO855034W in Calhoun Co. Probably named for the mountain about 12 miles to the northeast. PO est. in 1860. Inc. in 1907 (Jolly).

BLUE (RIDGE) MOUNTAINS   See TALLADEGA MOUNTAINS.

BLUES OLD STAND   Community with discontinued PO at 315905NO854301W in Bullock Co. Name refers to the general store of Hector Blue, who was also the first postmaster, appointed in 1887 (Harris 1982, 26).

BLUE SPRINGS   Settlement with discontinued PO at 313949NO853024W in Barbour Co. Descriptive and environmental name for the waters from the nearby lime springs. PO est. in 1902. Inc. in 1907 (M. B. Owen 1:365).

BLUEWATER CREEK   Stream rising in Franklin Co., TN, and flowing into the Tennessee River at 344838NO872446W in Lauderdale Co. Name, descriptive of the stream's mineral waters, appears on B. Tanner's 1796 map (Sockwell).

BLUFF   Settlement with discontinued PO at 334914NO875423W in Fayette Co. Named for a nearby ridge. PO est. in 1897 (Peoples 4).

BLUFF PARK   Settlement with PO on a high bank of Shades Creek at 332405NO-865122W in Jefferson Co. Probably a descriptive and reminiscent name. PO est. in 1971.

BLUFF SPRING   Community with discontinued PO on a high bank of the Enitachopco Creek, near a spring, at 330948NO854939W in Clay Co. Descriptive and environmental name. PO est. in 1843 (Waldrop).

BLUFFTON   See LANETT in Chambers Co.

BLUFFTON   Community with discontinued PO at 340025NO852624W in Cherokee Co. In Nov. 1888, the Bluffton Land, Ore, and Furnace Co. was founded here, but the area never became an important iron-manufacturing center. Name is descriptive of the location of the settlement on iron bluffs. PO est. in 1888 (Cherokee Co. Historical Society 3:99–100; M. T. Stewart 1958, 1:33).

BOAZ   Inc. town with PO at 341202NO-860959W in Marshall Co. Henry McCord of Albertville suggested the name to his son-in-

20

law, G. M. E. Mann, the first postmaster, appointed in 1887. The biblical character Boaz was a wealthy inhabitant of Bethlehem, who married Ruth, the Moabite woman. Inc. in 1897 (Roden 52).

BODKA CREEK ['bɑdkə] Stream rising in MS and flowing into the Noxubee River at 325000NO881312W in Sumter Co. BODCA C. on La Tourette's 1844 map. "The name seems to have been shortened . . . from Choctaw *hopatka*, 'wide,' a plural form used perhaps with reference to the numerous branches of Bodka Creek. . . . A literal translation, then, would be 'wide creek,' from Choctaw *bok hopatka*" (Read 8).

BOGUECHITTO CREEK [ˌbog't∫itə] Stream rising at 324055NO872432W in Perry Co. and flowing into the Alabama River at 320959NO871359W in Dallas Co. On La Tourette's 1844 map. Name means 'big creek,' from Choctaw *bok* 'creek' and *chito* 'big' (Read 8).

BOGUE CREEK [bog] Stream rising at 335250NO880133W in Lamar Co. and flowing into the Buttahatchee River. Name is pleonastic because *bogue* is derived from Choctaw *bok* 'creek' (McMillan in Read 96).

BOGUELOOSA CREEK [ˌbogə'lusə] Stream rising at 320450NO882151W in Choctaw Co. and joining Okatuppa Creek at 315305NO881807W. BOGUE LOOSA on La Tourette's 1844 map. Name, meaning 'black creek,' comes from Choctaw *bok* 'creek' and *lusa* 'black' (McMillan in Read 100; Read 8).

BOLIGEE ['bolɪˌdʒɪ] Inc. town with PO at 324521NO880144W in Greene Co. Settled in 1816 by John McKee and given the name of a nearby creek, for which Read suggests several possible Choctaw sources: *balichi* 'to stab,' *baluhchi* 'hickory bark,' *abolichi* 'to hit,' *apalichi* 'a hewer of wood,' *apolichi* 'to hill corn,' *aboli* 'thicket' plus *ushi* 'little.' PO est. in 1838. Inc. in 1926 (Read 9; Rich 1979, 117).

BOLINGER ['bolɪndʒər] Settlement with PO at 314642NO881952W in Choctaw Co. Named for Sanford Henry Bolinger of Redfield, KS, who acquired land here and founded the Choctaw Lumber Co. in 1915. PO est. in 1921 (Choctaw Co. Bicentennial Commission 2).

BOLLING ['bolɪŋ] Settlement with PO at 314331NO864221W in Butler Co. that grew up around a sawmill founded by the Flowers family and was named for Samuel Jackson

Bolling, probate judge of the co. during the 1860s. PO est. in 1872 (Dugas [Butler Co.] 78).

BOLTON'S CROSSROADS See WATTSVILLE in St. Clair Co.

BOMAR Community with discontinued PO at 340631NO853449W in Cherokee Co. Probably named for a local family. PO est. in 1890.

BON AIR [ˌban'æjr] Inc. town with PO at 331549NO862008W in Talladega Co. This textile mill village was given its subjectively descriptive name, which is French for 'good air,' by the mill's founder, Jonathan T. Lewis. Its Central of Georgia RR station was est. in 1901 and its PO in 1908. Inc. in 1932 (McMillan).

BON SECOUR [ˌbansə'kjur] Settlement with discontinued PO at 301855NO874346W in Baldwin Co. Named for the river and bay. PO est. in 1875 (Bush 34).

BON SECOUR BAY Bay at 301833NO875213W in Baldwin Co. The bay and the river emptying into it were given the same name c. 1700 by French explorers, a reduced form of the French phrase *bon secours* meaning 'good succor or help,' a subjective description. The Spaniards retained this designation for the river in the form *Rio del Socorro*, 1780–1813 (Bush 35).

BONITA Community with discontinued PO at 323240NO864942W in Autauga Co. Probably a personal name, but it might be subjectively descriptive, because the word is the Spanish feminine adjective meaning 'pretty or attractive.' PO est. in 1898.

BOOKER See DOCENA in Jefferson Co.

BOONE See KINSTON in Coffee Co.

BOOTH Settlement with PO at 323001NO863419W in Autauga Co. Probably named for Charles Booth, a local landowner. PO est. in 1899 (Biggs 22).

BOOT HILL Settlement at 315233NO853833W in Barbour Co. Probably a reminiscent name suggesting that the village is dead (G. R. Stewart 1970, 54).

BOOTSVILLE Dead town located 5 miles southwest of Fort Payne in DeKalb Co. The second temporary seat of justice, during 1837 while the co. was being organized. Named for an Indian chief called "Boots," who had lived in the area (Raughton 21).

BORDEN CREEK Stream rising at 342605NO872021W in Lawrence Co. and flowing into Sipsey Fork of Mulberry Fork of the Black Warrior River at 341733NO-872400W in Winston Co. Probably named for a family in the area (U.S.G.S., 1966 Base Maps).

BORDEN SPRINGS Settlement with discontinued PO that grew up around a resort hotel at 335547NO852813W in Cleburne Co. In the 1890s the Borden-Wheeler Co. built the hotel here and gave it the designation of the PO est. in 1876. The PO had been named for the springs discovered by John A. Borden, the earliest settler. The hotel burned in 1935 (Sulzby 78–79).

BOSTON See BRILLIANT in Marion Co.

BOSWELL Community on the Central of Georgia RR at 314440NO855938W in Bullock Co. Probably named for a local resident or for an employee of the RR (U.S.G.S., 1966 Base Maps).

BOTTLE, THE Settlement at the intersection of U.S. Highway 280 and state Highway 147 at 324034NO852911W in Lee Co. Received its name because of a large wooden sign in the shape of a Coca-Cola bottle that once stood here (Harris 1982, 28).

BOYD Settlement with discontinued PO at 323710NO881815W in Sumter Co. Named for John Boyd, who came here in 1832 from SC. PO est. in 1912 (Foscue 24).

BOYD SWITCH See LIM ROCK in Jackson Co.

BOYKIN Settlement with discontinued PO at 310845NO865228W in Escambia Co. Named for Robert Hayne Boykin, an early settler, who came to the area c. 1871. PO est. in 1883 (Waters 180).

BOYKIN Settlement with PO at 320440NO871653W in Wilcox Co. Named for Frank W. Boykin (1885–1968), member of the U.S. House of Representatives from the First District (1935–62). PO est. in 1971 (Harris 1982, 28).

BOYLSTON Settlement with PO at 322542NO861646W in Montgomery Co. Probably named for a local family. PO est. in 1827.

BOZEMAN See MARBURY in Autauga Co.

BRADFORD Community with discontinued PO at 325941NO860506W in Coosa Co. Named for Joseph H. Bradford, who erected a textile mill here in 1839. PO est. in 1850 (Harris 1982, 28).

BRADFORD Settlement in 334507NO-864214W in Jefferson Co. Named for a town near Leeds, England, by Jim Justice, fore-

man of the mines opened here in 1880 (Hagood 7).

BRADLEY Settlement with discontinued PO at 310200NO864332W in Escambia Co. First called BRADLEY DAM because the Simpson Co., a lumber firm, built a dam across Panther Creek to form a reservoir for running logs and named it for the W. C. Bradley family. Bradley Dam PO est. in 1892, the word *dam* being dropped in 1894 (Waters 180–81).

BRADLEYTON Settlement with discontinued PO at 315406NO861432W in Crenshaw Co. Named for John Bradley, who settled in the area in 1828. PO est. in 1884 (Harris 1982, 29).

BRAGGS Settlement with discontinued PO at 320301NO864744W in Lowndes Co. Named for the family of the first postmaster, Peter N. Braggs, appointed in 1833 ("Record of Appointment of Postmasters").

BRAGGVILLE Settlement with discontinued PO at 324056NO875950W in Greene Co. Named for Richard Bragg, who settled nearby in 1817. PO est. in 1890 (Rich 1979, 124).

BRANCHVILLE Inc. town with discontinued PO at 333931NO862557W in St. Clair Co. Area called *The Branch* by the first settlers in 1819 because of its location near the headwaters of Kelly Creek. Town given the descriptive and environmental name BRANCHVILLE. Branchville PO est. in 1834. Inc. in 1968 (Rich).

BRANDON See COLLBRAN in DeKalb Co.

BRANNON SPRINGS See SOUTHSIDE in Etowah Co.

BRANTLEY Inc. town with PO at 313456NO861526W in Crenshaw Co. Named for Thomas Kirvin Brantley (1833–1914), a town leader. PO est. in 1891. Inc. in 1895 (M. B. Owen 1:411).

BRANTLEYVILLE Settlement at 331257NO-865230W in Shelby Co. Founded c. 1930 by Thomas Brantley, a prominent citizen who prospered from his own efforts despite losing both legs at the age of ten in a freight train accident (Tamarin 3).

BREMEN ['brimɪn] Settlement with PO at 335940NO865812W in Cullman Co. Founded with the symbolic designation EMPIRE in 1860. To honor the city in Germany and to prevent confusion with another PO in the state, the name was changed by James

Macentepe, the first postmaster, appointed in 1879 (Jones 1972, 71–74).

BRENT Inc. town with PO at 325614NO-870953W in Bibb Co. Named for Brent H. Armstrong, the engineer who directed the construction of the Gulf, Mobile and Ohio RR bridge at this point across the Cahaba River. Armstrong also was first postmaster, appointed in 1899. Inc. in 1913 (Ellison 193–96).

BREWTON Inc. co. seat with PO at 310618NO870420W in Escambia Co. First known as CROSSROADS because two early roads intersected at this point; later called NEWPORT because it was a landing for two large creeks. When the Louisville and Nashville RR station was opened in 1861, the town was named for the first station agent, William Troupe Brewton, a great-nephew of the first settler of the area. PO est. in 1869. Became co. seat in 1880; inc. in 1885 (Waters 243–44).

BRIAR HILL Settlement at 315732NO-860748W in Pike Co. Descriptive and environmental name (Farmer 1973, 399–400; U.S.G.S., 1966 Base Maps).

BRICKYARD Community with discontinued PO at 322420NO850122W in Russell Co. Named for the nearby brick kilns operated by the Bickerstaffs. PO est. in 1892 (Maddox).

BRIDGE CREEK Stream rising at 323828NO863138W in Autauga Co. and joining Autauga Creek at 322933NO863210W. Descriptive and environmental name (Biggs 23; Geological Survey of Alabama, 1894 map).

BRIDGEPORT Inc. town with PO at 345651NO854252W in Jackson Co. Originally called JONESVILLE in the 1830s or 1840s for a local family. Renamed in the the 1850s because of the newly constructed RR bridge across the Tennessee River and because of the town's being an important port on this river. Jonesville PO est. in 1852, Bridgeport PO in 1854. Inc. in 1890 (M. B. Owen 1:440).

BRIDGEVILLE See ELBA in Coffee Co.

BRIERFIELD Settlement with PO at 330220NO865432W in Bibb Co. that grew up around ironworks built in the 1860s. A descriptive and environmental name. PO est. in 1881 (Ellison 109, 191).

BRIER FORK Stream rising in TN and flowing into the Flint River at 344924NO-862902W in Madison Co. Probably a descriptive and environmental name (U.S.G.S., 1966 Base Maps).

BRIGHT See BROOKLYN in Cullman Co.

BRIGHTON Settlement with PO at 332603NO865650W in Jefferson Co. First known as WOODWARD CROSSING because of the RR spur track running between it and Woodward, a nearby settlement named for W. H. Woodward, founder of the Woodward Iron Co. Renamed for the English seaside resort when PO est. in 1894 (Hagood 77).

BRILLIANT Inc. town with PO at 340131NO874530W in Marion Co. Earlier named BOSTON, for the MA city; then renamed for the Brilliant Coal Co., founded by Thomas H. Aldrich, Jr., who was also the first postmaster, appointed in 1899. Inc. in 1927 (Lawler).

BRINDLEY CREEK Stream rising at 341735NO864241W in Cullman Co. and flowing into the Broglen River at 340841NO-864608W. Probably named for Brindley Mountain. Designation approved by U.S. Board on Geographic Names in 1964.

BRINDLEY MOUNTAIN Mountain on which all of Cullman Co., the southern part of Morgan Co., and the western part of Marshall Co. are located. Named for Mace T. P. Brindley (1801–1871), an early settler of Cullman Co. (Ackley 15).

BRINN Community with discontinued PO at 341533NO87843W in Marion Co. Probably named for an early local family. PO est. in 1894.

BROCK See NEW BROCKTON in Coffee Co.

BROCKTON See NEW BROCKTON in Coffee Co.

BROCKTON See COVIN in Fayette Co.

BROCKVILLE See GRAHAM in Randolph Co.

BROGLEN RIVER ['brɑglən] Stream rising at 340841NO864607W in Cullman Co. and flowing into Mulberry Fork of the Black Warrior River at 340343NO864146W. Perhaps named for a local family. Designation approved by U.S. Board on Geographic Names in 1964.

BROMPTON Settlement with discontinued PO at 333455NO862810W in St. Clair Co. Probably named for a local family. PO est. in 1888 (Rich).

BROOKLYN Settlement with PO at 311545NO864616W in Conecuh Co. Named by founder, Edwin Robinson, for his former home, Brooklyn, CT. PO est. in 1829 (T. M. Owen 1:170).

BROOKLYN Settlement at 341333NO-863655W in Cullman Co. Originally named BRIGHT for a local family. Vert Schultz gave it the environmental name BROOKLYN for a nearby brook c. 1905, though he probably also had in mind the city in NY. Bright PO, 1890–1905 (Jones 1972, 53–54).

BROOKS Settlement with discontinued PO at 312854NO864106W in Covington Co. Probably named for a local family. PO est. in 1910.

BROOKSIDE Settlement with PO at 333816NO865500W in Jefferson Co. Name is probably descriptive of community's location by the side of a small stream. Inc. in 1896. PO est. in 1971 (Hagood 45).

BROOKSON See PLETCHER in Chilton Co.

BROOKSVILLE Settlement with discontinued PO at 340943NO862832W in Blount Co. Named for Henry Brooks, who settled here c. 1836 (Blount Co. Historical Society 19, 53).

BROOKWOOD Inc. town with PO at 331520NO871915W in Tuscaloosa Co. This coal-mining settlement, originally having the humorous designation HORSEHEAD, was given its present descriptive and environmental designation when the PO was est. in 1890. Inc. in 1977 (Rich 1979, 126–27).

BROWNEVILLE See PHENIX CITY in Russell Co.

BROWNS Settlement with PO at 322612NO872158W in Dallas Co. Named for Jesse Brown, who donated land here for the Southern RR station. PO est. in 1878 (Harris 1982, 30).

BROWNSBORO Settlement with PO at 344457NO862635W in Madison Co. Named for John Brown, a local miller. PO est. in 1866 (F. C. Roberts 143).

BROWNVILLE Inc. town at 332627NO-865443W in Jefferson Co. Probably named for a local family. Inc. in 1950.

BROWNVILLE Community with discontinued PO at 332342NO874242W in Tuscaloosa Co. Called SULPHUR SPRINGS because of its springs c. 1900; between 1900 and 1920 it had the pejoratively humorous name HOG EYE, referring to its small size; in the early 1920s known as RED VALLEY because of its location and because its houses were painted red. Name changed to BROWNVILLE for W. P. Brown after he founded a lumberyard here in 1925. PO est. in 1926 (Rich 1979, 128–29).

BRUNDIDGE Inc. town with PO at 314312NO854858W in Pike Co. Site of Collier's Store, a business operated by G. C. Collier. Town named for James McGinnis Brundidge, who founded the local Masonic lodge. PO est. in 1856. Inc. in 1893 (Farmer 1973, 87, 347; M. T. Stewart, *Pike Co.*, 17–18).

BRUSH CREEK The following streams have descriptive and environmental names probably because of the dense vegetation on their banks.
1. Stream rising at 330310NO875019W in Greene Co. and flowing into the Sipsey River at 330414NO880000W. Mentioned in the "Copies of the Field Notes of the Original Government Surveys" made c. 1820 (Rich 1979, 129–30).
2. Stream rising at 325540NO875340W in Greene Co. and flowing into the Tombigbee River at 324741NO880355W on the border between Greene Co. and Sumter Co. Located on Snedecor's 1856 *Map of Greene County* (Rich 1979, 129).
3. Stream rising at 345926NO875516W in Lauderdale Co. and flowing into the Tennessee River at 345413NO875911W. Located on 1878 General Land Office map. Earlier names were SUNDAY CREEK (Gardiner's c. 1817 map), for a local resident, and FOUR-MILE CREEK (Tuomey's 1849 map), whose significance is unknown (Sockwell).
4. Stream rising at 323108NO851846W in Lee Co. and flowing into the Uchee River at 322538NO851556W in Russell Co. (U.S.G.S., 1966 Base Maps).
5. Stream rising at 325149NO872251W in Perry Co. and joining Big Brush Creek at 324433NO873120W in Hale Co. (U.S.G.S., 1966 Base Maps).

BRUSHY CREEK Stream rising at 342322NO871842W in Lawrence Co. and flowing into Lewis Smith Lake at 340404NO-871533W in Winston Co. Probably a descriptive name for the dense vegetation in the area (U.S.G.S., 1966 Base Maps).

BRYANT Settlement with discontinued PO at 345637NO853756W in Jackson Co. Named for W. H. Bryant, a wealthy early settler. PO est. in 1891 (Kennamer 186).

BUCK CREEK Stream rising at 324224NO864926W in Chilton Co. and joining Mulberry Creek at 322731NO865155W between Autauga Co. and Dallas Co. Possibly an environmental name that is a translation of an Indian designation (Biggs 23; U.S.G.S., 1966 Base Maps).

BUCKHORN CREEK Stream rising at 315458NO854657W in Bullock Co. and flowing into the Pea River at 314427NO854207W between Pike Co. and Barbour Co. Probably a descriptive and environmental name that is a translation of an Indian designation (M. T. Stewart, *Pike Co.*, 27; U.S.G.S., 1966 Base Maps).

BUCKS Community with PO at 310037NO880127W in Mobile Co. Named for J. E. Bucks, a surveyor. PO est. in 1911 (Harris 1982, 31).

BUCKSNORT See BANKSTON in Fayette Co.

BUCKSVILLE Settlement with discontinued PO at 331642NO870508W in Tuscaloosa Co. Named for David Buck, who purchased land here in 1820 and founded a general store. PO est. in 1833 (Rich 1979, 133).

BUENA VISTA [ˌbjunəˈvɪstə] Community with discontinued PO at 314735NO-871455W in Monroe Co. Settled in 1818 by Andrew Rikard, who named it GERMANY for the country of his ancestors. Jacob W. Perrin, the first postmaster, appointed in 1847, renamed the village in honor of the Battle of Buena Vista in Mexico, in which he had fought in 1846 (Dugas [Monroe Co.] 94).

BUFFALO Settlement with discontinued PO at 325646NO852407W in Chambers Co. Originally BUFFALO WALLOW, the name is said to refer to the large bald spot shaped like a buffalo that is located on the earth here. PO est. in 1872 (Dugas [Chambers Co.] 56).

BUGHALL CREEK Stream rising at 320224NO854629W in Bullock Co. and joining Old Town Creek at 321729NO855240W between Bullock Co. and Macon Co. Name may be a humorous compound of *bug* and *hall* (U.S.G.S., 1966 Base Maps).

BUG TUSSLE See WILBURN in Cullman Co.

BUHL [bjul] Settlement with PO at 331525NO874510W in Tuscaloosa Co. Named for a Mr. Buhl, who was employed by the Mobile and Ohio RR (Gulf, Mobile and Ohio), which reached here in 1898. PO est. in 1900 (Rich 1979, 134).

BULL MOUNTAIN CREEK Stream rising at 341825NO875538W in Marion Co. and flowing into MS at 340603NO882527W. Designation comes from that of a nearby ridge, which probably has a descriptive and environmental name (U.S.G.S., 1966 Base Maps).

BULLOCK Community with discontinued PO at 313226NO861043W in Crenshaw Co. Perhaps named for Edward C. Bullock of Barbour Co., a Confederate officer who died in 1861. PO est. in 1864.

BULLOCK COUNTY Created by act of the state general assembly on Dec. 5, 1866. Bounded on the north by Macon Co., on the east by Russell Co., on the east and southeast by Barbour Co., on the south and southwest by Pike Co., and on the west by Montgomery Co. Named for Edward C. Bullock of Barbour Co., a Confederate officer who died in 1861. Union Springs was chosen to be the co. seat in 1867 (T. M. Owen 1:174–75; 2:1348).

BURBANK Settlement with discontinued PO at 311304NO882326W in Washington Co. Named for Luther Burbank, the famed horticulturist who had recommended the area to the German immigrants settling here. PO est. in 1903 (Matte 278).

BURCHFIELD Settlement with discontinued PO at 332041NO871755W in Tuscaloosa Co. Coal-mining town named for a family who settled here in 1830. PO est. in 1894 (Rich 1979, 136).

BURKVILLE Community with PO at 321941NO863213W in Lowndes Co. Probably named for the family of Timothy Burke, the first postmaster, appointed in 1876 ("Record of Appointment of Postmasters").

BURLINGTON Community with discontinued PO at 323449NO855620W in Elmore Co. Perhaps a name borrowed from an eastern city. PO est. in 1900.

BURNSVILLE Settlement with discontinued PO at 322828NO865330W in Dallas Co. Named for James H. Burns, who settled here in 1838. PO est. in 1841 (Harris 1982, 32).

BURNT CORN Settlement with PO at 313312NO870937W on the boundary between Monroe Co. and Conecuh Co. First called BURNT CORN SPRING because of its location near a spring of that name. Site of the Battle of Burnt Corn, which took place in 1813 between local militia and Creek Indians. PO est. in 1817 (Dugas [Monroe Co.] 94).

BURNT CORN CREEK Stream rising at 313244NO870924W in Conecuh Co. and flowing into the Conecuh River at 310547NO-870434W in Escambia Co. Named for the spring where James Cornells, a half-breed Creek Indian, is said to have found in the early 1800s burned or charred corn. Designation may, however, be a translation of an Indian incident name (T. M. Owen 1:179; G. R. Stewart 1970, 66).

BURNWELL Settlement with PO at 334228NO870515W in Walker Co. First called BURNWELL MINES, for the nearby coal mines, whose name may have been a descriptive compound. PO est. in 1909.

BUSHY CREEK Stream rising at 310530NO873858W in Baldwin Co. and joining Dyas Creek at 305623NO874123W. Probably a descriptive and environmental name referring to the dense vegetation in the area (U.S.G.S., 1966 Base Maps).

BUTLER Inc. co. seat with PO at 320522NO881319W in Choctaw Co. Formerly called HENDRIX CROSSROADS for a local family. Later named for Pierce Butler of SC, a colonel killed in the Mexican War in 1847. Inc. in 1847. PO est. in 1848 (Choctaw Co. Bicentennial Commission 1, 11–12, 18).

BUTLER COUNTY Created on Dec. 13, 1819, by act of the AL territorial general assembly. Bounded on the north by Lowndes Co., on the east by Crenshaw Co., on the south by Covington Co. and Conecuh Co., and on the west by Conecuh Co., Monroe Co., and Wilcox Co. Named for William Butler, a militia captain killed by Creek Indians in 1818. Fort Dale served as the tempo-

rary co. seat until Greenville was chosen to be the permanent one in 1822 (Dugas [Butler Co.] 78–79).

BUTLER SPRINGS Settlement with discontinued PO at 314807NO865158W in Butler Co. This resort town, which developed around mineral springs, was named for the co. PO est. in 1850 (Dugas [Butler Co.] 78).

BUTTAHATCHEE, LAKE [ˌbʌtəˈhætʃɪ] Artificial lake at 340659NO874206W in Marion Co. Named for the river impounded since the early 1960s (U.S.G.S., 1966 Base Maps).

BUTTAHATCHEE RIVER Stream rising at 341113NO873719W in Winston Co. and flowing into the Tombigbee River in MS. Joined at 340714NO874455W by the West Branch of Buttahatchee River, which rises at 341246NO874042W in Winston Co. BUTTAHATCHEE R. on La Tourette's 1844 map. Name is derived from Choctaw *bati* 'sumac' and *hacha* 'river' (Read 10).

BUTTSVILLE See GREENVILLE in Butler Co.

BUXAHATCHIE See CALERA in Shelby Co.

BUZBEEVILLE See VICTORIA in Coffee Co.

BYLER See BANKSTON in Fayette Co.

BYNUM [ˈbaɪnəm] Settlement with PO at 333647NO855740W in Calhoun Co. Named for the family of Ely Bynum, who settled in the area in the 1840s. PO est. in 1883 (Jolly).

BYRD SPRING LAKE Artificial lake at 343844NO863605W in Madison Co. Named for the spring, on land owned by the Byrd family in the 1880s, whose waters are the source of the stream impounded c. 1960 to form the lake (Green).

CADDO [ˈkædo] Settlement with discontinued PO at 343409NO870824W in Lawrence Co. Circumstances of naming unknown, but the word is the designation of a group of Indian tribes found in LA and TX who spoke Caddoan, the language of the Kadohadacho Confederacy. The term *kadohadacho* means 'real chiefs.' PO est. in 1901 (Harder 73).

CAGLE'S CROSSROADS See DOG TOWN in DeKalb Co.

CAHABA [kəˈhabə] Dead town with discontinued PO on the west bank of the Alabama River just north of the mouth of the Cahaba River at 321900NO870605W in Dallas Co. Founded by the Frenchman Crozat as a trading post on a large land grant from Louis XV. Named for the river. Served as the first official state capital, 1819–26, and first co. seat, 1819–65. When the co. seat of justice was moved to Selma after several devastating floods, the town's inhabitants moved away. PO est. in 1819 (Harris 1977, 66–67; C. H. Stewart 10–12).

CAHABA HEIGHTS   Inc. town with PO on a high bank of the Cahaba River at 332750NO864355W in Jefferson Co. Named for the river. Inc. in 1954. Now merged with Homewood. PO est. in 1971 (League of Municipalities).

CAHABA RIVER   Stream rising at 334115NO863600W in St. Clair Co. and flowing into the Alabama River at 321909NO-870541W in Dallas Co. CABO R. on D'Anville's 1732 map. CAHAWBA R. on *Early's Map of Georgia*, c. 1818. Name seems to be derived from Choctaw *oka* 'water' and *aba* 'above' (T. M. Owen 1:188).

CAHAWBA COUNTY See BIBB COUNTY.

CAIRO ['kero]   Settlement with discontinued PO at 345214NO870840W in Limestone Co. Name is that of the ancient city in Egypt, but it is probably merely reminiscent here. Caro [*sic*] PO est. in 1888.

CALCIS ['kælsɪs]   Settlement with discontinued PO at 332535NO862554W in Shelby Co. Name is derived from *calcium*, the designation of one of the components of the limestone upon which the mining town is located. PO est. in 1899 (Tamarin 4).

CALDWELL   Community at 335245NO-855509W in Calhoun Co. Incorrectly spelled COLWELL on the 1966 U.S.G.S. Base Maps. Named for Swan Caldwell, who owned and developed the area in the 1940s (Jolly).

CALEBEE CREEK [kə'libɪ]   Stream rising at 321424NO853310W in Macon Co. and flowing into the Tallapoosa River at 322634NO855652W between Macon Co. and Elmore Co. CALOEBEE in Benjamin Hawkins's "A Sketch of the Creek Country in 1798 and 1799" (49). Name seems to come from Creek *kalapi* 'overcup oak' (Read 11).

CALERA [kə'lɪrə]   Inc. town with PO at 330610NO864513W in Shelby Co. John R. Gambel, one of Andrew Jackson's soldiers who settled here soon after the Creek Indian War ended in 1814, gave the community its environmental name, the Spanish word for 'lime kiln.' Before 1814 area was known as BUXAHATCHIE, probably a different form of BUXIHATCHEE, the name of a creek in Chilton Co. that is derived from Creek *pakacha* 'commander' and *hachi* 'creek.' During 1853–54, when the Alabama and Tennessee Rivers RR (Southern) reached here, the station and newly established PO were called LIME STATION. Calera PO est. in 1869. Town inc. in 1887 (Read 10; Tamarin 5).

CALHOUN   Settlement with discontinued PO at 320300NO863242W in Lowndes Co. Probably named for the SC statesman John C. Calhoun (1782–1850). PO est. in 1859.

CALHOUN COUNTY   Created by act of the state general assembly on Dec. 18, 1832. Now bounded on the north by Etowah Co. and Cherokee Co., on the east by Cleburne Co., on the south by Talladega Co., and on the west by St. Clair Co. First named for Thomas Hart Benton (1782–1858) from SC, later a U.S. senator from MO, who had fought here during the Creek Indian War of 1813–14. Because Benton's political views by 1858 differed from those of most people in this area, the name was changed on Jan. 29 of that year to honor John C. Calhoun of SC, a spokesman for southern causes. The co. seat was Jacksonville until 1899, when the present one, Anniston, was chosen (Jolly).

CALUMET   Settlement with discontinued PO at 334741NO871713W in Walker Co. Name probably refers to the long ornamental pipe used by Indians for the ceremonial smoking of tobacco, though the word is the Norman-Picard term meaning 'tobacco pipe.' PO est. in 1902 (Read xiv).

CALVERT   Settlement with PO at 310918NO880036W on the border between Mobile Co. and Washington Co. Possibly named for the Calverts of MD. PO est. in 1929.

CAMDEN   Community with discontinued PO located about 10 miles south of Fort

Payne in DeKalb Co. Named for Camden, SC, where Baron de Kalb, for whom the co. was named, was killed during the American Revolution. PO est. in 1835. Served as the third co. seat, in 1838 (Raughton 24).

CAMDEN   See PAINT ROCK in Jackson Co.

CAMDEN   Inc. co. seat with PO at 315927NO871726W in Wilcox Co. Founded in the early 1830s and named BAR-BOURSVILLE for an early local family. Became co. seat in 1832. Inc. in 1841 as CAMDEN, for Camden, SC, the former home of many of the town's settlers. PO est. in 1842 (T. M. Owen 1:196).

CAMPBELL   Settlement with PO at 315524NO875852W in Clarke Co. Settled during the early 1800s and named MIL-LERSVILLE for a family from SC. Later renamed for a physician who lived in the area. PO est. in 1886 (Clarke Co. Historical Society 70–72).

CAMP CREEK   Stream rising at 341434NO874852W in Marion Co. and joining Williams Creek at 340831NO875229W. Name probably refers to a nearby place where Indians or settlers camped (U.S.G.S., 1966 Base Maps).

CAMP HILL   Inc. town with PO at 324801NO853913W in Tallapoosa Co. Name refers to the practice in the 1830s and 1840s of people from the north and east on their way to Wetumpka camping on a small hill near a large spring, now in the eastern part of the town. The settlement that grew up here was also once called ASHBANK because of the grayish sandy soil surrounding it. Camp Hill PO est. in 1849. Inc. in 1895 (Dugas [Tallapoosa Co.] 86).

CAMP SMITH   See LITTLEVILLE in Colbert Co.

CANDUTCHKEE CREEK   See EN-ITACHOPCO CREEK.

CANE CREEK   The names of the following streams are probably descriptive of the grass on their banks having long stiff stems and forming dense thickets or canebrakes.
1. Stream rising at 334341NO854420W in Calhoun Co. and flowing into the Coosa River at 334354NO860619W between Calhoun Co. and St. Clair Co. Name in use since 1836 (Jolly).
2. Stream rising at 343510NO874811W in Colbert Co. and flowing into the Tennessee River

at 344516NO875137W (Tuomey, 1849 map).
3. Stream rising at 335211NO872130W in Walker Co. and flowing into Mulberry Fork of the Black Warrior River at 334532NO871008W (U.S.G.S., 1966 Base Maps).

CANOE   Settlement with discontinued PO at 310134NO872443W in Escambia Co. on the Louisville and Nashville RR. Founded in 1852 when Andrew Jackson Hall (1820–1885) and his family moved from FL across the state line and bought land to settle here. First called CANOE STATION. Name refers to the long narrow boat used by Indians and later by many of the early settlers. PO est. in 1915 (Waters 181).

CANOE CREEK   See CYPRESS CREEK.

CANTON BLUFF   Community with discontinued PO on the high west bank of the Alabama River at 320312NO872056W in Wilcox Co. Probably named for either Canton, NC, or Canton, GA. Co. seat, 1819–32. Canton PO est. in 1824 (Harris 1982, 35).

CAPPS   Settlement with discontinued PO at 312949NO851843W in Henry Co. Named for the first postmaster, Daniel W. Capps, appointed in 1849 ("Record of Appointment of Postmasters").

CAPSHAW   ['kæpʃɔ]   Settlement with PO at 344623NO864734W in Limestone Co. Although some residents believe the town was named for an early settler, most authorities think the name is of Indian origin, deriving it from Chickasaw *bok kapassa* 'cold creek' or *oka kapassa* 'cold water.' PO est. in 1918 (McMillan in Read 100; Read 12).

CARBON HILL   Inc. town with PO at 335330NO873134W in Walker Co. Name probably refers to the coal that was mined from the hills here. PO est. in 1888. Inc. in 1891 (M. B. Owen 1:517).

CARDIFF   Inc. town with PO at 333844NO865601W in Jefferson Co. Named for the city in Wales. PO est. in 1890. Inc. in 1900 (Hagood 5).

CARLOWVILLE   Settlement with discontinued PO at 320513NO870203W in Dallas Co. Named for the first postmaster, Sylvester Carlow, appointed in 1832 ("Record of Appointment of Postmasters").

CARLTON   Settlement with PO at 312035NO875044W in Clarke Co. Original PO known as HAL'S LAKE, for impoundment beside which a runaway slave built a log stockade, was est. in 1892. Name changed to

28

honor an early family when Carlton PO was est. in 1902 (Clarke Co. Historical Society 77).

CARNS   Settlement at 344833NO855827W in Jackson Co. Name is a mispronunciation and consequent misspelling of the possessive form of the name of the Corn family, who settled in the area c. 1820 (Chambless).

CAROLINA   Inc. town with discontinued PO at 311426NO863140W in Covington Co. Named for the Carolinas, former home of many of the early settlers. PO est. in 1900 (Harris 1982, 36).

CARPENTER   Community with discontinued PO at 305125NO875158W in Baldwin Co. Named for Auretius M. Carpenter, killed while serving in the army during the Spanish-American War. PO est. in 1898 (Bush 36).

CARPENTER   See LONG ISLAND in Jackson Co.

CARROLL CREEK   Stream rising at 332210NO874140W in Tuscaloosa Co. and flowing into the North River at 331857NO-873210W. Named for an early local family. Mentioned in John Coffee's 1820 survey of the county (Rich 1979, 145).

CARROLLSVILLE   First seat of justice for Jefferson Co., 1819–21. The area where the settlement was located is now part of southwestern Birmingham. Named for either the town's first schoolmaster, Thomas Carroll from SC, or William Carroll, Andrew Jackson's inspector general (Harris 1977, 69).

CARROLLTON   Inc. co. seat with PO at 331522NO880505W in Pickens Co. Founded in 1830 after the U.S. government provided eighty acres of land for a permanent seat of justice. Named for Charles Carroll (1737–1832), MD patriot and signer of the Declaration of Independence. Inc. in 1831. PO est. in 1832 (N. F. Brown 29).

CARRVILLE   Inc. town with discontinued PO at 323259NO855212W in Tallapoosa Co. Named for Jesse A. Carr, the first postmaster, appointed in 1894. Inc. in 1903 (Dugas [Tallapoosa Co.] 86).

CARSON   Settlement with discontinued PO at 312820NO875629W in Washington Co. Named for the family of Thomas Carson, an early settler who bought land here in 1802. PO est. in 1888 (Matte 281).

CARTHAGE   See MOUNDVILLE in Hale Co.

CASTLEBERRY   Inc. town with PO at 311756NO870121W in Conecuh Co. Area first known as *Wilson's Field* for an early landowner; settlement named for the Castleberry family, whose dwelling served as a relay house on the stage route from Pensacola, FL, to Montgomery. PO est. in 1869. Inc. in 1912 (M. B. Owen 1:401).

CATALPA   [kə'tɔlpə]   Settlement with discontinued PO at 315246NO854959W in Pike Co. Probably an environmental name, for the catalpa trees growing in the area. PO est. in 1888.

CATHERINE   Settlement with PO on the Southern RR at 321104NO872810W in Wilcox Co. Named for the wife of a RR official. PO est. in 1888 (Harris 1982, 36–37).

CATOMA CREEK   [kə'tomə]   Stream rising at 320950NO860644W in Montgomery Co. and flowing into the Alabama River at the northwestern border of the co. at 322227NO-862744W. A tributary, Little Catoma Creek, rises at 320548NO860034W in the same co. and joins the larger stream at 321617NO-861102W. AUKE THOME on De Crenay's 1733 map. CATOMA on La Tourette's 1844 map. The name is derived from Alabama *oki* 'water' and *Tohome*, the name of a Muskhogean tribe that was living near Mobile in 1729. Meaning of *Tohome* is uncertain (Read 12).

CATOOSA   See WILTON in Shelby Co.

CAVE SPRING   See OLD BETHEL in Colbert Co.

CAVE SPRINGS   See SMITHSONIA in Lauderdale Co.

CECIL   ['sisəl]   Settlement with PO at 321809NO860031W in Montgomery Co. Possibly named for Cecil McDade, member of a prominent local family. PO est. in 1895 (Freeman).

CEDAR BEND   See SOUTHSIDE in Etowah Co.

CEDAR BLUFF   Inc. town with PO on the high east bank of the Coosa River at 341312NO853628W in Cherokee Co. Inc. in 1837 as JEFFERSON, probably to honor Thomas Jefferson (1743–1826), third president of the U.S. (1801–09). Its current name is a descriptive and environmental one. First co. seat, 1837–44. Cedar Bluff PO est. in 1842 (Harris 1982, 37).

CEDAR CREEK   The following streams have environmental names, some of which may be translations of Indian designations.

1. Stream rising at 312029NO865830W in Conecuh Co. and joining Burnt Corn Creek at 310809NO870118W in Escambia Co. (U.S.G.S., 1966 Base Maps).

2. Stream rising at 342551NO873605W in Franklin Co. and joining Little Bear Creek at 343859NO880758W (U.S.G.S., 1966 Base Maps).

3. Stream rising at 311929NO852424W in Houston Co. and flowing into the Chattahoochee River at 311719NO852153W (U.S.G.S., 1966 Base Maps).

4. Stream rising at 310617NO881342W in Mobile Co. and flowing into the Mobile River at 310321NO875954W (U.S.G.S., 1966 Base Maps).

CEDAR CROSSING   See LACON in Morgan Co.

CEDAR GROVE   Settlement on the Southern RR at 345000NO855222W in Jackson Co. Descriptive and environmental name for once-abundant cedar trees in the area. Also called CEDAR SWITCH. Settled around 1840 (Melancon).

CEDAR GROVE   See LEEDS in Jefferson Co.

CEDAR LAKE   Settlement at 343316NO-865825W in Morgan Co. Probably a descriptive and environmental name (U.S.G.S., 1966 Base Maps).

CEDAR POINT   Cape on Mississippi Sound at 301841NO880815W in Mobile Co. Probably a descriptive and environmental name (U.S.G.S., 1966 Base Maps).

CEDARVILLE   Community with discontinued PO at 323645NO874010W in Hale Co. Probably a descriptive and environmental name. PO est. in 1879.

CENTER   See DEARMANVILLE in Calhoun Co.

CENTER HILL   Settlement at 340522NO-864329W in Cullman Co. Probably a descriptive or locational name (*Official 1959 Alabama Highway Map*).

CENTER POINT   Settlement with PO at 333717NO864136W in Jefferson Co. Robert Franklin, owner of a store located here in 1898, when asked by Birmingham merchants where to ship the supplies he had purchased from them, gave the place this name, because it was halfway between the road to Chalkville and the one to Pinson. PO est. in 1938 (Hagood 44).

CENTER STAR   Settlement with discontinued PO in the center of land once disputed by the Cherokees and the Chickasaws at 345141NO872720W in Lauderdale Co. Founded before the Civil War as CENTRE. Renamed for the PO est. in 1850 that was on a *star* 'major' postal route (Sockwell).

CENTERVILLE   Community at 312425NO-865158W in Conecuh Co. Probably a locational name (*Official 1983–84 Alabama Highway Map*).

CENTERVILLE   See MONROEVILLE in Monroe Co.

CENTRAL   Settlement with PO at 324056NO860551W in Elmore Co. Probably originally named for the Central Plank Road, a toll road from Montgomery heading north. Between 1870 and 1890 the community was known as CENTRAL INSTITUTE, because the Central Southern Mechanical and Literary Institute, organized in 1852, was located here. Central Institute PO est. in 1870, *institute* being dropped in 1890 (Brannon 1929, 3).

CENTRAL CITY   Settlement at 311435NO-855306W in Coffee Co. Probably a locational name (*Official 1959 Alabama Highway Map*).

CENTRAL MILLS   Community with discontinued PO on the Louisville and Nashville RR at 321710NO872627W in Dallas Co. A mill was probably once located in this west-central RR stop. PO est. in 1878 (Nelms).

CENTRE   Inc. co. seat with PO at 340907NO854044W in Cherokee Co. Name is descriptive of town's central location in the co. Chosen co. seat in 1844. PO est. in 1865. Inc. in 1897 (*Alabama: A Guide*, 390).

CENTRE   See CENTER STAR in Lauderdale Co.

CENTREVILLE   Inc. co. seat with PO on the Cahaba River at 325640NO870819W in Bibb Co. With its original descriptive and environmental name FALLS OF THE CAHAWBA, the settlement served as the first co. seat, 1819–22. When PO est. in 1821, name changed to CENTREVILLE COURT HOUSE, later CENTREVILLE, because of the town's location between two points in a land survey. Under this designation, co. seat, 1829–. Inc. in 1832 (Ellison 21–22).

CENTREVILLE   See TROY in Pike Co.

CHALKVILLE   Settlement at 333911NO-863852W in Jefferson Co. Name descriptive of the outcroppings of chalk rock in the area

(Hagood 37–38; *Official 1959 Alabama Highway Map*).

CHAMBERS COUNTY   Created by act of the state general assembly on Dec. 18, 1832. Bounded on the north by Randolph Co., on the east by GA, on the south by Lee Co., and on the west by Tallapoosa Co. Named for Henry Chambers (1790–1826), a Huntsville physician who was one of the first U.S. senators elected from the state following its admission to the Union. Chambers Court House was the temporary co. seat, Apr.–Oct. 1833, when the present one, Lafayette, was chosen (Dugas [Chambers Co.] 56).

CHAMBERS COURT HOUSE   Dead town with discontinued PO located 3 1/2 miles northeast of Lafayette in Chambers Co. James Thompson, the probate judge, who was also the first postmaster, chose the house of Baxter Taylor to serve as the temporary seat of justice for the co., Apr.–Oct. 1833. PO, 1830–49 (Harris 1977, 70).

CHAMBERSVILLE   See LAFAYETTE in Chambers Co.

CHAMPION   Community with discontinued PO at 335608NO862644W in Blount Co. Probably given the name of the nearby mines. PO est. in 1890 (Weaver).

CHANCE   Settlement with PO at 314455NO873155W in Clarke Co. Called CANE CREEK for a nearby stream, 1880–92. Site of McDuffie's Gin. The traditional explanation of the current name is that the first postmaster, Butler V. Dozier, appointed in 1892, said he would "take another chance" after *Cane Creek* and several other names proposed for the PO were not approved by the PO Dept. (Clarke Co. Historical Society 83–89).

CHANCELLOR   Settlement with PO at 311053NO855238W in Geneva Co. Named for Wiley J. Chancellor, an early settler. PO est. in 1900 (Harris 1982, 37).

CHANDLER MOUNTAIN   Mountain whose summit is at 335504NO861804W in St. Clair Co. Named for Joel Chandler, who brought his family to this area soon after the Creek Indians were removed in 1814 (Rich).

CHANDLER SPRINGS   Community with discontinued PO at 331950NO855954W in Talladega Co. A former summer resort named for the original owner, James Chandler (1801–1885). PO est. in 1852 (McMillan).

CHANNAHATCHEE CREEK   [tʃɪnɪˈhætʃɪ] Stream rising at 324200NO8605525W in Tallapoosa Co. and flowing into the Tallapoosa River at 323801NO855333W on the border between Elmore Co. and Tallapoosa Co. Name derived from Creek *achina* 'cedar' and *hachi* 'creek' (McMillan in Read 100; Read 13).

CHAPMAN   Community with PO at 314016NO864244W in Butler Co. When the Louisville and Nashville RR reached here in the 1880s, it was referred to as CHAPMAN'S STATION in honor of John R. Chapman, a stockholder in the Rocky Creek Lumber Co. Name officially changed to CHAPMAN on Sept. 1, 1887, when PO was est. (Dugas [Butler Co.] 78).

CHARLESTON   See ARITON in Dale Co.

CHASE   Community with discontinued PO at 344700NO863248W in Madison Co. Originally called MERCURY, possibly for the Roman messenger of the gods, its PO was est. with this name in 1889. Later named for the Chase family who moved here from ME. Chase PO est. in 1908 (Harris 1982, 38).

CHASTANG   Settlement with discontinued PO at 310215NO880124W in Mobile Co. Named for nearby Chastang Bluff, which honors Dr. John Chastang, who settled here in the 1750s. PO est. in 1890 (Harris 1982, 38).

CHATAHOSPEE CREEK   [ˌtʃætəˈhɑspɪ] Stream rising at 325558NO852343W in Chambers Co. and flowing into the Tallapoosa River at 325826NO853756W in Tallapoosa Co. The name is derived from Creek *chato* 'rock,' *ak* 'down,' and *sufki* 'deep' (Read 13; U.S.G.S., 1966 Base Maps).

CHATOM   Inc. co. seat with PO at 312754NO881516W in Washington Co. The name is a reduced form of that of a co. in VA honoring William Pitt, the first earl of Chatham (1708–1778). PO est. in 1904. Chosen co. seat in 1907. Inc. in 1949 (G. R. Stewart 1970, 88).

CHATTAHOOCHEE RIVER   [ˌtʃætəˈhutʃɪ] Stream that forms the lower half of the boundary between AL and GA, rising at 344828NO834730W and flowing into Lake Seminole in

Florida at 304230NO845145W. CHAT-TOHO-CHE in Benjamin Hawkins's "A Sketch of the Creek Country in 1798 and 1799" (52). The name, descriptive of the rocks on the bed of the river, is derived from Creek *chato* 'rock' and *huchi* 'marked' (Read 14).

CHATTASOFKA CREEK [ˌtʃɔtəˈsɔfkə] Stream rising at 325521NO853651W in Tallapoosa Co. and flowing into the Tallapoosa River at 324822NO854601W. CHATOKSOFKE in Albert S. Gatschet's *A Migration Legend of the Creek Indians*, 1884, 1888. Name is derived from Creek *chato* 'rock,' *ak* 'down,' and *sufki* 'deep' (Read 13).

CHEAHA CREEK [ˈtʃihɔ] Stream rising at 332844NO854856W in Clay Co. and joining Choccolocco Creek at 333229NO860246W in Talladega Co. Mentioned in 1832 "Field Notes of the Original Government Surveyor." CHEHAWHAW or POTATOE CR. on La Tourette's 1833 map. Possibly from Choctaw *chaha* 'high' (McMillan; Read 14).

CHEAHA MOUNTAIN Mountain whose summit is 2,407 feet above sea level at 332908NO854833W in Cleburne Co. The tallest mountain in AL, its name may be derived from Choctaw *chaha* 'high.' Approved by U.S. Board on Geographic Names in 1906 (McMillan in Read 87; Read 14).

CHELSEA Settlement with PO at 332024NO863749W in Shelby Co. Named for either the London district or the towns in the eastern part of the U.S. that have borrowed its name. PO est. in 1908 (Tamarin 6).

CHEPULTEPEC See ALLGOOD in Blount Co.

CHEROKEE Inc. town with PO at 344525NO875822W in Colbert Co. Founded in 1856 after the completion of the Memphis and Charleston RR (Southern) and named for the Indians who had once claimed the land upon which it is located. PO est. in 1856. Inc. in 1871 (Sockwell).

CHEROKEE COUNTY Created by act of the state general assembly on Jan. 9, 1836.

Bounded on the northwest by DeKalb Co., on the east by GA, on the south by Calhoun Co. and Cleburne Co., and on the west by Etowah Co. The name, that of a powerful Iroquoian tribe, is probably derived from Creek *Tciloki* or *Chilokee* 'people of a different speech.' The first co. seat was Cedar Bluff, until 1844, when the present one, Centre, was chosen (Read 15; Swanton 1937, 213).

CHESSER See SHADY GROVE in Pike Co.

CHESSON Settlement with discontinued PO at 321737NO855528W in Macon Co. Perhaps named for a local family. PO est. in 1892.

CHESTNUT Settlement with discontinued PO at 314827NO871356W in Monroe Co. A large chestnut tree at the crossroads where the town is located suggested the descriptive and environmental name. PO est. in 1886 (Dugas [Monroe Co.] 94).

CHESTNUT CREEK Stream rising at 324801NO862428W in Chilton Co. and flowing into the Coosa River at 324619NO862428W on the border between Chilton Co. and Coosa Co. An environmental name (Covington 6; U.S.G.S., 1966 Base Maps).

CHESTNUT CREEK See COOPER in Chilton Co.

CHEWACLA CREEK [tʃiˈwæklə] Stream rising at 323707NO852049W in Lee Co. and joining Uphapee Creek at 322534NO853720W in Macon Co. SAWACKLAHATCHEE C. on La Tourette's 1844 map. Name is derived from Hitchiti *sawi* 'raccoon,' *ukli* 'town,' and *hahchi* 'stream' (Read 15).

CHEWALLEE See ELK RIVER.

CHICKASAW See RIVERTON in Colbert Co.

CHICKASAW Inc. town with PO at 304549NO880429W in Mobile Co. The name is that of a Muskhogean tribe at one time living in the area. Though the full designation cannot be translated, Swanton believes the ending is the Choctaw and Chickasaw locative -*asha* 'it sits there' or 'it is there.' PO est. in 1924. Inc. in 1946 (Read 16; Swanton 1937, 213).

CHICKASAW BOGUE Stream rising at 321400NO873133W in Marengo Co. and flowing into the Tombigbee River at 321733NO875545W on the border between Marengo Co. and Choctaw Co. On La Tourette's 1844 map.

Named for the Indian tribe. *Bogue* comes from Choctaw *bok* 'creek' (Read 17).

CHICKASAW CREEK   Stream rising at 310253NO881333W in Mobile Co. and flowing into the Mobile River at 304418NO880240W. On La Tourette's 1844 map. Named for the Indian tribe (Read 17).

CHIGGER HILL   Settlement at 342351NO860059W in DeKalb Co. Traditional explanation is that the town was named in 1918 for the larvae of mites that infested the hill on which it is located. Once known as ELROD MILL (Landmarks 94).

CHIKASANOXEE CREEK   [,tʃɪkəsɔ'nɑksɪ] Stream rising at 330726NO852206W in Chambers Co. and flowing into the Tallapoosa River at 330301NO853316W. COHOASANOCSA CR. on La Tourette's 1833 map. Name is probably derived from Creek *koha* 'cane' and *chanaksi* 'ridge,' the first element being later confused with the tribal name *Chickasaw* (Read 16).

CHILATCHEE CREEK   [tʃɪ'lætʃɪ] Stream rising at 322459NO872838W in Perry Co. and flowing into the Alabama River at 320833NO871508W on the border between Dallas Co. and Wilcox Co. CHILATCHEE CR. on E. A. Smith's 1891 map in Berney. Name derived from Choctaw *chula* 'fox' and *hacha* 'stream' or 'river' (Read 17).

CHILDERSBURG   Inc. town with PO at 331641NO862118W in Talladega Co. Named for Thomas Childress, an early settler. PO est. in 1855. Inc. in 1889 (McMillan).

CHILTON COUNTY   Created by act of the state legislature on Dec. 30, 1868, from part of Bibb Co. Bounded on the north by Shelby Co., on the east by Coosa Co. and Elmore Co., on the south by Autauga Co. and Dallas Co., and on the west by Perry Co. and Bibb Co. First named BAKER COUNTY for Alfred Baker, a prominent local citizen who owned the land where the co. seat was located. Renamed CHILTON COUNTY on Dec. 17, 1874, for William Parrish Chilton

(1810–1871), a member of the Confederate Congress and a chief justice of the state supreme court. Clanton is the co. seat (Covington iii).

CHINA GROVE   Settlement with discontinued PO at 320146NO855641W in Pike Co. Name is probably a descriptive and environmental one referring to the chinaberry trees in the area. PO est. in 1857 (Farmer 1973, 11).

CHINNEBY   ['tʃɪnɪbɪ]   Settlement with discontinued PO on the Louisville and Nashville RR at 332746NO855801W in Talladega Co. One of the locations of FORT CHINNEBY, used by white settlers and friendly Creeks in the Creek Indian War of 1813–14. Honors Chinnibee, a Creek chief, whose name is probably derived from Creek *achina* 'cedar' and *api* 'tree.' PO est. in 1840 (McMillan; Read 17).

CHISCA   ['tʃɪskə]   Community on the St. Louis and San Francisco RR at 334848NO872920W in Walker Co. Name is derived from Creek *chisca* 'base of a tree,' a term applied to a place occupied by the Yuchi Indians, an ancient subtribe of whom were known as 'the Root People' (Read 18; Semmes, 1929 map; Swanton 1937, 213).

CHOCCOLOCCO   [tʃɑkə'lɑkə]   Settlement with PO at 333933NO854213W in Calhoun Co. Named for the nearby creek. PO est. in 1878 (Jolly; McMillan in Read 100).

CHOCCOLOCCO   See WHITE PLAINS in Calhoun Co.

CHOCCOLOCCO CREEK   Stream rising at 334754NO853447W in Calhoun Co. and flowing into Logan Martin Lake of the Coosa River on the border between Talladega Co. and St. Clair Co. at 333212NO861200W. CHOCKOLOCKO CR. on La Tourette's 1833 map. Name is derived from Creek *chahki* 'shoal' and *lako* 'big.' The translation BIG SHOALS CREEK appears on some early maps (Read 18).

CHOCTAW   Settlement with discontinued PO at 321232NO880539W in Choctaw Co. Named for the co. Also known as CHOCTAW CITY. PO est. in 1912 (Choctaw Co. Bicentennial Commission 18).

CHOCTAW BLUFF   Community with discontinued PO on a high bank of the Alabama River at 312135NO874601W in Clarke Co. Oldest settlement in the co. Founded by the James and the Darrington families in 1789.

Named for the river bluff on which it is located. PO est. in 1878 (Clarke Co. Historical Society 49).

CHOCTAW COUNTY   Created by act of the state general assembly on Dec. 29, 1847, from portions of Washington Co. and Sumter Co. Bordered on the north by Sumter Co., on the east by Marengo Co. and Clarke Co., on the south by Washington Co., and on the west by MS. Name is that of the Indian tribe who lived in southeast MS and southwest AL. It is derived from the Choctaw term *chahta*, whose meaning is unknown. Butler is the co. seat (T. M. Owen 1:252; Read 18).

CHOCTAWHATCHEE RIVER   [ˌtʃɑktɔˈhætʃi] Stream formed by the confluence, at 312140NO853301W in Dale Co., of the East Fork of the Choctawhatchee River, which rises at 315207NO852150W in Barbour Co., and the West Fork, which rises at 314513NO852947W in Barbour Co. River flows south into Choctawhatchee Bay of the Gulf of Mexico at 302413NO860725W. First part of the designation, *Choctaw* (*Chahta*), was apparently confused with *Chatot*, the name of an Indian tribe living near Mobile about 1706, whose meaning is unknown. The second element is from Creek *hachi* 'river' or 'stream.' Designation approved by U.S. Board on Geographic Names in 1892. A tributary, Little Choctawhatchee River, rises at 311902NO852514W in Henry Co. and flows into the larger river at 311519NO854032W in Dale Co. (Read 19).

CHRISTIAN HOME   Community at 345207NO854252W in Jackson Co. Named for an early church once located here (Melancon; U.S.G.S., 1966 Base Maps).

CHRYSLER   Settlement with discontinued PO at 311818NO874204W in Monroe Co. Name may be that of a local family or possibly of the automobile manufacturer. PO est. in 1926.

CHUBBEHATCHEE CREEK   [ˌtʃʌbɪˈhætʃi] Stream rising at 323842NO860708W in

Elmore Co. and flowing into the Tallapoosa River at 322519NO860507W on the border between Elmore Co. and Montgomery Co. HATCHEE CHUBBEE on La Tourette's 1844 map. Name is derived from Creek *hachi* 'creek' and *chaba* 'halfway.' The elements were reversed to distinguish this creek from Hatchechubbee, the stream in Russell Co. (Read 19–20).

CHULAFINEE   See ROANOKE in Randolph Co.

CHUNCHULA   [tʃʌnˈtʃulə]   Settlement with PO on the Mobile and Ohio RR at 305518NO881202W in Mobile Co. On G. W. Colton's 1855 map. Owen derives the name from Choctaw *hachunchoba* [*hachunchuba*] 'alligator.' Read says that though the name may be a hybrid of *hachunchuba* and Choctaw *chula* 'fox,' he thinks it may be the Spanish masculine plural noun *chunchullos* (meaning 'tripe,' the lining of the stomach of cattle or sheep used as a food), which, in turn, comes from Kechuan *ch'unchull.* PO est. in 1873 (T.M. Owen 1:256; Read 20–21).

CITRONELLE   [ˌsɪtrəˈnɛl]   Inc. town with PO at 310526NO881341W in Mobile Co. Named for the citronella grass growing in the area. PO est. in 1852. Inc. in 1892 (M. B. Owen 1:476).

CLAIBORNE   Community with discontinued PO at 313224NO873056W in Monroe Co. The settlement grew up around the fort built in 1813 on a bluff overlooking the Alabama River to serve as a military and supply post for troops under the command of Ferdinand L. Claiborne, general of the MS militia sent to fight the hostile Creek Indians. Served as co. seat, 1815–32. PO est. in 1831 (Dugas [Monroe Co.] 94).

CLAIBORNE LAKE   Artificial lake formed by the impoundment of the Alabama River by Claiborne Lock and Dam at 313653NO873308W in 1968. Named for the military fort and supply depot that was located a few miles to the south in Monroe Co. (Dugas, "Recreation Guide for Monroe Co.," 84–86).

CLAIRMONT SPRINGS   Settlement on the Atlantic Coast Line at 332101NO855549W in Clay Co. First called JENKINS SPRINGS because Bill Jenkins in 1854 bought the land where the springs were located. By 1904 both the springs and community were identified with the subjectively descriptive and reminiscent name *Clairmont* 'clear mountain.' In 1909 the Clairmont Springs Co. bought the property and erected the first wing of a resort hotel here (1904 AL RR Commission map; Sulzby 103).

CLANTON   Inc. co. seat with PO at 325019NO863746W in Chilton Co. First identified by the humorously descriptive name GOOSE POND. In 1870 when Alfred Baker began laying out the town that was to be the co. seat, he changed the name to honor the former Confederate brigadier general James Holt Clanton (1827–1871), a prominent state politician. PO est. in 1871. Inc. in 1873 (Covington 6).

CLARENCE   See SUSAN MOORE in Blount Co.

CLARKE COUNTY   Created by act of the MS territorial legislature on Dec. 10, 1812. Bordered on the north by Marengo Co., on the east by Wilcox Co. and Monroe Co., on the south by Baldwin Co., and on the west by Washington Co. and Choctaw Co. Named for John Clarke, a Georgian who served as a general in the Creek Indian War of 1813–14. After AL became a state, Clarkesville was the co. seat until 1831 when the present one, Grove Hill, was chosen (T. M. Owen 1:269).

CLARKESVILLE   Community with discontinued PO at 314344NO875335W in Clarke Co., for which it was named. Became the seat of justice for the co. in 1819 and received its PO in 1820. Co. seat moved to Grove Hill in 1831 (T. M. Owen 1:269–70).

CLAUDE   [klɔd]   Settlement with discontinued PO at 322444NO860414W in Elmore Co. Probably named for a local resident. PO est. in 1894.

CLAY   Settlement with PO at 334209NO-863559W in Jefferson Co. When PO was est. in 1878, Bill McCoy, a local resident, suggested the environmental name descriptive of the clay hills in the area (Hagood 38).

CLAY BANK   See DALEVILLE in Dale Co.

CLAY CITY   Settlement at 302908NO-874824W in Baldwin Co. Probably a descriptive and environmental name (U.S.G.S., 1966 Base Maps).

CLAY COUNTY   Created by act of the state general assembly on Dec. 7, 1866. Bounded on the north by Cleburne Co., on the east by Randolph Co., on the south by Tallapoosa Co. and Coosa Co., and on the west by Talladega Co. Named for Henry Clay (1777–1852), the great KY statesman. Lineville was the temporary co. seat until 1867, when the courthouse was built at Ashland (Waldrop).

CLAYBANK CREEK   Stream rising at 313426NO854414W in Geneva Co. and flowing into the Choctawhatchee River at 311038NO854405W in Dale Co. Probably a descriptive and environmental name (U.S.G.S., 1966 Base Maps).

CLAYHATCHEE   [kleˈhætʃɪ]   Inc. town with discontinued PO at 311408NO854322W in Dale Co., about 6 miles from where Claybank Creek joins the Choctawhatchee River. Name is a blend of *Clay* from *Claybank* and *-hatchee* from *Choctawhatchee*. PO est. in 1878. Inc. in 1967 (Read 21; U.S.G.S., 1966 Base Maps).

CLAY'S STATION   See CUBA in Sumter Co.

CLAYSVILLE   Community at 342428NO-861619W in Marshall Co. Named for Henry Clay (1777–1852), great KY statesman. Co. seat, 1836–38. PO est. in 1837 (Roden 52).

CLAYTON   Inc. co. seat at 315241NO-852659W in Barbour Co. Settled between 1818 and 1827. Named for a prominent local family in 1834 when selected to be co. seat. PO est. in 1834. Inc. in 1841 (Griffith 162).

CLEAR CREEK   Descriptive name for the following streams.

1. Stream rising at 310902NO861640W in Covington Co. and flowing into Yellow River at 310611NO862545W (U.S.G.S., 1966 Base Maps).

2. Stream rising at 340918NO860910W in Etowah Co. and flowing into Locust Fork of the Black Warrior River at 340712NO861933W on the border between Marshall Co. and Blount Co. (U.S.G.S., 1966 Base Maps).

3. See SHOAL CREEK in Lauderdale Co.

4. Stream rising at 341324NO873647W in Winston Co. and flowing into the backwaters of Lewis Smith Lake at 340136NO871456W. Its tributary Right Fork of Clear Creek rises at 341508NO873421W and joins Clear Creek at 340858NO872828W (U.S.G.S, 1966 Base Maps).

CLEAR FORK OF BIG NANCE CREEK Stream rising at 343325NO871608W in Lawrence Co. and joining Big Nance Creek at 343504NO871950W. Descriptive name (U.S.G.S., 1966 Base Maps).

CLEAR SPRINGS See GALLANT in Etowah Co.

CLEBURNE COUNTY ['klibərn] Created by act of the state legislature on Dec. 6, 1866. Bounded on the north by Cherokee Co., on the east by GA, on the south by Clay Co. and Randolph Co., and on the west by Talladega Co. and Calhoun Co. Named for Patrick R. Cleburne (1828–1864) of AR, a Confederate general killed at the Battle of Franklin, TN, Nov. 20, 1864. Its co. seat was Edwardsville until 1906 when the present one, Heflin, replaced it (M. B. Owen 1:394).

CLEMENTS DEPOT See COALING in Tuscaloosa Co.

CLEMMONS CITY See HARTFORD in Geneva Co.

CLEVELAND Inc. town with PO at 335927NO863439W in Blount Co. Originally called DRY CREEK CROSSROADS because of the roads intersecting near the stream having this name; then BLACKWOODS CROSSROADS for John Blackwood, who bought a store in this area in 1884. In 1890 when the PO was est., it and the town were named for Grover Cleveland (1837–1908),

president of the U.S. (1885–89, 1893–97). Inc. in 1912 (Weaver).

CLEVELAND See SARALAND in Mobile Co.

CLEVELAND CROSSROADS Community where state Highway 9 crosses co. Highway 4 at 330647NO855915W in Clay Co. In 1886 when a PO was est. here, it and the settlement were named ELIAS for the postmaster, Elias B. Cleveland. Became known as CLEVELAND CROSSROADS, also in honor of Cleveland, after the PO was discontinued in 1905 ("Record of Appointment of Postmasters"; Waldrop).

CLINTON Settlement with PO at 325449NO875933W in Greene Co. Named for a pioneering family in the area. PO est. in 1826 (Rich 1979, 164).

CLINTONVILLE Settlement with discontinued PO at 312425NO855339W in Coffee Co. First called INDIGO HEAD because of the indigo plants being grown in the area. Name changed to CLINTONVILLE, probably for a local family, in 1860 when PO was est. (F. S. Watson 1970, 34).

CLIO ['klaɪo] Inc. town with PO at 314231NO853638W in Barbour Co. Settlement was originally located approximately 1 mile east of present site and called ADKINSON HEAD. Name changed, in 1860 when the PO was est., to CLIO for a town in SC, the former home of some of the early settlers. After the Central of Georgia RR reached the area in 1888, most of the town was relocated in its present site beside the RR. As a result of this move, town sometimes called NEW CLIO. Inc. in 1890 (Ellis 26).

CLOPTON Settlement with PO at 313630NO852548W in Dale Co. Probably named for David Clopton, a member of Congress before the Civil War and a justice of the state supreme court. PO est. in 1853 (F. S. Watson 1949, 46).

CLOUD'S TOWN See NEW HOPE in Madison Co.

CLOVERDALE Settlement with PO at 345619NO874617W in Lauderdale Co. PO known as WAVELAND (origin unknown) est. here in 1872. PO and town renamed RAWHIDE in 1874 for the local tannery owned and operated by Jonathan Paulk. In 1889 both PO and town were given the descriptive and commendatory name CLOVER-

DALE because relatives and friends of some newcomers to the town were said to have objected to addressing letters for them to RAWHIDE (Sockwell).

COAL CITY See WATTSVILLE in St. Clair Co.

COAL FIRE CREEK See COLD FIRE CREEK in Pickens Co.

COALING Settlement with PO on the Alabama Great Southern RR at 330932NO-872027W in Tuscaloosa Co. The RR station here and the PO est. in it in 1871 were named CLEMENTS DEPOT for Hardy Clements, a prosperous landowner. In 1879 both the settlement around the depot and the PO were called COALING, a name descriptive of the coal mining in the area (Rich 1979, 161).

COALMONT Settlement with discontinued PO at 331517NO865259W in Shelby Co. Named for the coal mines founded by the Ruffin brothers in 1878. PO est. in 1903 (Tamarin 6).

COAL VALLEY Settlement with discontinued PO at 334424NO872505W in Walker Co. Descriptive and environmental name. PO est. in 1891 (Gant).

COATOPA [koə'topə] Community with discontinued PO at 322906NO880410W in Sumter Co. Founded by J. R. Larkins in 1847 as a stop on the old East Tennessee, Virginia and Georgia RR and given the name of the nearby creek, derived from Choctaw *koi* 'panther,' *a* 'there,' *hotupa* 'wounded.' PO est. in 1866 (Foscue 27; Read 22).

COBBS FORD Community on the west bank of Still Creek at 322643NO862307W in Elmore Co. Designation probably comes from a fording place named for a local family (U.S.G.S., 1966 Base Maps).

COBB TOWN See WEST END in Calhoun Co.

COBB TOWN See HENSON SPRINGS in Lamar Co.

COCHRANE ['kɑkrən] Settlement with discontinued PO at 330355NO881504W in Pickens Co. Named for John T. Cochrane, president of the Tuscaloosa Belt Line (Alabama, Tennessee and Northern RR). PO est. in 1907 (N. F. Brown 30).

CODEN ['kodɛn] Settlement with PO at 302258NO881418W in Mobile Co. Name is a reduced form of the French *coq d'Inde* 'turkey cock.' Before its PO was est. in 1880, known as PORTERSVILLE, probably in honor of a local family (*Alabama: A Guide*, 388).

COFFEE COUNTY Created by act of the state general assembly on Dec. 29, 1841. Bounded on the north by Pike Co., on the east by Dale Co., on the south by Geneva Co., and on the west by Covington Co. and Crenshaw Co. Named for John Coffee (1772–1833), a general in the War of 1812 and the Creek Indian War of 1813–14 and later a surveyor for the state. Its seat of justice was at Wellborn until 1852 when it was moved to Elba (M. B. Owen 1:395–96).

COFFEE SETTLEMENT See LANGSTON in Jackson Co.

COFFEE SPRINGS Inc. town with PO at 310952NO855434W in Geneva Co. A well-known resort for a number of years because of its mineral springs named for a nearby creek. PO est. in 1876. Inc. in 1900 (M. B. Owen 1:430).

COFFEEVILLE See ALEXANDRIA in Calhoun Co.

COFFEEVILLE Settlement with PO on the bank of the Tombigbee River at 314528NO880523W in Clarke Co. Earlier known as COFFEEVILLE LANDING and COFFEEVILLE FERRY. Named for John Coffee (1772–1833), a general in the Creek Indian War of 1813–14. PO est. in 1830 (D. S. Akens 9, 40).

COHABADIAH CREEK [ko,habə'daɪə] Stream rising at 332925NO852944W in Cleburne Co. and flowing into Little Tallapoosa River at 332456NO852517W in Randolph Co. Name composed of Creek *koha* 'cane' and *apata-i* 'covering,' referring to a canebrake. Designation approved by U.S. Board on Geographic Names in 1901 (Read 23).

COHASSET [ko'hæsɪt] Community with discontinued PO at 312341NO864136W in Conecuh Co. Designation possibly borrowed from the town in MA whose name is Algonquian for 'high place or promontory.' PO est. in 1880 (Harder 113).

COKER   Settlement with PO at 331445NO-874116W in Tuscaloosa Co. Formerly known as BIG CREEK, for a nearby stream; then KOSTER for a local German family. When PO was est. in 1888, in order to prevent confusion with another place in the state, it and the town were named COKER for a family who settled in the area in the 1840s (Rich 1979, 168, 321).

COLBERT COUNTY ['kɑlbərt]   Created by act of the state general assembly on Feb. 6, 1867, out of part of Franklin Co. Abolished in Nov. 1867 but again est. in Dec. 1869. Bounded on the north by Lauderdale Co., on the east by Lawrence Co., on the south by Franklin Co., and on the west by MS. Named for the Chickasaw chief George Colbert. Co. seat is Tuscumbia (Sockwell).

COLBERT HEIGHTS   Settlement on Colbert Mountain at 343939NO874140W in Colbert Co. Named for the ridge. Laid out in 1918 (Sockwell).

COLD   CREEK   Stream   rising   at 305835NO880717W in Mobile Co. and flowing into the Mobile River at 305926NO-880021W. Descriptive name (U.S.G.S., 1966 Base Maps).

COLD   FIRE   Community with discontinued PO at 332414NO880505W in Pickens Co. First known as FUNDEE, a blend of the names of two local families, the Funderburks and the DeLoaches. Renamed for the nearby creek, whose designation has also been recorded as COAL FIRE. Colefire [sic] PO est. in 1834 (N. F. Brown 30).

COLD FIRE CREEK   Stream rising at 333459NO875421W in Fayette Co. and flowing into the Tombigbee River at 331527NO-881739W on the border between Pickens Co. and Sumter Co. COAL FIRE CREEK on La Tourette's 1856 map. Traditional explanation of the name is that settlers fording the creek in the winter experienced a feeling of warmth

after emerging from the water (N. F. Brown 30).

COLD SPRING   See COLE SPRING in Morgan Co.

COLD SPRINGS   Settlement at 335854NO-870200W in Cullman Co. Descriptive and environmental name chosen c. 1890 because of the cold spring water running down the side of a nearby mountain. Became known, unofficially, c. 1940 as NEW BREMEN (Jones 1972, 70–71).

COLD WATER   See TUSCUMBIA in Colbert Co.

COLDWATER   MOUNTAIN   Ridge   at 333737NO855324W in Calhoun Co. Name descriptive of the spring water flowing down it (Jolly; U.S.G.S., Topographical Maps, 1900 Anniston Quad.).

COLE SPRING   Settlement at 342114NO-864958W in Morgan Co. COLD SPRING on *Official 1959 Alabama Highway Map*, but COLE SPRING on 1966 U.S.G.S. Base Maps and *Official 1983–84 Alabama Highway Map*. Explanation of name or names is unknown.

COLEFIRE PO   See COLD FIRE in Pickens Co.

COLLBRAN ['kɑlbrən]   Community with discontinued PO at 342233NO834643W in DeKalb Co. Called BRANDON, 1870–1903, in honor of an early settler. Renamed for a nearby Alabama Great Southern RR station built c. 1890. Its designation is possibly a combination of *collis*, Latin for 'hill,' and *Brandon*. Collbran PO est. in 1903 (Raughton 27).

COLLINSVILLE   Inc. town with PO at 341550NO855138W in DeKalb Co. Named for Alfred Collins, who moved here from TN in 1842. PO est. in 1869. Inc. in 1901 (Raughton 27).

COLLIRENE [,kɑlə'rin]   Settlement with discontinued PO at 321033NO864925W in Lowndes Co. Earlier HAYES HILL for Dick Hayes, a former owner of the land. Present name is a descriptive blend of Latin *collis* 'hill' and *arena* 'sand.' Collirene PO est. in 1842 (Harris 1982, 46).

COLOMA [kə'lomə]   Community with discontinued PO at 340212NO853645W in Cherokee Co. Although the circumstances of the naming are not known, the designation, whose meaning has been forgotten, is that of

a Maidu Indian village in CA. PO est. in 1851
(G. R. Stewart 1970, 106).

COLUMBIA Inc. town with discontinued
PO at 311733NO850642W in Houston Co.
Settled in 1820 when H. W. Attaway founded
a trading post here. Probably given what was
commonly regarded as the feminine form, ap-
propriate for towns, of the name of
Christopher Columbus. Served as co. seat for
Henry Co., 1824–30, before Houston Co. was
created. PO est. in 1826. Inc. in 1870 (F. S.
Watson 1972, 48).

COLUMBIA See COLUMBIANA in
Shelby Co.

COLUMBIANA [kə,lʌmbɪ'ænə] Inc. co.
seat with PO at 331041NO863626W in Shelby
Co. First known as COONSBORO, probably
an animal-incident name. Also sometimes
called GERMAN HILL because the first family settling here was from Germany. Given the
name COLUMBIA, a variant of *Columbus*, in
1826 when chosen to be the co. seat and when
its PO was est. Name officially changed to
COLUMBIANA, another variant of *Columbus*, on Nov. 18, 1832. Inc. in 1837 (Tamarin
7).

COLUMBUS CITY Settlement with discontinued PO at 342738NO861400W in Marshall Co. Founded with the never realized
hope that it would become an industrial center. Named for Christopher Columbus. PO
est. in 1891 (Harris 1982, 46).

COLVIN MOUNTAIN See GREEN
CREEK MOUNTAIN in Etowah Co.

COLWELL See CALDWELL in Calhoun
Co.

COMER ['komər] Settlement with discontinued PO at 320158NO852300W in Barbour Co. Called HARRIS, 1889–1907,
probably for an early local family. Renamed
for Braxton Bragg Comer (1848–1927), who
was born in this area and served as governor
of the state, 1907–11. PO est. in 1907 (Ellis
27).

CONCORD ['kankərd] Community at
333059NO874435W in Fayette Co. Named for
Concord, MA, the site of an early battle of
the American Revolution, after land grants
were made here during the 1820s to veterans
of that war (Sartwell).

CONCORD Settlement at 332803NO-
870152W in Jefferson Co. Name is an inspirational one, connoting the importance of the

residents' working harmoniously together
(Hagood 51; *Official 1959 Alabama Highway
Map*).

CONECUH COUNTY [kə'nekə] Created
by act of the AL territorial general assembly
on Feb. 13, 1818. Bounded on the west and
north by Monroe Co., on the east by Butler
Co. and Covington Co., and on the south by
Escambia Co. Named for the river. The co.
seats have been Hampden Ridge, until 1820;
Sparta, 1820–66; and Evergreen, the present
one (Riley 1881, 2, 30).

CONECUH RIVER Stream rising at
320820NO854038W in Bullock Co. and flowing southward into FL at 305946NO871037W
in Escambia Co. KO-O-NE-CUH in Benjamin Hawkins's "Sketch of the Creek Country in 1798 and 1799" (23). Name may be a
compound of Creek *koha* 'canebrakes' and
anaka 'near' or of Creek *kono* and *ika* 'polecat's head' or of Choctaw *kuni* 'young canes'
and *akka* 'below' (Read 23–24).

CONSUL Settlement with discontinued
PO at 321551NO873224W in Marengo Co.
Origin of name unknown, but it might refer to
a U.S. consul who once lived here. PO est. in
1898 (W. Smith).

CONVERSE LAKE See BIG CREEK
LAKE in Mobile Co.

COOKS SPRINGS Community with PO at
333524NO862340W in St. Clair Co. Former
health resort named for William Proctor
Cooke, who settled here in 1854. Name
shortened to fit on the instrument used to
cancel stamps when PO was est. in 1883
(Rich).

COONSBORO See COLUMBIANA in
Shelby Co.

COOPER ['kupər] Community with discontinued PO at 324630NO863244W in
Chilton Co. First called BARBOURSVILLE
for John Barbour, an early settler who
founded a store here. In 1833 CHESTNUT
CREEK PO, named for a nearby creek, was
est. The village was also identified with this

designation until 1879 when the South and North RR (Louisville and Nashville) reached here, and the names of both the PO and the community were changed to COOPER to honor Andy J. Cooper, who had a store near the RR station (B. D. Roberts).

COOSA   See CROPWELL in St. Clair Co.

COOSA BEND   See RAINBOW CITY in Etowah Co.

COOSA COUNTY   ['kusə]   Created by act of the state general assembly on Dec. 18, 1832, from lands relinquished by the Creek Indians earlier that year. Bounded on the north by Talladega Co. and Clay Co., on the east by Tallapoosa Co., on the south by Elmore Co., and on the west by Chilton Co. and Shelby Co. Named for the river. Its seat of justice was Lexington until 1835 when the present one, Rockford, was chosen (M. B. Owen 1:407).

COOSADA   [ku'sɑdə]   Inc. town with PO at 323025NO862054W in Elmore Co. on the Louisville and Nashville RR. Founded c. 1818 by colonists from GA. Named for an Upper Creek branch of the Alabama Indians known as the Koasati. Their designation may be derived from Choctaw *kusha* 'cane' and *hata* 'white.' Coosada Station PO est. in 1871. Inc. in 1970 (McMillan in Read 100; Read 24–25).

COOSAHATCHIE CREEK   See TERRAPIN CREEK in Cleburne Co.

COOSA RIVER   Stream formed by confluence of the Oostanaula and the Etowah rivers near Rome in northwest GA. It joins the Tallapoosa River at 323021NO861558W on the border between Elmore Co. and Montgomery Co. to form the Alabama River. COOSEE on Melish's 1814 map. Named for an Upper Creek town in Talladega Co. visited by the de Soto expedition in 1540. Designation is probably derived from Choctaw *kusha* 'cane' or 'canebrake.' In the 1700s also called the ARBACOOCHEE RIVER for Abihkuchi (for meaning see ARBACOOCHEE), an Up-

per Creek town in Talladega Co. (Read 5, 24).

COOSA VALLEY   See CROPWELL in St. Clair Co.

COPELAND   Community with discontinued PO at 313336NO882509W in Washington Co. Named for the family of the first postmaster, George C. Copeland, appointed in 1906 (Matte 295–98).

COPELAND'S BRIDGE   See CROSSVILLE in DeKalb Co.

COPPERAS GAP   See BANGOR in Blount Co.

COPPER'S GAP   See BANGOR in Blount Co.

CORCORAN   Settlement at 314953NO855659W in Pike Co. Founded during the early part of this century and named for J. B. Corcoran, a Central of Georgia RR freight agent at Troy for more than 45 years (Farmer 1973, 406–07).

CORDOVA   [kɔr'dovə]   Inc. town with PO at 334535NO871100W in Walker Co. Founded in 1859 by Benjamin M. Long, who had been stationed at Cordova in Mexico during the Mexican War. PO est. in 1885. Inc. in 1902 (Gant 5).

COREY   See FAIRFIELD in Jefferson Co.

CORNELIA   See ST. CLAIR SPRINGS in St. Clair Co.

CORNELIUS   See WALNUT GROVE in Etowah Co.

CORNER CREEK   Stream rising at 310028NO861903W in Covington Co. and flowing into the Pea River at 310336NO860744W in Geneva Co. Probably a descriptive and environmental name for its location in the corners of the counties (U.S.G.S., 1966 Base Maps).

CORONA   [kə'ronə]   Settlement with PO at 334230NO872810W in Walker Co. Founded when the Corona Coal Co. opened its mines here in the 1880s. Name is the Spanish noun meaning 'crown.' An ironic name, because the town is located at the foot of a hill rather than on its top. PO est. in 1884 (T. M. Owen 1:400).

CORTELYOU   [kɔr'tɛlju]   Settlement with discontinued PO on the Mobile and Birmingham RR (Southern) at 312524NO880030W in Washington Co. First known as RICHARDSON STATION for John A. Richardson, Jr., who settled here in the 1880s. Richardson PO est. in 1898. PO and settlement renamed in 1906 for George R. Cortelyou, then the U.S. postmaster general (Matte 298–300).

COTACO COUNTY See MORGAN COUNTY.

COTACO CREEK [ko'teko] Stream rising at 342026NO863427W in Marshall Co. and flowing into the Tennessee River at 343329NO864455W in Morgan Co. COTACO C. on Finley's 1826 map. Name is possibly Cherokee from *ikati* 'swamp' or 'thicket' and *kunahita* 'long' (Read 25).

COTAHAGA CREEK [ˌkotəˈhegə] Stream rising at 322512NO881314W in Sumter Co. and flowing into the Tombigbee River at 322046NO875938W. COTAHAGER C. on La Tourette's 1839 map. Name may be derived from Choctaw *kati* 'locust tree,' *a* 'there,' and *hikia* 'standing' (Read 26).

COTTAGE GROVE Settlement with discontinued PO at 325120NO860721W in Coosa Co. Descriptive and environmental name. PO est. in 1908 (Hopkins).

COTTONDALE Settlement with PO at 331122NO872706W in Tuscaloosa Co. Originally called KENNEDALE in 1868 for Joseph S. Kennedy when the Baugh, Kennedy, and Co. cotton mill was opened here. In 1876 name changed to COTTONDALE for the cotton mill. Cottondale PO est. in 1877 (Rich 1979, 175, 313).

COTTONTON Settlement with PO at 320848NO850426W in Russell Co. Named for the crop that once provided support for the town. PO est. in 1900 (Russell Co. Historical Commission C62–C63).

COTTONWOOD Inc. town with PO at 310255NO851818W in Houston Co. Named for the softwood (*Populus deltoides*) trees in the area. PO est. in 1873. Inc. in 1903 (F. S. Watson 1972, 53).

COUNTY LINE Inc. town in 334917NO-864307W on the boundary line between Jefferson Co. and Blount Co. Locational name. Inc. in 1957 (1967 General Highway Map of Jefferson Co.).

COUNTY LINE See LINEVILLE in Clay Co.

COURTLAND Inc. town with PO at 344008NO871834W in Lawrence Co. First known by the biblical name EBENEZER. Inc. as COURTLAND in 1819, because a federal court and land office were located

here. PO est. in 1825 (T. M. Owen 1:427).

COVE See HELENA in Shelby Co.

COVIN ['kovɪn] Settlement with discontinued PO on the Southern RR at 334124NO-875321W in Fayette Co. First called BROCKTON, for first postmaster, Reuben J. Brock, appointed in 1884; then, TALLULA, 1890–92, perhaps for Tallula, LA, which has a Cherokee name of unknown meaning; and finally COVIN, for L. E. Covin, an early settler who donated land for the RR depot. Covin PO est. in 1892 (Peoples 4, 18).

COVINGTON See MONTEZUMA in Covington Co.

COVINGTON COUNTY ['kʌvɪŋtən] Created by act of the state general assembly on Dec. 18, 1821. Bounded on the north by Butler Co. and Crenshaw Co., on the east by Coffee Co. and Geneva Co., on the south by FL, and on the west by Escambia Co. and Conecuh Co. Named for Wailes Covington from MD, a brigadier general in the Creek Indian War and the War of 1812 who was killed in 1813. Called JONES COUNTY, Aug.–Oct. 1868, for Josiah Jones, a political leader of the co., who, however, refused the honor. The co. seat was Montezuma (earlier known as COVINGTON) until floods forced the selection of a new site, Andalusia, in 1844 (W. D. Ward 9, 21, 43–44).

COWARTS ['kauərts] Inc. town with PO at 311200NO851817W in Houston Co. Probably named for the nearby creek. PO est. in 1880. Inc. in 1961.

COWARTS CREEK Stream rising at 311259NO851633W in Houston Co. and flowing into FL at 305436NO851617W. Named for a family settling in the area before 1880 (F. S. Watson 1972, 56).

COWDEN See SAMANTHA in Tuscaloosa Co.

COWHEAD See EVA in Morgan Co.

COWIKEE CREEK [kauˈægɪ] Stream formed by three branches: North Fork, which rises at 322023NO852209W in Russell

Co.; Middle Fork, which rises at 321218NO-852602W in Bullock Co. and joins North Fork at 320202NO850937W in Barbour Co.; and South Fork, which rises at 320359NO-853106W in Bullock Co. and joins the combined streams at 315933NO850840W in Barbour Co. Cowikee Creek then flows into the Walter F. George Reservoir of the Chattahoochee River at 315738NO8500511W. CO-WAG-GEE in Benjamin Hawkins's "Sketch of the Creek Country in 1798 and 1799" (65). Name means 'water-carrying [place],' from Hitchiti *oki* 'water' and *awaiki* 'hauling, carrying' (McMillan in Read 100; Read 27).

COXEY Settlement with discontinued PO at 344807NO871042W in Limestone Co. Probably named for the family of the first postmaster, William D. Cox, appointed in 1918 ("Record of Appointment of Postmasters").

COY Settlement with PO at 315341NO-872746W in Wilcox Co. Named for a local family. PO est. in 1891 (Harris 1982, 49).

CRAGFORD Settlement with PO at 331503NO854021W in Clay Co. In 1879 when known as WHEELERVILLE, probably for a local family, its PO was est. Given a descriptive and environmental designation, a compound of *crag* and *ford*, c. 1908 when the name of the PO was changed (McMillan; Waldrop).

CRANE HILL Settlement with PO at 340538NO870347W in Cullman Co. Name, given to the community by Jane and Ellen Nesmith, daughters of John B. Nesmith, the first settler here in 1851, refers to the area's being, during that period, the roosting place of migratory cranes. PO est. in 1874 (Jones 1972, 74–75).

CRAWFORD Settlement with discontinued PO at 322724NO851123W in Russell Co. Called CROCKETTSVILLE, 1832–37, in honor of David Crockett (1786–1836), hero of the Alamo who had fought in AL in the Creek Indian War of 1813–14. Named CRAWFORD for Joel Crawford from GA, who had also fought in the Creek Indian War. Co. seat, 1837–68. Crawford PO est. in 1843 (*Alabama: A Guide*, 282).

CREEK STAND Settlement with discontinued PO at 321740NO852839W in Macon Co. The name is said to refer to the town's location on the site of a Creek Indian village. PO est. in 1851 (Harris 1982, 50).

CREEL Settlement with discontinued PO at 334847NO865940W in Walker Co. Probably named for James T. Creel, the first postmaster, appointed in 1900 ("Record of Appointment of Postmasters").

CRENSHAW COUNTY Created by act of the state general assembly on Nov. 24, 1866. Bounded on the north by Montgomery Co., on the east by Pike Co. and Coffee Co., on the south by Covington Co., on the west by Butler Co., and on the northwest by Lowndes Co. Named for Anderson Crenshaw (1783–1847), a distinguished early settler of Butler Co. from SC. Rutledge was the co. seat until 1893 when the present one, Luverne, was chosen (M. B. Owen 1:410).

CREOLA [kri'olə] Inc. town with PO at 305330NO880223W in Mobile Co. Name is probably derived from the feminine form of the Spanish adjective *criollo* 'Creole,' a term for a descendant of the Spanish or, later, French settlers of the Gulf states. Feminine forms were considered appropriate for names of towns. PO est. in 1885. Inc. in 1978.

CREWS Settlement with discontinued PO on the St. Louis and San Francisco RR at 335447NO880450W in Lamar Co. Originally CREWS DEPOT. Named for Titus L. Crew, the first postmaster, appointed in 1888 (Acee 34).

CROCKETTSVILLE See CRAWFORD in Russell Co.

CROMWELL Community with PO at 321343NO881628W in Choctaw Co. Named for Cromwell Ulmer, a local resident. PO est. in 1906 (Rogers).

CROOKED CREEK Stream rising at 341809NO865831W in Cullman Co. and flowing into the backwaters of Lewis Smith Lake at 340402NO870745W. Probably a descriptive name (U.S.G.S., 1966 Base Maps).

CROPWELL Settlement with PO at 333308NO861609W in St. Clair Co., dating from the 1820s. Known as COOSA or COOSA VALLEY until 1837 when the subjectively descriptive compound of *crop* and *well*, referring to the prosperous farms surrounding the town, was chosen to be its name. Cropwell PO est. in 1837 (Rich).

CROSBY Community with discontinued PO at 310219NO850511W in Houston Co. Probably named for the first postmaster, John Crosby, appointed in 1886 ("Record of Appointment of Postmasters").

CROSS KEYS See SHORTER in Macon Co.

CROSS PLAINS See PIEDMONT in Calhoun Co.

CROSS ROADS See LEIGHTON in Colbert Co.

CROSS ROADS See PINCKARD in Dale Co.

CROSSROADS Community at intersection of co. highways 138 and 225 at 305005NO-875140W in Baldwin Co. Locational designation (Bush 39).

CROSSROADS See BREWTON in Escambia Co.

CROSS TRAILS See KINSTON in Coffee Co.

CROSSVILLE Inc. town with PO at 341715NO855939W in DeKalb Co. Earlier COPELAND'S BRIDGE, probably for a bridge built by James Alexander Copeland, who became the first postmaster of Crossville, appointed in 1869. Two explanations for the name chosen by Copeland for the PO have been proposed: it honors a man named *Cross* or it refers to the many crossroads in the locality. Inc. in 1942 (Raughton 29).

CROSSVILLE Settlement at 334438NO-880008W in Lamar Co. Known as JEWELL for a local family while it had a PO, 1875–1905. Present name is probably a locational one, referring to the intersection here of state Highway 18 and co. Highway 49 (Acee 25).

CROW CREEK Stream rising in TN and flowing into the Tennessee River at 344850NO854934W in Jackson Co. Name may be a translation of an Indian animal-incident name (U.S.G.S., 1966 Base Maps).

CROW MOUNTAIN Summit at 345133NO-860037W in Jackson Co. Probably named for the creek (U.S.G.S., 1966 Base Maps).

CRUMP See SAMANTHA in Tuscaloosa Co.

CRYSTAL LAKE Community at 342807NO854122W in DeKalb Co. Earlier known as RAWLINGSVILLE in honor of Rezin Rawlings, the first postmaster, appointed in 1837. Under that name, served as first co. seat for a brief period during 1836. After PO was discontinued in 1871, name changed to CRYSTAL LAKE for a nearby artificial lake. Following the drowning of Creed Clayton in the impoundment in 1926, the owner of the land on which it was located had it drained (Raughton 29, 66).

CUBA ['kjubə] Inc. town with PO at 322541NO882235W in Sumter Co. First called CLAY'S STATION, but R. A. Clay objected to the town's being named for him. In 1856 when he gave the right-of-way to the Southern RR, he suggested that the station be given the name of a settlement that had existed before 1850 on land a few miles to the southwest, the old town probably having been named for the Caribbean island. PO est. in 1866. Inc. in 1901 (Foscue 28).

CUBAHATCHEE CREEK [kju'be,hætʃi] Stream rising at 320941NO854015W in Bullock Co. and flowing into the Tallapoosa River at 322538NO855944W on the border between Elmore Co. and Tallapoosa Co. CUPIAHAT-CHEE C. on La Tourette's 1844 map. Name means either 'creek where the lye was made,' from Creek *kapi* 'lye drip' and *hachi* 'creek,' or 'mulberry tree creek,' from *ki-api* 'mulberry tree' and *hachi* 'creek' (Read 27).

CULLMAN Inc. town and PO at 341029NO865037W in Cullman Co. In the 1870s Johann Gottfried Cullmann (1823–1895), a Bavarian revolutionary who had fought against Bismarck, bought land from the Louisville and Nashville RR and founded here a German settlement and named it for himself. PO est. in 1873. Inc. in 1875. Became seat of justice when co. was created in 1877 (Whitehead 4).

CULLMAN COUNTY Created by act of the state legislature on Jan. 24, 1877.

Bounded on the north by Morgan Co. and Marshall Co., on the east and south by Blount Co., on the southwest by Walker Co., and on the west by Winston Co. Named for the town that is its co. seat (Whitehead 3).

CULLOM   See CULLOMBURG in Choctaw Co.

CULLOMBURG   Community with PO at 314249NO881749W in Choctaw Co. First called REDEMPTION because of the financial success here of an impoverished man. Later called CULLOM and then CULLOMBURG for the resort hotel built here at the mineral springs on land purchased in 1853 by Charles Cullum of Mobile. Few traces of the resort remain now. Cullomberg [*sic*] PO est. in 1912 (Sulzby 111–15).

CURRY   Settlement with discontinued PO on the Alabama and Tennessee Rivers RR (Southern) at 332911NO860102W in Talladega Co. From 1833 until 1844 called KELLY'S SPRINGS for James Kelley, an Indian land grantee. By 1844 renamed CURRY'S STATION for William Curry, who had settled here in 1838 and opened a store. Curry PO est. in 1858 (McMillan).

CUSSETA   [kə'sitə]   Settlement with PO at 324705NO851821W in Chambers Co. COSETA on La Tourette's 1844 map. *Cusseta* is synonymous with *Kasihta*, the name of an ancient Lower Creek tribe. The meaning of the latter term is unknown, but the Creeks relate the word to *hasihta* 'coming from the sun.' PO est. in 1837 (Read 28).

CUTTACOOCHEE CREEK   See VALLEY CREEK in Jefferson Co.

CYPRESS   Settlement with PO at 325652NO874001W in Hale Co. Name comes from the endeavors of George Brigden, who moved here c. 1910 and built a shingle mill at which were made ties of durable cypress wood for the Southern RR. PO est. in 1900 (Wilson).

CYPRESS CREEK   Stream rising at 350642NO874524W in Lauderdale Co. and joining, at 345026NO874328W, Little Cypress Creek, which rises in TN. The combined streams, known as THE FORKS OF CYPRESS, empty into the Tennessee River at 344644NO874140W. TEKETANOAH was the Indian name, whose meaning is unknown. Also called CANOE CREEK and PAYTON'S CREEK for John Payton, who

explored the area in 1785. Present name, mentioned in the Hopewell Treaty of 1806, is an environmental one (Sockwell 25).

DADEVILLE   See BATTLES WHARF in Baldwin Co.

DADEVILLE   Inc. co. seat with PO at 324952NO854549W in Tallapoosa Co. Named for Francis Langhorne Dade (1793–1835), a major in the U.S. army from VA killed after being ambushed by Osceola, leader of the Indians in the Seminole War (1835–42). PO est. in 1837. Became the co. seat in 1838 and was inc. in 1841 (Dugas [Tallapoosa Co.] 86).

DALE COUNTY   Created by act of the state legislature on Dec. 22, 1824. Bounded on the north by Pike Co. and Barbour Co., on the east by Henry Co., on the south by Houston Co. and Geneva Co., and on the west by Coffee Co. Named for Samuel Dale (1772–1841), general in the Indian wars and legislator for both MS and AL. Its co. seats have been Richmond, until 1827; Dale Court House, until 1841; and Newton, until 1871 when Ozark, the present one, was chosen (Harder 133).

DALE COURT HOUSE   See DALEVILLE in Dale Co.

DALEVILLE   Inc. town with PO at 311836NO854247W in Dale Co. First called DALE COURT HOUSE when the settlement served as co. seat, 1827–41. During 1841–48 given the environmental designation CLAY BANK, borrowed from a nearby creek. Its current name DALEVILLE was chosen in 1848 because of the town's location in the center of the co., a fact that had also led to its earlier selection as co. seat. Daleville PO est. in 1848. Inc. in 1958 (Harder 133).

DALLAS   Settlement at 335058NO863938W in Blount Co. Given this name when the South and North RR (Louisville and Nashville) reached this point c. 1870. Probably honors Dallas Morton, a prominent early citizen, though some residents think the name refers to a kind of grass growing in the area (Weaver).

DALLAS COUNTY   Created by act of the AL territorial general assembly on Feb. 9, 1818. Bounded on the north by Perry Co. and Chilton Co., on the east by Autauga Co. and Lowndes Co., on the south by Wilcox Co., and on the west by Marengo Co. Named for Alexander James Dallas (1759–1817), an attorney and statesman from PA who served as U.S. secretary of state (1814–16) and acting secretary of war in 1815 under President James Madison. Its co. seat was Cahaba until 1865 when Selma, the present one, was chosen (T. M. Owen 1:447–48).

DAMASCUS   Community at 311022NO865125W in Escambia Co. Settled before 1825 when Damascus Baptist Church, for which it was named, was officially organized. This church probably was given the name of the ancient capital city of Syria (Waters 184).

DAN   Community with discontinued PO at 345556NO864454W in Madison Co. PO est. in 1885 and named for Daniel H. Turner, who was the postmaster, 1887–1901 (Green).

DANCY   Settlement with discontinued PO at 330040NO881734W in Pickens Co. Named for E. C. Dancy, a local physician. PO est. in 1892 (N. F. Brown 31).

DANLEY   Settlement where state highways 12 and 141 intersect at 312508NO861004W in Coffee Co. Also known as DANLEYS CROSSROADS. Probably named for a local family (U.S.G.S., Topographic Maps, 1968 Danleys Crossroads Quad.).

DANVILLE   Settlement with PO at 342452NO870515W in Morgan Co. In 1828 a PO was est. in Houston's Store, operated by Robert Houston. Later named for Danville, VA, the former home of some of the town's residents. Danville PO est. in 1852 (Ackley 21).

DAPHNE   Inc. town with PO at 302012NO875413W in Baldwin Co. During the 1850s given the descriptive and environmental name HOLLYWOOD. Following the Civil War named DAPHNE, probably for a type of laurel shrub growing here. Co. seat, 1868–1901. Daphne PO est. in 1874. Inc. in 1927 (Bush 39–40).

DARLINGTON   See ISBELL in Franklin Co.

DARLINGTON   Community with PO at 315839NO870750W in Wilcox Co. Perhaps named for the town in SC. PO est. in 1904.

DAUPHIN ISLAND   ['dɔfɪn]   Island between the Gulf of Mexico and Mississippi Sound at 301458NO881102W in Mobile Co. Called MASSACRE ISLAND by the French after Iberville in 1699 found a pile of some sixty headless skeletons here. Given for its name, c. 1702, the title of the wife of the French royal Dauphin, the final *e* later being dropped (Griffith 13).

DAUPHIN ISLAND   Settlement with PO on Dauphin Island at 301519NO880635W in Mobile Co. Named for the island. PO est. in 1896 (*Alabama: A Guide*, 400).

DAVENPORT   Settlement at 320356NO862423W in Lowndes Co. Recorded on an unidentified 1892 map of Alabama. Designation sometimes spelled DEVENPORT. Named for Jack Davenport, a local merchant (Harris 1982, 53).

DAVIS CREEK   Stream rising at 331419NO871027W in Tuscaloosa Co. and flowing into the Black Warrior River at 332435NO872324W. Probably named for Dr. Daniel Davis, who moved to the co. in 1822. Also given the descriptive and environmental designation ROCK CASTLE CREEK, both names appearing on Tuomey's 1849 map (Rich 1979, 188–89).

DAVISTON   Inc. town with PO at 330310NO853823W in Tallapoosa Co. Named for John O. Davis, the first postmaster, appointed in 1853. Inc. in 1887 (Dugas [Tallapoosa Co.] 86).

DAVISVILLE   Settlement at 321939NO854011W in Macon Co. Named for a local family (Harris 1982, 53; *Official 1983–84 Alabama Highway Map*).

DAWES   Settlement with discontinued PO at 302627NO881519W in Mobile Co. Named for T. R. Dawes, a land promoter from IL. PO est. in 1912 (Harris 1982, 53).

DAWSON   Settlement with PO at

341814NO855534W in DeKalb Co. Probably named for a local family. PO est. in 1887.

DAY'S GAP   See OAKMAN in Walker Co.

DAYTON   Inc. town with PO at 322103NO873831W in Marengo Co. Laid out in 1836. Probably named for Dayton, TN, which had borrowed the designation of the city in OH honoring Jonathan Dayton, the youngest delegate to the U.S. Constitutional Convention in 1787. PO est. in 1837. Inc. in 1844 (W. Smith).

DEANS   Community at 313936NO865620W in Conecuh Co. Probably named for a local family (*Official 1983–84 Alabama Highway Map*).

DEAN'S STATION   See ARITON in Dale Co.

DEANSVILLE   See JACK in Coffee Co.

DEARMANVILLE [dɪˈɑrmənvəl]   Settlement with PO at 333735NO854505W in Calhoun Co. Originally called CENTER because it was a central trading place. Named in 1873, when PO est., for John DeArman, an original settler of the area in 1833 (Lindsey 28).

DEAS [dez]   Community at 321345NO880550W in Choctaw Co. Station on the Meridian and Bigbee RR (Burlington Northern) during the early 1920s. Probably named for a local family (Gay).

DEATSVILLE [ˈditsvəl]   Settlement with PO at 323629NO862345W in Elmore Co. Named for W. S. Deats, who founded the town in 1840. PO est. in 1871 (T. M. Owen 1:474).

DECATUR   Inc. co. seat with PO at 343621NO865900W in Morgan Co. In 1820 President James Monroe directed the surveyor general to set aside land for a town to be named DECATUR in honor of Stephen F. Decatur (1779–1820), hero of the Battle of Tripoli in 1804 and a commodore of the U.S. navy during the War of 1812. PO est. in 1825. Inc. in 1826. Became co. seat in 1891 (Ackley 22).

DECATUR COUNTY   Created by act of the state general assembly on Dec. 7, 1821, from the western part of Jackson Co., it was named for the naval hero Stephen F. Decatur (1779–1820). Woodville was chosen to serve as co. seat. Abolished in 1824, its lands were divided among Jackson Co., Madison Co. and Marshall Co. (Kennamer 159–62).

DEER PARK   Settlement with PO at 311300NO881902W in Washington Co. Name refers to the area's being a spot frequented by deer. PO est. in 1859 (Avant 45).

DEER RANGE STATION   See RANGE in Conecuh Co.

DEES [diz]   Community at 304352NO882935W in Mobile Co. Honors Dewitt Dees, son of Charlie Dees, who opened a store here in 1909. Also called UNION CHURCH COMMUNITY for a local church organized in 1868 (Harris 1982, 55).

DEKALB COUNTY [dɪˈkæb]   Created by act of the state general assembly on Jan. 9, 1836. Bounded on the north by Jackson Co., on the east by GA, on the south by Cherokee Co. and Etowah Co., and on the west by Marshall Co. Named for Johann Kalb, known as Baron de Kalb (1721–1780), German-born French soldier who fought beside the Americans during the Revolution. He was killed at the Battle of Camden in SC. The co. seats have been Rawlingsville, Bootsville, Camden, Portersville (each serving for only a few months), and Lebanon, 1840–76. Fort Payne, the present one, was chosen in 1876 (Raughton 2).

DELCHAMPS [ˈdɛl,tʃæmps]   Settlement with discontinued PO at 302402NO880856W in Mobile Co. Named for first postmaster, Julius Delchamps, appointed in 1899 ("Record of Appointment of Postmasters").

DELMAR   Settlement with PO at 341012NO873621W in Winston Co. Originally designated with the descriptive and environmental name FROG LEVEL. *Del mar*, a Spanish phrase meaning 'of the sea,' became its name in 1887 when the PO was est. The reason for this choice, with its suggestion of vague attractiveness, is no longer remembered (Gant; G. R. Stewart 1970, 132).

DELTA   Settlement at 332624NO854126W in Clay Co. Descriptive and environmental name given because of the town's location on the delta of a stream. Appears on E. A. Smith's 1891 map in Berney (McMillan; Waldrop).

DEMMICK See WATERFORD in Dale Co.

DEMOPOLIS [dɪ'mɑpolɪs] Inc. town at 323103NO875011W in Marengo Co. When the Bonapartist Vine and Olive Colony made their settlement on White Bluff, the high limestone bank of the Tombigbee River, in 1817, they named it DEMOPOLIS at the suggestion of Count Pierre François Real of Philadelphia, who had helped the group obtain a land grant. The word is a Greek compound that means 'the people's city.' In a short time most of the French were forced to leave their town to the English and American settlers living nearby because they had located their settlement on land not included in their claim. Inc. in 1821. PO est. in 1832 (Johnson and Alexander 10; W. Smith).

DEMOPOLIS, LAKE Artificial lake made in 1954 by the impoundment of the Black Warrior River with Demopolis Lock and Dam at 323116NO875245W between Marengo Co. and land on the boundary between Hale Co. and Greene Co. Named for the town (Johnson and Alexander 10).

DENNIE KILN See LIME KILN in Colbert Co.

DEPOSIT Community with discontinued PO at 345108NO862729W in Madison Co. Located on Deposit Road built by Andrew Jackson's troops for transporting supplies to New Market from Deposit Ferry on the north bank of the Tennessee River opposite Fort Deposit in Marshall Co., their supply depot during the Creek Indian War of 1813–14. PO est. in 1888 (T. J. Taylor 1976, 96).

DE SOTO RIVER See LITTLE RIVER.

DETROIT ['ditrɔɪt] Inc. town with PO at 340141NO881012W in Lamar Co. Originally called MILLVILLE because of the many water mills once here. Renamed for the city in MI when PO est. in 1874. Inc. in 1955 (Acee 15).

DEVENPORT See DAVENPORT in Lowndes Co.

DEVIL'S HALF ACRE See KELLY'S CROSSROADS in Coosa Co.

DEXTER Settlement with discontinued PO at 323821NO860859W in Elmore Co. Origin of name unknown, but it might have some locational significance, because the adjective *dexter* in Latin means 'right.' PO est. in 1891.

DIAMOND Community with discontinued PO at 341808NO862347W in Marshall Co. Name is said to refer to the discovery of diamond pebbles on the farm owned by Washington W. Griffin when an exploratory oil well was being dug. PO est. in 1891 (Roden 52).

DICKERT ['dɪkərt] Settlement with discontinued PO at 330754NO852823W in Randolph Co. Possibly named for a local person. PO est. in 1908.

DICKINSON Settlement with PO at 314548NO874238W in Clarke Co. Founded in the 1880s, when the Southern RR reached this point. Named for the Dickinson family, early settlers of the co. PO est. in 1888 (Clarke Co. Historical Society 155).

DILL Settlement at 313039NO853913W in Dale Co. Although origin of name is not known, it might be that of either a local family or the herb plant (*Official 1983–84 Alabama Highway Map*).

DITTO'S LANDING See WHITESBURG in Madison Co.

DIXIANA PO for BRADFORD in Jefferson Co. This name, regarded as a feminine form of *Dixie*, a term symbolic of the South, was chosen in 1880 after another Bradford PO was discovered to be in the state (Hagood 7).

DIXIE Settlement with discontinued PO at 324323NO865421W in Escambia Co. The name is a term symbolic of the South. PO est. in 1874 (Waters 184).

DIXON CORNER Settlement at 302707NO-881431W in Mobile Co. Name, which has some locational significance, probably refers to a local family (U.S.G.S., 1966 Base Maps).

DIXONS MILL Settlement with PO at 320329NO874715W in Marengo Co. Named for the gristmill on a nearby creek operated by Joel Dixon, Sr., who was born in NC and settled here c. 1836. PO est. in 1845 (W. Smith).

DIXONVILLE Settlement with discontinued PO at 310001NO870210W in Escambia Co. Named for John T. Dixon, an early settler. PO est. in 1893 (Waters 184).

DOCENA [do'sinə] Settlement with PO at 333334NO865552W in Jefferson Co. Originally named BOOKER in honor of Booker T. Washington (1856–1915), the black educator who founded Tuskegee Institute in east AL in 1881. The current name is the Spanish feminine determiner *docena* 'twelfth,' for a nearby mine. Ed F. Stallingworth, who had worked in Mexico as a RR dispatcher and was later a train master here, is credited with suggesting the Spanish name. PO est. 1952 (Hagood 5).

DOG RIVER POINT   Cape on Mobile Bay at 303558NO880345W in Mobile Co. Named for the nearby river called *Rivière au chien* 'Dog River' by the French. The traditional explanation is that one of the French settlers lost a favorite dog in this area (Harris 1982, 57).

DOG TOWN   Settlement at 342110NO854413W in DeKalb Co. First called CAGLE'S CROSSROADS for a local family, it is said to have acquired its present name because it was frequented by hunters and their dogs. Some of its residents, however, prefer RUHAMA, the name of the local Baptist church organized in 1900. Ruhamah in the Bible is Hosea's daughter (Raughton 31; U.S.G.S., 1966 Base Maps).

DOGWOOD   Settlement at 330904NO865223W in Shelby Co. Probably named for the Dogwood Grove Baptist Church, organized in 1858. The church has a descriptive and environmental name because it was erected in a grove of dogwood trees (Tamarin).

DOLOMITE   ['dolǝmaɪt]   Settlement with PO at 332746NO865741W in Jefferson Co. Named by the early local industrialists, probably during the 1880s, for the limestone, rich in magnesium carbonate, found here and used in the production of steel. PO est. in 1971 (Brown and Nabers 190).

DORA   Inc. town with PO at 334343NO870525W in Walker Co. Called SHARON, possibly for the region named in the Bible, in the early 1880s. First inc. as HORSE CREEK for a nearby stream in 1897. Name officially changed to DORA in 1906 to honor Dora Freil, the wife of Hugh Freil, the operator of the local Victory Mines. Sharon PO est. in 1886; Horse Creek PO in 1890; Dora PO in 1905 (Gant).

DORSEY CREEK   Stream rising at 335940NO865610W in Cullman Co. and flowing into Mulberry Fork of the Black Warrior River on the border between Cullman Co. and Walker Co. at 335135NO865814W. Probably named for a local family (U.S.G.S., 1966 Base Maps).

DOSTER   Settlement with discontinued PO at 313851NO854026W in Barbour Co. Named for the Doster family, early settlers of the area. PO est. in 1912 (Ellis 29).

DOTHAN   Inc. co. seat with PO at 311323NO852326W in Houston Co. Cawthon's Cowpen, the corral built to hold cattle to be sold to William Cawthon, an important cattle dealer in GA, was located here. Given the environmental designation POPLAR HEAD c. 1858. Name changed to DOTHAN after the existence of another Poplar Head in the state was discovered when the first PO was est. in 1871. J. Z. S. Connelly suggested this biblical name, that of a plain on the caravan route from Syria to Egypt. Inc. in 1885. Became the co. seat in 1903 (F. S. Watson 1972, 59–60).

DOUBLE BRIDGES CREEK   Stream rising at 312406NO855409W in Coffee Co. and flowing into the Choctawhatchee River at 310142NO855121W in Geneva Co. Name refers to the two bridges only about 8 miles apart in Coffee Co. that cross the creek (U.S.G.S., 1966 Base Maps; F. S. Watson 1970, 17).

DOUBLEHEAD   Community with discontinued PO at 330539NO852339W in Chambers Co. Possibly named for Double Head, a famed Cherokee chief who was living in north AL in 1835. PO est. in 1888 (Dugas [Chambers Co.] 57).

DOUBLE OAK MOUNTAIN   Mountain whose summit is at 333035NO862815W in Shelby Co. Name is descriptive of two large oak trees that were on one of its slopes (Tamarin; U.S.G.S., 1966 Base Maps).

DOUBLE SPRINGS   See GADSDEN in Etowah Co.

DOUBLE SPRINGS   Inc. co. seat with PO at 340847NO872408W in Winston Co. between Clear Creek and Sipsey Fork. Environmental name given because of the settlement's location between the sources of the two streams. Chosen co. seat in 1882. PO est. in 1883. Inc. in 1943 (T. M. Owen 1:520).

DOUGLAS   Inc. town with PO at 341025NO861925W in Marshall Co. Named for Stephen Douglas, a pioneer settler of this area, before the Civil War, from Douglasville, GA, who gave land for the first school. PO est. in 1936. Inc. in 1970 (Roden 52).

DOWNING   Community with discontinued PO at 320839NO860031W in Montgomery Co. Probably named for the family of Joseph

P. Downing, the first postmaster, appointed in 1893 ("Record of Appointment of Postmasters").

DOWNS   Settlement with discontinued PO on the Seaboard Air Line RR at 321553NO-854703W in Macon Co. Probably named for a local Down family. PO est. in 1902.

DOZIER   Inc. town with PO at 312931NO-862154W in Crenshaw Co. Named for Daniel Dozier, a pioneer settler from SC. PO est. in 1887. Inc. in 1907 (Harris 1982, 58).

DRAG   See PARAGON in Choctaw Co.

DRAKE EYE   See ENTERPRISE in Coffee Co.

DRAYTON   See JACKSONVILLE in Calhoun Co.

DREWERY   Community with discontinued PO at 312910NO871511W in Monroe Co. First known as WAIT (possibly for a local family). A PO called HATTER'S MILL for the sawmill operated by D. J. Hatter was est. here in 1898 with Mr. Hatter the postmaster. Renamed DREWERY a few years later for John Drew McMillan, a pioneer born in 1807 who built the first store here, where the PO was located. Drewery PO est. in 1901 with McMillan as the postmaster (Dugas [Monroe Co.] 94–95).

DRY CEDAR CREEK   Stream rising at 320507NO864135W in Lowndes Co. and flowing into the Alabama River at 320744NO-865844W in Dallas Co. Probably a descriptive and environmental name (U.S.G.S., 1966 Base Maps).

DRY CREEK   The following streams have a name that is probably descriptive during dry seasons.
1. Stream rising at 311350NO861633W in Covington Co. and joining Clear Creek at 311219NO861300W (U.S.G.S., 1966 Base Maps).
2. Stream rising at 344722NO854755W in Jackson Co. and flowing into Guntersville Lake at 344442NO854749W (U.S.G.S., 1966 Base Maps).
3. Stream rising at 320136NO874414W in Marengo Co. and joining Chickasaw Bogue at 320207NO873737W. A smaller stream, Little Dry Creek, rises at 322602NO873655W and joins Chickasaw Bogue at 321935NO-874254W (U.S.G.S., 1966 Base Maps).

DRY CREEK CROSSROADS   See CLEVELAND in Blount Co.

DRY FORKS   Community at 315405NO-872200W in Wilcox Co. Probably named for the plantation home of John Asbury Tait that was built nearby in 1833 (Harris 1982, 58).

DUBLIN   Settlement at 320155NO860933W in Montgomery Co. Probably named for Dublin Co., NC, from which came many settlers of the area (Harris 1982, 58; U.S.G.S., 1966 Base Maps).

DUCK CREEK   Stream rising at 341818NO-864153W in Cullman Co. and flowing into Mulberry Fork of the Black Warrior River at 341445NO863906W on the border between Cullman Co. and Blount Co. Name probably refers to migratory ducks that fed here (U.S.G.S., 1966 Base Maps).

DUCK SPRINGS   Settlement at 340845NO-855957W in Etowah Co. Named for either Young Duck, an Indian living in the area, according to the Cherokee Roll of 1835, or wild ducks that fed at the nearby springs (Jolly; *Official 1959 Alabama Highway Map*).

DUDLEY   Settlement with discontinued PO at 330939NO871800W in Tuscaloosa Co. Coal-mining operations began here in the early 1880s. Named for a local family. PO est. in 1882 (Rich 1979, 200).

DUDLEYVILLE   Settlement with discontinued PO at 325454NO853600W in Tallapoosa Co. The town developed around a trading post here in the early nineteenth century. By 1835 when a PO was est. it was known as PITTSBOROUGH, perhaps for a local Pitts family. The next year the name of the town was changed to DUDLEYVILLE for Peter Dudley, an early trader with the Creek Indians. PO est. in 1836 (Dugas [Tallapoosa Co.] 86–87).

DUGGAR MOUNTAIN   Ridge at 335016NO-853846W in Calhoun Co. and Cleburne Co. Named for Hiram Duggar, an early settler of the area. Also identified with the descriptive and environmental name TERRAPIN MOUNTAIN (General Land Office, 1915 map; Jolly).

DUKE   Settlement with discontinued PO at 335102NO855409W in Calhoun Co. Named for the first postmaster, William Green Duke, who was also one of the earliest settlers. PO est. in 1883 (Jolly).

DUMAS   See NANAFALIA in Marengo Co.

DUNAVANT   Community with discontinued PO at 332936NO863239W in Shelby Co. Probably named for a local family. PO est. in 1897.

DUNCANVILLE   Settlement with PO at 330342NO872632W in Tuscaloosa Co. that developed when the Gulf, Mobile and Ohio RR reached this point in 1898. Named for either William M. Duncan, a local property owner, or W. Butler Duncan, an official of the RR. PO est. in 1890 (Rich 1979, 202).

DUNN   CREEK   Stream   rising   at 332725NO875108W in Tuscaloosa Co. and flowing into the Sipsey River at 332026NO-874539W. Named for the local Dunn family (Geological Survey of Alabama, 1894 map; Rich 1979, 202–03).

DUTTON   Inc. town with PO at 343639NO-855501W in Jackson Co. Named for M. M. Dutton, an early settler. PO est. in 1889. Inc. in 1962 (Kennamer 180).

DYAS   ['daɪəz]   Community with discontinued PO near the Louisville and Nashville RR at 305744NO874034W in Baldwin Co. Designation is probably a variant form reflecting the local pronunciation of *Dyer's*, the name of the RR station. Both forms probably honor a local family. PO est. in 1898.

DYAS CREEK   Stream rising at 310258NO-874050W in Baldwin Co. and flowing into the Perdido River at 305157NO873806W between Baldwin Co. and FL. Probably named for a local Dyer family (U.S.G.S., 1966 Base Maps).

EAGAN   See MALVERN in Geneva Co.

EASONVILLE   Settlement with discontinued PO at 333136NO861729W in St. Clair Co. flooded by Logan-Martin Lake in 1964. While the area was a Methodist campground, 1820–72, it was known as *Eat-and-camp*. When the settlement acquired a PO in 1872, it was named EASONVILLE, for Bolivar Eason, the first postmaster (Rich).

EASTABOGA   [ˌistə'bogə]   Community with discontinued PO at 333621NO860117W in Talladega Co. and Calhoun Co. Mentioned in 1848 *Acts of the General Assembly*. Named for an Upper Creek village, Istapoka, whose designation is derived from Creek *isti* 'people' and *apoga* 'dwelling place,' [b] resulting from the assimilation of [p] to the vowels surrounding it. PO est. in 1854 (McMillan; Read 31).

EAST BRANCH OF FISH RIVER   See MAGNOLIA RIVER in Baldwin Co.

EAST BREWTON   Inc. town with PO at 310535NO870346W in Escambia Co. It grew up around old FORT CRAWFORD, a military fortification serving as a supply base for federal troops fighting against hostile Indians, 1816–18. The fort was named for William H. Crawford (1772–1834), secretary of war (1815–16) under James Madison. Town was named for its location in relation to the town Brewton. Inc. in 1918. PO est. in 1971 (Waters 266–70).

EASTERN VALLEY   Settlement at 332134NO-865807W in Jefferson Co. Name is probably a descriptive and environmental one (U.S.G.S., 1966 Base Maps).

EASTON   Community with discontinued PO at 325433NO854148W in Tallapoosa Co. Probably named for the pioneering family of Stephen B. East, the first postmaster, appointed in 1840 (Dugas [Tallapoosa Co.] 87).

EBENEZER   See COURTLAND in Lawrence Co.

ECHO   Inc. town with discontinued PO at 312832NO852757W in Dale Co. The traditional explanation of the name is that the settlers building the first cabin here heard an echo each time the logs struck one another. PO est. in 1851. Inc. in 1903 (F. S. Watson 1968, 120–26).

ECHOLA   [ɛ'kolə]   Settlement with PO at 332041NO874722W in Tuscaloosa Co. Settled in the 1850s and named FOX for a prominent local family. In 1899 the designation was changed to ELBERT, probably also for a local family. Because of possible confusion with Elberta, AL, Golden · Mayfield, the postmaster, created a new name, a combination of *Echo* and *Alabama*, when the PO was est. in 1912 (Rich 1979, 208–09).

ECLECTIC   Inc. town with PO at 323807NO860204W in Elmore Co. Traditional explanation for the name is that M. L. Fielder, who had taken an "eclectic" course of study in school, suggested this designation because the word *eclectic* meant to him 'that which is best.' PO est. in 1879. Inc. in 1907 (Harris 1982, 59).

EDDY   Settlement with discontinued PO at 342119NO863034W in Marshall Co. Perhaps named for a local resident. PO est. in 1894.

EDGEWATER   Settlement at 333136NO-865728W in Jefferson Co. Descriptive and environmental name (Hagood 46–47; U.S.G.S., 1966 Base Maps).

EDGEWOOD Inc. town at 332803NO-864839W in Jefferson Co. Probably a descriptive and environmental name. Inc. in 1920. Now merged with Homewood (League of Municipalities).

EDSONS Settlement on the Western RR of Alabama at 321905NO864631W in Lowndes Co. Probably named for a local Edson family (U.S.G.S., 1966 Base Maps).

EDWARDSVILLE Inc. town with PO at 334226NO853033W in Cleburne Co. Chosen to be the seat of justice after the co. was created in 1866. Named for William Edwards, who donated land for the courthouse and other co. buildings. PO est. in 1869. Inc. in 1891. Co. seat changed to Heflin in 1906 (M. B. Owen 1:395).

EDWIN Settlement with discontinued PO at 313955NO852231W in Henry Co. Probably the name of a person, but identity unknown. PO est. in 1892.

EIGHT MILE Settlement with PO at 304548NO880737W in Mobile Co. Said to have received this name because the town is located 8 miles northeast of Mobile. PO est. in 1943 (Harris 1982, 60).

EIGHTMILE CREEK Stream rising at 341933NO864520W in Morgan Co. and flowing into the Broglen River at 340841NO-864609W in Cullman Co. Probably a descriptive name (U.S.G.S., 1966 Base Maps).

ELAMVILLE Settlement with discontinued PO at 314003NO853923W in Barbour Co. Named for the old Elam Church to commemorate the ancient kingdom in Asia. PO est. in 1875 (Ellis 31).

ELBA Inc. co. seat with PO at 312452NO-860404W in Coffee Co. During 1840–50 known as BRIDGEVILLE, probably a descriptive name. For a few months during 1850–51 called BENTONVILLE for Thomas Hart Benton, an officer serving in AL during the 1813–14 war with the Creek Indians. In 1851 named ELBA for the island where Napoleon was exiled. John B. Simmons, the postmaster, suggested the designation while reading a biography of the French emperor. PO est. in 1851. Chosen co. seat in 1852. Inc. in 1893 (F. S. Watson 1970, 36–37).

ELBERT See ECHOLA in Tuscaloosa Co.

ELBERTA Inc. town with PO at 302451NO873552W in Baldwin Co. Founded in 1903 by a group of German businessmen from Chicago. Town named for the Elberta peaches grown in N. C. Bartling's orchard. PO est. in 1928. Inc. in 1952 (Bush 42–43).

ELDERVILLE See MONTEREY in Butler Co.

ELDRIDGE Inc. town with PO at 335522NO873702W in Walker Co. While John Byler was building the road through this area that bears his name, his son-in-law, Eldridge Mallard, built an inn and PO on this site and became the first postmaster. PO est. in 1836. Inc. in 1970 (Gant).

ELGIN ['ɛldʒɪn] Settlement with discontinued PO where state Highway 101 crosses U.S. Highway 72 at 345055NO872328W in Lauderdale Co. First called INGRAM'S CROSSROADS for Benjamin Ingram, who owned the land in 1818. Then named ELGIN CROSSROADS and finally ELGIN, for Elgin, IL, when PO was est. in 1901 (Sockwell).

ELIAS See CLEVELAND CROSSROADS in Clay Co.

ELISKA Community with discontinued PO at 312109NO874059W in Monroe Co. Name may be that of a local person, or it may honor the rabbi of the synagogue of Safed in Upper Galilee during the sixteenth century. PO est. in 1899 (Read xv).

ELK COUNTY Created from lands now in Lauderdale Co. and Limestone Co. by the MS territorial legislature on May 24, 1817. Never materialized. Named for the river (Sockwell).

ELKMONT Inc. town with PO at 345544NO865826W in Limestone Co. Probably a descriptive and environmental name, which is a combination of *Elk*, from nearby Elk River, and *mont*, for the settlement's elevated location. PO est. in 1872. Inc. in 1873 (U.S.G.S., 1966 Base Maps).

ELK RIVER Stream rising in TN that forms part of the border between Limestone Co. and Lauderdale Co. before it flows into the Tennessee River at 344541NO871556W. Called CHEWALLEE or CHUWALEE by the Indians of the area. ELK RIVER on B. Tanner's 1796 map. Given this name because of the large number of elk on its banks (Sockwell).

ELKWOOD Settlement with discontinued PO at 345839NO864325W in Madison Co. Name is probably a descriptive and environmental compound. PO est. in 1899.

ELLIOTT'S CREEK Stream rising at

325607NO872727W in Hale Co. and flowing into the Black Warrior River at 325913NO-874229W. Named, c. 1825, for David Elliott, who is credited with being the first white man to cross this creek (Holliman).

ELMORE   Settlement with PO at 323219NO-861859W in Elmore Co. Named for Albert Stanhope Elmore (1827–1909), member of a prominent local family. PO est. in 1873 (Harris 1982, 61).

ELMORE COUNTY   Created by act of the state general assembly on Feb. 15, 1866. Bordered on the north by Coosa Co., on the east by Tallapoosa Co., on the south by Macon Co. and Montgomery Co., on the west by Autauga Co., and on the northwest by Chilton Co. Named for John Archer Elmore, a veteran of the American Revolution from VA who settled here in 1821 and was later a state legislator. The co. seat is Wetumpka (M. B. Owen 1:421).

ELROD   Settlement with PO at 331522NO-874732W in Tuscaloosa Co. Known c. 1830 as MITCHELL for a local family, then in the 1850s as SIPSEY TURNPIKE for the road named for the river. In 1898 after the Mobile and Ohio RR reached this point, named ELROD for William W. Elrod, a local physician. PO est. in 1898 (Rich 1979, 212–13, 377, 507).

ELROD MILL   See CHIGGER HILL in DeKalb Co.

ELSANOR ['ɛlsə,nor]   Community at 303242NO873501W in Baldwin Co. Named for the school that honors Elsa Norton, the wife of a Chicago dentist who donated land and money for the school with the condition that it be named for his wife (Bush 43; *Official 1959 Alabama Highway Map*).

ELYTON ['ilətən]   Settlement with discontinued PO once located at 333000NO-865027W in Jefferson Co., now part of the western section of Birmingham. Named for William H. Ely, a commissioner for the Connecticut Asylum for the Deaf and Dumb, who came here in 1819 after the federal government gave land in this area to the institution. The village located here before 1820 was called FROG LEVEL, a humorously descriptive name. When the settlement was chosen to become co. seat in 1821, Ely donated land for a courthouse and jail. Inc. in 1820. PO est. in 1821. Birmingham replaced it as co. seat in 1873 (Brown and Nabers 183).

EMELLE [ɪm'ɛl]   Settlement with PO at 324345NO881852W in Sumter Co. Honors Emelle Dial, whose father, Joseph Dial, gave land to the Alabama, Tennessee and Northern RR with the provision that the station be named for his daughter. Emelle Dial, said to have been named for her two aunts, Emma and Ella, but having none with these names, seems, instead, to have been named for Emelle Spencer, an acquaintance of her family living a few miles away in MS who attended the same church as they. Possibly it was Mrs. Spencer who was named for two aunts: *Em* for *Emma* and *-elle* for *Ella*. PO est. in 1912 (Stegall).

EMPIRE   See BREMEN in Cullman Co.

EMPIRE   Settlement with PO at 334830NO870038W in Walker Co. Probably named for a coal-mining co. in the area. PO est. in 1901 (Gant).

EMUCKFAW CREEK [i'mʌkfɔ]   Stream rising at 330929NO854255W in Clay Co. and flowing into the Tallapoosa River at 325913NO854511W in Tallapoosa Co. Benjamin Hawkins records the name as IMMOOKFAU and interprets it as 'gorget made of a conch' in his "Sketch of the Creek Country in 1798 and 1799" (46). In Hitchiti, *imukfa* means 'a shell or a concave metallic ornament' (Read 30).

ENITACHOPCO CREEK [i,nɪtə'tʃapko]   Stream rising at 331733NO855553W in Clay Co. and joining Hillabee Creek at 330444NO-855321W in Tallapoosa Co. CANDUTCHKEE CR. on La Tourette's 1844 map. This early name means 'boundary creek,' from Creek *ikana* or *kan* 'earth' and *tachki* 'line.' Now called ENITACHOPCO for an ancient Hilibi village that Benjamin Hawkins, in his "Sketch of the Creek Country in 1798 and 1799" (43), calls AU-NET-TE CHAP-CO. This name means 'Long Thicket Creek,' from Creek *anati* 'thicket' and *chapko* 'long' (Read 11, 30).

ENON   Settlement with PO at 320919NO-852948W in Bullock Co. Named by James

Glenn for the springs located in Judea. PO est. in 1842 (Harris 1982, 62).

ENTERPRISE Inc. town with PO at 311854NO855119W in Coffee Co. Originally DRAKE EYE, probably an environmental name. Renamed ENTERPRISE at the suggestion of W. J. Hatcher, a Baptist minister who considered the settlement an enterprising undertaking. PO est. in 1878. Inc. in 1896 (M. B. Owen 1:533–34).

EODA [i'odə] Settlement at 312228NO-861909W in Covington Co. Origin of name unknown (*Official 1983–84 Alabama Highway Map*).

EOLINE [i'olɪn] Settlement with PO at 325942NO871356W in Bibb Co. that developed around the Mobile and Ohio RR in 1898. Named for the daughter of Edward Russell of New Orleans, vice-president of the RR. PO est. in 1898 (Ellison 192, 196–97).

EPES [ɛps] Inc. town with PO located on the high west bank of the Tombigbee River at 324125NO880734W in Sumter Co. Formerly called JONES BLUFF in honor of John B. Jones, one of the first physicians of the co. Inc. in 1874 as EPES STATION, it was named for John W. Epes from Lunenburg, VA, who gave the right-of-way to the Alabama Great Southern RR. PO est. in 1874 (Foscue 31).

EQUALITY Settlement with PO at 324543NO860607W in Coosa Co. Probably an inspirational and symbolic name. PO est. in 1849.

ERIE Dead town with discontinued PO 4 miles southwest of Sawyerville in Hale Co. Co. seat of Greene Co., 1819–38. Since 1867 site has been in Hale Co. Named by early immigrants to this area for their former homeland, Erie (Ireland). Inc. and its PO est. in 1820 (Rich 1979, 215).

ERIN Community with discontinued PO at 332145NO855431W in Clay Co. Name is another designation for Ireland, the former home of many of the early settlers. PO est. in 1906 (Waldrop).

ESCAMBIA COUNTY [ɛs'kæmbiə] Created by act of the state legislature on Dec. 10, 1868. Bordered on the north by Monroe Co. and Conecuh Co., on the east by Covington Co., on the south by FL, and on the west by Baldwin Co. Named for Escambia Creek. The co. seats have been Pollard, 1868–80, and Brewton, the present one (M. B. Owen 1:23).

ESCAMBIA CREEK Stream rising at 312718NO871352W in Monroe Co. and flowing across the Escambia Co. boundary line at 311628NO872025W into FL where it joins Little Escambia Creek to form the Escambia River. Sometimes called BIG ESCAMBIA CREEK to distinguish it from Little Escambia Creek, which rises at 311920NO871436W in Conecuh Co. and flows across the Escambia Co. line into FL at 305949NO871037W. Both are on *Early's Map of Georgia*, c. 1818. Swanton suggests Choctaw *uski* 'cane' and *amo* 'to gather' as the source of the name. T. M. Owen proposes *oski* 'cane' and *ambeha* 'therein' as its origin (Read 30–31).

ESCATAWPA [,ɛskə'tɔpə] Settlement with discontinued PO at 311722NO882314W in Washington Co. Named for the river. PO est. in 1858 (Read 31).

ESCATAWPA RIVER Stream rising at 313348NO882540W in Washington Co. and flowing southwest through Mobile Co. into MS at 302530NO883333W. ESCATAWPA C. on La Tourette's 1844 map. Name refers to a creek where cane was cut, from Choctaw *uski* 'cane,' *a*, 'there,' and *tapa* 'cut' (Read 31).

ESTELLE Settlement at 315809NO-871209W in Wilcox Co. Name of a person, but identity not known (U.S.G.S., 1966 Base Maps).

ESTILL FORK ['ɛstəl] Stream rising in TN and joining Larkin Fork at 345353NO-861014W in Jackson Co. to form Paint Rock River. Named for a pioneering family who settled between the two branches of the river (Kennamer 136; U.S.G.S., 1966 Base Maps).

ESTILLFORK Settlement with PO at 345436NO861014W in Jackson Co. Named for the river branch. PO est. in 1858 (Melancon).

ETHELSVILLE Inc. town with PO on the Gulf, Mobile and Ohio RR at 332456NO-881300W in Pickens Co. Founded as a RR station c. 1900 and named for Ethel Hancock, a local resident. PO est. in 1899. Inc. in 1956 (N. F. Brown 33).

ETOMBIGABEE CREEK See FACTORY CREEK in Sumter Co.

ETOWAH COUNTY ['ɛtoˌwɔ] Created as BAINE COUNTY by act of the state general assembly on Dec. 7, 1866, but abolished on Dec. 3, 1867. Recreated as ETOWAH COUNTY on Dec. 1, 1868. Bordered on the north by DeKalb Co., on the east by Cherokee Co., on the south by Calhoun Co. and St. Clair Co., on the west by Blount Co., and on the northwest by Marshall Co. Originally named for David W. Baine, a Confederate officer from Cherokee Co. who was killed in the Civil War. Co. was abolished by the Reconstruction legislature because Baine had been a secessionist. When recreated, the co. was named for the Etowah mound in GA. The meaning of the Cherokee name *Itawa*, found in several places in GA, is unknown, but it may be related to the Creek word *italwa* 'town, tribe.' The co. seat is Gadsden (Jolly; McMillan in Read 100; Read 31).

EUFAULA [ju'fɔlə] Inc. town with PO at 315328NO850844W in Barbour Co. Inc. in 1832 as IRWINTON for William Irwin, a general in the Creek Indian War and the War of 1812, but because of confusion with a town in GA having the same name, in 1843 the name was changed to that of the Creek Indian settlement earlier located near here. *Eufaula* has never been satisfactorily translated. Irwinton PO est. in 1832; Eufaula PO in 1844 (Ellis 31–38; Read 31–32).

EUFAULA CREEK See TALLADEGA CREEK.

EUFAULA, LAKE See WALTER F. GEORGE RESERVOIR.

EULATON ['julətən] Settlement with discontinued PO at 333844NO855445W in Calhoun Co. Named for Eula, daughter of Lewis M. Ford, the first postmaster, appointed in 1884 (Lindsey 31).

EUNOLA [ju'nolə] Inc. town with PO at 310223NO855051W in Geneva Co. Possibly the name of a person, but identity not known. Inc. in 1885. PO est. in 1886.

EUPHAUBE CREEK See UPHAPEE CREEK in Macon Co.

EUTAW ['juˌtɔ] Inc. co. seat with PO at 325026NO875315W in Greene Co. Founded in 1838 when the co. seat was moved here from Erie. Named for Eutaw Springs, SC, where Nathaniel Greene, for whom the co. was named, won a victory over the British in Sept. 1781. PO est. in 1839. Inc. in 1840 (Rich 1979, 218).

EVA Inc. town with PO at 341956NO864532W in Morgan Co. Name is said to be that of either the wife or daughter of the first postmaster, William J. Rooks, Jr., appointed in 1887. PO first called COWHEAD (possibly a reference to livestock raised in the area), Sept. 1887–Oct. 1887. Inc. in 1963 (Ackley 24).

EVANSVILLE See MOUNT MEIGS in Montgomery Co.

EVERGREEN Inc. co. seat with PO at 312600NO865725W in Conecuh Co. When first settled c. 1820, area was known as *Cosey's Old Field* because it had once been part of a field cleared by the revolutionary war veteran John Cosey. Settlement was named EVERGREEN at the suggestion of Alexander Travis because of the surrounding evergreen (pine) trees. PO est. in 1840. Became co. seat in 1866. Inc. in 1873 (*Alabama: A Guide*, 268; T. M. Owen 1:552).

EWELL ['juəl] Settlement with discontinued PO at 312517NO853429W in Dale Co. Named by the first postmaster, Dallas Windham, appointed in 1891, for his son Ewell (Harris 1982, 64).

EXCEL Inc. town with PO at 312540NO872029W in Monroe Co. When the PO was est. in 1884, M. D. Harrison, who the next year became the owner of the land on which it was located, suggested the inspirational name because he felt the area had a "potential for excellence." Inc. in 1948 (Dugas [Monroe Co.] 94).

EZRA See OAK GROVE in Jefferson Co.

FABIUS Settlement with PO at 344839NO854639W in Jackson Co. Formerly located a few miles away, the PO was moved to present site in 1922. Though its origin is unknown, the name may refer to Fabius Maximus, the Roman general who opposed Hannibal. PO est. in 1881 (Melancon).

FACLER Settlement with PO at 344733NO855436W in Jackson Co. Named for a prominent landowner in the region. PO est. in 1869 (Kennamer 169).

FACTORY CREEK Stream rising at 324618NO881838W in Sumter Co. and flowing into the Tombigbee River at 324209NO880651W. ETOMBA-IGABY on Romans's 1772 map of FL. *Etombigabee* means 'coffin-makers,' from Choctaw *itombi* 'box, coffin' and *ikbi* 'makers.' An Indian who made boxes to contain the bones of the dead lived along the banks of this creek. FACTORY CREEK on La Tourette's 1839 map. By that time the name had been changed to FACTORY to commemorate the place where George S. Gaines, the Indian agent, conducted business with the Choctaws. This factory was built in May 1816, near where the creek empties into the Tombigbee River (Foscue 31–32; Read 69).

FADETTE Settlement with discontinued PO at 310240NO853215W in Geneva Co. H. A. Smith, a local merchant, opened the PO in his store and gave the town its name, whose origin is now forgotten. PO est. in 1891 (Harris 1982, 64).

FAIRFAX Settlement with PO at 324746NO851102W in Chambers Co. This model mill town built during the 1880s may have a merely euphonious name; however, it is said to have been named for either Lord Fairfax of England or the town Fairfax, VA. PO est. in 1971 (Dugas [Chambers Co.] 57).

FAIRFIELD Settlement with PO at 311506NO863844W in Covington Co. Probably a subjectively descriptive name. PO est. in 1872.

FAIRFIELD Inc. town with PO at 333346NO864753W in Jefferson Co. Called COREY in honor of William Ellis Corey, president of U.S. Steel (1910–13). After Mr. Corey became involved in a divorce scandal, the name was changed to FAIRFIELD for the CT hometown of James A. Farrell, a later president of the same organization. Corey PO est. in 1912, Fairfield PO in 1913. Inc. in 1918 (Brown and Nabers 195).

FAIRFORD Settlement with discontinued PO at 311005NO880351W in Washington Co. Probably a subjectively descriptive compound name. PO est. in 1889.

FAIRHOPE Inc. town with PO at 343122NO875412W in Baldwin Co. Founded c. 1890 by a group of followers of the economist Henry George (1839–1897) from Des Moines, IA. They chose this inspirational and symbolic name because they felt they had a "fair hope" of success. PO est. in 1889. Inc. in 1908 (*Alabama: A Guide*, 397).

FAIRVIEW Community at 324628NO864317W in Chilton Co. Founded during the 1880s and named for the home of Shelby Jones, owner of a cotton plantation here before the Civil War (B. D. Roberts).

FAIRVIEW Community at 311417NO860240W in Coffee Co. Named for the Fairview Baptist Church, founded in 1887 as Siloam Baptist Church (Lowe).

FAIRVIEW Inc. town at 341519NO864117W in Cullman Co. Originally called LAWRENCE CHAPEL for a Methodist church that developed from a prayer meeting organized by the Lawrence family c. 1880. Inc. with the subjectively descriptive name FAIRVIEW in 1967 (Jones 1972, 43–46).

FAKITCHIPUNTA CREEK See TURKEY CREEK in Choctaw Co.

FALKVILLE Inc. town with PO at 342206NO865431W in Morgan Co. Named for Louis M. Falk, a local merchant born in Prussia in 1839, who immigrated to the U.S. in 1857 and served in the Confederate army. PO est. in 1868. Inc. in 1898 (Knox 134–37).

FALLS OF THE BLACK WARRIOR See TUSCALOOSA in Tuscaloosa Co.

FALLS OF THE CAHAWBA See CENTREVILLE in Bibb Co.

FALLS OF TUSCALOOSA See TUSCALOOSA in Tuscaloosa Co.

FARLEY Settlement with PO at 343543NO863344W in Madison Co. Probably named for John B. Farley, the first postmaster, appointed in 1893 ("Record of the Appointment of Postmasters").

FARMERSVILLE Settlement with PO at 320441NO865331W in Lowndes Co. A symbolic name because farming was the main occupation of the area. PO est. in 1834 (Harris 1982, 65).

FATAMA [fə'tɑmə] Settlement with discontinued PO at 315356NO871408W in Wilcox Co. Although its origin is unknown, the designation may be a variant of *Fatima*, the name of a village with a religious shrine in Portugal. PO est. in 1855.

FAUNSDALE Inc. town with PO at 322735NO873538W in Marengo Co. Named for Thomas A. Harrison's nearby plantation, whose designation is a combination of *faun*, for either the Roman god Faunus or the young deer that were plentiful in the area, and the subjectively descriptive term *dale*. PO est. in 1841. Inc. in 1886 (W. Smith).

FAYETTE   Inc. co. seat at 334104NO-874951W in Fayette Co. First called, for only a short time, LAFAYETTE in honor of the Marquis de Lafayette (1757–1834), the French hero of the American Revolution; then after being chosen co. seat FAYETTE COURT HOUSE, 1824–80; and FAYETTE-VILLE, 1880–91. The town had two sections, 1838–90. The newer one growing up around the Georgia RR (Southern) was called FAYETTE DEPOT TOWN and also, because the area was wet and marshy, FROG LEVEL. The older section was called LATONA (origin unknown), 1891–97. In 1898, the residents voted to name the entire town FAYETTE. Fayette PO est. in 1892. Inc. in 1899 (Peoples 8).

FAYETTE COUNTY   Created by act of the state general assembly on Dec. 20, 1824. Bordered on the north by Marion Co., on the east by Walker Co., on the south by Tuscaloosa Co. and Pickens Co., and on the west by Lamar Co. Named for the Marquis de Lafayette (1757–1834), the French officer who came to the aid of American forces during the Revolution. Fayette is the co. seat (Peoples i).

FAYETTEVILLE   See   FAYETTE   in Fayette Co.

FAYETTEVILLE   Settlement with discontinued PO at 330844NO862421W in Talladega Co. Named for Fayetteville, TN, the home of Andrew Jackson's militia, some of whom settled here after the Creek Indian War of 1813–14. PO est. in 1837 (McMillan).

FENNEL'S TURNOUT   See TRINITY in Morgan Co.

FERNBANK   Settlement with PO at 333445NO880830W in Lamar Co. First called BALTIMORE for the city in MD. Given the descriptive name FERNBANK because of the ferns growing in the area. PO est. in 1884 (Acee 11, 71).

FINCHBURG   Community with discontinued PO at 313833NO873039W in Monroe Co. Named for J. C. Finch, a local merchant who was the first postmaster, appointed in 1891 (Dugas [Monroe Co.] 95).

FISCHER CROSSROADS   Community at 342752NO853847W in DeKalb Co. Named for Gustavus Fischer, a German who settled in the area in 1842 and operated a tannery, a gristmill, a cobbler's shop, and a cotton mill (Raughton 35).

FISH BAY   See WEEKS BAY in Baldwin Co.

FISHPOND   Community with discontinued PO at 325204NO860124W in Escambia Co. Named for a large fish pond at this site. PO est. in 1906 (Waters 186).

FISH RIVER   Stream rising at 304427NO-874756W in Baldwin Co. and flowing into Weeks Bay at 302448NO874931W. Descriptive and environmental name (Bush 44; U.S.G.S., 1966 Base Maps).

FISK   Community with discontinued PO at 345741NO863424W in Madison Co. Named for an early settler. PO est. in 1885 (Green).

FITZPATRICK   Settlement with PO at 321259NO855320W in Bullock Co. During the 1840s and 1850s, area was known as MOCCASIN GAP, probably an allusion to its earlier Indian inhabitants. By the time its PO was est. in 1869, the town was named for the Fitzpatrick brothers, especially Phillips Fitzpatrick, who came here from GA in the 1820s (T. M. Owen 1:592).

FIVE MILE CREEK   Stream rising at 325235NO872312W in Bibb Co. and flowing into the Black Warrior River at 325403NO-874537W in Hale Co. It received its name because it is approximately 5 miles north of Greensboro, the seat of justice for Hale Co. (Holliman; U.S.G.S., 1966 Base Maps).

FIVE POINTS   Inc. town with PO at 330105NO852101W in Chambers Co. First called LYSTRA, for the Baptist church of that name, which commemorates the ancient biblical city. Renamed FIVE POINTS for the five roads that once met in the center of town. Lystra PO est. in 1882, Five Points PO in 1888. Inc. in 1916 (Crump).

FIVE POINTS   Settlement at 342828NO-870927W in Lawrence Co. Given this descriptive name because five roads once met here (Harris 1982, 67; *Official 1959 Alabama Highway Map*).

FIVE RUNS CREEK Stream rising at 310346NO863033W in Covington Co. and flowing into the Yellow River at 310346NO863033W. Probably a name descriptive of the small runs (streams) that feed it (U.S.G.S., 1966 Base Maps).

FLAT CREEK Name is descriptive of the level bed of the streams.
1. Stream rising at 311248NO861643W in Covington Co. and flowing into the Pea River at 310219NO860511W in Geneva Co. (U.S.G.S., 1966 Base Maps).
2. Stream rising at 314706NO870511W in Monroe Co. and flowing into the Alabama River at 314659NO871236W. Also called BIG FLAT CREEK. Enoch Riley, who built his home near the banks of this creek, gave it this name (Dugas [Monroe Co.] 97).

FLAT CREEK Settlement with discontinued PO at 333839NO870533W in Walker Co. Probably named for a nearby creek that has a designation descriptive of its bed. PO est. in 1926.

FLAT ROCK Settlement with PO at 344611NO854140W in Jackson Co. First known as KOSH for a local family. Renamed for a nearby creek that has a flat rock bottom. PO est. in 1912 (Melancon).

FLATWOOD Settlement at 322701NO861540W in Montgomery Co. Probably a compound name descriptive of its location in a flat wooded area (U.S.G.S., 1966 Base Maps).

FLATWOOD Settlement with discontinued PO at 320857NO873123W in Wilcox Co. Possibly named for the plantation owned before the Civil War by Aaron Burr Cooper, who seems to have given it a descriptive and environmental name. PO est. in 1901 (Harris 1982, 67).

FLATWOODS See NATCHEZ in Monroe Co.

FLEA HOP See SANTUCK in Elmore Co.

FLINT CITY Settlement with discontinued PO at 343123NO865813W in Morgan Co. First known as MORGANSBURG in honor of Daniel Morgan (1736–1802), the revolutionary war general for whom the co. was named, when the PO was first est. in 1878. The next year named FLINT CITY for the creek beside which it is located. Flint City PO est. in 1879 (Ackley 25).

FLINT CREEK Stream known as EAST FORK OF FLINT CREEK as it rises at 342022NO864538W in Morgan Co. becomes FLINT CREEK as it reaches 341728NO865316W in Cullman Co. and flows into the backwaters of Wheeler Lake at 343506NO865532W in Morgan Co. Its tributary West Flint Creek rises at 342211NO870753W in Lawrence Co. and joins Flint Creek at 342924NO865801W in Morgan Co. Named for the quartz stone still to be found in the area (Ackley 25; U.S.G.S., 1966 Base Maps).

FLINT RIVER Stream rising in TN, crossing the state boundary line into Madison Co. at 350507NO862333W, and flowing into the Tennessee River between Madison Co. and Marshall Co. at 343009NO863146W. Named for the flint rocks nearby (*Alabama: A Guide*, 259; U.S.G.S., 1966 Base Maps).

FLOMATON ['flomətən] Inc. town with PO at 310000NO871539W in Escambia Co. that grew up at the junction of three rail lines. First called REUTERSVILLE in honor of a man named *Reuter*, the contractor who drove in the last spike joining the rail lines in 1869; next, PENSACOLA JUNCTION, alluding to the origin of one of the roads. Then a director of one of the RR companies named the settlement WHITING for himself in 1870. Because REUTERSVILLE and WHITING were both used as PO names in 1871 and 1872, the mail was often misdirected. Finally in 1884, a permanent name was chosen for both the town and PO: FLOMATON, a combination of the first syllable of *Florida*, the last one of *Alabama*, and *-ton* 'town.' Inc. in 1908 (Waters 274).

FLORA See PEACHBURG in Bullock Co.

FLORALA Inc. town with PO at 310018NO861941W in Covington Co. Name is a combination of clipped forms of *Florida* and *Alabama*. PO est. in 1891. Inc. in 1901 (Harder 178).

FLORENCE See WALLACE in Escambia Co.

FLORENCE Inc. co. seat with PO at 344759NO874038W in Lauderdale Co. Ferdinand Sannoner, the architect who planned the city, named it for Florence, Italy, his home. Became the co. seat and obtained its PO in 1818. Inc. in 1826 (Sockwell).

FLORETTE Settlement with PO at 342459NO864211W in Morgan Co. First called NUNN'S MILL for a mill operated by S. W. Nunn, a former Confederate officer. When PO est. in 1878, name changed to FLO-

RETTE, probably a personal name, but origin unknown (Ackley 25).

FOLEY Inc. town with PO at 302423NO-874101W in Baldwin Co. Named for J. B. Foley of Chicago, who bought a large tract of land here in 1901 and founded a farming community. PO est. in 1905. Inc. in 1915 (Bush 45–46).

FOLSOM Settlement with discontinued PO at 324057NO872421W in Perry Co. During the first term of Grover Cleveland (1837–1908) as president of the U.S. (1885–89), the area was a voting precinct known as *Cleveland Beat*. In 1887 when a PO was est. here, it was named FOLSOM for Frances Folsom, who had married Cleveland the year before (Harris 1982, 68).

FORESTER CHAPEL Community with discontinued PO at 330940NO853220W in Randolph Co. Probably named for the nearby Methodist church. PO est. in 1887 (1974 General Highway Map of Russell Co.).

FOREST HOME Settlement with PO at 315144NO865034W in Butler Co. Hattie Stewart, who served as the community's first teacher in 1871, is credited with choosing the name because of its suggestion of tranquility. PO est. in 1875 (Dugas [Butler Co.] 78).

FORKLAND Inc. town with PO in the fork, the area between the Black Warrior and Tombigbee rivers, at 323853NO875300W in Greene Co. First settled c. 1818. Named for its location. PO est. in 1840. Inc. in 1970 (Rich 1979, 234).

FORKS OF CYPRESS, THE See CYPRESS CREEK in Lauderdale Co.

FORKVILLE Settlement at 341609NO-873305W in Winston Co. A locational name for its position either between two highways here or near the West Fork of the Sipsey River (Gant; *Official 1959 Alabama Highway Map*).

FORNEY Settlement with discontinued PO at 340510NO852743W in Cherokee Co. Named for either John Horace Forney or his brother William Henry, both Confederate officers from adjoining Calhoun Co. PO est. in 1878 (Harris 1982, 68).

FORT BOWYER See FORT MORGAN in Baldwin Co.

FORT CHARLOTTE See MOBILE in Mobile Co.

FORT CHINNEBY See CHINNEBY in Talladega Co.

FORT CONDE DE LA MOBILE See MOBILE in Mobile Co.

58

FORT CRAWFORD See EAST BREWTON in Escambia Co.

FORT DALE Community with discontinued PO at 315329NO863927W in Butler Co. Settlement around the former military fortification was first identified with the descriptive and environmental name POPLAR SPRING. Samuel Dale (1772–1841), officer in the Indian wars, erected here in 1818 the log fort named for him. PO est. in 1818. Temporary co. seat, 1819–22 (Harris 1982, 68).

FORT DAVIS Settlement with PO at 321435NO854235W in Macon Co. Named for the first postmaster, Fort M. Davis, appointed in 1891 ("Record of Appointment of Postmasters").

FORT DEPOSIT Inc. town with PO at 315904NO863443W in Lowndes Co. Area was first known as *Ballard's Precinct* (identity of person unknown). In 1813 during the war with the Creek Indians, Andrew Jackson had a military fortification built here for storing supplies. PO est. in 1855. Inc. in 1891 (Harris 1982, 69).

FORT GAINES LAKE See WALTER F. GEORGE RESERVOIR.

FORT JACKSON Dead town with discontinued PO on the east bank of the Coosa River 5 miles south of Wetumpka in Elmore Co. It grew up around the military fortification built at the command of Andrew Jackson during the Creek Indian War of 1813–14 and named for him. This fort was on the same site as FORT TOULOUSE, built by the French for trading with the Alabama Indians in July 1717, and abandoned in 1763. It was named for the Count of Toulouse, a son of Louis XIV. Fort Jackson was abandoned in 1818. The town named for the fort was the original co. seat of Montgomery Co. when it was created by the MS territorial legislature in 1816. PO est in 1818 (Brannon 1951, 132).

FORT LESLIE See TALLADEGA in Talladega Co.

FORT LOUIS DE LA MOBILE See MOBILE in Mobile Co.

FORT MADISON See ALLEN in Clarke Co.

FORT MITCHELL Settlement with PO at 322029NO850118W in Russell Co. that grew up around a military fortification built by the GA militia in 1813 but soon taken over by federal troops. Town was named for the fort, which honored David Brydie Mitchell, the governor of GA at the time. PO est. in 1833 (Brannon 1959, 100).

FORT MORGAN   Community with discontinued PO at 301342NO880123W in Baldwin Co. It grew up around the fortified post erected on Mobile Point in 1833. This fort, named for Daniel Morgan (1736–1802), American general during the Revolution, replaced a wooden fortress, built in 1813 and destroyed by a storm in 1819, named FORT BOWYER for John Bowyer, a major in the Indian wars. The later fort was the scene of much fighting during the Civil War. The PO for the community named for this fort was est. in 1892 (Harris 1982, 115).

FORT PAYNE   Inc. co. seat at 342639NO-854311W in DeKalb Co. named for the fort built by a captain named *Payne*, sent here by the federal government in 1837 to provide a defensive fortification for the white settlers in case there was trouble moving the Indians west. PO est. in 1869. Became co. seat in 1876. Inc. in 1889 (Raughton 36).

FORT TALLADEGA   See TALLADEGA in Talladega Co.

FORT TOULOUSE   See FORT JACKSON in Elmore Co.

FORT WHITE   See GROVE HILL in Clarke Co.

FOSTERS   Community with PO at 330541NO874109W in Tuscaloosa Co. Named for the family of James Foster, who settled here in 1818. PO est. in 1833 (Rich 1979, 236).

FOSTORIA   Settlement with discontinued PO at 320511NO864948W in Lowndes Co. Probably named for the family of William Foster, a local resident. PO est. in 1813 (Harris 1982, 69).

FOUNTAIN   Settlement with PO at 313540NO872432W in Monroe Co. When the Gulf, Florida and Alabama RR (St. Louis and San Francisco) reached this point, a mile from the town of Hixon, c. 1914, because there was already a Hixon Station on the line, the new station here was called FOUNTAIN, the maiden name of Mrs. A. C. Hixon, a prominent local resident. PO est. in 1922 (Dugas [Monroe Co.] 95).

FOUR-MILE CREEK   See BRUSH CREEK in Lauderdale Co.

FOWL RIVER   Stream rising at 303321NO-881407W in Mobile Co. and flowing between the mainland and Mon Louis Island into Mississippi Sound at 302549NO880809W. Called

RIVIÈRE DE L'ILE AUX OIES 'River of the Isle of Geese [wild fowl]' by the French, a name that might have been a translation of an Indian designation. Approved by U.S. Board on Geographic Names in 1960 (Harris 1982, 69).

FOWL RIVER   Settlement with discontinued PO at 302744NO881008W in Mobile Co. Probably named for the nearby river. PO est. in 1878.

FOWL RIVER POINT   Cape on Mobile Bay at 302818NO880548W in Mobile Co. Probably named for the nearby river (U.S.G.S., 1966 Base Maps).

FOWL RIVER STATION   See THEODORE in Mobile Co.

FOX   See ECHOLA in Tuscaloosa Co.

FRANCISCO   Community with discontinued PO at 345914NO861457W in Jackson Co. Named for Francisco Rice, a captain in the Confederate army and later a state senator. PO est. in 1875 (Kennamer 143).

FRANKFORT   Settlement with discontinued PO at 343348NO875032W in Franklin Co. The name, a combination of *Frank-* from *Franklin* and *fort*, was chosen because it was similar to that of the co. Co. seat, 1849–78. PO est. in 1852 (Knight 22).

FRANKLIN   Dead town located a little to the north of old St. Stephens, which was 2 miles north of the present settlement with this name in Washington Co. Settled by Americans who did not wish to live in old St. Stephens, then a Spanish town, and probably named for Benjamin Franklin (1706–1790), American patriot. Served as co. seat, 1809–15, shortly thereafter merging with old St. Stephens (Matte 50, 62).

FRANKLIN   Inc. town at 322842NO-854809W in Macon Co. Possibly named for Benjamin Franklin (1706–1790), American patriot. Inc. in 1976 (*Official 1959 Alabama Highway Map*).

FRANKLIN   Settlement with PO at 314252NO872441W in Monroe Co. Named for a local woodcutter. PO est. in 1897 (Dugas [Monroe Co.] 95).

FRANKLIN COUNTY   Created by act of the AL territorial legislature on Feb. 4, 1818. Bounded on the north by Colbert Co., on the east by Lawrence Co., on the south by Winston Co. and Marion Co., and on the west by MS. Named for Benjamin Franklin (1706–1790), American patriot. The co. seats have been Russellville, 1818–49; Frankfort, 1849–78; Belgreen, 1878–81; and, since 1881, Russellville, for the second time (Knight 22).

FRANKLIN SPRING   See GOOD SPRING in Franklin Co.

FRANKVILLE   Community with PO at 313847NO880851W in Washington Co. Named for Frank Granade, the first postmaster, appointed in 1888 (Matte 307).

FREDONIA   Settlement with discontinued PO at 325923NO851719W in Chambers Co. Hurst's Store, a business operated by John A. Hurst, who traded with the Indians, was located here. FREDONIA is said to refer to either "Free" McDonald, one of Hurst's in-laws, or to the land's being a "free donation" to Hurst by the Indians (the name was sometimes spelled without an *i*). PO est. in 1834 (Dugas [Chambers Co.] 57).

FREEMANVILLE   Community with discontinued PO at 310418NO873115W in Escambia Co. Settled mostly by homesteading blacks in the early 1840s. PO est. in 1908 (Waters 185–86).

FRISCO CITY   Inc. town with PO at 312600NO872405W in Monroe Co. First called JONES MILL for the sawmill and gristmill operated by James W. Jones and his family, who moved here from Butler Co. in 1888. For a few years after the Muscle Shoals, Birmingham and Pensacola RR Co. built a rail line through this community, it was called ROY for Roy C. MeGargel, the RR president. After a change in the RR's management, the town was renamed JONES MILL. In 1925, the St. Louis and San Francisco RR took over the rail line. By 1928 the town became known as FRISCO CITY for this RR, often designated as the *Frisco* line. Jones Mill PO est. in 1890; Roy PO in 1913; Jones Mill PO est. again in 1915; Frisco City PO in 1928. Inc. as JONES MILL in 1909 and as FRISCO CITY in 1928 (Dugas [Monroe Co.] 95).

FROGGY BOTTOM   See MADISON in Montgomery Co.

FROG LEVEL   See FAYETTE in Fayette Co.

FROG LEVEL   See ELYTON in Jefferson Co.

FROG LEVEL   See DELMAR in Winston Co.

FROG POND   See PLEASANT GROVE in Jefferson Co.

FRUITDALE   Settlement with PO at 312033NO882428W in Washington Co. on the Mobile and Ohio RR. Founded as a lumbering center but given the compound name of *fruit* plus *dale* for the orchards once here. PO est. in 1894 (Matte 309–13).

FRUITHURST   Inc. town with PO at 334351NO852602W in Cleburne Co. on the Southern RR. Originally designated with the descriptive name SUMMIT CUT because of the grading needed for the rail line in 1882. In the early 1890s known as ZIDONIA, possibly what was thought to be the feminine form of the biblical name *Zidon*. Finally, it was given the subjectively descriptive compound name *fruit* plus *hurst* by the Alabama Fruit Growers and Winery Association, who hoped their endeavors would succeed here. Fruithurst PO est. in 1895. Inc. in 1895 (V. V. Hamilton 169; D. Stewart).

FULFORD'S CROSSROADS   See PEROTE in Bullock Co.

FULLERS CROSSROADS   Settlement at the intersection of co. Highway 50 and U.S. Highway 331 at 314904NO861840W in Crenshaw Co. Probably named for a local family (*Official 1959 Alabama Highway Map*).

FULTON   Inc. town with PO at 314718NO874338W in Clarke Co. on the Mobile and Birmingham RR (Southern). Originally called WADE'S STATION in honor of John A. Wade, a local businessman; then BEHRMAN, 1889–96, for Marcus B. Behrman, a local lumberman. In 1896 inc. as FULTON for the city in NY, the home of George R. Hannon and George C. and James S. Burr, partners in the town's most important lumber business. Behrman PO est. in 1889, Fulton PO in 1896 (Clarke Co. Historical Society 166–67).

FULTONDALE   Inc. town with PO at 333617NO864738W in Jefferson Co. Designation is a blend of the names of two rival communities: *Fulton Springs*, for the springs on land owned by an early local family, and *Glendale*, a subjectively descriptive name. Inc. in 1947. PO est. in 1950 (Hagood 22).

FUNDEE See COLD FIRE in Pickens Co.

FURMAN Settlement with PO at 320024NO865801W in Wilcox Co. Originally known as OLD SNOW HILL because it grew up on the first site of the town Snow Hill that was moved 2 miles westward to be on the Louisville and Nashville RR. Named for Furman, SC, in 1884 when PO was est. (Harris 1982, 71).

FYFFEE [faɪf] Inc. town with PO at 342648NO855415W in DeKalb Co. Name is an elaborate spelling of *fife*, a designation for a musical wind instrument, devised by a Mr. Ayers, a local resident. PO est. in 1900. Inc. in 1956 (Raughton 37).

GABRIEL CREEK Stream rising at 325429NO873334W in Hale Co. and joining Millians Creek at 325707NO874351W. A personal name, perhaps intended to be that of the archangel (U.S.G.S., 1966 Base Maps).

GADSDEN Inc. co. seat with PO at 340051NO860024W in Etowah Co. Originally known as DOUBLE SPRINGS because of the two springs on the site. Later, John S. Morague, an early settler, named the settlement for his personal friend James D. Gadsden (1788–1858), who had served in AL with Andrew Jackson during the Creek Indian War of 1813–14. While minister to Mexico under Franklin Pierce (1804–1869), president of the U.S. (1853–57), he made the Gadsden Purchase of land comprising the southern parts of AZ and NM. Double Springs PO est. in 1833, Gadsden PO in 1846. Inc. in 1871 (Jolly).

GAINESTOWN ['genz,taʊn] Community with PO at 312420NO874153W in Clarke Co. Named for the Choctaw Indian agent George S. Gaines and his brother E. P. Gaines. PO est. in 1848 (T. M. Owen 1:643).

GAINESVILLE ['genzvəl] Inc. town with PO at 324915NO880932W in Sumter Co. John Coleman, the half-Choctaw owner of the site, had promised to sell his land to George S. Gaines, the Indian agent, but because Moses Lewis made a better offer for it, Gaines urged Coleman to accept the better offer. In 1832 Lewis and John C. Whitsett laid out the town and named it for Gaines. PO est. in 1833. Inc. in 1835 (Foscue 33).

GAINO ['gaɪno] Community with discontinued PO at 315028NO852039W in Barbour Co. Named for Gaino Watson, a local resident. PO est. in 1897 (Ellis 34).

GALLANT Settlement with PO at 335955NO861443W in Etowah Co. Originally known as CLEAR SPRINGS, a descriptive and environmental designation. Renamed GALLANT for John A. Gallant, the first postmaster, appointed in 1889 (Jolly).

GALLION ['gæljən] Settlement with PO at 322948NO874258W in Hale Co. Named for Jo Gallion, a RR road master who lived in Demopolis. PO est. in 1883 (W. Smith).

GAMBLE Settlement with discontinued PO at 335246NO872004W in Walker Co. Named for Franklin A. Gamble, owner of the coal mines located here. PO est. in 1879 (Gant).

GANER ['genər] Settlement with discontinued PO at 310459NO860625W in Geneva Co. Possibly named for a local family. PO est. in 1902.

GANTT Inc. town with PO at 312424NO862903W in Covington Co. Probably named for either I. F. Gantt, first postmaster of what was the nearest PO, HAMPTONVILLE, located across the Conecuh River, 1879–1900, or William Gantt, first postmaster of Gantt PO, est. in 1899. Inc. in 1970 ("Record of Appointment of Postmasters").

GANTT LAKE Artificial lake formed by the impoundment before 1960 of the Conecuh River at 312412NO862847W in Covington Co. Probably named for the nearby town (U.S.G.S., 1966 Base Maps).

GANTT'S QUARRY Inc. town at 330854NO861722W in Talladega Co. Named for the marble quarry operated by Edward Gantt, 1838–65. Inc. in 1910 (McMillan).

GARDEN CITY Inc. town with PO at 340052NO864449W in Cullman Co. Name resulted from Johann G. Cullmann's calling this spot, in 1876, "the garden center of the world." PO est. in 1898. Inc. in 1911 (Jones 1972, 65–68).

GARDENDALE Inc. town with PO at 333936NO864846W in Jefferson Co. Originally known as JUGTOWN because of a jug factory located here. Name changed, it is said, because a citizen called the settlement "the garden spot of the state." PO est. in 1935. Inc. in 1955 (Hagood 41).

GARLAND Settlement with discontinued PO at 313323NO864924W in Butler Co. In 1831 when the Mobile and Montgomery RR (Louisville and Nashville) reached this point, the station was named for W. P. Garland, one of the RR's chief engineers. PO est. in 1875 (Dugas [Butler Co.] 78).

GARTH   Settlement with discontinued PO at 344331NO861811W in Jackson Co. Named for a U.S. congressman who caused the postal route to reach this point in 1878 (Kennamer 136).

GASQUE   [gæsk]   Community with discontinued PO at 301511NO874911W in Baldwin Co. Named for a member of a local family, probably William H. Gasque, a representative in the 1842 state general assembly. PO est. in 1880 (Bush 49).

GASTONBURG   Settlement with discontinued PO at 321226NO872615W in Wilcox Co. First known as PARIS, probably for the French city. When the Southern RR reached this point in 1887, name was changed to GASTONBURG. Named for the Gaston family, who were early settlers. John W. Gaston was the first postmaster, appointed in 1891 (T. M. Owen 1:644).

GATESWOOD   Community at 304315NO873451W in Baldwin Co. Name is a compound of *Gates*, for a local family, plus *wood* (Bush 49; *Official 1959 Alabama Highway Map*).

GAYLESVILLE   Inc. town with PO at 341606NO853325W in Cherokee Co. First identified with the descriptive and environmental name SULPHUR SPRINGS. Renamed GAYLESVILLE for John Gayle (1792–1858), sixth governor of the state, when PO was est. in 1836. Inc. in 1887 (T. M. Owen 1:644).

GEIGER   ['geigər]   Inc. town with discontinued PO at 325205NO881818W in Sumter Co. Founded by John A. Pinson, a state senator, who named it for his wife's family. PO est. in 1904. Inc. in 1912 (Foscue 34).

GENEVA   Inc. co. seat at 310158NO855150W in Geneva Co. Named for Geneva, Switzerland, by the first postmaster, Walter H. Yonge, a native of Switzerland, appointed in 1840. Became the seat of justice when the co. was created in 1868. Inc. in 1875 (Harder 195).

GENEVA COUNTY   Created by act of the state legislature on Dec. 26, 1868. Bounded on the north by Coffee Co. and Dale Co., on the north and east by Houston Co., on the south by FL, and on the west by Covington Co. Named for the town Geneva, which became the co. seat (T. M. Owen 1:645).

GEORGETOWN   Settlement at 305318NO881613W in Mobile Co. Possibly named for a city in the east (*Official 1959 Alabama Highway Map*).

GEORGIANA   Inc. town with PO at 313813NO864431W in Butler Co. Founded in 1855 by Pitt S. Milner, a Baptist minister from GA who was also the first postmaster, appointed the same year. He is said to have named the town for his native state and for his youngest daughter, Anna, who was drowned as a child. Inc. in 1872 (Dugas [Butler Co.] 78).

GERALDINE   Inc. town with PO at 342105NO860003W in DeKalb Co. Name of a person, but identity unknown. PO est. in 1882. Inc. in 1957 (Raughton 37).

GERMAN HILL   See COLUMBIANA in Shelby Co.

GERMANY   See BUENA VISTA in Monroe Co.

GIBSON   Community with discontinued PO at 320536NO860922W in Montgomery Co. Probably named for a local family. PO est. in 1899.

GILBERTOWN   Inc. town with PO at 315237NO881917W in Choctaw Co. Named for the local Gilbert family. PO est. in 1911. Inc. in 1913 (Choctaw Co. Bicentennial Commission 1, 19).

GILMER   See HANCEVILLE in Cullman Co.

GILMERVILLE   See HILLSBORO in Lawrence Co.

GILMORE   Settlement at 333059NO870848W in Jefferson Co. Named for Irvin Gilmore, a settler who operated a store here, probably during the 1830s (Hagood 24; U.S.G.S., 1966 Base Maps).

GINTOWN   See GRAYSVILLE in Jefferson Co.

GIRARD   Settlement with discontinued PO now part of PHENIX CITY in Russell Co. Founded in 1832 and named for Stephen Girard, a Philadelphia philanthropist who owned land in the area. Served as co. seat until 1837. PO est. in 1840. Merged with Phenix City in 1923 (*Alabama: A Guide*, 339).

GLEN ALLEN Inc. town with PO at 335454NO874430W in Fayette Co. Previously known as STEWART'S GAP, probably for a local family. GLEN ALLEN is said to be composed of the names of two engineers on the Kansas City, Memphis and Birmingham RR (St. Louis and San Francisco), which reached the settlement in 1889, but because *gap* and *glen* both refer to a narrow valley, and the Glen Allen PO was est. in 1876, thirteen years before the rail line was completed, it is more likely that the name really means 'Allen's valley' and that Allen was a local resident. Inc. in 1959 (Peoples 10).

GLENCOE Inc. town with PO at 333014NO864430W in Etowah Co. Named for Glencoe, Scotland, by the Scottish immigrants Taylor and Zachary Spencer. PO est. in 1915. Inc. in 1939 (Jolly).

GLENNVILLE Settlement with discontinued PO at 320743NO851037W in Russell Co. Named for James E. Glenn, who settled in the area in 1835. PO est. in 1837 (M. B. Owen 3:419).

GLENWOOD Inc. town with PO at 313952NO861017W in Crenshaw Co. on the Central of Georgia RR. Designation is said to be a combination of *Glenn*, the name of a RR man, and the descriptive and environmental word *wood*. Inc. in 1907 (Harris 1982, 74).

GOAT ROCK LAKE Artificial lake formed by the impoundment of the Chattahoochee River with Goat Rock Dam at 323633NO850449W between Lee Co. and GA. Dam built in 1912 by the Columbus [GA] Electric and Power Co. Descriptive phrase may be a translation of an Indian animal-incident name (Blackmon).

GOBBLERSVILLE See MONTEREY in Butler Co.

GOLD HILL Settlement with discontinued PO at 324318NO853028W in Lee Co. One explanation of the name is that the word *gold* refers to traces of the mineral found here, and another is that it honors a Mr. Goldsmith, an early settler of this hilly region. PO est. in 1837 (Nunn 21).

GOLD MINE Settlement with discontinued PO at 340221NO874437W in Marion Co. Received its name because a fine grade of coal known as "black gold" was discovered here. PO est. in 1850 (Lawler).

GOLDVILLE Inc. town with discontinued PO at 330501NO854702W in Tallapoosa Co. Environmental name referring to the discov-

ery of gold here in 1842. Received its PO and was inc. in 1843 (Dugas [Tallapoosa Co.] 87).

GOOD HOPE Inc. town at 340657NO863149W in Cullman Co. Named for the Good Hope Baptist Church, organized in 1842. Inc. in 1962 (Jones 1972, 78–80).

GOODMAN Settlement at 311646NO855937W in Coffee Co. Named for the Goodman family, who were early settlers, probably in the 1840s (*Official 1959 Alabama Highway Map*; F. S. Watson 1970, 60).

GOOD SPRING Community at 343230NO874149W in Franklin Co. Originally FRANKLIN SPRING, probably for a spring named for the co. Later given the subjectively descriptive name GOOD SPRING (*Official 1959 Alabama Highway Map*).

GOOD SPRINGS Settlement with discontinued PO at 345650NO871139W in Limestone Co. Probably a subjectively descriptive name alluding to nearby springs. PO est. in 1854.

GOODSPRINGS Settlement with PO at 334008NO871354W in Walker Co. Subjectively descriptive name alluding to nearby springs. PO est. in 1924 (Gant).

GOODWATER Inc. town with PO at 330356NO860312W in Coosa Co. Originally called ADKINS GAP in honor of the first settler in the area in the 1830s. Name changed to GOODWATER, descriptive of the large spring that provides water for the town and that is also one of the sources of Hatchet Creek, when PO est. in 1850. Inc. in 1894 (M. B. Owen 2:408).

GOODWAY Settlement with PO at 312012NO872533W in Monroe Co. Name is subjectively descriptive of the roads leading to its main buildings. PO est. in 1904 (Dugas [Monroe Co.] 95).

GOOSE CREEK Stream rising at 321109NO873907W in Marengo Co. and joining Beaver Creek at 320019NO873141W in Wilcox Co. Descriptive and environmental designation, which may be a translation of an animal-incident name (U.S.G.S., 1966 Base Maps).

GOOSE POND See CLANTON in Chilton Co.

GORDO Inc. town with PO at 331912NO875410W in Pickens Co. Probably named by a veteran of the Mexican War for the Battle of Cerro Gordo, an American victory at a mountain pass north of Vera Cruz in 1847. Alabamians fought there under Winfield Scott. PO est. in 1847. Inc. in 1901 (N. F. Brown 35–36).

GORDON Inc. town with PO at 310828NO850548W in Houston Co. When first settled in the 1830s known as WOOD-VILLE, possibly an environmental designation; then in the 1850s called OPEN ROAD, a subjectively descriptive name. By 1866 when PO was est., it honored Dan Gordon, the probate judge of the co. Inc. in 1872 (F. S. Watson 1972, 80).

GORDONSVILLE Community with discontinued PO at 320946NO864357W in Lowndes Co. Probably named for the family of Francis Gordon (1795–1867), a prominent local citizen. PO est. in 1877 (Harris 1982, 75).

GORGAS Settlement with discontinued PO at 333857NO871229W in Walker Co. Named for William Crawford Gorgas (1854–1920), the army surgeon, a native of AL, who conquered yellow fever in the Panama Canal Zone. PO est. in 1918 (Gant).

GOSHEN Inc. town with PO at 314322NO-860706W in Pike Co. Located a few miles from the present site and known as GOSHEN HILL c. 1830–93. When the settlement was moved, the word *hill* was dropped. The name *Goshen*, that of the home of the Israelites in Egypt, has also acquired the connotation 'land of plenty.' Goshen Hill PO est. in 1877, Goshen PO in 1893. Inc. in 1905 (Farmer 1973, 122, 373; Harder 203).

GOSPORT ['gɑsport] Settlement with discontinued PO at 313457NO873501W in Clarke Co. Named for the plantation Gosport Retreat founded by Samuel Forwood of MD in the early 1830s. *Gosport*, a reduced form of *God's Port*, is the name of a place in England. PO est. with Samuel Forwood as postmaster in 1834 (Clarke Co. Historical Society 172–74).

GRABALL Community at the intersection of state Highway 10 and U.S. Highway 431 at 313511NO851633W in Henry Co. First known as HART'S CROSSROADS for Vance Hart, who built his home here between 1816 and 1820, and later HUDSPETH'S CROSSROADS for Joel Abbott Hudspeth, who bought Hart's house and land in 1866. The traditional explanation of the current name is that during a surprise raid by officers of the law on a chicken fight being bet on by gamblers, someone cried, "Grab all the money and run!" *Graball* is thus, supposedly,

a compound of *grab* and *all* (*Official 1959 Alabama Highway Map*; Warren, *Henry's Heritage*, 333).

GRADY Settlement with PO at 315941NO-861204W in Montgomery Co. Named for Henry W. Grady (1850–1889), the GA journalist who helped to promote the "New South" during the 1880s. PO est. in 1890 (Harder 204).

GRAHAM Settlement with discontinued PO at 332727NO851915W in Randolph Co. Originally named BROCKVILLE, then GRAHAM, both probably for local families. Graham PO est. in 1880.

GRAND BAY Bay at head of Mobile Bay at 304527NO880011W in Baldwin Co. Name is probably descriptive, the French form of which would have been *La grande baie*, the feminine adjective *grande* meaning 'great' or 'large.' (U.S.G.S., 1966 Base Maps).

GRAND BAY Settlement with PO at 302834NO882032W in Mobile Co. Probably named for the nearby bay. PO est. in 1870.

GRANGEBURG Settlement with discontinued PO at 310028NO851242W in Houston Co. First named GRANGER for John W. Granger; later, GRANGEBURG. Granger PO est. in 1882; Grangeburg PO in 1917 (F. S. Watson 1972, 85).

GRANGER See GRANGEBURG in Houston Co.

GRANT Inc. town with PO at 343143NO-861512W in Marshall Co. Named for Ulysses S. Grant (1822–1885), president of the U.S. (1869–77), by the first postmaster, Henry Walls, who was a Republican. PO est. in 1887. Inc. in 1945 (Roden 52).

GRANTLEY Community with discontinued PO at 335114NO853246W in Cleburne Co. Possibly named for a local family. PO est. in 1871.

GRAVEL HILL Settlement at 342907NO-874431W in Franklin Co. Name is descriptive of the town's location (Knight 23; *Official 1959 Alabama Highway Map*).

GRAYSON Settlement with PO at 335534NO863030W in Winston Co. in the William B. Bankhead National Forest. Founded by the Grayson Lumber Co. of Birmingham, for which the town is named. PO est. in 1943 (Harris 1982, 77).

GRAYSTONE Community at 335534NO-863030W in Blount Co. Named for the home of the Cheney family, who quarried and crushed limestone for many years in this area and built their house of this material. A descriptive name (U.S.G.S., 1966 Base Maps; Weaver).

GRAYSVILLE   Inc. town with PO at 333714NO865817W in Jefferson Co. Originally called GINTOWN because a cotton gin was located here. Later named GRAYSVILLE for a local family. PO est. in 1942. Inc. in 1946 (Hagood 20).

GREAT POINT CLEAR   Cape on Mobile Bay at 302859NO875612W in Baldwin Co. The descriptive name, an English translation of the Spanish designation PUNTA CLARA 'point clear,' refers to the large clearly visible cape (Bush 50; U.S.G.S., 1966 Base Maps).

GREELEY   Community at 331525NO870730W in Tuscaloosa Co. Named for the Horace Greeley School located here, c. 1890–1963 (Rich 1979, 257).

GREEN BAY   Community with discontinued PO at 311040NO861722W in Covington Co. Name is descriptive of the bay trees in the area. PO est. in 1879 (Harris 1982, 77).

GREENBRIER   Settlement with PO at 344015NO865037W in Limestone Co. Probably named for Greenbrier, VA, because a number of settlers of the co. came from VA. PO est. in 1869 (T. M. Owen 1:880–85).

GREEN CREEK MOUNTAIN   Mountain whose summit is at 335418NO855808W in Etowah Co. and Calhoun Co. Also called GREEN MOUNTAIN. Named for the nearby creek, itself honoring the family of Jacob Green, a revolutionary war veteran. The east side is known as COLVIN MOUNTAIN for Alford Colvin, an early resident of the area (Jolly).

GREENE COUNTY   Created by act of the AL territorial general assembly on Dec. 13, 1819, out of parts of Marengo Co. and Tuscaloosa Co. Until 1867 it included the western part of Hale Co. Now bordered on the north by Pickens Co. and Tuscaloosa Co., on the east by Hale Co., on the south by Marengo Co., and on the southwest by Sumter Co.

Named for Nathaniel Greene (1742–1786), the revolutionary war general who defeated the British at the Battle of Eutaw Springs in SC in Sept. 1781. The co. seat was Erie until 1838 when the present one, Eutaw, was chosen (Rich 1979, 257–58).

GREEN HILL   Settlement with discontinued PO at 345823NO873044W in Lauderdale Co. Named for Green Berry Hill, a Mexican War veteran. PO est. in 1850 (Sockwell).

GREEN MOUNTAIN   See GREEN CREEK MOUNTAIN.

GREEN MOUNTAIN   Mountain whose summit is at 343740NO863141W in Madison Co. Named for a family who settled in the area during the 1840s or 1850s (Green; U.S.G.S., 1966 Base Maps).

GREEN POND   Settlement with PO at 331330NO870735W in Bibb Co. Named for a nearby pond whose designation refers to the green algae in the water. PO est. in 1872 (Hubbs).

GREENSBORO   Inc. co. seat at 324216NO873545W in Hale Co. First called RUSSELL SETTLEMENT for a local family. Known as TROY or NEW TROY, 1817–23, probably to commemorate the ancient city in Asia Minor. In 1823 name changed to GREENSBORO for Greene Co., in which it was located at that time. PO est. in 1825. Became the co. seat of Hale Co. following its creation in 1867. Inc. in 1870 (Holliman).

GREENSPORT   Dead community with discontinued PO at 334825NO860740W in St. Clair Co. that was flooded by Neely Henry Lake in 1968. A compound of *Green's* and *port*, the name refers to the landing place for the ferry Jacob Green was chartered to operate on the Coosa River in 1832. PO est. in 1847 (Rich).

GREENVILLE   Inc. co. seat at 314946NO863704W in Butler Co. In 1818 called BUTTSVILLE for Samuel Butts of GA, an officer killed fighting hostile Creek Indians in Macon Co. in 1814. Name changed to GREENVILLE for Greenville, SC, the former home of a number of its early residents, including Hilary Herbert, who suggested the name change when the town was selected to be co. seat in 1822. Inc. in 1823. PO est. in 1825 (Dugas [Butler Co.] 78–79).

GREENWOOD See KEENER in Etowah Co.

GREENWOOD   Settlement at 331933NO-865610W in Jefferson Co. Name is a compound of *green* plus *wood*, probably given c. 1910 because of the trees in the area by either Bill or Charles Martin of the Martin Investment Co. (Hagood 40–41).

GRIFFIN MILL   Community at 323133NO-851559W in Lee Co. Named for a mill operated here by an early settler named *Griffin* c. 1833–35 (Harris 1982, 78).

GRIMES   Inc. town with discontinued PO on the Atlantic Coast Line at 311816NO-852653W in Dale Co. First called ABBEVILLE JUNCTION because of its location on the rail line from Abbeville. Then named GRIMES, probably for a local family. PO est. in 1893. Inc. in 1968 (F. S. Watson 1968, 127).

GROSSE POINTE ISLAND   See MON LOUIS ISLAND in Mobile Co.

GROVE HILL   Inc. co. seat with PO at 314231NO874638W in Clarke Co. During the Creek Indian War of 1813–14, a defensive fortification called FORT WHITE, possibly because it was intended to provide protection for the white settlers, was located here. In 1815 a small settlement grew up around Magoffin's Store, operated by James Magoffin from Philadelphia. By 1828 this settlement was known as GROVE HILL, a name descriptive of the grove of oak trees on the plateau where it was located. A few years later another small settlement, called SMITHVILLE in some documents and MACON in others (both *Smith* and *Macon* may have been local family names) grew up nearby. In the 1830s, after the two settlements merged, the entire town became known as GROVE HILL. Grove Hill PO est. in 1828. Became co. seat in 1831. Inc. in 1929 (Clarke Co. Historical Society 175–77).

GROVE OAK   Settlement with PO at 342617NO860309W in DeKalb Co. Name is a compound of *grove* and *oak*, descriptive of the grove of oak trees across from the PO, est. in 1873 (Raughton 40).

GUERRYTON   ['gɛrɪtən]   Settlement with discontinued PO on the Central of Georgia RR at 321315NO853005W in Bullock Co. Probably honors a local person or RR employee named *Guerry*. PO est. in 1872.

GUESS CREEK   Stream rising at 345134NO860745W in Jackson Co. and flowing into the Paint Rock River at 344443NO-861343W. Named for George Guess (c. 1760–1843), better known as Sequoya, the

half-Cherokee inventor of the Cherokee syllabary in 1821 (Raughton 71; U.S.G.S., 1966 Base Maps).

GUEST   Settlement with discontinued PO at 342527NO855224W in DeKalb Co. Probably named for the local Guest family. PO est. in 1892 (Raughton 40).

GUIN   ['gjuɪn]   Inc. town with PO at 335756NO875453W in Marion Co. Founded by the J. M. Guin family c. 1873. PO est. in 1888. Inc. in 1893 (Lawler).

GUINN CROSSROADS   Community at 342912NO875527W in Franklin Co. where two roads once intersected. Probably named for a local family (Knight 24; *Official 1959 Alabama Highway Map*).

GULF CREST   Community with discontinued PO at 305943NO881425W in Mobile Co. An environmental name that is suggestive rather than literal because the settlement is located almost 50 miles away from the Gulf of Mexico. PO est. in 1906.

GUM SPRINGS   Settlement with discontinued PO at 340255NO863950W in Blount Co. Name is descriptive of the nearby gum trees and springs. PO est. in 1879 (Weaver).

GUNTER'S FERRY, LANDING, VILLAGE   See GUNTERSVILLE in Marshall Co.

GUNTERS MOUNTAIN   Mountain whose summit is at 343358NO861039W in Marshall Co. Named for John Gunter, the first white man to settle in the area c. 1784 (Roden 53; U.S.G.S., 1966 Base Maps).

GUNTERSVILLE   Inc. co. seat with PO at 342129NO861741W in Marshall Co. Named for a Scotsman, John Gunter, the first white settler in this area, c. 1784, who was adopted into the Indian tribe after he married a Cherokee woman. The village where he lived, at the bend of the Tennessee River, was first known as GUNTER'S VILLAGE; then GUNTER'S FERRY for the ferry he began operating in 1818; also GUNTER'S LANDING; then WHITE HOUSE, possibly referring to the dwelling of this white man; HELICON in 1836 for the mountain in Greece inhabited by the Muses of mythology; MARSHALL in 1838 for the co.; and finally, in 1848, GUNTERSVILLE. As MARSHALL, served as co. seat, 1838–41. Name changed to GUNTERSVILLE when the town was again chosen to be co. seat in 1848. Inc. first as MARSHALL in 1838 and again as GUNTERSVILLE in 1848. Helicon PO est. in 1836; Marshall PO in 1839; Gunter's

Landing PO in 1844; Guntersville PO in 1854 (T. M. Owen 1:678).

GUNTERSVILLE LAKE Artificial lake formed by impoundment of the Tennessee River with Guntersville Dam at 342523NO-862332W in Marshall Co. in 1939. Named for the town (Dugas, "Recreation Guide for Marshall Co.," 34–37).

GURLEY Inc. town with PO at 344206NO-862233W in Madison Co. Known as GURLEYSVILLE when the Memphis and Charleston RR (Southern) reached this point in 1857. Named for the family of John Gurley, pioneers in this area. Gurleysville PO est. in 1866, Gurley PO in 1883. Inc. in 1891 (T. J. Taylor 1976, 85).

GURLEYSVILLE See GURLEY in Madison Co.

GU-WIN ['gju͵wɪn] Inc. town at 335704NO875159W in Marion Co. Its designation consists of the first syllables of *Guin* and *Winfield*, chosen because this settlement is located between the two towns having these names. Inc. in 1958 (Lawler).

HACKLEBURG Inc. town with PO at 341638NO874943W in Marion Co. Said to have been named by men from TN who had difficulty driving their sheep to market in AL through the thick plants called "hackles" growing here. These tore the sheep's fleece and poisoned the ones eating them. PO est. in 1857. Inc. in 1909 (T. M. Owen 1:679).

HACKNEYVILLE Settlement with PO at 330337NO855559W in Tallapoosa Co. Named for the family of Joe Hackney, who operated a gristmill here. PO est. in 1859 (Dugas [Tallapoosa Co.] 87).

HACODA [he'kodə] Settlement with discontinued PO at 310429NO860959W in Geneva Co. First named MARTHA in honor of the wife of D. I. B. Atkinson, the first postmaster, appointed in 1882. Given the designation HACODA, an acronym formed from the names of three local businessmen—Hart, Coleman, and Davis—in 1904 when Hacoda PO was est. (Harris 1982, 79).

HAGLER ['heglər] Settlement with discontinued PO at 330202NO872024W in Tuscaloosa Co. Named for Isaac S. Hagler, the first postmaster, appointed in 1880 (Rich 1979, 264).

HAGOOD'S CROSSROADS See PINSON in Jefferson Co.

HALAWAKEE CREEK [͵hælə'wækɪ] Stream rising at 324503NO852417W in Chambers Co. and flowing into Lake Harding in Lee Co. HOLLOWACKEE in Benjamin Hawkins's "Letters," Jan. 20, 1797. Name comes from Creek *holwaki* 'bad' (McMillan in Read 100; Read 34).

HALBERTS PO See NEW LEXINGTON in Tuscaloosa Co.

HALEBURG Inc. town with discontinued PO at 312423NO850814W in Henry Co. Named for Jonathan Hale, an early settler. PO est. in 1889. Inc. in 1911 (E. C. S. Scott 9, 70).

HALE COUNTY Created out of the eastern half of Greene Co. and parts of Tuscaloosa Co., Marengo Co., and Perry Co. by act of the state general assembly in 1867. Bordered on the north by Tuscaloosa Co., on the east by Bibb Co. and Perry Co., on the south by Marengo Co., and on the west by Greene Co. Named for Stephen F. Hale, a prominent lawyer who had lived at Eutaw in Greene Co. and was killed at Gaines Mill, VA, while leading the Eleventh Alabama Infantry Regiment of the Confederate army. The co. seat is Greensboro (Holliman).

HALEYS ['helɪz] Community with discontinued PO at 340711NO874406W in Marion Co. Named for Greene M. Haley, who settled here in 1855 and was the first postmaster, appointed in 1857 (Lawler).

HALEYVILLE Inc. town with PO at 341335NO873717W in Winston Co. Originally called ARK for what was then the nearest PO, located about 1 mile east of the town. Ark PO, est. in 1881, may have been named for the biblical ark of Noah. Inc. as ARK in 1889; renamed HALEYSVILLE in 1891 for C. L. Haley, the settlement's first merchant. Now known as HALEYVILLE. Haleysville PO est. in 1891, Haleyville PO in 1918 (Ford).

HALF ACRE Community with discontinued PO at 321140NO875444W in Marengo Co. The traditional explanation of the name is that after completing their work surveyors found they had made a half-acre error. They assigned the extra half acre to the devil, calling it HELL'S HALF ACRE. Later, the residents shortened the name to HALF ACRE. Half Acre PO est. in 1855 (W. Smith).

HALLS CREEK Stream rising at 315644NO863558W in Butler Co. and joining Pigeon Creek at 314921NO863002W. Probably named for Joseph Hall, who owned land in the area as early as 1822 (J. Taylor).

HALLS CREEK Stream rising at 310103NO874422W in Baldwin Co. and flowing into the Tensaw River at 310315NO875203W. Probably named for Charles Hall, owner of land on the east side of the Tensaw c. 1849 (Bush 51; U.S.G.S., 1966 Base Maps).

HALLS CROSSROADS See JENKINS CROSSROADS in Bullock Co.

HALLS MILL CREEK Stream rising at 303818NO881448W in Mobile Co. and flowing into the Dog River at 303532NO880701W. Probably named for a gristmill operated in the 1880s by a Mr. Hall (Boudousquie, 1889 map).

HALLTOWN Settlement at 342711NO880341W in Franklin Co. First named A-LANTHUS for the PO est. here in 1881. Origin of this name is unknown, but it may have resulted from a misidentification by postal officials of a handwritten *c* in *Acanthus*, the name of a plant, as an *l*. Renamed HALL-TOWN in the late 1890s, probably for the family of the first Alanthus postmaster, John T. Hall (Knight 24).

HALSELL ['hɔlsəl] Settlement with discontinued PO at 321702NO881638W in Choctaw Co. Named for Mart V. B. Halsell, an early settler. PO est. in 1912 (Choctaw Co. Bicentennial Commission 19).

HALSO MILL ['hɔlso] Community at 312920NO860610W in Butler Co. Named for a gristmill operated by a Mr. Halso on Pigeon Creek (Dugas [Butler Co.] 79; *Official 1959 Alabama Highway Map*).

HAL'S LAKE PO See CARLTON in Clarke Co.

HAMILTON Inc. co. seat with PO at 340832NO875919W in Marion Co. Originally known as TOLL GATE because a station for collecting tolls from vehicles traveling on the road between Washington, D.C., and New Orleans was located here. Renamed HAMILTON for Albert J. Hamilton, an early settler who gave the land for the courthouse when the town was selected to become the co. seat in 1882. Toll Gate PO est. in 1838,

Hamilton PO in 1872. Inc. in 1896 (T. M. Owen 1:682).

HAMMAC ['hæmæk] Community with discontinued PO at 310720NO871323W in Escambia Co. Named for the family of Solomon W. Hammac, the first postmaster, appointed in 1891 (Waters 186).

HAMMONDVILLE Inc. town at 343454NO853736W in DeKalb Co. Named for William Cook Hammond, who settled here in 1832. Inc. in 1937 (Raughton 41).

HAMNER Settlement with discontinued PO at 324436NO881609W in Sumter Co. Founded by a free black man, Tom, who because of his marriage to an Indian woman was granted the land by the Treaty of Dancing Rabbit Creek with the Choctaw Indians in 1830. Probably a family name, but origin unknown. PO est. in 1890 (Foscue 36).

HAMPDEN Community with discontinued PO at 320453NO873744W in Marengo Co. Probably named for Hampden, MA, itself named for John Hampden (1594–1643), a member of the English Parliament who encouraged the founding of Puritan colonies in New England. Henry W. Hatch, merchant and first postmaster, was from the MA town. PO est. in 1846 (W. Smith).

HAMPDEN RIDGE Dead town located on a hill approximately 10 miles south of Belleville in Conecuh Co. Founded and named by Alexander Autrey, probably for a town in the east honoring the English member of Parliament, John Hampden. First co. seat, 1818–20. After the Indians living across Murder Creek from this settlement left the area, the inhabitants moved from this place to the site of the Indian village and founded Sparta, the next co. seat (Harris 1977, 82–83).

HAMPTONVILLE See LEESBURG in Cherokee Co.

HAMPTONVILLE PO First PO, 1879–1900, for GANTT, located across the Conecuh River in Covington Co. Probably named for a local family.

HANCEVILLE Inc. town with PO at 340338NO864603W in Cullman Co. First called GILMER, probably for a local citizen. Renamed for Horace Kinney, the first postmaster, appointed in 1872, who came here from Ireland. Inc. in 1878 (Jones 1972, 59–65).

HANCOCK COUNTY See WINSTON COUNTY.

HANNON Settlement with discontinued PO at 321421NO853134W in Macon Co. Probably named for a local family. PO est. in 1892.

HANOVER Settlement with discontinued PO at 330017NO861209W in Coosa Co. Possibly named for Hanover, VA, itself having the name of one of the English royal houses. PO est. in 1847 (Harder 220).

HARDAWAY Settlement with PO at 321711NO855056W in Macon Co. Named for local family. PO est. in 1853 (Harris 1982, 81).

HARDING, LAKE Artificial lake in Lee Co. and GA formed by the impoundment of the Chattahoochee River at 323946NO-850527W with Bartletts [Bartley's] Ferry Dam, named for the ferry operated by Walter Bartley. Lake honors R. M. Harding, general manager during the early 1900s of the Columbus [GA] Electric and Power Co. (Blackmon).

HARDYVILLE See KEYSTONE in Shelby Co.

HARPERSVILLE Inc. town with PO at 332038NO862617W in Shelby Co. Named for its founder, James W. Harper. PO est. in 1843. Inc. in 1945 (Tamarin).

HARRIS See COMER in Barbour Co.

HARRIS Community with discontinued PO on the Louisville and Nashville RR at 343931NO865813W in Limestone Co. Probably named for a local family. PO est. in 1868.

HARRISBURG Settlement with discontinued PO at 325233NO871328W in Bibb Co. Named for the family of Phelan Harris, a prominent local resident. PO est. in 1876 (Ellison 108).

HARRIS CREEK Stream rising at 315449NO880047W in Clarke Co. and flowing into the Tombigbee River at 314632NO-875911W. Probably named for a local family (U.S.G.S., 1966 Base Maps).

HARTFORD Inc. town with PO at 310608NO854149W in Geneva Co. Originally called CLEMMONS CITY for William F. Clemmons, a local resident. Renamed for Hartford, CT, when the PO was est. in 1895. Inc. in 1897 (Harris 1982, 81).

HART'S CROSSROADS See GRABALL in Henry Co.

HARTSELLE ['hɑrtsəl] Inc. town with PO at 342636NO865607W in Morgan Co. Named for George S. Hartselle, who settled in this area before 1834. PO est. in 1872. Inc. in 1875 (Ackley 27).

HARVEST Settlement with PO at 345120NO864503W in Madison Co. Originally called KELLY for Thomas B. Kelly, later the first postmaster of Harvest PO, est. in 1905. HARVEST is probably a name symbolic of the farming in the area (Green).

HATCHECHUBBEE [ˌhætʃi'tʃʌbɪ] Settlement with PO at 321614NO851633W in Russell Co. Named for the lower Creek village that was located nearby and for the stream. PO est. in 1858 (Read 34).

HATCHECHUBBEE CREEK Stream rising at 322059NO851737W in Russell Co. and flowing into the Chattahoochee River at 320817NO-850319W. HAT-CHE CHUB-BAU in Benjamin Hawkins's "A Sketch of the Creek Country in 1798 and 1799" (34). Name is derived from two Creek forms: *hachi* 'creek' and *chaba* 'halfway' (Read 34).

HATCHET CREEK Stream rising at 331425NO860241W in Clay Co. and flowing into the Coosa River at 325103NO862639W in Coosa Co. Its West Fork rises at 331846NO-860320W in Talladega Co. and flows into Hatchet Creek at 331426NO860240W in Clay Co., while its East Fork rises at 331427NO-860241W in Clay Co. and flows into Hatchet Creek at 331705NO855919W. PO-CHUSE-HAT-CHE in Benjamin Hawkins's "A Sketch of the Creek Country in 1798 and 1799" (50). HATCHET C. on La Tourette's 1833 map. Name is the English translation of either *pochuswuchi hachi* 'hatchet creek' or *pochuswa hachi* 'ax creek' (Read 35).

HATTER'S MILL See DREWERY in Monroe Co.

HATTON Settlement with PO at 343346NO-872455W in Lawrence Co. Originally SANDERSON TOWN for Johnnie Sanderson, who came to the community in 1850. Renamed HATTON, possibly for a local family, when PO est. in 1882 (Gentry 57, 117).

HAVANA Settlement with PO at 325342NO-873715W in Hale Co. Because of its location near a mineral spring, it was founded as a resort village and named for Havana, Cuba. PO est. in 1831 (Holliman).

HAWK Community with discontinued PO at 332604NO852207W in Randolph Co. Origin of name unknown, but it is probably either an environmental one or a personal one. PO est. in 1898.

HAWTHORN Community with discontinued PO at 311959NO880518W in Washington Co. Probably named for the hawthorn bush or tree. PO est. in 1894.

HAYDEN ['hedən]   Inc. town with PO at 335333NO864528W in Blount Co. Formerly identified with the descriptive name ROCKLAND because of the many rocks in the area. Renamed HAYDEN to honor an early settler. Hayden PO est. in 1817. Inc. in 1949 (Blount Co. Historical Society 67).

HAYES HILL   See COLLIRENE in Lowndes Co.

HAYNES MOUNTAIN   Mountain whose summit is at 340800NO865528W in Cullman Co. Probably named for a local family (U.S.G.S., 1966 Base Maps).

HAYNEVILLE   Inc. co. seat with PO at 321102NO863449W in Lowndes Co. In the 1820s called BIG SWAMP for the nearby creek. Named HAYNEVILLE for Robert Y. Hayne (1791–1839), governor of SC and U.S. senator, after being chosen co. seat in 1830. Big Swamp PO est. in 1826, Hayneville PO in 1832. Inc. in 1841 (Harder 228).

HAYSOP CREEK ['hesαp]   Stream rising at 330417NO871633W in Bibb Co. and flowing into the Cahaba River at 325250NO871035W. HAYSOPPY on La Tourette's 1844 map. If Indian, name may be derived from *hushi* 'birds' plus *apa* 'eat,' the Choctaw designation for the black gum tree; or from Choctaw *ahe* 'potatoes' plus *osapa* 'field' (Read 35).

HAZEL GREEN   Settlement with PO at 345556NO863419W in Madison Co. Name is probably descriptive of the hazelnut trees in the area. PO est. in 1829 (*Alabama: A Guide*, 329).

HAZEN ['hezən]   Settlement with discontinued PO on the Louisville and Nashville RR at 322024NO871214W in Dallas Co. Possibly a personal name, but identity of individual or family not known. PO est. in 1881.

HEADLAND   Inc. town with PO at 312104NO852032W in Henry Co. Named for James J. Head, who founded the settlement upon land that he owned. PO est. in 1871. Inc. in 1893 (M. B. Owen 1:437).

HEALING SPRINGS   Settlement with discontinued PO at 313756NO882012W in Washington Co. Name is the subjectively descriptive one of the former health resort founded by William Wooten in 1872 at mineral springs thought to have therapeutic powers. PO est. in 1883 (Sulzby 148–49).

HEATH   Inc. town with discontinued PO at 312138NO862811W in Covington Co. Named for Kate Heath, the first postmaster, appointed in 1900. Inc. in 1967 ("Record of Appointment of Postmasters").

HEBRON ['hibrən]   Settlement at 342907NO862249W in Marshall Co. Possibly named for the biblical city in western Jordan (U.S.G.S., 1966 Base Maps).

HECTOR   Settlement with discontinued PO at 320644NO855432W in Bullock Co. Said to be named for the Trojan hero killed by Achilles in the *Iliad*. PO est. in 1885 (Harris 1982, 82).

HEDGEMAN TRIPLETT'S FERRY   Dead town named for the ferry operated across the Little Tallapoosa River north of Wedowee in Randolph Co. by the first co. surveyor. First co. seat, 1832–35 (Harris 1982, 137).

HEFLIN   Inc. co. seat with PO at 333856NO853515W in Cleburne Co. Named for Wilson L. Heflin, an early settler and the father of U.S. Senator J. Thomas Heflin (1920–31). PO est. in 1868. Inc. in 1886. Became co. seat in 1906 (M. B. Owen 1:395).

HEIBERGER ['haɪbərgər]   Settlement with discontinued PO at 324529NO871712W in Perry Co. Named by a German immigrant for a town in his former homeland. PO est. in 1904 (Harris 1982, 82).

HELENA [hɛ'linə]   Inc. town with PO at 331746NO865037W in Shelby Co. A crossroads stage stop first known as COVE, probably a descriptive and environmental name; then HILLSBORO, said to be for a local family. Name changed to HELENA c. 1864 to honor Helen Lee Boyle, the wife of Peter Boyle, an engineer making surveys for the Louisville and Nashville RR. Cove PO est. in 1849; Hillsboro PO in 1856; and Helena PO in 1872. Inc. in 1877 (Tamarin 10).

HELICON   See GUNTERSVILLE in Marshall Co.

HELICON   Settlement with discontinued PO at 340734NO870818W in Winston Co. Probably named for the mountain in Greece, home of the muses of Greek mythology. PO est. in 1895.

HELLS CREEK   Stream rising at 335230NO875442W in Fayette Co. and joining Yellow Creek at 334418NO880614W in Lamar Co. Designation is a reduction of *Herald's*, the possessive form of the name of a local family (Peoples 10; U.S.G.S., 1966 Base Maps).

HELL'S HALF ACRE   See HALF ACRE in Marengo Co.

HENAGAR [ˈhɛnəgər]   Inc. town with PO at 343806NO854602W in DeKalb Co. Named for Owen Henagar, an early settler. PO est. in 1878. Inc. in 1966 (Raughton 42).

HENDERSON   Settlement with discontinued PO at 313959NO860424W in Pike Co. Site of Gainer's Store. Town probably named for Eli Henderson, an early settler. PO est. in 1860 (M. T. Stewart, *Pike Co.*, 17–18).

HENDRIX   Settlement at 340217NO862712W in Blount Co. Named for a local family. Approved by U.S. Board on Geographic Names in 1964 (Weaver).

HENDRIX CROSSROADS   See BUTLER in Choctaw Co.

HENRY COUNTY   Created by act of the AL territorial general assembly on Dec. 13, 1819. Bordered on the north by Barbour Co., on the east by GA, on the south by Houston Co., and on the west by Dale Co. Named for the American patriot Patrick Henry (1736–1799). The co. seats have been Richmond, 1819–24; Columbia, 1824–30; and the present one, Abbeville (Warren, *Henry's Heritage*, 13).

HENSON SPRINGS   Community with discontinued PO at 340109NO880351W in Lamar Co. First called COBB TOWN for a local family, then WEBB for another local family. Named HENSON SPRINGS for the resort owned and operated by the Henson family at the nearby mineral springs. PO est. in 1892 (Acee 30–31).

HERBERT   Community with discontinued PO at 315009NO864819W in Conecuh Co. Probably the name of a person, but identity unknown. PO est. in 1879.

HERON BAY   Settlement on Mon Louis Island at 302116NO880749W in Mobile Co. Named for the nearby bay, which has an environmental designation (Boudousquie, 1889 map).

HEWITT   See PARRISH in Walker Co.

HIAGGEE CREEK   See IHAGEE CREEK in Russell Co.

HICKMAN   See RALPH in Tuscaloosa Co.

HICKORY FLAT   Settlement with discontinued PO at 330539NO851718W in Chambers Co. Name is descriptive of the location of a large hickory tree. PO est. in 1854 (Dugas [Chambers Co.] 57).

HIGDON   Settlement with PO at 345044NO853659W in Jackson Co. Originally MOUNT OLIVE. A Methodist minister stipulated that his church be named for his daughter Olive before he would make a donation for its relocation in this place. After the PO was est. in 1882, it and the town were named for Thomas W. Higdon, the first postmaster (Melancon).

HIGHLAND HOME   Settlement with PO at 315712NO861850W in Crenshaw Co. Named for the school founded as Barnes School in 1881, later the Highland Home Male and Female College. A descriptive and environmental name. PO est. in 1885 (Harris 1982, 84).

HIGHLAND, LAKE   Artificial lake at 335252NO862604W in Blount Co. formed by the impoundment of the Blackburn Fork of the Black Warrior River. Originally LAKE SHUFF for Hugh Shuff, who developed the recreational facilities here. Given the descriptive and environmental name LAKE HIGHLAND in 1956 (Blount Co. Historical Society 68).

HIGHLAND LAKE   Inc. town at 340345NO862330W in Blount Co. Named for the nearby lake. Inc. in 1967 (Blount Co. Historical Society 68).

HIGH PINE   See ROANOKE in Randolph Co.

HIGH POINT   Settlement at 341432NO861643W in Marshall Co. Name is probably descriptive of town's location on Sand Mountain (*Official 1959 Alabama Highway Map*).

HIGH RIDGE   Settlement with discontinued PO at 320345NO855342W in Bullock Co. Probably a descriptive and environmental name. PO est. in 1892.

HIGHTOGY [ˌhaɪˈtodʒɪ]   Settlement with discontinued PO at 334142NO880541W in Lamar Co. Area first known as *Ridge Beat*, an environmental name for the voting precinct, and settlement was called SIMMON TOWN, probably for a local family. Origin of current name unknown, but it may have been derived from the compound *high* plus *tor*, a Middle English noun meaning 'high, craggy hill' that occurs in several English place names. PO est. in 1890 (Acee 27).

HIGHTOWER   Settlement with discontinued PO at 333154NO852344W in Cleburne Co. Named for a local family. PO est. in 1879 (Harris 1982, 84).

HILL CREEK   Stream rising at 330839NO-871251W in Tuscaloosa Co. and joining Schultz Creek at 330146NO871056W in Bibb Co. Named for James Hill, who settled in Tuscaloosa Co. near the creek c. 1817 (Rich 1979, 280).

HILL PO   See REECE CITY in Etowah Co.

HILLABEE   See MILLERVILLE in Clay Co.

HILLABEE CREEK   ['hɪləbɪ]   Stream formed by the junction of Little Hillabee and Enitachopco creeks at 330444NO855320W in Tallapoosa Co. and flowing into the Tallapoosa River at 325752NO855112W. Little Hillabee Creek rises at 331611NO855647W in Clay Co. Hilibi was an ancient Upper Creek town near these creeks. Name is derived from Creek *hilapki* or *hilikbi* 'quick' (Read 36; U.S.G.S., 1966 Base Maps).

HILLSBORO   Inc. town with PO at 343821NO871130W in Lawrence Co. A small settlement nearby, Gilmerville, honoring William Gilbert, a local resident, absorbed Hillsboro in 1873 and took the latter's descriptive name. Hillsboro PO est. in 1837. Inc. in 1899 (T. M. Owen 1:694).

HILLSBORO   See HELENA in Shelby Co.

HILLVIEW   Settlement at 333432NO-865303W in Jefferson Co. Formerly called KATZ MOUNTAIN for a ridge named for early settlers. Later given the descriptive and environmental name HILLVIEW (Hagood 48; U.S.G.S., 1966 Base Maps).

HILLWOOD   Community with discontinued PO at 325531NO862141W in Coosa Co. Descriptive and environmental compound. PO est. in 1943 (Hopkins).

HINES MOUNTAIN   Mountain whose summit is located at 335052NO860702W in St. Clair Co. Probably a local family name (U.S.G.S., 1966 Base Maps).

HISSOP   ['hɪsəp]   Settlement with PO at 325332NO860912W in Coosa Co. Origin of name unknown, but it may be a misspelling of *hyssop*, the designation for the herb mixed with vinegar given to Christ upon the cross. PO est. in 1880.

HOBART   See BERLIN in Cullman Co.

HOBOKEN   Settlement with discontinued PO at 320133NO875237W in Marengo Co. Perhaps named for Hoboken, NJ, a city on the banks of the Hudson River, by Richard Henry

Hudson (1828–1879), an early settler who may have had some connection with the NJ city. PO est. in 1877 (W. Smith).

HOBSON CITY   Inc. town at 333717NO-855039W in Calhoun Co. An all-black community when inc. in 1899. Named for Richmond Pearson Hobson (1870–1943), Spanish-American War naval hero born in Greensboro, AL (Jolly).

HODGE   Community at 343710NO855658W in Jackson Co. Named for a family living in the area in the 1880s (Melancon).

HODGES   Inc. town with PO at 341937NO-875535W in Franklin Co. Named for Stephen Hodge, a local resident. PO est. in 1897. Inc. in 1913 (Knight).

HODGESVILLE   Settlement at 310457NO-852223W in Houston Co. Named in honor of Forman Hodges, who built a gristmill, a sawmill, and a cotton gin here in the 1890s. In 1906 called LISBON for the city in Portugal, but because this designation was not popular, soon renamed HODGESVILLE (F. S. Watson 1972, 89).

HODGEWOOD   Settlement at 315614NO-881808W in Choctaw Co. A sawmill town, possibly named for mill owner. If so, then the name may be a compound of *Hodge* and *wood* (Rogers; U.S.G.S., 1966 Base Maps).

HOG EYE   See BROWNVILLE in Tuscaloosa Co.

HOGOHEGEE CREEK   See LIMESTONE CREEK in Limestone Co.

HOKES BLUFF   Settlement with PO at 335953NO855159W in Etowah Co. Area first called *The Bluff*, with reference to the steep bank of the Coosa River where it is located. Named in 1854 for Daniel Hoke, Jr., at the suggestion of William B. Wynne, his partner in the general merchandise business. PO est. in 1855. Inc. in 1946 (Jolly).

HOLLAND GIN   Community at 345748NO-865314W in Limestone Co. Named for the cotton gin operated by a father and son, Hezzie and Egbert Holland (U.S.G.S., 1966 Base Maps; Wellden).

HOLLEY CREEK   Stream rising at 311029NO874215W in Baldwin Co. and flowing into the Alabama River at 311055NO-875118W. Current name is probably a reduced form of HOLLOW CREEK, an earlier one. The creek name predates the organization in 1839 of Holley Creek Methodist Church (Bush 53).

HOLLINGER CREEK   Stream rising at

305227NO874558W in Baldwin Co. and flowing into the Styx River at 303855NO873658W. Probably named before 1928 for Adam Hollinger, an early landowner in the area (Comminge and Albers 512).

HOLLINS Settlement with PO at 330703NO860840W in Clay Co. Named for an official of the Kaul Lumber Co., founder of the sawmill town. PO est. in 1887 (Harris 1982, 85).

HOLLIS Community where U.S. Highway 431 crosses state Highway 9 at 333125NO853814W in Cleburne Co. Also HOLLIS CROSSROADS. Named for Benjamin Hollis, a local landowner (Harris 1982, 85; *Official 1959 Alabama Highway Map*).

HOLLOW CREEK See HOLLEY CREEK in Baldwin Co.

HOLLY POND Inc. town with PO at 341027NO863659W in Cullman Co. First settled in 1875. The pond no longer exists, but the name when first given was descriptive of town's location. PO est. in 1888. Inc. in 1912 (Jones 1972, 57).

HOLLYTREE Settlement with PO at 344810NO861459W in Jackson Co. Descriptive and environmental compound. PO est. in 1878 (Kennamer 143).

HOLLYWOOD See DAPHNE in Baldwin Co.

HOLLYWOOD Inc. town with PO at 344327NO855821W in Jackson Co. on the Alabama Great Southern RR. First BELLEFONTE STATION, the depot for the nearby former co. seat; then SAMPLES for the merchant who owned the land where the town was located. He divided it into lots and sold it after the rail line reached here. Current name is a descriptive and environmental compound of *holly* and *wood*. Samples PO est. in 1883, Hollywood PO in 1887 (Kennamer 167).

HOLT Settlement with PO at 331402NO872904W in Tuscaloosa Co. Named for Frank Holt, who purchased property here in 1901. PO est. in 1903 (Rich 1979, 286–87).

HOLTVILLE Settlement with discontinued PO at 323810NO861936W in Elmore Co. Named for Samantha Holt, the first postmaster, appointed in 1889 ("Record of Appointment of Postmasters").

HOLY TRINITY Settlement with PO at 321320NO850019W in Russell Co. Named for a Catholic school founded here in 1920. Inspirational and symbolic name. PO est. in 1923 (Russell Co. Historical Commission 5–10).

HOMEWOOD Inc. town with PO at 332818NO864803W in Jefferson Co. Originally · inc. in 1921 as EDGEWOOD for the Edgewood Land Co., which laid out the settlement. In 1926 inc. as HOMEWOOD. This name is a subjectively descriptive environmental compound. PO est. in 1971 (Hagood 41).

HONORAVILLE [hə'norəvəl] Community with PO at 315102NO862422W in Crenshaw Co. John Holloway, a local landowner, is said to have named it for the heroine of John Dryden's *Theodore and Honoria*. PO est in 1858 (Harris 1982, 86–87).

HOOD'S CROSSROADS Settlement at 335918NO862513W in Blount Co. Named for William Thompson Hood, owner of a store located here (Blount Co. Historical Society 68–69; U.S.G.S., 1966 Base Maps).

HOOKS Community with discontinued PO at 321130NO851357W in Russell Co. Named for John J. Hooks, the first postmaster, appointed in 1893 ("Record of Appointment of Postmasters").

HOOVER Inc. town with PO at 332419NO864841W in Jefferson Co. Named for William H. Hoover of the Employers Insurance Co. Inc. in 1967. PO est. in 1971 (Harris 1982, 86).

HOPE HULL Settlement with PO at 321611NO862126W in Montgomery Co. First MCGEHEE'S SWITCH, a stop on the Mobile and Montgomery RR honoring Abner McGehee, a prominent planter. Shorty afterward, McGehee named the town for Hope Hull, a Methodist circuit rider who had influenced McGehee while he was growing up in GA. PO est. in 1882 (Harris 1982, 86).

HOPEFUL Community at 332938NO855445W in Talladega Co. Named for Hopeful Church of Christ, founded in 1878. Also known as HOPEWELL. Both are inspirational and symbolic names (McMillan).

HOPEWELL Community at 342228NO860251W in DeKalb Co. Probably named for Hopewell Baptist Church, organized in 1896. An inspirational and symbolic name (Landmarks 106–07).

HOPEWELL See WEST GREENE in Greene Co.

HOPEWELL See HOPEFUL in Talladega Co.

HORSEBLOCK MOUNTAIN Mountain whose summit is at 333355NO854224W in Cleburne Co. Name probably refers to a natural rock formation used by early settlers to contain their horses (U.S.G.S., 1966 Base Maps).

HORSE CREEK Stream rising at 315610NO874531W in Clarke Co. and flowing into the Tombigbee River at 320437NO-880315W in Marengo Co. Probably a descriptive and environmental name (U.S.G.S., 1966 Base Maps).

HORSE CREEK See DORA in Walker Co.

HORSEHEAD See BROOKWOOD in Tuscaloosa Co.

HORTON Settlement with PO at 341203NO861749W in Marshall Co. Named for the Horton family from GA, pioneer settlers of this area. PO est. in 1890 (Roden 52).

HORTON'S MILL Community at 340052NO862712W in Blount Co. Named for Thurmon Horton (1893–1915), owner of a mill, blacksmith shop, and general store here (Weaver).

HOUSTON Settlement with PO at 340829NO871529W in Winston Co. Named for Sam Houston (1793–1863), president of the Republic of Texas before its annexation by the U.S. in 1846. Served as co. seat, 1850–82. PO est. in 1851 (Gant).

HOUSTON COUNTY Created by act of the state legislature on Feb. 9, 1903. Bordered on the north by Dale Co. and Henry Co., on the east by GA, on the south by FL, and on the west by Geneva Co. Named for George Smith Houston (1808–1879), who was elected to the U.S. Senate in 1865 but not seated. He served as governor of AL, 1874–78. Co. seat is Dothan (Harder 241).

HOUSTON COUNTY See LAUDERDALE COUNTY.

HOWARD Settlement with discontinued PO at 335115NO873403W in Fayette Co. Also called HOWARD MINES. Howard was probably the head of the coal-mining operation or the owner of the land where it was located. PO est. in 1927 (Peoples 11).

HOWEL CROSSROADS See HOWELTON in Etowah Co.

HOWELTON ['hauəltən] Settlement with discontinued PO where state Highway 179 meets U.S. Highway 278 at 340321NO-861101W in Etowah Co. Formerly HOWEL

CROSSROADS. Named for George W. Howell, the first postmaster, appointed in 1852, who was a member of a pioneering family (Jolly).

HOWTON ['hautən] Settlement and station for the Louisville and Nashville RR at 331532NO872025W in Tuscaloosa Co. By 1912 named for the local Howton family (Rich 1979, 292).

HUDSPETH'S CROSSROADS See GRAB-ALL in Henry Co.

HUEYTOWN Inc. town with PO at 332704NO865948W in Jefferson Co. Named for John M. Huey, a Confederate army captain. PO est. in 1873. Inc. in 1960 (Brown and Nabers 188).

HUGO Community with discontinued PO at 321600NO874120W in Marengo Co. Probably named for a local person or possibly for the French writer Victor Hugo (1802–1885). PO est. in 1903.

HULACO [hju'leko] Community with discontinued PO at 341844NO863555W in Morgan Co. Though its origin is unknown, the designation may be an acronym of a business name such as Hutcheson or Humphrey (both early settlers) Land Co. PO est. in 1855 (Knox 120).

HUNNICUT Community at 331129NO-865716W in Shelby Co. Probably named for a local family. Also called SAWMILL TOWN (*Official 1959 Alabama Highway Map*; Tamarin).

HUNTER Settlement on the Gulf, Mobile and Ohio RR at 322344NO862344W in Montgomery Co. Formerly HUNTER STATION. Probably named for a local family (*Official 1959 Alabama Highway Map*).

HUNT'S SPRING See HUNTSVILLE in Madison Co.

HUNTSVILLE Inc. co. seat at 344349NO-863510W in Madison Co. First HUNT'S SPRING for John Hunt, a revolutionary war veteran who built his cabin near Big Spring in 1802. Then TWICKENHAM for the home of English poet Alexander Pope. Finally HUNTSVILLE once more, in honor of Hunt. Chosen co. seat in 1808. Inc. and received its PO in 1811. Served as temporary state capital in 1819 (Griffith 68).

HURRICANE Settlement with discontinued PO at 305027NO875407W in Baldwin Co. on Hurricane Bayou. Formerly called HURRICANE BAYOU for the backwaters of the Tensaw River whose designation probably refers to one of the devastating storms that have occurred in this area. Hurricane Bayou PO est. in 1888, the word *bayou* being dropped in 1895 (Bush 54).

HURRICANE CREEK   Name probably refers to severe storms that occurred in the two areas.

1. Stream rising at 315620NO853440W in Barbour Co. and joining Pea Creek at 314916NO853806W (U.S.G.S., 1966 Base Maps).

2. Stream rising at 310336NO853737W in Geneva Co. and flowing into the Choctawhatchee River at 311044NO854336W (U.S.G.S., 1966 Base Maps).

HURTSBORO   Inc. town with PO at 321430NO852459W in Russell Co. Originally HURTSVILLE for Joel Hurt, the founder, but confusion with HUNTSVILLE caused the name to be changed to HURTSBORO. Hurtsville PO est. in 1860, Hurtsboro PO in 1881. Inc. in 1872 (T. M. Owen 1:720).

HURTSVILLE   See HURTSBORO in Russell Co.

HUSTLE   See HUSTLEVILLE in Marshall Co.

HUSTLEVILLE   Settlement at 341842NO861003W in Marshall Co. Originally HUSTLE. Name is said to refer to the "hustling" nature of its residents. Hustle PO, 1902–08 (Roden 52; *Official 1959 Alabama Highway Map*).

HUXFORD   Settlement with PO at 311312NO872743W in Escambia Co. Originally LOCAL, a station on the St. Louis and San Francisco RR. That designation probably refers to the kind of train service then available. Later named for C. C. Huxford, a dealer in naval stores. Local PO est. in 1903, Huxford PO in 1928 (Waters 194).

HYATT   Settlement with discontinued PO at 341403NO862035W in Marshall Co. Named for the Hyatt family, early settlers of the area. PO est. in 1883 (Roden 52).

HYBART   Settlèment with PO at 314935NO872255W in Monroe Co. Named for the French Huguenot family of James W. Hybart, the first postmaster, appointed in 1926 (Dugas [Monroe Co.] 95).

HYTOP   Community with PO at 345458NO860517W in Jackson Co. The name, a combination of *hy* 'high' and *top*, is probably descriptive of the settlement's location on the Cumberland Plateau. PO est. in 1894 (Kennamer 153–54).

IDER ['aɪdər]   Inc. town with PO at 344251NO854051W in DeKalb Co. A very old settlement on Sand Mountain. Name is said to be a "pretty" form of the name *Ida*, perhaps honoring either Ida Stallings or Ida Deavonport, both local residents. PO est. in 1877. Inc. in 1971 (Raughton 44).

IHAGEE CREEK [aɪ'hædʒɪ]   Stream rising at 321851NO850835W in Russell Co. and flowing into the Chattahoochee River at 321305NO845734W. IHAGEE CR. on E. A. Smith's 1891 map in Berney. Also HIAGGEE CREEK. *Ihagi* or *Haihagi*, the name of a Lower Creek town meaning 'the groaners,' is derived from Creek *haihkita* 'to groan' (Read 35).

INDEPENDENCE   Settlement with discontinued PO at 323123NO864205W in Autauga Co. Settled c. 1825 by the family of the first postmaster, David Newton, appointed in 1830. Inspirational and patriotic name (Biggs 29).

INDIAN CREEK   Stream rising at 344928NO864257W in Madison Co. and flowing into the Tennessee River at 343330NO864500W. Named for the early inhabitants of the area (U.S.G.S., 1966 Base Maps).

INDIGO HEAD   See CLINTONVILLE in Coffee Co.

INDUSTRY   Settlement with discontinued PO at 313615NO863646W in Butler Co. The traditional explanation of the name is that it is an inspirational and symbolic one, referring to the industry of the early settlers in destroying the dog fennel weed to prepare the land for cultivation. PO est. in 1888 (Dugas [Butler Co.] 79).

INGLE MILLS   See NAUVOO in Walker Co.

INGRAM'S CROSSROADS   See ELGIN in Lauderdale Co.

INLAND LAKE   Artificial lake formed by the impoundment of the Blackburn Fork of the Black Warrior River at 335011NO863300W in Blount Co. before 1950. Descriptive name (*Official 1959 Alabama Highway Map*).

INO ['aɪno]   Settlement with discontinued PO at 311616NO860541W in Coffee Co. The traditional explanation is that when the postmaster asked for suggestions for names from a group of people, all of whom were talking at the same time, one person kept saying, "I know." Finally, the group proposed, "Let's call it 'I know' and spell the name *Ino*." PO est. in 1894 (F. S. Watson 1970, 63).

INTERCOURSE   Community with discontinued PO at 322458NO881425W in Sumter Co. A symbolic name. Two roads originally intersected here enabling persons from four parts of the co. to have 'intercommunication' (one of the meanings of *intercourse*) with one another. Some of its residents now prefer to say that they are from Siloan, the community surrounding Siloan (Siloam) Baptist Church, or from Sandtuck, the south-central part of the co. where Intercourse is located. Its informal designation refers to its poor sandy soil. PO est. in 1840 (Foscue 38, 57–59).

INVERNESS ['ɪnvərnɛs]   Settlement with PO at 320053NO854446W in Bullock Co. When the Girard and Mobile RR (Central of Georgia) reached here after the Civil War, a Mr. Thomas gave land for the station that was then named for him. Later renamed INVERNESS for the home in Scotland of the ancestors of John C. Graham, a local resident. Thomas Station PO est. in 1867, Inverness PO in 1883 (Harris 1982, 89).

IRONATON   [a'rɑnətən]   Community with discontinued PO at 332536NO855816W in Talladega Co. During the Civil War Fain's Creek Forge (named for the nearby creek), also called *Vulcan Forge* (for the Roman god associated with metalworking), was located here. OWEN'S TANYARD on La Tourette's 1856 map. Stephen N. Noble founded IRONATON c. 1880 and named it for the bank of iron ore in the area. PO est. in 1884 (McMillan).

IRON CITY   Settlement and discontinued PO at 334004NO853951W in Calhoun Co. Named for the abundant iron ore in the vicinity. PO est. in 1889 (Jolly).

IRONDALE   Inc. town with PO at 333217NO864226W in Jefferson Co. In 1863 W. S. McElwain built an iron furnace here to supply pig iron to the Confederate arsenal at Selma. This furnace ceased operations in 1873. Name of the town is a compound of *iron*, for the furnace, and *dale*. PO est. in 1872. Inc. in 1887 (Hagood 48).

IRVINGTON   Settlement with PO at 303024NO881402W in Mobile Co. Probably named for a local Irving family. PO est. in 1910.

IRWINTON   See EUFAULA in Barbour Co.

ISBELL   Settlement with discontinued PO at 342719NO874514W in Franklin Co. First named DARLINGTON by T. L. Fossick, Sr., for a town in England where he had lived. In the 1880s John Ellis Isbell divided the town's land into lots and changed the name to honor his father, one of the area's original settlers. Isbell PO est. in 1885 (Knight 25).

76

ISLAND   CREEK   Stream   rising   at 322955NO851441W in Lee Co. and joining Uchee Creek at 322255NO851100W in Russell Co. Name probably refers to an island in the creek (U.S.G.S., 1966 Base Maps).

ISLE AUX HERBES   ['aləhɜrb]   Island at 302036NO881524W in Mobile Co. in Mississippi Sound of the Gulf of Mexico. The name, probably given by the early French settlers, means 'Herb Island' (U.S.G.S., 1966 Base Maps).

ISNEY   Settlement with discontinued PO at 314656NO882720W in Choctaw Co. Name, given by M. Gardinière, a French merchandiser, is assumed to be an anglicized form of *Aisne*, the name of a river in France. PO est. in 1840 (Rogers).

JACHIN   ['dʒekɪn]   Settlement with discontinued PO at 314656NO882720W in Choctaw Co. Name given by R. M. Moore, a local mason, probably for the grandson of Jacob in the Bible, whose name means 'God makes firm.' PO est. in 1892 (Choctaw Co. Bicentennial Commission 19).

JACK   Community with PO at 313426NO860001W in Coffee Co. First named DEANSVILLE, probably for a local family; then JACK for the first postmaster, John T. Stanton, appointed in 1899 (F. S. Watson 1970, 65).

JACKS   CREEK   Stream   rising   at 325204NO860535W in Coosa Co. and joining Hatchet Creek at 325639NO861059W. Named for the John Jacks family, early settlers in the area (Hopkins; U.S.G.S., 1966 Base Maps).

JACKSON   Inc.   town   with   PO   at 313032NO875340W in Clarke Co. Called REPUBLICVILLE, a symbolic name, c. 1813; then in 1816 PINE LEVEL, a descriptive name. A few years later renamed to honor Andrew Jackson (1767–1845) of TN, general in the Creek Indian War of 1813–14. PO est. in 1821. Inc. in 1887 (Clarke Co. Historical Society 189).

JACKSON COUNTY   Created by act of the AL territorial general assembly on Dec. 13, 1819. Bordered on the north by TN, on the east by GA, on the southeast by DeKalb Co., on the south by Marshall Co., and on the west by Madison Co. Named for Andrew Jackson (1767–1845) of TN, commanding general in the Creek Indian War of 1813–14, who was visiting Huntsville at the time the general assembly was meeting. The co. seats have been Sauta Cove, 1819–21; Bellefonte, 1821–59; and Scottsboro, the present one (Kennamer 17).

JACKSON CREEK Stream rising at 314251NO874942W in Clarke Co. and flowing into the Tombigbee River at 313300NO880025W. Probably named for Andrew Jackson (1767–1845), hero of the Creek Indian War of 1813–14 (U.S.G.S., 1966 Base Maps).

JACKSON CREEK Stream rising at 303311NO881600W in Mobile Co. and flowing into MS at 302904NO882605W. Possibly named for Andrew Jackson (1767–1845), general in the Creek Indian War of 1813–14 (U.S.G.S., 1966 Base Maps).

JACKSONS GAP Settlement with PO at 325310NO854842W in Tallapoosa Co. Named for the Mr. Jackson who built a cabin in the 1830s at this point in a gap between the hills. PO est. in 1874 (Dugas [Tallapoosa Co.] 87).

JACKSONVILLE Inc. town with PO at 334849NO854541W in Calhoun Co. First DRAYTON, probably for the prominent SC family; then, briefly, MADISON, probably for James Madison (1751–1836), president of the U.S. (1809–17). In the fall of 1835, named JACKSONVILLE for Andrew Jackson (1767–1845), whose troops under John Coffee had fought here during the Creek Indian War of 1813–14. Drayton PO est. in 1833, Jacksonville PO in 1834. Inc. in 1836. Co. seat, 1832–99 (Jolly).

JACOBS MOUNTAIN Mountain whose summit is at 344851NO861104W in Jackson Co. Named for the Jacobs family, early settlers in the area (Melancon; U.S.G.S., 1966 Base Maps).

JAMESTOWN Settlement with discontinued PO at 342352NO853439W in Cherokee Co. Perhaps named for Jamestown, VA, the first permanent English colony in the U.S. PO est. in 1891.

JAMESTOWN See WARSAW in Sumter Co.

JAMISON See JEMISON in Chilton Co.

JASPER Inc. co. seat at 334952NO871639W in Walker Co. Settled c. 1815 by E. G. Musgrove, who then laid out the town and gave it to the co. for its seat of justice in 1824. Named for William Jasper (1750–1779), a revolutionary war sergeant from SC famed for replacing the American battle flag when it was shot down by the British during the battle at Fort Moultrie in 1776. Inc. in 1840. PO est. in 1842 (Gant).

JAY VILLA Settlement with discontinued PO at 311946NO865725W in Conecuh Co. Named for the house owned by Andrew Jay, a Baptist minister and state legislator. PO est. in 1870 (Harris 1982, 91).

JEFFERS CROSSROADS See LEIGHTON in Colbert Co.

JEFFERSON See CEDAR BLUFF in Cherokee Co.

JEFFERSON See KIMBERLY in Jefferson Co.

JEFFERSON Settlement and PO at 322312NO875353W in Marengo Co. Settled in 1810 by three veterans of the Revolution—John Gilmore, Reuben Hildreth, and John Samples—who named their village for Thomas Jefferson (1743–1826), author of the Declaration of Independence and president of the U.S. (1801–09). PO est. in 1848 (Johnson and Alexander 15).

JEFFERSON COUNTY Created by act of the AL territorial general assembly on Dec. 13, 1819, out of the southern part of Blount Co. Bordered on the north by Blount Co., on the east by St. Clair Co., on the southeast by Shelby Co., on the south by Bibb Co., on the southwest by Tuscaloosa Co., and on the west by Walker Co. Named for the third president of the U.S. (1801–09), Thomas Jefferson (1743–1826). The co. seats have been Carrollsville, 1819–21; Elyton, 1821–73; and Birmingham, the present one (Brown and Nabers 182).

JEMISON Inc. town with PO on the Louisville and Nashville RR at 323735NO864448W in Chilton Co. Originally called LANGSTON STATION or LANGSTONSVILLE for Louise Langston, owner of most of the land occupied by the settlement. Name changed to JEMISON (briefly JAMISON) for

Robert Jemison, who operated a stage line through here between Montgomery and Tuscaloosa. Langston Station PO est. in 1870; Jamison PO in 1873; Jemison PO shortly thereafter the same year (B. D. Roberts).

JENA ['dʒinə] Settlement and discontinued PO at 330750NO875049W in Greene Co. and Tuscaloosa Co. Probably named by the local Huffman family, who had immigrated from Germany, for the city in East Germany where Napoleon won a military victory. PO est. in 1837 (Rich 1979, 302–03).

JENIFER Settlement with discontinued PO at 333257NO855611W in Talladega Co. Village grew up around a blast furnace, now dismantled. Named for Jenifer Ward Noble, mother of Samuel Noble, one of the town's developers. PO est. in 1881 (McMillan).

JENKINS CROSSROADS Community at 320134NO854628W in Bullock Co., where two roads once intersected. Named for the original owners of the land. Also known as HALLS CROSSROADS for the present owners (Harris 1982, 91; *Official 1983–84 Alabama Highway Map*).

JENKINS SPRINGS See CLAIRMONT SPRINGS in Clay Co.

JEWELL See CROSSVILLE in Lamar Co.

JOHNS Mining settlement with discontinued PO at 332142NO870635W in Jefferson Co. Named for Llewelyn Johns, a Welch mining engineer for the nearby DeBardeleben coal and iron mines. Johns PO est. in 1889. Though inc. in 1912 as NORTH JOHNS, now usually called JOHNS (Hagood 30).

JONES Settlement with PO at 323502NO-865351W in Autauga Co. on the Southern RR. Probably named for a local family. Jones Switch PO est. in 1878, *switch* being dropped in 1903 (Biggs 30).

JONES BLUFF See EPES in Sumter Co.

JONESBORO See TOWN CREEK in Lawrence Co.

JONESBORO See PARRISH in Walker Co.

JONES CHAPEL Settlement with discontinued PO at 341237NO870307W in Cullman Co. Probably named for a church that honored "Turkeytail" Jones (1812–1860), an early settler. PO est. in 1877 (Jones 1972, 82).

JONES COUNTY See COVINGTON COUNTY.

JONES COUNTY See LAMAR COUNTY.

JONES CROSSROADS See VINA in Franklin Co.

JONES MILL Community with discontinued PO at 324502NO875034W in Fayette Co. Named for a local miller, probably Giles W. Jones, the first postmaster, appointed in 1895 ("Record of Appointment of Postmasters").

JONES MILLS See FRISCO CITY in Monroe Co.

JONESVILLE See BRIDGEPORT in Jackson Co.

JOPPA Settlement with PO at 341752NO-863322W in Cullman Co. A Mrs. Berry is credited with naming the town for the biblical seaport, now part of Tel Aviv. PO est. in 1888 (Jones 1972, 49–53).

JORDAN Settlement with discontinued PO at 324219NO860008W in Elmore Co. Probably named for John L. Jordan, the first postmaster, appointed in 1891 ("Record of Appointment of Postmasters").

JORDAN, LAKE ['dʒɜrdən] Artificial lake at 323707NO861528W in Elmore Co. formed by the impoundment of the Coosa River with Jordan Dam. In 1929 both the lake and dam were given the maiden name of the mother of Reuben A. and Sidney Z. Mitchell, officers of Alabama Power Co. (T. W. Martin 68; U.S.G.S., 1966 Base Maps).

JOSEPHINE Settlement with discontinued PO at 301935NO873152W in Baldwin Co. Name of a person, but identity unknown. Perhaps it honors Napoleon's first wife. PO est. in 1881.

JUDY CREEK Stream rising at 314109NO-853726W in Barbour Co. and flowing into the Choctawhatchee River at 312612NO853247W in Dale Co. Its tributary Little Judy Creek rises at 314245NO853612W in Barbour Co. and joins the larger stream at 313107NO-853433W in Dale Co. Possibly named for the Judie family, early settlers who lived in Barbour Co. near the larger stream (Godfrey 1:178; U.S.G.S., 1966 Base Maps).

JUGTOWN See GARDENDALE in Jefferson Co.

KANSAS Settlement with PO at 335406NO873307W in Walker Co. Probably named for the state. PO est. in 1855. Inc. in 1955 (Gant).

KATZ MOUNTAIN See HILLVIEW in Jefferson Co.

KEEGO Settlement at 310338NO870739W

in Escambia Co. Said to have been named in the 1890s by the wife of J. J. McKenny, superintendent of the Louisville and Nashville RR. The word meaning 'fish' is from Henry W. Longfellow's narrative poem *The Song of Hiawatha* (Waters 192).

KEEL'S MOUNTAIN Mountain in Madison Co. and Jackson Co. whose summit is at 343711NO862042W in Madison Co. The Keel family settled in this area after the Civil War (Green).

KEENER Settlement with discontinued PO at 340922NO855704W in Etowah Co. Formerly GREENWOOD, possibly a descriptive compound. Renamed for George W. Keener, who donated land for the Alabama Great Southern RR station. Greenwood PO est. in 1870, Keener PO in 1888 (Jolly).

KELLERMAN Settlement with PO at 332026NO871817W in Tuscaloosa Co. Probably named for a civil engineer with the Kellerman Mine Co. c. 1900. PO est. in 1902 (Rich 1979, 213).

KELLY See HARVEST in Madison Co.

KELLY CREEK Stream rising at 333907NO862350W in St. Clair Co. and flowing into the Coosa River at 332427NO862138W in Talladega Co. Named for a Creek Indian chief who called himself "Toe Kelly" (Rich; U.S.G.S., 1966 Base Maps).

KELLY'S CREEK See LONDON in St. Clair Co.

KELLY'S CROSSROADS Community at 325014NO862004W in Coosa Co. where state Highway 22 crosses co. Highway 29. First known as TRAVELER'S REST or DEVIL'S HALF ACRE, designations for the store in the center of town that was also a distillery and saloon where brawls occurred. Later named for the store's owner, John Kelly (1953 General Highway Map of Coosa Co.; Harris 1982, 93).

KELLY'S SPRINGS See CURRY in Talladega Co.

KELLYTON Settlement with PO at 325847NO860201W in Coosa Co. Named for Archibald Kelly, a local physician. PO est. in 1874 (G. E. Brewer 87).

KEMPVILLE See TUNNEL SPRINGS in Monroe Co.

KENNEDALE See COTTONDALE in Tuscaloosa Co.

KENNEDY Inc. town with PO at 333513NO875904W in Lamar Co. Named for a family of early settlers. PO est. in 1883. Inc. in 1895 (Acee 17).

KENNEDY'S CROSSROADS See MIDLAND CITY in Dale Co.

KENT Settlement with PO at 323708NO855655W in Elmore Co. Probably named for Cicero B. Kent, the first postmaster, appointed in 1891 ("Record of Appointment of Postmasters").

KENTUCK See NORTHPORT in Tuscaloosa Co.

KENTUCK MOUNTAIN ['kɛn,tʌk] Mountain whose summit is at 333148NO855010W in Talladega Co. Named before 1872 for a nearby settlement whose designation may be a shortened form of *Kentucky* (McMillan).

KEYSTONE Settlement with discontinued PO at 331604NO864835W in Shelby Co. First called HARDYVILLE for Fred Hardy, the founder of the Keystone Lime Plant and the first postmaster. Then named for the lime plant. Hardyville PO est. in 1898; Keystone PO in 1904 (Tamarin 11).

KILLEN Inc. town with PO at 345146NO873715W in Lauderdale Co. Named for James Killen, who had the PO est. in his dry-goods store in 1896. Inc. in 1857 (Sockwell).

KILPATRICK Settlement at 341605NO860435W in DeKalb Co. Named for James R. Kilpatrick, who arrived here from Walker Co., GA, in 1856 (Raughton 46).

KIMBERLY Inc. town with PO at 334624NO864850W in Jefferson Co. Originally called JEFFERSON for the Jefferson seam of coal tapped here in the 1890s. When the PO was est. in 1901, the town was renamed for Kimberly, Union of South Africa, a famed diamond-mining area. Inc. in 1951 (Hagood 4).

KIMBRELL Settlement at 331634NO870402W in Jefferson Co. Named for Miles Kimbrell, a storekeeper and sewing-machine agent in the late 1880s (Hagood 24).

KIMBROUGH Settlement with PO at 320200NO873355W in Wilcox Co. Probably named for the first postmaster, Flavius Kimbrough, appointed in 1889 ("Record of Appointment of Postmasters").

KINCAIDE CREEK Stream rising at 332722NO880852W in Pickens Co. and flowing southwest into MS. KINCADE on La Tourette's 1856 map. Probably named for a local family (N. F. Brown 39).

KING COVE Small valley or gap at 345641NO861639W between the mountains in Madison Co. and Jackson Co. Probably named for a local family (U.S.G.S., 1966 Base Maps).

KINGSTON Community with discontinued PO at 323639NO863253W in Autauga Co. Probably named for Kingston, GA, whose name is a combination of *king's* and *-ton* 'town,' chosen to honor the then-reigning king of England. Co. seat, 1830–68. PO est. in 1831 (Harder 275).

KINGSVILLE See LINCOLN in Talladega Co.

KINGVILLE Community with discontinued PO at 334043NO880226W in Lamar Co. Probably named for a local family. PO est. in 1877.

KINSEY Inc. town with PO at 311756NO852040W in Houston Co. Named for Eliza Kinsey, the first postmaster, appointed in 1866. Inc. in 1957 (F. S. Watson 1972, 92).

KINSTON Inc. town with PO on the Louisville and Nashville RR at 311257NO861016W in Coffee Co. In the 1890s known as CROSS TRAILS because of the intersection here of two roads; in 1900, BOONE, the maiden name of Pink Hickman, wife of the donor of land for the town's depot; next PINK for Pink Hickman; then because of confusion with other places in the state, KINSTON, for Kinston, NC, the former home of a Mr. Pride, another resident of the town. Cross Trails PO est. in 1878, Kinston PO in 1912. Inc. in 1920 (F. S. Watson 1970, 17, 66).

KINTERBISH CREEK ['kɪntərbɪʃ] Stream rising at 321915NO882556W in Sumter Co. and flowing into the Tombigbee River at 321604NO880107W in Choctaw Co. KINTABUSH C. on La Tourette's 1844 map. Derived from Choctaw *kinta* 'beaver' and *ibish* 'lodge' (Read 39).

KIRBY CREEK See SECTION in Jackson Co.

KIRK Community at 331429NO875315W in Pickens Co. Formerly RALEIGH for the city in NC named for Sir Walter Raleigh (c. 1552–1618), English courtier. Then named for A. A. Kirk, a local physician. Locally known as KIRK TOWN (N. F. Brown; 1971 General Highway Map of Pickens Co.).

KIRKLAND Community with discontinued PO at 342456NO862029W in Escambia Co. Named for the first station agent for the Alabama and Florida RR (Louisville and Nashville), which reached this point in 1836. PO est. in 1883 (Waters 193).

KNIGHTS STATION See PHENIX CITY in Russell Co.

KNOXVILLE Community with PO at 325932NO874726W in Greene Co. Named for the pioneering Knox families in the area, especially Matthew Knox, the first postmaster, appointed in 1833 (Rich 1979, 320).

KOENTON ['koɪntən] Settlement with discontinued PO at 313824NO881534W in Washington Co. Named for the Koen family, who moved here from Germany. PO est. in 1886 (Matte 325–27).

KOSH See FLAT ROCK in Jackson Co.

KOSTER See COKER in Tuscaloosa Co.

KYMULGA CREEK See TALLADEGA CREEK.

LABUCO [lə'buko] Community with discontinued PO at 333634NO870521W in Jefferson Co. Name is an acronym of Lacy-Buck [Iron] Co. PO est. in 1918 (Brown and Nabers 199).

LACEYS SPRING Settlement with PO at 343203NO863615W in Morgan Co. Named for the spring near where John Lacy, a veteran of the American Revolution, and his brothers settled in 1818. PO est. in 1831 (Ackley 30).

LACON ['lekən] Settlement with discontinued PO at 342005NO865412W in Morgan Co. First called CEDAR CROSSING; then name changed to LACON by G. P. Orendorff for his former home in IL, itself named for Laconia, Greece. Cedar Crossing PO est. in 1888, Lacon PO in 1891 (Ackley 30).

LADONIA [lə'donjə] Settlement with discontinued PO at 322805NO850445W in Russell Co. Probably named for Ladonia, TX, whose name is an anglicized form of the Spanish noun phrase *la dona* 'the lady.' PO est. in 1889 (G. R. Stewart 1970, 47).

LAFAYETTE [lə'feət] Inc. co. seat at 325339NO852404W in Chambers Co. Originally called CHAMBERSVILLE for the co.; then inc. in 1835 as LAFAYETTE in honor of the French general Marquis de Lafayette (1757–1834), who had visited AL ten years earlier. Became permanent co. seat in Oct. 1833. PO est. in 1875 (Dugas [Chambers Co.] 57).

LAFAYETTE See FAYETTE in Fayette Co.

LAKEVIEW Inc. town at 342327NO855842W in DeKalb Co. Descriptive and en-

80

vironmental compound name. Inc. in 1968 (Raughton 46).

LAMAR See WOODLAND in Randolph Co.

LAMAR COUNTY Created by act of the state general assembly as JONES COUNTY, named for E. P. Jones of Fayette Co., out of parts of Marion Co. and Fayette Co. on Feb. 4, 1867. Abolished the same year; then recreated as SANFORD COUNTY in honor of H. C. Sanford of Cherokee Co. on Oct. 8, 1868. Bounded on the north by Marion Co., on the east by Fayette Co., on the south by Pickens Co., and on the west by MS. Name changed to LAMAR on Feb. 8, 1877, for Lucius Quintus Cincinnatus Lamar (1825–1893), GA-born MS soldier and statesman. Vernon is the co. seat (Acee 4).

LAMISON Settlement with PO on the Mobile and Birmingham RR (Southern) at 320716NO873400W in Wilcox Co. Named for the first depot agent here. PO est. in 1888 (Harris 1982, 96).

LAND Settlement with discontinued PO at 320143NO881942W in Choctaw Co. Named for a local family. PO est. in 1913 (Choctaw Co. Bicentennial Commission 19).

LANDERSVILLE Settlement with discontinued PO at 342808NO872403W in Lawrence Co. Named for John Landers, a local citizen. PO est. in 1851 (Gentry 58, 62).

LANETT [lə'nɛt] Inc. town with PO at 325207NO851126W in Chambers Co. First inc. in 1865 as BLUFFTON because of its location on a bluff overlooking the Chattahoochee River. Inc. again in 1895 as LANETT, a blend of the last names of two early textile mill developers, Lafayette Lanier and Theodore Bennett. PO est. in 1900 (Dugas [Chambers Co.] 57).

LANGDALE Settlement with PO at 324913NO851020W in Chambers Co. Name is a compound of *Lang*, for Thomas Lang, an Englishman who managed the local textile mill for many years, plus *dale*. PO est. in 1892 (Dugas [Chambers Co.] 57).

LANGSTON Settlement with PO at 343220NO860428W in Jackson Co. Originally called COFFEE SETTLEMENT for the Coffee brothers, early settlers. Renamed LANGSTON for Langston Coffee, the first postmaster, appointed in 1835 (Melancon).

LANGSTON STATION See JEMISON in Chilton Co.

LANGSTONSVILLE See JEMISON in Chilton Co.

LANIERS Settlement with discontinued PO at 332253NO861939W in Talladega Co. Named for the J. C., J. D., and Walter Lanier families, who settled here c. 1890. Also known as LANIERSVILLE. PO est. in 1903 (McMillan).

LANIERSVILLE See LANIERS in Talladega Co.

LAPINE [lə'paɪn] Settlement with PO at 315756NO861704W in Montgomery Co. and Crenshaw Co. Given its pseudo-French name by Robert A. Hardaway because of the longleaf pine trees in the area. PO est. in 1887 (Harris 1982, 96).

LAPLACE [lə'plæs] Settlement with discontinued PO at 322242NO855146W in Macon Co. An early settler is said to have given the area where the town is located the French noun phrase *La place*, meaning 'the place,' for its name. PO est. in 1858 (Harris 1982, 96).

LARKIN FORK Stream rising in TN and joining Estill Fork to form Paint Rock River at 345353NO861014W in Jackson Co. Named for William Larkin, an early settler (Melancon; U.S.G.S., 1966 Base Maps).

LARKINSVILLE Settlement with discontinued PO at 344127NO860729W in Jackson Co. Named for David Larkin, an early settler in the area and the first postmaster, appointed in 1832 (Kennamer 18, 164).

LASCA ['læskə] Settlement with discontinued PO at 320059NO875730W in Marengo Co. First settled by J. P. Lambert, who built a sawmill and cotton gin here. Possibly the name is derived from the Spanish feminine noun meaning 'chip of stone.' PO est. in 1899 (W. Smith).

LATHAM Community with discontinued PO at 310505NO875003W in Baldwin Co. Probably named for Latham Cooper, the first postmaster, appointed in 1880 ("Record of Appointment of Postmasters").

LATHAMVILLE Settlement at 341624NO860200W in DeKalb Co. Probably named for the family of Jonathan Latham, whose deed for 100 acres of land bought in 1836 for $125 was the first legal paper recorded in the co. (Raughton 47).

LATONA   See FAYETTE in Fayette Co.

LAUDERDALE COUNTY   Originally included in HOUSTON COUNTY, created to honor John Houston (1744–1796), governor of GA, by land speculators in 1784; then made a part of ELK COUNTY, named for the river, by the MS territorial legislature before 1817; however neither of these materialized. The present co. was est. by the AL territorial general assembly on Feb. 3, 1818. Bordered by TN on the north, Limestone Co. on the east, Colbert Co. and Lawrence Co. on the south, and MS on the west. Named at the suggestion of John Coffee for James Lauderdale, a lieutenant colonel who died from wounds received while fighting under Coffee at the Battle of Talladega in 1814. The co. seat is Florence (Sockwell).

LAVACA   [lə'vækə]   Settlement with PO at 320825NO880448W in Choctaw Co. Name was suggested by a resident who had visited Port Lavaca, TX. *La vaca* is the Spanish feminine noun phrase meaning 'the cow.' PO est. in 1925 (Choctaw Co. Bicentennial Commission 19).

LAWLEY   Settlement with PO est. in 325134NO865705W in Bibb Co. Probably named for the family of Joseph Lawley, an early settler from Randolph Co., NC. PO est. in 1898 (Abrams 20–21).

LAWRENCE CHAPEL   See FAIRVIEW in Cullman Co.

LAWRENCE COUNTY   Created by the AL territorial general assembly on Feb. 4, 1818. Bordered on the north by Lauderdale Co. and Limestone Co., on the east by Morgan Co., on the south by Winston Co., and on the west by Franklin Co. and Colbert Co. Named for James Lawrence (1781–1813), NJ naval commander who fought at Tripoli (1801–05) and in the War of 1812. He was killed while commanding his ship off Boston Harbor on June 1, 1813. The co. seat was Marathon until 1820 when Moulton, the present one, was chosen (Gentry 1).

LAWRENCEVILLE   Settlement with discontinued PO at 313927NO851609W in Henry Co. Named for Joseph Lawrence, who donated land for the Lawrenceville Male and Female Academy in the 1840s and was also the first postmaster, appointed in 1849 (Warren, *Henry's Heritage*, 329).

LAY LAKE   Artificial lake formed by the impoundment of the Coosa River at 325749NO863103W between Chilton Co. and Coosa Co. with Lay Dam, completed in 1912. Both dam and lake were named for William P. Lay (1853–1940), an engineer and promoter of river navigation (McMillan).

LEBANON   Settlement with discontinued PO at 342157NO854857W in DeKalb Co. Founded c. 1825 by James and Bud Baxter. Named for Lebanon, TN, the former home of the Carden family, also early settlers. PO est. in 1834. Co. seat, 1840–76 (Raughton 48).

LEE COUNTY   Created by act of the state general assembly on Dec. 15, 1866. Bordered on the north by Chambers Co., on the east by GA, on the south by Russell Co., on the southwest by Macon Co., and on the west by Tallapoosa Co. Named for Robert E. Lee (1807–1870), commander-in-chief of the Confederate armies during the Civil War. The co. seat is Opelika (Harder 294).

LEE STATION   See LILITA in Sumter Co.

LEEDS   Inc. town with PO at 333253NO-863240W in Jefferson Co. The first community here was known as CEDAR GROVE, then OAK RIDGE, both descriptive names. When the Georgia Pacific RR (Southern) reached here in 1881, E. M. Tutwiler and

James A. Montgomery, engineers building the road, founded the settlement of LEEDS and named it for the city in Yorkshire, England, also known for its iron industry. Cedar Grove PO est. in 1835; Oak Ridge PO in 1869; Leeds PO in 1884. Inc. in 1887 (Hagood 7).

LEESBURG Inc. town with PO at 341047NO854541W in Cherokee Co. Formerly called HAMPTONVILLE for Joseph Hampton, the first postmaster, appointed in 1836. Later named LEESBURG, probably for a local Lee family. Leesburg PO est. in 1839. Inc. in 1960 ("Record of Appointment of Postmasters").

LEESDALE Settlement with discontinued PO at 342323NO865442W in Morgan Co. Probably named for a local Lee family. PO est. in 1879.

LEGG See LEGGTOWN in Limestone Co.

LEGGTOWN Community with discontinued PO at 345721NO870356W in Limestone Co. Named for the local Legg family. PO est. in 1894 (R. H. Walker 82).

LEHIGH Community with discontinued PO at 335102NO864100W in Blount Co. Named for nearby Lehigh Coal Mines by an engineer on the branch rail line to the mines. PO est. in 1905 (Weaver).

LEIGHTON ['litən] Inc. town with PO at 344203NO873144W in Colbert Co. In the early 1830s known as CROSS ROADS because of the intersection here of two roads or JEFFERS CROSSROADS, probably for a local family. Given the name consisting of *Leigh* plus *-ton* 'town' for William Leigh (1790–1873) of VA and, later, Florence, AL, who was grand master of the Masonic Grand Lodge of AL in 1834. PO est. in 1831. Inc. in 1891 (Sockwell).

LENOX Settlement with PO at 312011NO871108W in Conecuh Co. The name, that of a town in MA honoring one of the earls of Lennox who was also duke of Richmond, is a frequently occurring one throughout the U.S. because it is short and distinctive. PO est. in 1902 (G. R. Stewart 1970, 255).

LEON ['liɑn] Community with discontinued PO at 313327NO862334W in Crenshaw Co. Possibly for Leon Co., FL or TX, both of which were named for the Spanish explorer Ponce de Leon (1460?–1521). PO est. in 1856 (Harder 296).

LEROY Community with PO at 313016NO-

875905W in Washington Co. Named for Leroy Bowling, one of the hosts to the Marquis de Lafayette, revolutionary war hero, who visited the area in 1825. PO est. in 1896 (Matte 331–37).

LESTER Inc. town with PO at 345926NO870912W in Limestone Co. Named for a local family. PO est. in 1938. Inc. in 1959 (Wellden).

LETOHATCHEE [ˌlitoˈhætʃɪ] Settlement with PO at 320746NO862909W in Lowndes Co. Named for a nearby creek, whose designation means 'wooden arrow creek,' from Creek *li* 'arrow,' *ito* 'wood,' and *hachi* 'stream.' PO est. in 1858 (McMillan in Read 100; Read 41).

LEVEL PLAINS Inc. town with discontinued PO at 311758NO854641W in Dale Co. Name is descriptive of settlement's location. PO est. in 1891. Inc. in 1965 (F. S. Watson 1968, 129–30).

LEVEL ROAD Community with discontinued PO at 33108NO853056W in Randolph Co. Name is probably descriptive of a road leading to the settled area. PO est. in 1875.

LEWIS CREEK Stream rising at 312015NO880528W in Washington Co. and flowing into the Tombigbee River at 311904NO875825W. Probably named for a local family (U.S.G.S., 1966 Base Maps).

LEWIS SMITH LAKE Artificial lake formed by the impoundment of the Sipsey Fork of the Mulberry Fork of the Black Warrior River at 335632NO870621W between Cullman Co. and Walker Co. in 1961. Both dam and lake were named for Lewis M. Smith, an official of Alabama Power Co. (U.S.G.S., 1966 Base Maps; Whitehead 15).

LEWISTON Settlement with discontinued PO at 330227NO880113W in Greene Co. Named either for one of the local Lewis families or for the town in Inverness, Scotland. PO est. in 1891 (Rich 1979, 329).

LEWISVILLE See LOUISVILLE in Barbour Co.

LEXINGTON Dead town on the bank of Hatchemadega Creek 8 miles from the center of Coosa Co. Probably named for either Lexington, VA, or Lexington, MA, the latter being the site of the first battle of the American Revolution. Co. seat, 1832–35 (Harris 1977, 89).

LEXINGTON Inc. town with PO at 345809NO872216W in Lauderdale Co. Probably named for Lexington, VA, or Lexington,

MA. PO est. in 1832. Inc. in 1959 (Sockwell).

LEXINGTON   See NEW LEXINGTON in Tuscaloosa Co.

LIBERTY   Community with PO at 340628NO863057W in Blount Co. First called MUSTER because Confederate troops assembled at the big spring here to drill or parade during the Civil War; then WOOTEN in honor of James M. Wooten, postmaster at Blountsville, 1871–83; finally LIBERTY, probably an inspirational and symbolic name. Liberty PO est. in 1884 (Blount Co. Historical Society 70).

LIBERTY   See ODENVILLE in St. Clair Co.

LIBERTYVILLE   Inc. town at 311429NO-862741W in Covington Co. Name is probably inspirational or symbolic. Inc. in 1967.

LICKSKILLET   See OXFORD in Calhoun Co.

LIGHTWOOD KNOT CREEK   ['laɪtəd,nɑt] Stream rising at 313129NO861122W in Crenshaw Co. and flowing into the Yellow River at 311453NO861954W in Covington Co. Probably an environmental name referring to pine kindling wood found in the area (U.S.G.S., 1966 Base Maps).

LILITA   [lə'litə]   Community with discontinued PO at 322901NO880742W in Sumter Co. on the old East Tennessee, Virginia and Georgia RR. Settlement originally called LEE STATION for a local family. The PO for Allison Lumber Co., named BELLAMY, was located here, 1901–06. When this PO was moved to the settlement around the sawmill, both then being named BELLAMY, C. A. Larkin, the postmaster here, named the new PO for his daughter Lilita. Shortly thereafter the settlement here also assumed this name. Lilita PO est. in 1907 (Foscue 42).

LILLIAN   Settlement with PO at 302446NO872613W in Baldwin Co. The first postmaster, William Thomas Kee, appointed in 1884, named the PO and town for his daughter (Bush 56–57).

LIME KILN   Settlement at 344554NO-880221W in Colbert Co. Formerly known as DENNIE KILN for a lime kiln operated by a local businessman during the 1880s. Later named LIME KILN (Sockwell).

LIME ROCK   See LIM ROCK in Jackson Co.

LIME STATION   See CALERA in Shelby Co.

LIMESTONE COUNTY   Originally part of ELK COUNTY (named for the river), created by the MS territorial legislature before 1817, but it never materialized. LIMESTONE COUNTY was created by act of the AL territorial general assembly on Feb. 6, 1818. Bordered on the north by TN, on the east by Madison Co., on the south by Morgan Co. and Lawrence Co., and on the west by Lauderdale Co. Named for the creek flowing through it. Co. seat is Athens (M. B. Owen 1:458).

LIMESTONE CREEK   Both streams have descriptive and environmental names referring to their limestone beds.
1. Stream rising in TN and flowing through Limestone Co. into Wheeler Lake at 343438NO865313W. Said to have been called HOGOHEGEE 'Black Creek' by the Indians (Harris 1982, 99; U.S.G.S., 1966 Base Maps).
2. Stream rising at 312917NO871207W in Monroe Co. and flowing into the Alabama River at 313329NO873045W (Dugas [Monroe Co.] 97; U.S.G.S., 1966 Base Maps).

LIM ROCK   [laɪm]   Settlement with PO at 344020NO861118W in Jackson Co. on the Southern RR. Originally called BOYD SWITCH for John Boyd, a local merchant. Later Walter S. Gordon made a contribution to the Methodist church on the condition that the village be named LIM(E) ROCK, a name descriptive of the rocks used in the local lime kiln. Boyd Switch PO est. in 1870, Lim Rock PO in 1882 (Kennamer 162–63).

LINCOLN   Inc. town with PO at 333647NO-860706W in Talladega Co. Originally called KINGSVILLE, possibly for Robert M. King (1820–1888). One tradition is that the town was renamed for Benjamin Lincoln (1733–1810), a general commanding American troops in GA during the Revolution, who was U.S. secretary of war (1781–84). However, according to Ida Groce Newman, her father, B. W. Groce, named it for his former home, Lincoln Co., GA, which was, however, named for Gen. Lincoln. Kingsville PO est. in 1850, Lincoln PO in 1856. Inc. in 1911 (McMillan).

LINDEN Inc. co. seat with PO at 321822NO874753W in Marengo Co. Originally called TOWN OF MARENGO for the co. In 1820 when the French were settling the area around Demopolis, Abner Lipscomb, a prominent local judge, suggested naming the town *Hohenlinden*, shortened to LINDEN, in honor of the victory of the French general Moreau over the Austrian forces of Archduke John at Hohenlinden in Bavaria in 1800. The town received this name and became the co. seat on Dec. 19, 1823. PO est. in 1832. Inc. in 1839 (M. B. Owen 1:467–68).

LINE CREEK Stream rising at 320455NO-855939W in Bullock Co. and flowing into the Tallapoosa River at 322505NO860123W between Macon Co. and Montgomery Co. OAK-FUSKEE or LINE C. on La Tourette's 1844 map. *Oakfuskee* 'point between streams,' from Creek *ak* 'down in' and *faski* 'sharp, pointed.' Now called LINE CREEK because it is the boundary between Macon Co. and Montgomery Co. (Read 47).

LINEVILLE Inc. town with PO at 331838NO854516W in Clay Co. First known as LUNDIES CROSSROADS for William Y. and Thomas Lundie; next called COUNTY LINE, probably for the County Line Baptist Church, founded in 1848 and located on what was then the boundary line between Talladega Co. and Randolph Co. Name changed to LINEVILLE when the town became the temporary co. seat for Clay Co. in 1866. County Line PO est. in 1856, Lineville PO in 1870. Inc. in 1898 (McMillan; Waldrop).

LINWOOD Settlement with discontinued PO on the Central of Georgia RR at 315536NO-855151W in Pike Co. Origin of name unknown, possibly that of a person. PO est. in 1869.

LIPSCOMB Inc. town at 332532NO-865536W in Jefferson Co. Named for a local family whose house was located at a frequently used streetcar stop. Inc. in 1910 (Hagood 20).

LISBON See HODGESVILLE in Houston Co.

LISMAN ['lɪsmən] Inc. town with PO at 321007NO881651W in Choctaw Co. Named by John T. Cochrane, the president of the Tuscaloosa Belt Line (Alabama, Tennessee and Northern), for a backer of the RR. PO est. in 1912. Inc. in 1971 (Choctaw Co. Bicentennial Commission 19).

LISTER See LISTERHILL in Colbert Co.

LISTERHILL Community at 344527NO-873456W in Colbert Co. Originally called LISTER for Lister Hill (1895–1985), U.S. senator from AL (1938–68), who had helped to persuade Reynolds Aluminum Co. to locate a defense plant here in early 1941. By June of that year, the village was known as LIS-TERHILL (Sockwell).

LITTLE COON MOUNTAIN Mountain whose summit is at 345523NO860020W in Jackson Co. Probably a descriptive and environmental name (U.S.G.S., 1966 Base Maps).

LITTLE LAGOON A tidal-spill pond at 301438NO874512W in Baldwin Co. Name is descriptive of its size (Bush 57–58; U.S.G.S., 1966 Base Maps).

LITTLE POINT CLEAR Cape at 301542NO875610W in Baldwin Co. Named for the larger cape, Great Point Clear (U.S.G.S., 1966 Base Maps).

LITTLE RIVER Name is probably descriptive of the size of the following watercourses.
1. Stream formed by confluence of East Fork and West Fork at 342732NO853500W between DeKalb Co. and Cherokee Co. that flows into Weiss Reservoir at 341329NO853842W in Cherokee Co. The East Fork rises in GA, entering AL at 343405NO852722W in DeKalb Co., while the West Fork rises in GA, entering AL at 344238NO852818W in DeKalb Co. Also known as DE SOTO RIVER in honor of the Spaniard who explored this area in 1540 (Raughton 49; U.S.G.S., 1966 Base Maps).
2. Stream rising at 312316NO872608W in Monroe Co. and flowing into the Alabama River at 311752NO874551W. Serves as the boundary line between Monroe Co. and Baldwin Co. and as a partial one between Monroe Co. and Escambia Co. (U.S.G.S., 1966 Base Maps).

LITTLE RIVER Settlement with discontinued PO at 341653NO854024W in Cherokee Co. Probably named for the nearby river. PO est. in 1858.

LITTLEVILLE Inc. town at 343526NO-874037W in Colbert Co. Founded by and named for a Capt. Little who had marched through here under the command of Andrew Jackson in 1813 and who later returned to the area to settle. Listed as CAMP SMITH (identity of person unknown), a voting precinct, in 1870. Both names used, 1888–92. Inc. in 1956 (Sockwell).

LIVELY See PHENIX CITY in Russell Co.

LIVINGSTON Inc. co. seat with PO at 323503NO881114W in Sumter Co. This site for the co. seat was selected by William Anderson, John C. Whitsett, Charles J. Puckett, Andrew Ramsey, William O. Winston, Edward B. Colgin, and Warham Easley in 1832. Named for Edward Livingston (1764–1836), secretary of state (1831–33) under Andrew Jackson (1767–1845), president of the U.S. (1829–37). PO est. in 1833. Inc. in 1867 (Foscue 42–43).

LOACHAPOKA [ˌlotʃəˈpokə] Inc. town with PO at 323615NO853536W in Lee Co. Named for the Upper Creek town Lutchapoga in Randolph Co. Name is derived from Creek *locha* 'turtle' and *poga* 'killing place.' PO est. in 1853. Inc. in 1910 (Read 41).

LOANGO [loˈæŋgo] Settlement with discontinued PO at 311946NO863856W in Covington Co. The traditional explanation of the name is that it is a combination of the words *load*, *and*, and *go* used to describe the actions of the farmers at the store containing the PO, est. in 1856 (W. D. Ward 159).

LOCAL See HUXFORD in Escambia Co.

LOCKHART Inc. town with PO at 310037NO862059W in Covington Co. Founded c. 1910 when the Jackson Lumber Co. built a mill here. Named for Aaron Lockhart, a co. commissioner in 1821. PO est. in 1924. Inc. in 1931 (Harris 1982, 100).

LOCUST FORK Inc. town with PO at 335427NO863655W in Blount Co. Named for the Locust Fork of the Black Warrior River. Inc. and PO est. in 1970 (Blount Co. Historical Society 71).

LOCUST FORK Stream rising at 341203NO861643W in Marshall Co. and joining Mulberry Fork at 333325NO871109W in Jefferson Co. to form the Black Warrior River. An environmental name mentioned in the 1818 *Acts of the General Assembly of the Alabama Territory* (Jolly).

LOGAN Settlement with PO at 315909NO862926W in Cullman Co. Named for John Alexander Logan (1826–1886), a Union army general, by James Robert Freeman, a former Union army officer who was the first postmaster, appointed in 1884 (Jones 1972, 80).

LOGAN MARTIN, LAKE Artificial lake formed by the impoundment of the Coosa River with Logan Martin Dam at 332531NO862010W between St. Clair Co. and Talladega Co. Both lake and dam named in 1960 for Logan Martin, an official of Alabama Power Co. (McMillan).

LOG CREEK Stream rising at 320344NO855516W in Pike Co. and flowing into the Conecuh River at 315505NO855220W. Name possibly refers to the creek's being used by lumbermen to float logs to a mill (U.S.G.S., 1966 Base Maps).

LOLA See CAIRO in Limestone Co.

LOMAX Settlement with discontinued PO at 325244NO863939W in Chilton Co. Named for Tennent Lomax, a colonel in the Third Alabama Infantry Regiment of the Confederate army who was killed June 1, 1862, at the Battle of Seven Rivers, VA. PO est. in 1873 (Harris 1982, 101).

LONDON Settlement with discontinued PO at 311751NO870516W in Conecuh Co. Probably named for the city in England. PO est. in 1895.

LONDON Community at 332854NO862134W in St. Clair Co. Originally called KELLY'S CREEK for the creek named for the Indian "Toe Kelly." Renamed NEW LONDON after the Civil War, probably for London, England. By the late 1880s known primarily as LONDON. Kelly's Creek PO, 1841–61 (Rich).

LONG CREEK Stream rising at 314554NO865137W in Butler Co. and flowing into the Sepulga River at 313440NO865228W. Probably a descriptive name (U.S.G.S., 1966 Base Maps).

LONG ISLAND Settlement with discontinued PO at 345825NO854016W in Jackson Co. Earlier called CARPENTER for the family who moved into the area from AR. Then given the English form of the name of the Cherokee village on the long island in the Tennessee River dating from 1783. Long Island PO est. in 1852 (Kennamer 173).

LONG STREET See TUNNEL SPRINGS in Monroe Co.

LOOKOUT MOUNTAIN Mountain in east TN, northwestern GA, and DeKalb Co., Cherokee Co., and Etowah Co. in northeastern AL. Descriptive name for a place used as a lookout. Mentioned in the Sept. 10, 1792, *American State Papers* (Jolly; G. R. Stewart 1970, 263).

LOPER Community with discontinued PO at 313453NO881800W in Washington Co. Named for the family of George T. Loper, the first postmaster, appointed in 1906 (Matte 337).

LOREE [lo'rɪ] Community with discontinued PO at 312914NO870524W in Conecuh Co. Named for the daughter of a Mr. Davis, probably Archie F. Davis, the first postmaster, appointed in 1904 (Harris 1982, 101).

LOST CREEK See RANBURNE in Cleburne Co.

LOST CREEK Stream rising at 335631NO873521W in Walker Co. and flowing into the Mulberry Fork of the Black Warrior River at 333723NO871418W. Name probably alludes to the disappearance of a person or animal occurring nearby (U.S.G.S., 1966 Base Maps).

LOTTIE Settlement with discontinued PO at 310744NO873720W in Baldwin Co. Named for the nearby Langham Lottie School. PO est. in 1903 (Bush 59).

LOU Community at 315508NO881240W in Choctaw Co. Named for Lou Downey, an early resident (Rogers; U.S.G.S., 1966 Base Maps).

LOUISVILLE ['luɪsvəl] Inc. town with PO at 314700NO853321W in Barbour Co. Originally named LEWISVILLE for Daniel Lewis, who settled here c. 1821. Spelling soon changed to LOUISVILLE. During 1821–27 before Barbour Co. was created, town served as the co. seat for Pike Co.; then during 1832–34 it was the seat of justice for Barbour Co. PO est. in 1831. Inc. in 1834 (Ellis 41).

LOVETTS CREEK Stream rising at 312436NO872610W in Monroe Co. and flowing into the Alabama River at 312553NO873434W. Named for the family of John F. Lovett, a farmer who operated a river landing south of the mouth of this creek (Harris 1982, 102; U.S.G.S., 1966 Base Maps).

LOVICK ['lʌvɪk] Settlement with discontinued PO at 333332NO863650W in Jefferson Co. Named for Lovick L. Stevenson, a brick mason and contractor who was also the first postmaster, appointed in 1902 (Hagood 26).

LOWDER SPRINGS See TALLAHATTA SPRINGS in Clarke Co.

LOW DIE See NATURAL BRIDGE in Winston Co.

LOWER PEACH TREE Settlement with PO at 315026NO873243W in Wilcox Co. Given the same designation as that of one of the two Indian villages once in this area. Benjamin Hawkins, the Creek Indian agent, had introduced peaches to the Indians around 1800. During the Creek war of 1813–14, the soldiers finding peaches at these two abandoned Indian settlements called the southernmost one LOWER PEACH TREE and the other one UPPER PEACH TREE. PO est. in 1825 (Harris 1982, 102).

LOWER TUSCALOOSA See NEWTOWN in Tuscaloosa Co.

LOWERY Settlement with discontinued PO at 311002NO860834W in Geneva Co. Probably named for a local family. PO est. in 1903.

LOWNDESBORO Inc. town with PO at 321630NO863641W in Lowndes Co. Formerly called MCGILL'S HILL for John and Selma McGill, early settlers. Renamed for the co. Inc. and received its PO in 1832 (Harris 1982, 102).

LOWNDES COUNTY Created by act of the state general assembly on Jan. 20, 1830. Bounded on the north by Autauga Co., on the east by Montgomery Co. and Crenshaw Co., on the south by Butler Co., and on the west by Wilcox Co. and Dallas Co. Named for William Jones Lowndes (1782–1822), SC legislator and U.S. representative (1811–22). The co. seat is Hayneville (Harder 310).

LOWREYTOWN See STATESVILLE in Bibb Co.

LOXLEY Inc. town with PO at 303705NO874511W in Baldwin Co. Named for an early family in the lumbering business. PO est. in 1893. Inc. in 1957 (Bush 60).

LUBBUB ['lʌbəb] Community with discontinued PO at 332406NO875321W in Pickens Co. Named for the nearby creek. PO est. in 1834 (N. F. Brown 42).

LUBBUB CREEK Stream rising at 333129NO875406W in Fayette Co. and flowing into the Tombigbee River at 330421NO881138W in Pickens Co. LUBBUB C. on La Tourette's 1844 map. The full name, derived from Choctaw *lahba* 'warm,' is probably either *oka lahba* 'warm water' or *bok lahba* 'warm creek' (Read 42).

LUCILLE Dead town at 330518NO870851W in Bibb Co. Once a mining community named in the 1880s for a relative of a RR man (Ellison 177; Hubbs).

LUGO   Settlement at 315756NO851254W in Barbour Co. Origin of name unknown, possibly a personal one (*Official 1983–84 Alabama Highway Map*).

LUNDIES CROSSROADS   See LINE-VILLE in Clay Co.

LUVERNE   [lu'vɜrn]   Inc. co. seat with PO at 314259NO861550W in Crenshaw Co. Named for Luverne, the wife of M. P. LeGrand of Montgomery, owner of a real estate business. PO est. in 1887. Inc. in 1891. Co. seat since 1893 (Harder 311).

LUXAPALLILA   See WINFIELD in Marion Co.

LUXAPALLILA CREEK   [ˌlʌksəpəˈlaɪlə] Stream rising at 340305NO874749W in Marion Co. and crossing the state boundary at 332725NO882558W in Lamar Co., after which it flows into the Tombigbee River c. 20 miles from Columbus, MS. LUXAPALLILA on E. A. Smith's 1891 map in Berney. Name is derived from Choctaw *luksi* 'turtle,' *a* 'there,' *balali* 'crawls' (Read 42).

LYEFFION   ['laɪfɪən]   Settlement at 313233NO865910W in Conecuh Co. Origin unknown, but possibly the name of a family (*Official 1983–84 Alabama Highway Map*).

LYNN   Settlement with discontinued PO at 340249NO873259W in Winston Co. Named for John Lynn, descendant of a revolutionary war soldier. PO est. in 1888 (Gant).

LYSTRA   See FIVE POINTS in Chambers Co.

MCCALLA   [məˈkɔlə]   Settlement with PO at 332055NO870051W in Jefferson Co. Named for R. C. McCalla, chief engineer on the South and North RR (Louisville and Nashville). PO est. in 1873 (Brown and Nabers 189).

MCCALLS CREEK   Stream rising at 315123NO871722W in Wilcox Co. and flowing into the Alabama River at 314810NO872546W in Monroe Co. Probably named for a local family (U.S.G.S., 1966 Base Maps).

MCCOLLUM   Settlement with discontinued PO at 334904NO871931W in Walker Co. Named for a family of early settlers. PO est. in 1903 (Gant).

MCCOY MOUNTAIN   Mountain whose summit is at 343934NO861236W in Jackson Co. Probably named for a local family (U.S.G.S., 1966 Base Maps).

MCCULLEY   Settlement at 330821NO-870521W in Bibb Co. Founded c. 1929 as mining town. Probably named for a local family (Ellison 177, 188).

MCCULLOH   Community at 324223NO-850859W in Lee Co. Founded when the Chattahoochee Valley RR (Central of Georgia) reached this point in 1898. Named for Calvin McCulloh, whose home was nearby (Nunn 100–01).

MCCULLOUGH   Settlement with PO at 311000NO873135W in Escambia Co. Named for the family of Warren Hill McCullough, who settled here c. 1893. PO est. in 1914 (Waters 195).

MCDADE   Community at 321856NO-860247W in Montgomery Co. Settled in the 1820s and named for a prominent early local family (Freeman).

MCDONALD   See WEDOWEE in Randolph Co.

MCDONALD'S STATION   See TANNER in Limestone Co.

MCDUFFIE ISLAND   Island in Mobile Bay at 303922NO880217W in Mobile Co. Probably named for a local family (U.S.G.S., 1966 Base Maps).

MCELDERRY   [mək'ɛldərɪ]   Settlement with discontinued PO at 332911NO855749W in Talladega Co. on the Anniston and Atlantic RR (Louisville and Nashville). Formerly MCELDERRY(S) STATION. Named for Thomas W. McElderry (1790–1883), pioneer settler. PO est in 1884 (McMillan).

MCGEHEE'S SWITCH   See HOPE HULL in Montgomery Co.

MCGILL'S HILL   See LOWNDESBORO in Lowndes Co.

MCINTOSH   Inc. town with PO at 311558NO880153W in Washington Co. Named for the nearby bluff overlooking the Tombigbee River. PO est. in 1903. Inc. in 1970 (Matte 345–48).

MCINTOSH BLUFF   Dead town on the high west bank of the Tombigbee River between the place where this stream joins the Alabama River and the site of old St. Stephens in Washington Co. The land was an English grant to John McIntosh, a Scotsman who built his home here in 1778. Served as the co. seat of Washington Co., 1800–1805. Later, when the southern part of Washington Co. was included in Baldwin Co., 1809–20, it was the seat of justice for Baldwin Co. (Avant 4).

MCKENDREE   See MASSEY in Morgan Co.

MCKENZIE   Settlement with PO at 313232NO864254W in Butler Co. Named for Bethune B. McKenzie, a Confederate veteran

88

who became engineer-in-chief for the Louisville and Nashville RR. PO est. in 1900 (Dugas [Butler Co.] 79).

MCKINLEY Settlement at 321754NO-873225W in Marengo Co. first identified with the ironic designation NEW RUIN because it seemed to be a "new" rather than an "old" ruin. Probably named for John McKinley (1780–1852), U.S. senator from AL (1826–31). PO est. in 1838 (W. Smith).

MCKINNEY MOUNTAIN Mountain whose summit is at 343048NO862718W in Madison Co. Named for a local family (Green; U.S.G.S., 1966 Base Maps).

MCLARTY Settlement with PO at 341036NO862407W in Blount Co. Named for the family of Thomas S. McLarty, the first postmaster, appointed in 1883 ("Record of Appointment of Postmasters").

MCMULLEN Inc. town at 331230NO-880730W in Pickens Co. Probably named for a local family. Inc. in 1971.

MACON See GROVE HILL in Clarke Co.

MACON See PRAIRIEVILLE in Hale Co.

MACON COUNTY Created by act of the state general assembly on Dec. 18, 1832. Bordered on the north by Tallapoosa Co. and Lee Co., on the east by Russell Co., on the south by Bullock Co., and on the west by Montgomery Co. and Elmore Co. Named for Nathaniel Macon (1757–1837), U.S. senator from NC (1815–28). The co. seat is Tuskegee (Harder 314).

MCSHAN Settlement with PO at 332251NO880830W in Pickens Co. Area settled c. 1820. Named for W. S. McShan, who had a road built to the town. PO est. in 1898 (N. F. Brown 43).

MCVAY Settlement with discontinued PO at 313624NO875344W in Clarke Co. Named for a local family. PO est. in 1910 (Clarke Co. Historical Society 284).

MCVILLE Settlement with discontinued PO at 349710NO860740W in Marshall Co. Possibly named for a local family. PO est. in 1890.

MCWILLIAMS Settlement with PO at 314951NO870538W in Wilcox Co. Probably named for the family of Evander T. McWilliams, the first postmaster, appointed in 1900 ("Record of Appointment of Postmasters").

MADISON See JACKSONVILLE in Calhoun Co.

MADISON Inc. town with PO at 344157NO864454W in Madison Co. on the Southern RR. Settled c. 1818 and named for the co. PO est. in 1856. Inc. in 1869 (Harder 314).

MADISON Settlement and station on the Western RR of Alabama at 322525NO861335W in Montgomery Co. Also known as FROGGY BOTTOM. Probably named for James Madison (1751–1836), fourth president of the U.S. (1809–17) (Sartwell; 1926 Soil Map).

MADISON COUNTY Created by act of the MS territorial legislature on Dec. 13, 1808. Bordered on the north by TN, on the east by Jackson Co., on the south by Marshall Co. and Morgan Co., and on the west by Limestone Co. Named for James Madison (1751–1836), then U.S. secretary of state (1801–09). The co. seat is Huntsville (M. B. Owen 1:463).

MADKIN MOUNTAIN Mountain whose summit is at 344000NO863838W in Madison Co. Named for a local family (Green; U.S.G.S., 1966 Base Maps).

MADRID ['mædrɪd] Inc. town with PO at 310208NO852336W in Houston Co. Named by J. B. Dell for the capital of Spain. PO est. in 1907. Inc. in 1911 (F. S. Watson 1972, 74).

MAGBY CREEK Stream rising at 333008NO880653W in Pickens Co. and flowing across the state line at 333025NO882338W into MS. Designation may have been derived from an Indian form or it may be a family name (U.S.G.S., 1966 Base Maps).

MAGNOLIA See STANLEYS CROSSROADS in Escambia Co.

MAGNOLIA Settlement with PO at 320808NO874005W in Marengo Co. The Jones family laid out the town and named it for the magnolia trees they had planted around their house. PO est. in 1873 (Johnson and Alexander 18; W. Smith).

MAGNOLIA RIVER Stream rising at 302752NO874148W in Baldwin Co. and flowing into Weeks Bay at 302324NO874900W. Originally known as EAST BRANCH or EAST PRONG OF FISH RIVER, but as the nearby settlement of Magnolia Springs developed during the 1880s, it was called MAGNOLIA RIVER for this town (Bush 60).

MAGNOLIA SPRINGS Settlement with PO at 302358NO874634W in Baldwin Co. Originally called MAGNOLIA PLANTATION for the nearby plantation, then renamed MAGNOLIA SPRINGS. Probably a descriptive and environmental name. Magnolia Plantation PO est. in 1878, Magnolia Springs PO in 1885 (Bush 60–61).

MAGNOLIA TERMINAL Community around the station built c. 1928 for the St. Louis and San Francisco RR some 3 miles southwest of the settlement of Magnolia in Marengo Co. Also known as MAGNOLIA STATION (Johnson and Alexander 18).

MAHAN CREEK Stream rising at 325725NO864931W in Chilton Co. and flowing into the Little Cahaba River at 330335NO865626W in Bibb Co. Probably named for the family of John Mahan, an army major who settled near the stream shortly after the Battle of New Orleans in 1815 (Abrams 43).

MAJESTIC Settlement with discontinued PO at 334458NO864538W in Jefferson Co. Named for a nearby mine, now closed. PO est. in 1927 (Hagood 52).

MAJORS CREEK Stream rising at 310615NO873959W in Baldwin Co. and flowing into the Tensaw River at 310851NO875206W. Possibly honors Robert Farmer, the British governor of Mobile (1763–80), a former army major who owned land in the area of the Tensaw River (Bush 61).

MALBIS Community at 303920NO875107W in Baldwin Co. Named for Jason Malbis, who founded a Greek colony here in 1907 (Comminge and Albers 79).

MALCOLM Settlement with PO at 311128NO880027W in Washington Co. Known as ROSEBUD when founded as a flag stop on the Southern RR. Renamed for Malcolm McRea, a prominent local resident. PO est. in 1892 (Matte 344–45).

MALONE Community with discontinued PO at 331155NO853503W in Randolph Co. Probably named for a local family. PO est. in 1908.

MALVERN Inc. town with PO at 310821NO853109W in Geneva Co. Originally known as EAGAN, possibly for a local family. Inc. in 1904 as MALVERN in honor of the Civil War Battle of Malvern Hill in VA. Eagan PO est. in 1901, Malvern PO in 1902 (Harris 1982, 105).

MANACK Settlement with discontinued PO at 321942NO863040W in Lowndes Co. Named for Sam Manack (or Moniac), a half-Indian landowner in the area. PO est. in 1851 (Harris 1982, 105).

MANACK'S CREEK See PINTLALLA CREEK.

MANCHESTER Settlement with discontinued PO at 335423NO871805W in Walker Co. The Western Electric Co. founded the town as a lumber center and obtained a charter for the Alabama Central RR to build a rail line here. Now almost deserted because of the depletion of the lumber supply in 1926. PO est. in 1907 (Gant).

MANILA Dead town with discontinued PO at 322654NO865516W in Clarke Co. Probably named for the capital of the Philippine Islands, frequently in the news during the Spanish-American War of 1898. PO est. in 1898 (Clarke Co. Historical Society 366–68).

MANTUA ['mænt/u,e] Community with PO at 330313NO875544W in Greene Co. Probably named for Mantua, a city in northern Italy. PO est. in 1880 (Rich 1979, 360).

MAPLESVILLE Inc. town with PO at 324718NO865218W in Chilton Co. Named for Steven W. Maples, who settled here in the 1820s and ran a store. PO est. in 1830. Inc. in 1914 (Abrams 17).

MARATHON Dead town with discontinued PO located at the head of Elk River Shoals on the south bank of the Tennessee River in Lawrence Co. It was the first settlement in the co., originally known as MELTON'S BLUFF, named for John Melton, an early settler. Renamed MARATHON for the plain in Greece where the Athenians and Plataeans defeated the Persians in 490 BC. PO est. in 1818. Co. seat, 1818–20. Abandoned shortly after the co. seat was relocated at Moulton (Harris 1982, 106).

MARBLE VALLEY Community with discontinued PO at 330238NO862707W in Coosa Co. Name is descriptive and environmental. PO est. in 1852 (G. E. Brewer 95).

MARBURY Settlement with PO at

324204N0862816W in Autauga Co. Originally BOZEMAN, probably honoring the family of Jeff Bozeman, who lived near here in 1861. Renamed MARBURY for Josiah H. Marbury, who started a lumber business in this area in 1876. Bozeman PO est. in 1883, Marbury PO in 1898 (Biggs 22, 32).

MARENGO   Settlement with discontinued PO at 320325N0874851W in Marengo Co. Named for the co. PO est. in 1914 (W. Smith).

MARENGO COUNTY   Created by act of the AL territorial legislature on Feb. 7, 1818. Bounded on the north by Hale Co. and Greene Co.; on the east by Perry Co., Dallas Co., and Wilcox Co.; on the south by Clarke Co.; and on the west by Choctaw Co. and Sumter Co. Abner Lipscomb, a prominent local judge, suggested the name to honor Napoleon's victory over the Austrian army at Marengo in northern Italy on June 14, 1800. The co. seat is Linden (Johnson and Alexander 18).

MARENGO, TOWN OF   See LINDEN in Marengo Co.

MARGARET   Inc. town with PO at 334110N0862830W in St. Clair Co. Founded by Charles F. DeBardeleben as a coal-mining town and named by him for his wife. PO est. in 1907. Inc. in 1960 (Rich).

MARGERUM ['mardʒərəm]   Settlement at 344601N0880406W in Colbert Co. on the Southern RR. Called MARGERUM SWITCH in the 1876 Colbert Co. Commissioners Minutes. Probably named for the Mr. Margerum who operated a quarry here (Sockwell).

MARIETTA   Settlement with discontinued PO at 334202N0872338W in Walker Co. Founded by J. E. Cook of Columbus, MS, who purchased the mineral land where it is located. Either a personal name or a transfer from another town, possibly Marietta, GA. PO est. in 1885 (Gant).

MARION   Inc. co. seat with PO at 323756N0871909W in Perry Co. Formerly called MUCKLE'S RIDGE for Michael Muckle, who settled here in 1817. Renamed for Francis Marion (c. 1732–1795), revolutionary

war general known as "the Swamp Fox" because of his evasive tactics in the SC swamps. Became the co. seat in 1822. Inc. in 1835. PO est. in 1845 (England; Harder 321).

MARION COUNTY   Created by act of the AL territorial general assembly on Dec. 13, 1818. Bordered on the north by Franklin Co., on the east by Winston Co. and Walker Co., on the south by Fayette Co. and Lamar Co., and on the west by MS. Named for Francis Marion (c. 1732–1795) of SC, revolutionary war general. The co. seat was Pikeville until 1882 when Hamilton, the present one, was chosen (M. B. Owen 1:472).

MARION JUNCTION   Settlement with PO at 322614N0871420W. Name is descriptive of the town's location at the junction of the Marion and Cahaba RR and the Alabama and Mississippi RR (precursors of the Southern RR). PO est. in 1874 (Harris 1982, 107).

MARLOW   Community with discontinued PO at 302739N0874757W in Baldwin Co. The name, that of a nearby Methodist church organized before the Civil War, was the one chosen from a list submitted to the PO Dept. by the first postmaster, Thomas Thompson, appointed in 1887 (Bush 62).

MAROS   See URIAH in Monroe Co.

MARSHALL   Community at 322603N0871930W in Dallas Co. Named for either I. Abraham Marshall, who lived in this area in the 1800s, or his brother Massillon, who lived a short distance away during the same period (Nelms).

MARSHALL   See GUNTERSVILLE in Marshall Co.

MARSHALL COUNTY   Created by act of the state general assembly on Jan. 9, 1836.

Bounded on the north by Madison Co. and Jackson Co., on the east by DeKalb Co., on the south by Blount Co. and Etowah Co., on the southwest by Cullman Co., and on the west by Morgan Co. Named for John Marshall (1755–1835), fourth chief justice of the U.S. (1801–35). The co. seats have been Claysville, 1836–38; Marshall, later renamed GUNTERSVILLE, 1838–41; Warrenton, 1841–48; and Guntersville, the present one, chosen again in 1848 (Harder 323).

MARTHA   See HACODA in Geneva Co.

MARTIN CREEK   Stream rising at 320607NO853051W in Bullock Co. and flowing into the Middle Fork of Cowikee Creek at 320853NO852030W in Russell Co. Probably named for a local family (U.S.G.S., 1966 Base Maps).

MARTIN, LAKE   Artificial lake formed by the impoundment of the Tallapoosa River at 324048NO855442W between Tallapoosa Co. and Elmore Co. with Martin Dam. Both the dam and lake were named c. 1960 for Thomas W. Martin, then president of Alabama Power Co. (Dugas [Tallapoosa Co.] 88; U.S.G.S., 1966 Base Maps).

MARTIN'S STAND   See SUMMIT in Blount Co.

MARTINTOWN   Settlement at 344437NO-855514W in Jackson Co. Named for the William Martin family, who settled in this area after the Civil War and founded the community (Chambless).

MARTLING   Settlement with discontinued PO at 342202NO861003W in Marshall Co. Possibly named for a local family. PO est. in 1884.

MARVEL   Settlement with discontinued PO at 330848NO870011W in Bibb Co. Named by Elizabeth Roden, wife of Benjamin Franklin Roden, the operator of the coal mines here, for her favorite poet, Andrew Marvell. PO est. in 1929 (Ellison 177; Hubbs).

MARVYN   Settlement at 322620NO-852151W in Lee Co. Named for Enoch Mather Marvin, a bishop of the Methodist church from 1866 until his death in 1877 (M. B. Owen 1:418).

MASSACRE ISLAND   See DAUPHIN ISLAND in Mobile Co.

MASSEY   Settlement with discontinued PO at 342213NO870120W in Morgan Co. Founded in 1820 and named MCKENDREE for the McKendree Methodist Church, itself honoring William McKendree, a bishop of the Methodist church. In 1886 the town's designation was changed to MASSEY for W. D. Massey, a local resident. PO est. in 1888 (Ackley 32).

MATHEWS   Community with PO at 321555NO860014W in Montgomery Co. Probably named for George Mathews from Oglethorp Co., GA, one of the largest landowners in the co. PO est. in 1868 (Freeman).

MATHILDAVILLE   See TUSCALOOSA in Tuscaloosa Co.

MAYLENE   Settlement with PO at 331212NO865142W in Shelby Co. C. C. Vandergrift, a banker and merchant of Montevallo, named it for his eldest daughter. PO est. in 1892 (Tamarin).

MAYSVILLE   Settlement with discontinued PO at 344611NO862549W in Madison Co. Settled c. 1838. *May* was probably the name of a local family or woman. PO est. in 1850 (T. J. Taylor 1976, 38).

MAYTOWN   Inc. town at 333209NO-865950W in Jefferson Co. Named for a local person or, possibly, for the month of the year. Inc. in 1956.

MEGARGEL   [mə'gɑrgəl]   Settlement with PO at 312247NO872542W in Monroe Co. Founded when the Muscle Shoals, Birmingham and Pensacola RR reached here c. 1910. Named for the president of the RR, Roy C. McGargel. PO est. in 1923 (Dugas [Monroe Co.] 95).

MELLOW VALLEY   Community with discontinued PO at 331109NO854453W in Clay Co. Probably a subjectively descriptive name. PO est. in 1866.

MELROSE   Community at 332342NO-880632W in Pickens Co. Named c. 1840 for a plantation that had been given the name of a town in Scotland mentioned by Sir Walter Scott in his narratives (N. F. Brown 43).

MELTON   Community at 324424NO-874100W in Hale Co. Named for Billy Melton, who settled here, probably before 1860 (Wilson).

MELTON'S BLUFF   See MARATHON in Lawrence Co.

MELVIN   Settlement with PO at 315549NO-882732W in Choctaw Co. Nicholson's Store was the center of the community when first settled c. 1840. Town named for a Methodist preacher. PO est. in 1883 (Choctaw Co. Bicentennial Commission 1, 5, 19).

MEMPHIS   Inc. town with discontinued PO on the west bank of the Tombigbee River at

330811NO881751W in Pickens Co. Named for either Memphis, TN, or the ancient city in Egypt. Now often called OLD MEMPHIS. PO est. in 1844. Inc. in 1971 (N. F. Brown 45; J. E. Hudgins).

MENTONE [ˌmɛn'ton] Inc. town with PO on Lookout Mountain at 343446NO853526W in DeKalb Co. Founded as a resort by John Mason and named by his daughter for Menton, a vacation spot in France then frequented by European aristocracy about which she had been reading. PO est. in 1888. Inc. in 1971 (Parker; Raughton 54).

MERCURY See CHASE in Madison Co.

MERIDIANVILLE Settlement with PO located at 345105NO863420W in Madison Co. on the Huntsville meridian. Named for this line, which marked the division between GA and the MS Territory in 1809. PO est. in 1831 (F. C. Roberts 146).

MERRELLTON Community with discontinued PO at 335148NO854431W in Calhoun Co. Named for Merrill Frank by her mother, Adelia E. Frank, then postmaster at Jacksonville. PO est. in 1884 (Jolly).

MERRICKS See OZARK in Dale Co.

MEXIA ['mɛkʃə] Settlement with PO at 313025NO872318W in Monroe Co. Named by Thomas S. Wiggins of Monroeville for a town in Limestone Co., TX, the latter honoring Thomas Mejia (1815–1857), who had donated the land upon which it was built. PO est. in 1893 (Dugas [Monroe Co.] 95; Read xv).

MIDDLETON Community with PO at 334611NO855905W in Calhoun Co. Name is descriptive of town's location midway between Ohatchee and Morrisville. PO est. in 1858 (Lindsey 48).

MIDFIELD Inc. town with PO at 332741NO865432W in Jefferson Co. Name is descriptive of the town's location between Birmingham and Bessemer. Inc. in 1953. PO est. in 1972 (Hagood 44).

MIDLAND CITY Inc. town with PO at 311908NO852938W in Dale Co. Formerly KENNEDY'S CROSSROADS, named in 1859 for Shep Kennedy, who had settled here in 1850 and opened a store. In 1890 inc. as MIDLAND CITY because it is located between Pinckard and Grimes on the RR that became known as the Atlantic Coast Line. PO est. in 1890 (F. S. Watson 1968, 130–33).

MIDWAY Inc. town with PO at 320437NO853120W in Bullock Co. Site of Feagin's Store,

operated by Samuel Feagin, who became the first postmaster of Midway PO, appointed in 1838. Name is descriptive of the town's location midway between Union Springs and Clayton in Barbour Co. Inc. in 1871 (McNair 26).

MIDWAY Settlement at 314848NO862749W in Butler Co. According to tradition, the town received its name because it was located between two places in the co.: McBride's and Pine School (Dugas [Butler Co.] 79; *Official 1959 Alabama Highway Map*).

MIDWAY Community at 314308NO870257W in Monroe Co. Its settlement probably predates the organization of the co. in 1815. Name is thought to refer to the town's location on the old Federal Road, from which Indian trails branched in several northerly directions (Dugas [Monroe Co.] 95).

MIFLIN Settlement with discontinued PO at 302213NO873639W in Baldwin Co. Probably named for the Miflin family, who owned land in the area in 1840. PO est. in 1930 (Bush 63).

MILLBROOK Inc. town with discontinued PO at 322847NO862143W in Elmore Co. The wife of Hines Hall is said to have given the settlement its name, which is descriptive of the local gristmill's location by a small stream. PO est. in 1896. Inc. in 1971 (Harris 1982, 110).

MILL CREEK Stream rising at 335854NO871123W in Walker Co. and joining Lost Creek at 335442NO870503W. Probably named for a water-operated mill once located on its banks (U.S.G.S., 1966 Base Maps).

MILLER Community with discontinued PO at 320923NO874708W in Marengo Co. Probably named for Charles H. Miller, a state senator, who was also the first postmaster, appointed in 1898 (W. Smith).

MILLER CREEK Stream rising at 304058NO881355W in Mobile Co. and joining Big Creek at 303646NO882258W. Probably honors either a person who was a miller or one whose name was *Miller* (U.S.G.S., 1966 Base Maps).

MILLERS FERRY Settlement with PO on the eastern bank of the Alabama River at 320558NO872203W in Wilcox Co. Named for the ferry operated by Abijah Miller before the Civil War. PO est. in 1890 (Harris 1982, 110).

MILLERSVILLE See CAMPBELL in Clarke Co.

MILLERVILLE Settlement with PO at

331129NO855533W in Clay Co. Formerly called HILLABEE for the creek. Probably renamed for a person who was a miller or who was named *Miller*. PO est. in 1889 (Waldrop).

MILLPORT Inc. town with PO at 333348NO880453W in Lamar Co. Originally located 3 miles west on the south bank of Luxapallila Creek. Moved to present site in 1882 when the Georgia Pacific RR (Southern) was built. Named for the sawmill, planing mill, and gristmill once in the town. PO est. in 1878. Inc. in 1887 (Acee 19–24).

MILLRY Inc. town with PO at 313802NO-881848W in Washington Co. Named for nearby Mill Creek. PO est. in 1859. Inc. in 1848 (Matte 348–49).

MILLSTEAD Community with discontinued PO at 323633NO855351W in Macon Co. Name refers to the place by the Tallapoosa River where a gristmill once stood. PO est. in 1896 (Harris 1982, 111).

MILLTOWN Settlement with discontinued PO at 330316NO852905W in Chambers Co. Graggs Mill, a gristmill operated by William Graggs, was located here. The community was first known as WOODVILLE, a descriptive and environmental name; finally, in 1848 when the PO was est. with Graggs as postmaster, name was changed to MILLTOWN, for Graggs's mill, because there was already a Woodville PO in the state (Dugas [Chambers Co.] 58).

MILLVILLE See DETROIT in Lamar Co.

MIMS CREEK Stream rising at 314253NO-854903W in Pike Co. and joining Whitewater Creek at 313921NO855435W. Probably named for a local family (U.S.G.S., 1966 Base Maps).

MINTER Settlement with PO at 320440NO-865937W in Dallas Co. Named for William Townsend Minter (1805–1865), a local planter and the president of the Selma and Gulf RR. PO est. in 1876 (Harris 1982, 111).

MIRIAMVILLE See WALLACE in Escambia Co.

MISSISSIPPI SOUND Bay emptying into the Gulf of Mexico at 301500NO890000W in Mobile Co. Named for the territory of which AL was a part, 1798–1817. *Mississippi* means 'big river,' from Algonquian *misi* 'big' and *sipi* 'river' (Read 42–43; U.S.G.S., 1966 Base Maps).

MISSOURI See PEROTE in Bullock Co.

MITCHELL Community on the Central of Georgia RR at 321446NO855616W in Bullock Co. Formerly known as MITCHELL STA-
94

TION. Named for a family of early settlers. PO est. in 1875 (Harris 1982, 111).

MITCHELL See ELROD in Tuscaloosa Co.

MITCHELL LAKE Artificial lake formed by the impoundment of the Coosa River with Mitchell Dam at 324820NO862642W between Chilton Co. and Coosa Co. Both lake and dam were named in 1921 for James Mitchell, a well-known promoter of water power (B. D. Roberts).

MOBILE [ˌmoˈbil] Inc. co. seat with PO at 304139NO880235W in Mobile Co. In 1702 FORT LOUIS DE LA MOBILE, honoring Louis XIV of France, was built by Bienville near where the town Mount Vernon is now located; in 1716 the fort was relocated at its present site; in 1720 its name was changed to FORT CONDE DE LA MOBILE to honor the Prince de Conde (1621–1686), a French general; in 1763 the British captured the fort and named it FORT CHARLOTTE for the wife of the British king, George III; in 1780 the fort and the town surrounding it were captured and occupied by the Spaniards led by Galvez; finally in 1813 both came under the control of American forces led by James Wilkinson. MOBILE, also the name of an Indian tribe once living below the point at which the Tombigbee and Alabama rivers join to form the Mobile River, probably is derived from Choctaw *moeli* 'to row, to paddle,' the noun *moeli* meaning 'the rowers.' Chosen to be co. seat in 1812. PO est. in 1818. Inc. in 1819 (Read 43–44).

MOBILE BAY Bay at 302633NO880033W between Mobile Co. and Baldwin Co. The Spanish names BAHIA DE OCHUSE (BAY OF ICHUSA), from Choctaw *ichusa* 'river-little' and BAHIA DEL ESPIRITU SANTO 'Bay of the Holy Spirit,' the latter dating from c. 1519, did not last. The French, naming the bay for the Mauvila Indians, called it MOBILE (Griffith 2; Moore 38; G. R. Stewart 1970, 217).

MOBILE COUNTY Created by act of the MS terrritorial legislature on Aug. 1, 1812. Bounded on the north by Washington Co., on the east by Baldwin Co. and Mobile Bay, on the south by Mississippi Sound, and on the west by MS. Named for the city and bay. The co. seat is the city Mobile (M. B. Owen 1:476).

MOBILE POINT   Cape at 301319NO-880142W in Baldwin Co. at the entrance to Mobile Bay. Named for this bay (Read 43–44; U.S.G.S., 1966 Base Maps).

MOBILE RIVER   Stream formed by the confluence of the Alabama and Tombigbee rivers at 310810NO875638W between Baldwin Co. and Washington Co. and flowing into Mobile Bay at 303921NO880152W between Baldwin Co. and Mobile Co. De Soto, c. 1519, called it RIO DEL ESPIRITU SANTO 'River of the Holy Spirit.' The French, c. 1700, gave it the name of the Mauvila Indians, whom they called *Mobile* (M. B. Owen 1:476).

MOCCASIN GAP   See FITZPATRICK in Bullock Co.

MOLLOY   Community with discontinued PO at 334553NO881245W in Lamar Co. Area formerly called *Betts Beat* for the Betts family. Settlement named MOLLOY for the family of Benjamin M. Molloy, the first postmaster, appointed in 1885 (Acee 34).

MON LOUIS [,man'luɪ]   Settlement with discontinued PO at 302625NO880621W in Mobile Co., 1 mile north of the island for which it was named. PO est. in 1890 (Harris 1982, 112–13).

MON LOUIS ISLAND   Island in Mobile Bay at 302202NO880826W in Mobile Co. In 1710 the French government granted the island, known then as GROSSE POINTE 'large cape' to Nicholas Bodin, Sieur de Miragouin. He changed the name to MON LOUIS 'my Louis,' probably in honor of Louis XIV (1638–1715), king of France (1643–1715) (Harris 1982, 113).

MONROE COUNTY   Created by act of the MS territorial legislature on June 29, 1815. Bordered on the north by Wilcox Co., on the east by Butler Co. and Conecuh Co., on the

south by Escambia Co. and Baldwin Co., and on the west by Clarke Co. Named for James Monroe (1758–1831), then secretary of state (1811–17) under James Madison and later president of the U.S. (1817–25). The co. seat was Claiborne, 1815–32; Monroeville, the present one, was chosen in 1832 (Harder 351).

MONROEVILLE   Inc. co. seat with PO at 313140NO871929W in Monroe Co. First settled in 1815 by a Maj. Walker who operated Walker's Store. When this site was chosen for the seat of justice because of its central location in the co., it was called for a short time CENTERVILLE. Renamed MONROE-VILLE for the co. in 1832 when it became the seat of justice. PO est. in 1833. Inc. in 1901 (Dugas [Monroe Co.] 96).

MONTEREY ['mantrɪ]   Settlement with discontinued PO at 315412NO865255W in Butler Co. Originally called ELDERVILLE for Dave Elder, who built the first house here in 1820. Later known as GOBBLERSVILLE because of the wild turkeys in the area. In 1847 named, at the suggestion of William H. Traweek, for Monterrey, Mexico, where a Mexican War battle was fought. PO est. in 1850 (Dugas [Butler Co.] 79).

MONTEVALLO [,mantə'vælə]   Inc. town with PO at 330602NO865151W in Shelby Co. Originally known as WILSON'S HILL because it was settled in 1815 by Jesse Wilson, one of Andrew Jackson's soldiers in the Creek Indian War. Inc. in 1848 as MONTEVALLO, a name that is a pseudo-Italian combination of *monte* 'mountain' and *valle* 'valley.' PO est. in 1829 (Tamarin).

MONTEZUMA   Community with discontinued PO on the east bank of the Conecuh River at 311829NO862648W in Covington Co. Originally called COVINGTON for the co. Renamed for Montezuma (?–1520), the Aztec emperor of Mexico (1479–1520), for Aaron Lockhart, a co. commissioner in 1821. Co. seat, 1822–44. PO est. in 1826. Town abandoned after 1844, following several devastating floods (W. D. Ward 146–49).

MONTGOMERY [,mʌn(t)'gʌmrɪ]   Inc. co. seat and state capital with PO at 322200NO-861800W in Montgomery Co. Named for Richard Montgomery (1736–1775), a major general killed in the Battle of Quebec on Dec. 31, 1775. Became co. seat in 1817. Inc. in 1819. PO est. in 1824. Chosen state capital in 1846 (*Alabama: A Guide*, 222; V. V. Hamilton 120).

MONTGOMERY COUNTY Created by act of the MS territorial legislature on Dec. 6, 1816. Originally included land now in Elmore Co. and Autauga Co., among others. Now bounded on the north by Elmore Co., on the east by Macon Co. and Bullock Co., on the south by Pike Co. and Crenshaw Co., on the west by Lowndes Co., and on the northwest by Autauga Co. Named for Lemuel Putnam Montgomery of TN, a major killed in the Battle of Horseshoe Bend by Creek Indians on March 27, 1814. Original co. seat was Fort Jackson Town, on land now in Elmore Co. It was replaced as seat of justice in 1817 by the city of Montgomery (M. B. Owen 1:488).

MONTICELLO [ˌmɑntə'sɛlo] Settlement with discontinued PO at 314931NO854643W in Pike Co. Probably named for Thomas Jefferson's plantation in VA. Served as co. seat, 1827–38. PO est. in 1833 (M. T. Stewart, *Pike Co.*, viii).

MONTROSE Settlement with PO at 303356NO875406W in Baldwin Co. An earlier designation, SIBLEY CITY, honored Cyrus Sibley, who purchased the land in 1839. In 1852 Theodore Graham suggested renaming the town for Montrose, Scotland. PO est. in 1879 (Bush 64).

MOODY Inc. town with discontinued PO at 333527NO862927W in St. Clair Co. Named for Epps Moody from NC, who settled here in 1820. Also called MOODY'S and MOODY'S CROSSROADS. PO est. in 1882. Inc. in 1962 (Rich).

MOORES BRIDGE Settlement with PO at 332655NO874737W in Tuscaloosa Co. Named for the bridge built by Duncan Taney Moore over the Sipsey River where he had earlier operated a ferry. PO est. in 1853 (Rich 1979, 382).

MOORE'S CROSSROADS See NOTASULGA in Macon Co.

MOORESVILLE Inc. town with PO at 343742NO865249W in Limestone Co. Named for William Moore, who settled here c. 1808. Inc. in 1818. PO est. in 1819 (R. H. Walker 37).

MORELAND Settlement with discontinued PO at 341428NO871802W in Winston Co. Perhaps named for John O. Moore, the first postmaster, appointed in 1899 ("Record of Appointment of Postmasters").

MORGAN CITY Settlement at 342819NO863411W in Morgan Co. Founded c. 1830 and named for the co. (Ackley 4).

MORGAN COUNTY Created by act of the AL territorial general assembly on June 8, 1818, as COTACO COUNTY. Name changed to MORGAN COUNTY in 1821. Bordered on the north by Madison Co. and Limestone Co., on the east by Marshall Co., on the south by Cullman Co., and on the west by Lawrence Co. First named for Cotaco Creek; then renamed for Daniel Morgan (1736–1802), the revolutionary war general. The co. seats have been Somerville, 1818–91, and Decatur, the present one (Ackley 3–4).

MORGANSBURG See FLINT CITY in Morgan Co.

MORGAN'S CROSSROADS See RAINBOW CITY in Etowah Co.

MORGAN SPRINGS Settlement at 324443NO872457W in Perry Co. The town was named for the nearby springs, which probably honor the family of William Morgan, a local property owner who died in 1860 (Harris 1982, 115).

MORRIS Inc. town with PO at 334453NO864831W in Jefferson Co. According to some residents, the settlement was named for an engineer on the Louisville and Nashville RR, but others believe it honors George Lafayette Morris of Birmingham, who owned the Morris Mining Co. PO est. in 1872. Inc. in 1885 (Hagood 26; Harris 1982, 115).

MORTAR CREEK Stream rising at 324219NO863305W in Autauga Co. and flowing into the Coosa River at 323026NO861808W in Elmore Co. The name, which dates from 1837 or earlier, may refer to the large guns used in the area during the Indian wars (Biggs 33; DeVaughn).

MORTON HILL   Mountain whose summit is at 334135NO854420W in Calhoun Co. Located on land now occupied by Fort McClellan, a military base. Probably named for a local family (Jolly; U.S.G.S., 1966 Base Maps).

MORVIN ['mɔrvɪn]   Community with PO at 315908NO875936W in Clarke Co. The name is said to mean 'old red hill,' but the language from which it may have been derived is not specified. PO est. in 1851 (Clarke Co. Historical Society 281).

MOSSES   Inc. town at 321033NO864019W in Lowndes Co. Also known as MOSS. Probably either a family name or an environmental designation, for the plant. Inc. in 1979 (1975 General Highway Map of Lowndes Co.).

MOTLEY   Community with discontinued PO at 330701NO853932W in Clay Co. Probably named for a local family, one of whose members, John A. Motley, became the postmaster in 1905. PO est. in 1888 ("Record of Appointment of Postmasters").

MOULTON   Inc. co. seat with PO at 342852NO871736W in Lawrence Co. Named for Michael Moulton, an officer killed during the Creek Indian War of 1813–14. Inc. in 1819 and chosen co. seat in 1820. PO est. in 1824 (M. B. Owen 1:456).

MOULTON VALLEY   Valley extending from 342756NO873245W in Franklin Co. to 342854NO871807W in Lawrence Co. Probably named for the town in Lawrence Co. Also known as RUSSELLVILLE VALLEY, probably for the town in Franklin Co. (U.S.G.S., 1966 Base Maps).

MOUNDVILLE   Inc. town with PO at 325951NO873748W in Hale Co. Originally called CARTHAGE for the ancient city in north Africa. Renamed for the many Indian mounds nearby. Carthage PO est. in 1831, Moundville PO in 1893. Inc. in 1908 (Holliman).

MOUNTAINBORO   Settlement with discontinued PO at 340849NO860750W in Etowah Co. Settled and given its descriptive and environmental name before 1876. PO est. in 1891. Inc. in 1963 (Jolly).

MOUNTAIN CREEK   Settlement with PO at 324238NO862844W in Chilton Co. Named for the nearby creek. PO est. in 1875 (Covington 19).

MOUNTAIN CREEK   Inc. town with PO at 344330NO863252W in Jefferson Co. Developed during the late 1920s by Robert Jemison, the president of the Jemison Real Estate and Insurance Co. Inc. in 1942. PO est. in 1972 (Harris 1982, 117).

MOUNTAIN FORK   Stream rising at 345943NO861916W in Madison Co. and flowing into the Flint River at 345227NO862828W. Probably a descriptive and environmental name (U.S.G.S., 1966 Base Maps).

MOUNTAIN VIEW   Settlement at 341818NO861753W in Marshall Co. Probably a descriptive and environmental name (U.S.G.S., 1966 Base Maps).

MOUNT ANDREW   Settlement with discontinued PO at 315816NO853129W in Barbour Co. Named for the church that honors J. E. Andrew, a bishop of the Methodist church. PO est. in 1846 (Ellis 43).

MOUNT ARARAT   See ARARAT in Choctaw Co.

MOUNT CARMEL   Mountain whose summit is at 320016NO862022W in Crenshaw Co. Probably named for the biblical mountain range extending across northwestern Israel to the Mediterranean Sea (U.S.G.S., 1966 Base Maps).

MOUNT CARMEL   Settlement at 345611NO854633W in Jackson Co. Named for a local Church of Christ church, probably organized before 1880 (Melancon).

MOUNT CARMEL   Settlement with discontinued PO at 320339NO862155W in Montgomery Co. Named for the local Mount Carmel Methodist Church, the sanctuary having been built in 1830 but the organization dating from c. 1820. PO est. in 1872 (Harris 1982, 116).

MOUNT HEBRON   Settlement with discontinued PO at 340832NO861722W in Greene Co. The first people who reached this area in 1818 named this elevated site for the biblical town that was the last home of Abraham. PO est. in 1837 (Rich 1979, 389).

MOUNT HESTER   Community at 344342NO880043W in Colbert Co. Formerly known as MOUNT PLEASANT, a subjectively descriptive name that was changed after 1908 to avoid confusion with another settlement. The present designation honors the brothers Leighton Thomas Hester (1883–1960) and Walter Amos Hester (1887–1962) (Sockwell).

MOUNT HOPE Settlement with PO at 342730NO872854W in Lawrence Co. Probably an inspirational and symbolic name. PO est. in 1832 (Gentry 39).

MOUNT JEFFERSON Dead town with discontinued PO at 324334NO852221W in Lee Co. Probably named for Thomas Jefferson (1743–1826), third president of the U.S. (1801–09). After the Montgomery County RR, chartered in 1834, chose a route through Opelika because it was on a lower elevation than Mount Jefferson, this settlement was gradually abandoned. PO est. in 1839 (Blackmon; Nunn 28–29, 32).

MOUNT MEIGS [mɛgz] Settlement with PO at 322145NO860607W in Montgomery Co. First known as EVANSVILLE for Jesse Evans, the tavern owner. When Evans moved away in 1818 or 1819, the town was given the subjectively descriptive name MOUNT PLEASANT. The present designation honors a local family who operated a store and a gin. Mount Meigs PO est. in 1827 (Freeman).

MOUNT MEIGS STATION Settlement on the Western RR of Alabama at 322357NO-860625W in Montgomery Co. Grew up around the RR station for the town of Mount Meigs, located about 3 miles to the southeast (Freeman; 1926 Soil Map).

MOUNT OLIVE Settlement with discontinued PO at 330410NO860806W in Coosa Co. Named for the local Baptist church constituted in 1852. PO also est. in 1852 (G. E. Brewer 163).

MOUNT OLIVE See HIGDON in Jackson Co.

MOUNT PINSON See PINSON in Jefferson Co.

MOUNT PLEASANT See MOUNT HESTER in Colbert Co.

MOUNT PLEASANT See MOUNT MEIGS in Montgomery Co.

MOUNT ROZELL Settlement with PO at 345606NO870825W in Limestone Co. Named for the Rozell family, pioneers in the area. PO est. in 1857 (Harris 1982, 117).

MOUNT STERLING Settlement with discontinued PO at 320537NO880947W in Choctaw Co. Named for a town in KY by the first postmaster, Sanford E. Catterlin, appointed

in 1838 (Choctaw Co. Bicentennial Commission 5, 19).

MOUNT VERNON Inc. town with PO at 310506NO880048W in Mobile Co. Named for the U.S. army cantonment located here in 1811. In 1828 an arsenal also was built here. In 1900 following release to the state, the military facilities, named for the home of George Washington in VA, were converted into a state mental institution. PO est. in 1832. Inc. in 1959 (Harris 1982, 117).

MOUNT WILLING Settlement with discontinued PO at 320336NO864205W in Lowndes Co. Named for a town in the part of SC where many of the local residents had lived. PO est. in 1833 (Harris 1982, 117).

MOUNT ZION See SECTION in Jackson Co.

MUCKLE'S RIDGE See MARION in Perry Co.

MUD CREEK Descriptive and environmental name for the following watercourses.
1. Stream rising at 342607NO880539W in Franklin Co. and flowing into Town Creek at 342734NO880648W in Lawrence Co. (Knight 28; U.S.G.S., 1966 Base Maps).
2. Stream rising at 345339NO860501W in Jackson Co. and flowing into the Tennessee River at 344406NO855313W (Kennamer 6; U.S.G.S., 1966 Base Maps).
3. Stream rising at 331927NO870812W in Jefferson Co. and joining Valley Creek at 332951NO871150W (Hagood 46; U.S.G.S., 1966 Base Maps).
4. Stream rising at 333908NO880302W in Lamar Co. and flowing across the state line at 333617NO881623W into MS (Acee 3; U.S.G.S., 1966 Base Maps).

MUDDY CREEK Stream rising at 345813NO865622W in Limestone Co. and joining Swan Creek at 345003NO865711W. Probably a descriptive name (U.S.G.S., 1966 Base Maps).

MUDDY FORK Stream rising at 342829NO871638W in Lawrence Co. and joining Clear Fork at 343505NO871950W to form Big Nance Creek. Probably a descriptive name (U.S.G.S., 1966 Base Maps).

MUDDY PRONG Stream rising at 332546NO863246W in Shelby Co. and joining South Fork at 332546NO863246W to form Yellowleaf Creek. Descriptive name (Tamarin; U.S.G.S., 1966 Base Maps).

MULBERRY Settlement with discontinued PO at 324015NO864303W in Autauga Co. Named for the creek. PO est. in 1831 (Biggs 34).

MULBERRY CREEK Stream rising at 325209NO864724W in Chilton Co. and flowing into the Alabama River at 323621NO-865130W between Autauga Co. and Dallas Co. Probably received its name from the mulberry trees once growing in the area. On Lucas's 1822 map. A smaller stream, Little Mulberry Creek (Morse and Breese's 1842 map), rising at 324844NO864239W in Chilton Co. and flowing into the Alabama River at 322607NO865043W between Autauga Co. and Dallas Co., is named for the larger one (Biggs 31, 34).

MULBERRY FORK Stream rising at 341435NO863015W in Cullman Co. and joining Locust Fork at 333325NO871115W in Jefferson Co. to form the Black Warrior River. Probably named for the mulberry trees that once grew in the area (U.S.G.S., 1966 Base Maps).

MULGA ['mʌlgə] Inc. town with PO at 333259NO865827W in Jefferson Co. Name may be that of an Indian or it may be derived from the Creek word *omalga* 'all.' PO est. in 1907. Inc. in 1947 (Read 44).

MULLET POINT Cape at 302434NO-875423W in Baldwin Co. Probably an environmental name referring to a type of fish found in Mobile Bay (U.S.G.S., 1966 Base Maps).

MUNFORD Settlement with PO at 333147NO855703W in Talladega Co. On the 1895 Cruikshank map. Named for a Mrs. Munford, who operated a boardinghouse for workmen building the Alabama and Tennessee Rivers RR (Southern). PO est. in 1867 (McMillan).

MURDER CREEK Stream rising at 314346NO870427W in Conecuh Co. and flowing into the Conecuh River in Escambia Co. at 310404NO870555W. Name commemorates the murder and robbery in 1788 of Joseph Kirkland and his party, who were camping on the bank of the creek on their way to LA by way of Pensacola, FL. The murderers, members of a trading party, were a white man called "Cat" by the Indians because of his ferocity and a Hilibi Indian called "Istillicha [the Manslayer]" because of the number of murders he had committed; and a black man named "Bob." Although these men escaped, Cat was later apprehended and executed here (Waters 16–19).

MUSCADINE Settlement with PO at 334404NO852310W in Cleburne Co. Named for the muscadine grapes growing in the region. PO est. in 1887 (*Alabama: A Guide*, 321).

MUSCADINE CREEK Stream rising at 334811NO852931W in Cleburne Co. and flowing into the Tallapoosa River at 334345NO-852220W. Probably named for the muscadine grapes growing in the area (U.S.G.S., 1966 Base Maps).

MUSCLE SHOALS Inc. town with PO at 344441NO874003W in Colbert Co. Laid out by backers of Henry Ford, who had planned to build an automobile plant here, and named for the shoals now inundated by the impounded water of the Tennessee River. The Cherokee Indians had called the shoals *dagunahi* 'mussel place,' from *daguna* 'mussel' and *-hi* 'place' and also *chustanaluyi* 'shoals place,' from *ustanalahi* 'place of rocks across a stream.' In 1892 the U.S. Board on Geographic Names chose *muscle*, an obsolete form of *mussel*, as the official spelling of the word. PO est. in 1918. Inc. in 1923 (Sockwell).

MUSH CREEK Stream rising at 321244NO864856W in Lowndes Co. and flowing into the Alabama River at 321306NO-870309W in Dallas Co. Probably a descriptive name referring to soft muddy bed and banks of the creek (U.S.G.S., 1966 Base Maps).

MUSTER See LIBERTY in Blount Co.

MYNOT ['maɪˌnɑt] Community with discontinued PO at 343844NO880302W in Colbert Co. Although its origin is unknown, the name might be a different spelling of *Minot*, the designation for a town in ND, chosen for the PO because it was short and easy to remember. PO est. in 1898 (Sockwell).

MYRTLEWOOD Inc. town with PO at 321501NO875659W in Marengo Co. Thomas Jefferson Beck (1865–1938), deputy sheriff (1888–92), suggested naming the settlement for the crepe myrtle bushes and the trees growing in the region. PO est. in 1886. Inc. in 1957 (W. Smith).

NADAWAH ['nædəwɔ] Community with discontinued PO at 314851NO871020W in Monroe Co. Founded as a sawmill town and named for the Nadawah Lumber Co. PO est. in 1900 (Harris 1982, 119).

NAHEOLA [neˈhiolə] Community with discontinued PO at 321339NO880144W in Choctaw Co. Named for the bluff on the west bank of the Tombigbee River called *Naheola* by the Indians. According to Swanton, Choctaw *nahollo*, the source of this name, means not only 'white man,' as Read says, but also 'something supernatural or remarkable' and was used to refer to mythic beings before it was applied to white men. PO est. in 1878 (McMillan in Read 92; Read 44).

NANAFALIA [ˌnænəfəˈlaɪə] Settlement with PO at 320646NO875917W in Marengo Co. Also known briefly as DUMAS for a local family. Named for the bluff on the east side of the Tombigbee River that the Choctaw Indians described as *nanih* 'hill' and *falaia* 'long.' Identified as the "hills of Nanafalaya" by Romans in 1772. PO est. in 1833 (Read 44; W. Smith).

NAPIER FIELD Inc. town with PO at 311855NO852715W in Dale Co. The settlement grew up around and was named for the airfield, used by Camp Rucker during World War II, that honored Edward L. Napier of Union Springs, an officer killed in an airplane crash in 1923. Inc. in 1968. PO est. in 1971 (Harris 1982, 119).

NARCISSUS See BATTLES WHARF in Baldwin Co.

NATCHEW CREEK See TALLASEE-HATCHEE CREEK.

NATCHEZ Community with discontinued PO at 314339NO871538W in Monroe Co. The area was first known as *The Fork* because of its location between Big and Little Flat creeks. Its residents called the southwest section AFRICA, perhaps because it was inhabited by black persons, and the central part FLATWOODS, a descriptive and environmental designation. Named NATCHEZ, probably for Natchez, MS, c. 1891. *Natchez* may be related to Caddo *na'htcha* 'forest wood' and *da'htcha'hi* 'timber.' If so, it may mean 'timber land.' PO est. in 1891 (Dugas [Monroe Co.] 96; Read 45).

NAT MOUNTAIN Mountain whose summit is at 344143NO861456W in Jackson Co. Named for Nat Wisdom, an early settler (Kennamer 152; U.S.G.S., 1966 Base Maps).

NATURAL BRIDGE Settlement with PO at 340536NO873607W in Winston Co. Formerly known as LOW DIE, a term from gambling. Renamed for the large natural rock

bridge located nearby. PO est. in 1890 (Elliott 1:176).

NAUVOO [ˈnɔˌvu] Inc. town with PO at 335922NO872920W in Walker Co. Earlier known as INGLE MILLS, probably for mills operated by a local family. Name changed to NAUVOO by a Mr. Carroll for a town in IL founded by Mormons in 1840. The word *nauvoo* is derived from the Hebrew adjective *naveh* 'pleasant.' Ingle Mills PO est. in 1858, Nauvoo PO in 1879. Inc. in 1906 (Gant; Read xv).

NEBO Settlement with discontinued PO at 343318NO862015W in Madison Co. A biblical name, that of the mountain near Jericho where Moses died. PO est. in 1890 (Green).

NECTAR Inc. town with PO at 335735NO863822W in Blount Co. Formerly called TIDMORE for Henry Tidmore, the first postmaster, appointed in 1877. Five months later the name of the PO was changed to NECTAR, probably symbolic of the flowers in the region. Inc. in 1970 (Blount Co. Historical Society 27, 77).

NEEDHAM Settlement with PO at 315916NO882012W in Choctaw Co. Named for E. W. Needham, an early resident. PO est. in 1910 (Choctaw Co. Bicentennial Commission 19).

NEEDMORE See PROVIDENCE in Cullman Co.

NEEDMORE See WINFIELD in Marion Co.

NEEDMORE Settlement at 315407NO855627W in Pike Co., which grew up around the Pleasant Hill Primitive Baptist Church, organized in 1842. Originally called ROUGH LOG, a designation descriptive of the rapidly built church. The present name is said to have been suggested a short time later by a local man who stated that the town needed more of everything (Farmer 1973, 404).

NEEL Settlement with discontinued PO at 342756NO870340W in Morgan Co. Named for the man who operated a general store for the early settlers. PO est. in 1890 (Ackley 35).

NEELY HENRY LAKE Artificial lake formed by the impoundment of the Coosa River with Neely Henry Dam at 334658NO860158W between St. Clair Co. and Etowah Co. Named in 1968 for H. Neely Henry, a former president of Alabama Power Co. (Rich).

NEENAH [ˈninə] Settlement with discontinued PO at 315452NO871041W in Wilcox

Co. NEENAH is said to be a "phonetic spelling" of the given name of Nina Olinsky, a local resident. PO est. in 1902 (Harris 1982, 120).

NEGRO CREEK Stream rising at 302957NO874251W in Baldwin Co. and flowing into the Blackwater River at 302907NO873336W. Because *negro* is a Spanish adjective meaning 'black,' this name may have been used during the 1780s by the Spanish settlers to describe the dark marsh waters (Bush 66).

NEWBERN ['njubən] Inc. town with PO at 323535NO873158W in Hale Co. Settled by persons from NC, who named their new settlement for Newberne, NC. PO est. in 1833. Inc. in 1859 (Holliman).

NEW BREMEN See COLD SPRINGS in Cullman Co.

NEW BROCKTON [,nju'braktən] Inc. town with PO at 312308NO855546W in Coffee Co. Originally named BROCK, then BROCKTON, for Huey E. Brock, who built the first residence on the town site, but because the Brockton PO was frequently confused with the Blockton one in Bibb Co., the postmaster, John T. Brock, added the word *new* to the name. Brockton PO est. in 1898; New Brockton PO in 1907. Inc. in 1902 (F. S. Watson 1970, 17, 71).

NEWBURG Settlement with discontinued PO at 342849NO873433W in Franklin Co. The compound name is descriptive of the newness of the town. PO est. in 1834 (Knight 28).

NEW BURLESON See VINA in Franklin Co.

NEW CASTLE Settlement with PO at 333856NO864607W in Jefferson Co. Founded and named for the English coal-mining center by John T. Milner, the organizer of the Newcastle Coal and Iron Co. PO est. in 1874 (Brown and Nabers 199; Hagood 6–7).

NEWELL Community with discontinued PO at 332559NO852601W in Randolph Co. Named for the family of W. P. Newell, a former sheriff, elected in 1845. PO est. in 1887 (Harris 1982, 121).

NEW HOPE Inc. town with PO at 343213NO862340W in Madison Co. Known as CLOUD'S TOWN, 1820–25, for William Cloud, the first settler, who traded with the Indians. In 1832 the town was to have been inc. as *Vienna*, but because there was already

a settlement with that name in the state, it was unofficially given the inspirational and symbolic name of the local Methodist church, NEW HOPE. New Hope PO est. in 1834. Inc. as NEW HOPE in 1956 (T. J. Taylor 1976, 45).

NEW HOPEWELL Community at 333803NO852301W in Cleburne Co. Given the inspirational and symbolic name of the New Hopewell Baptist Church, organized in 1911 (Harris 1982, 121).

NEW LEXINGTON Settlement with discontinued PO at 333344NO873927W in Tuscaloosa Co. A prosperous agricultural settlement dating from c. 1819, its PO, one of the earliest in the co., having been est. in 1826, was named HALBERTS PO in honor of the first postmaster, Joshua Halbert. In 1836 both the PO and the settlement became known as NEW LEXINGTON, probably for Lexington, SC, the former home of Isaac Cannon, a prominent early settler. Also known as LEXINGTON (Rich 1979, 406–07).

NEW LONDON See LONDON in St. Clair Co.

NEW MARKET Settlement with PO at 345436NO862540W in Madison Co. Settled c. 1809, it received its descriptive name because it was intended to serve as a "new market" for the merchants and farmers in the region. PO est. in 1826 (Harris 1982, 121; F. C. Roberts 185).

NEWPORT See BREWTON in Escambia Co.

NEW RIVER Stream rising at 340702NO873728W in Winston Co. and becoming the Sipsey River at 335451NO874114W in Fayette Co. Formerly called NINE ISLAND CREEK, a descriptive name. The current designation probably refers to the discovery of the stream by early settlers in the area (U.S.G.S., 1966 Base Maps).

NEW RUIN See MCKINLEY in Marengo Co.

NEW ST. STEPHENS See ST. STEPHENS in Washington Co.

NEW SITE See ANDALUSIA in Covington Co.

NEW SITE Inc. town with discontinued PO at 330214NO854627W in Tallapoosa Co. Name refers to a new settlement made by some former residents of Goldville who, it is said, moved a few miles away from their former community because it was too sinful for them. They probably left the older town after most of their neighbors, hearing of the CA gold rush, moved west to the more abundant fields. PO est. in 1859. Inc. in 1965 (Dugas [Tallapoosa Co.] 87).

NEWTON Inc. town with PO at 312006NO853619W in Dale Co. Probably named for the local Newton family. Co. seat, 1841–71. PO est. in 1843. Inc. in 1887 (F. S. Watson 1949, 16–18).

NEWTON See ATTALLA in Etowah Co.

NEWTONVILLE Settlement with discontinued PO at 333243NO874805W in Fayette Co. Named for E. B. Newton, who settled here soon after 1800 and operated a trading post. PO est. in 1851 (Peoples 14).

NEW TOWN See ATTALLA in Etowah Co.

NEWTOWN Former co. seat of Tuscaloosa Co., now part of Tuscaloosa. On March 3, 1819, the U.S. Congress granted this block of land to the Connecticut Asylum for the Deaf and Dumb. In an attempt to block the growth of Tuscaloosa, a group of investors bought the land and founded a new settlement called THE LOWER TOWN OF TUSCALOOSA, soon shortened to LOWER TUSCALOOSA and then changed to NEWTOWN. Co. seat, 1822–26. On March 4, 1842, the settlement was severely damaged by a tornado, after which many of its residents moved away (Rich 1979, 408).

NEW TROY See GREENSBORO in Hale Co.

NEWVILLE Inc. town with PO on the Alabama Midland RR (Atlantic Coast Line) at 312518NO852016W in Henry Co. First known as WELLS STATION, named for James Madison Wells, an early property owner. Later, the RR called the station NEWVILLE because they wanted it to have a new name. Newville PO est. in 1894. Inc. in 1903 (Warren, *Henry's Heritage*, 337).

NICHOLSVILLE Settlement with discontinued PO at 320029NO875407W in Marengo Co. Founded before 1850 and named for William Nichols from SC. PO est. in 1884 (Johnson and Alexander 21; W. Smith).

NINE ISLAND CREEK See NEW RIVER in Winston Co.

NIXBURG Community with PO at 324940NO860640W in Coosa Co. Founded in 1850 by Solomon Robbins from NC, who called the community ROBBINSVILLE.

Settlement was later named NIXBURG for the Nix family, who were among the early settlers. PO est. in 1836 (G. E. Brewer 82).

NORMAL Community with PO at 344720NO863419W in Madison Co. Named for the state Normal and Industrial School (now Alabama Agricultural and Mechanical University), founded first in Huntsville in 1873 and moved here in 1875. PO est. in 1891 (*Alabama: A Guide*, 329).

NORTH ELMORE Settlement at 323323NO861909W in Elmore Co. Town was given its name because of its location c. 2 miles north of Elmore (U.S.G.S., 1966 Base Maps).

NORTH JOHNS See JOHNS in Jefferson Co.

NORTHPORT Inc. town with PO at 331344NO873438W in Tuscaloosa Co. The first settlers reached the site on the north bank of the Black Warrior River in 1816 and called their community KENTUCK, either a shortened form of *Kentucky* or a descriptive compound of *cane* and *tuck*, a term for poor sandy soil. From c. 1837 to the early 1840s, also known as NORTH TUSCALOOSA because of its location north of the town Tuscaloosa and NORTHPORT because it was the port the farthest north on the Black Warrior River. Northport PO est. in 1832. Inc. in 1852 (Rich 1979, 314–15, 411–13).

NORTH RIVER Stream rising at 335027NO873352W in Fayette Co. and flowing into the Black Warrior River at 331440NO873012W in Tuscaloosa Co. The descriptive and locational name appears in John Coffee's 1820 survey of Tuscaloosa Co. (Rich 1979, 413).

NORTH TUSCALOOSA See NORTHPORT in Tuscaloosa Co.

NOTASULGA [ˌnotəˈsʌlgə] Inc. town with PO at 323338NO854021W in Macon Co. First known as MOORE'S CROSSROADS, probably for Amos Moore, the first postmaster, appointed in 1843. Present name is the Creek one for a group of angelica plants, *notosalgi*, a compound of *notosa* and the collective *algi*. Notasulga PO est. in 1849. Inc. in 1893 (McMillan in Read 92; Read 46).

NOTTINGHAM Community with discontinued PO at 332144NO861322W in Talladega Co. Named for Nottingham, England, by a group of promoters hoping to attract English capital to develop the nearby mineral deposits. Never became more than a village. Now only a scattered settlement. PO est. in 1887 (McMillan).

NOXUBEE RIVER [ˈnɑksjəbɪ] Stream rising in MS, entering AL at 331812NO-890851W in Sumter Co. and flowing into the Tombigbee River at 324942NO881045W. OKA ONOXUBBA or 'Strong Smelling Water' on Purcell's map, c. 1770. *Noxubee* is derived from Choctaw *nakshobi* 'stinking' (Read 46).

NUNN'S MILL See FLORETTE in Morgan Co.

OAKBOWERY Settlement with discontinued PO at 324502NO852611W in Chambers Co. In 1833 Webb Kidd founded a trading post here and gave it the descriptive name WOODLAWN. Two years later, the settlement was renamed OAK BOWERY, then OAKBOWERY, for a Methodist campground where a church with this subjectively descriptive name was later built. Oak Bowery PO est. in 1837, Oakbowery PO in 1883 (Dugas [Chambers Co.] 58).

OAKFUSKEE CREEK See LINE CREEK.

OAK GROVE Settlement at 332717NO-870913W in Jefferson Co. First known as EZRA, possibly the name of a local person, but also a biblical name, that of the fifth century BC Hebrew high priest. The present designation is descriptive of the grove of oak trees where the town is located. Ezra PO, 1886–92 (Hagood 40).

OAK GROVE Community with discontinued PO at 305125NO881055W in Mobile Co. Probably a descriptive and environmental name. PO est. in 1888.

OAK GROVE Inc. town at 331130NO-861758W in Talladega Co. Given the traditional and descriptive name of a local Baptist church organized in 1896. Inc. in 1966 (McMillan).

OAK HILL Settlement at 341857NO-860146W in DeKalb Co. Name is descriptive and environmental (Raughton 60; U.S.G.S., 1966 Base Maps).

OAK HILL Inc. town with PO at 315515NO870458W in Wilcox Co. Probably a descriptive and environmental name. PO est. in 1894. Inc. in 1940.

OAKLAND Settlement with discontinued PO at 345030NO874756W in Lauderdale Co. Probably named for Wyatt Collier's house,

The Oaks, built in 1836. PO est. in 1850 (Sockwell).

OAKLAND Settlement at 344939NO-870507W in Limestone Co., which grew up around a Church of Christ church erected c. 1907. Name is descriptive of the oak trees on the site, some of which were used to build the church (Harris 1982, 124).

OAKLEVEL Settlement with discontinued PO at 335058NO852841W in Cleburne Co. Dating from the 1840s, this was the largest town during the 1860s in what was to become Cleburne Co. A descriptive and environmental name. PO est. in 1845 (D. Stewart).

OAKMAN Inc. town with PO at 334248NO872319W in Walker Co. First called DAY'S GAP in honor of W. B. Day, the first settler here in 1862. Name changed to YORK when the application for a PO was submitted in 1884, but because there was already another York in the state, OAKMAN, in honor of W. G. Oakman, a director of the Sloss-Sheffield Iron and Steel Co., was the name finally chosen for the PO and then the town. Oakman PO est. in 1890 (Gant).

OAK MOUNTAIN Mountain whose summit is at 332603NO863759W in Shelby Co. and Jefferson Co. Name is descriptive of the trees in the area (Hagood 40; U.S.G.S., 1966 Base Maps).

OAKMULGEE CREEK [okˈmʌlgɪ] Stream rising at 325423NO865512W in Bibb Co. and flowing between Perry Co. and Dallas Co. into the Cahaba River at 322818NO870931W in Dallas Co. Its tributary Little Oakmulgee Creek rises at 324554NO865803W in Chilton Co. and flows between Perry Co. and Dallas Co. into the larger stream at 323412NO-870452W. The name, meaning 'bubbling water,' is derived from Hitchiti *oki* 'water' and *mulgi* 'boiling' (Read 47).

OAKOCHAPPA See (BIG) BEAR CREEK in Colbert Co.

OAK RIDGE See LEEDS in Jefferson Co.

OAKVILLE Community with discontinued PO at 342643NO870944W in Lawrence Co. Descriptive and environmental name. PO est. in 1830 (Gentry 60).

OAKWOOD Community with discontinued PO at 320733NO860424W in Montgomery Co. Descriptive and environmental name. PO est. in 1895 (Freeman).

OCHOCCOLA CREEK See PECKERWOOD CREEK.

OCOCOPOSO   See TUSCUMBIA in Colbert Co.

OCRE ['okrɪ]   Community with discontinued PO at 331129NO882602W in Randolph Co. Although the origin of the name is unknown, the form may be a spelling representing the local pronunciation of *okra*, the vegetable, or possibly it is the French word for the color ochre, which does have this spelling. PO est. in 1899.

OCTAGON   Community with discontinued PO at 321215NO874519W in Marengo Co. Named for the original structure of Bethlehem Baptist Church, built in 1868, which had eight sides. PO est. in 1876 (W. Smith).

ODEN RIDGE   Settlement at 342226NO864544W in Morgan Co. The PO located here, 1890–93, was named AIR, probably an environmental designation. After it was discontinued, the settlement was named ODEN RIDGE for James H. Oden, who had been the postmaster (Ackley 37).

ODENVILLE   Inc. town with PO at 334038NO862348W in St. Clair Co. The settlement, made in 1821 by persons from Chester Co., SC, developed around Hardin's Shop, a cabinet shop owned by Peter Hardin. Later the town was known as LIBERTY, an inspirational and symbolic name. When the PO was est. in 1874, it and the town were named ODENVILLE, probably for a local family. Inc. in 1914 (Rich).

OHATCHEE [o'hætʃɪ]   Inc. town with PO at 334700NO860009W at Calhoun Co. Named for Ohatchee Creek. PO est. in 1840. Inc. in 1956 (Read 48).

OHATCHEE CREEK   Stream in Calhoun Co. rising at 335722NO854920W and joining Tallaseehatchee Creek at 334544NO860237W. On Bradford's 1841 map. Because this stream is north of Tallaseehatchee Creek, the first element of the name may be Creek *oh* 'upper,' the second being *hachi* 'stream' (Read 48).

OKATUPPA CREEK [okə'tʌpə]   Stream rising in MS, entering AL at 320915NO882832W in Choctaw Co., and flowing into the Tombigbee River at 314919NO881048W. OKA TUPPAH on E. A. Smith's 1891 map in Berney. Name is derived from *oktapi* 'dam,' a contraction of Choctaw *oka* 'water' and *tapa* 'dammed up' (Read 49).

OKFUSKEE [ok'fʌskɪ]   Dead town with discontinued PO north of the junction of Little Kowaliga Creek and the Tallapoosa River in Tallapoosa Co. Named for the trading post, Fort Okfuskee, built by the British in 1735 near the Indian village Okfuskee, whose name means 'point, promontory, between streams,' from Creek *ak* 'down in' and *faski* 'sharp, pointed.' Co. seat, 1832–38. PO, 1832–40 (Read 47).

OLD BETHEL   Settlement at 343452NO873125W in Colbert Co. that grew up around Old Bethel Baptist Church, organized in 1819. Also designated during the 1890s with the descriptive and environmental name CAVE SPRING (Sockwell).

OLD CLIO   See ADKINSON HEAD in Barbour Co.

OLD MEMPHIS   See MEMPHIS in Pickens Co.

OLD ST. STEPHENS   See ST. STEPHENS in Washington Co.

OLD SNOW HILL   See FURMAN in Wilcox Co.

OLD SPRING HILL   Settlement with discontinued PO at 322615NO874625W in Marengo Co. Known as SPRING HILL when settled in the 1820s, the word *old* was added to distinguish the PO from one formerly in Mobile Co. A descriptive and environmental name. Spring Hill PO est. in 1838, Old Spring Hill PO in 1878 (W. Smith).

OLD TEXAS   Settlement with discontinued PO at 314528NO865909W in Monroe Co. First known as SIMPKINSVILLE for the house and store built in the early 1800s by J. J. Simpkins. When the PO was est. in 1857 in the store built by Simpkins, the name of the town was changed to OLD TEXAS, probably for the state (Dugas [Monroe Co.] 96).

OLD TOWN CREEK   Stream rising at 321043NO853548W in Bullock Co. and joining Line Creek at 321948NO855804W between Macon Co. and Montgomery Co. Named for an abandoned Indian village on its banks (Sartwell; U.S.G.S., 1966 Base Maps).

OLD WOODVILLE   Dead town located 3/4 mile east of the present town Woodville in Jackson Co. Founded by Henry Derrick c. 1815 and named for Richard Wood, an early settler. As WOODVILLE, served as co. seat of Decatur Co., 1821–24 (M. B. Owen 1:441).

OLEANDER   Settlement with discontinued PO at 342450NO863141W in Marshall Co. Probably an environmental name, for the evergreen shrub. PO est. in 1842.

OLIVER   Settlement with discontinued PO

at 344839NO871501W in Lauderdale Co. Named for a local family. PO est. in 1894 (Sockwell).

OLNEY ['olnɪ]   Community with discontinued PO at 330828NO880219W in Pickens Co. Probably named for a local family. PO est. in 1844 (N. F. Brown 48).

OLUSTEE CREEK [o'lʌstɪ]   Stream rising at 320428NO860036W in Montgomery Co. and joining Patsaliga Creek at 315226NO861046W between Pike Co. and Crenshaw Co. Name means 'black water,' from Creek *oi-wa* 'water' and *lasti* 'black' (Read 49; U.S.G.S., 1966 Base Maps).

OMAHA   Community with discontinued PO at 331809NO851837W in Randolph Co. Probably named for Omaha, NE. PO est. in 1877.

OMUSEE CREEK [o'mʌsɪ]   Stream rising in Houston Co. at 311719NO852153W and flowing north into Henry Co., then back south into the Chattahoochee River at 311633NO850653W between Houston Co. and GA. OMUSSEE C. on La Tourette's 1844 map. The name, a reduced form of the tribal name *Yamassee*, is derived from Creek *yamasi* 'gentle, quiet' (Read 49).

ONEONTA [anɪ'antə]   Inc. co. seat with PO at 335653NO862822W in Blount Co. Named by William Newbold for his former home in NY. Became co. seat and received its PO in 1889. Inc. in 1891 (T. M. Owen 1:156; Read ix).

ONYCHA [o'nikə]   Inc. town at 311250NO861700W in Covington Co. Name is the term used in the Bible for an ingredient of the sacred composition that gives off a sweet aroma when burned. Inc. in 1971 (Read xvi).

OPELIKA [ˌopə'laɪkə]   Inc. co. seat at 323843NO852242W in Lee Co. The name was recorded as OPELIKAN when the town was founded in the 1830s. In 1850 respelled as OPELIKA, the name of an Upper Creek town in Coosa Co., whose designation means 'big swamp,' from Creek *opilwa* 'swamp' and *lako* 'big.' Opelikan PO est. in 1839, Opelika PO in 1850. Inc. in 1854. Chosen co. seat in 1866 (Read 50).

OPEN ROAD   See GORDON in Houston Co.

OPINE [ˌo'paɪn]   Community with discontinued PO at 315417NO875602W in Clarke Co. Although its origin is unknown,

the name might be an apostrophe consisting of "O" and "pine" addressed to the trees growing abundantly in the region. PO est. in 1898.

OPINTLOCCO CREEK [ˌopɪnt'lako]   Stream rising at 322847NO852419W in Lee Co. and joining Chewacla Creek at 322533NO853721W in Macon Co. OPINTLOCO C. on La Tourette's 1844 map. Name is derived from the Creek *opillako* 'big swamp,' consisting of *opilwa* 'swamp' and *lako* 'big' (Read 50).

OPP [ɑp]   Inc. town with PO at 311657NO861520W in Covington Co. Named for Henry Opp, a lawyer and the settlement's principal promoter. PO est. in 1900. Inc. in 1901 (M. B. Owen 1:410).

ORANGE BEACH   Settlement with PO on the eastern part of the peninsula along the Gulf of Mexico at 301739NO873425W in Baldwin Co. Named for the fruit, probably first planted by the Spaniards, that once grew in this area. PO est. in 1910 (Bush 68).

ORCHARD   Settlement with PO at 304310NO881226W in Mobile Co. The environmental name apparently refers to the area where this town is located, shown on Boudousquie's 1889 map to be covered with turpentine orchards. PO est. in 1900.

ORION [o'raɪən]   Settlement with discontinued PO at 315731NO860020W in Pike Co. First identified with the descriptive and environmental name PROSPECT RIDGE. Then named for the mighty hunter slain by Artemis and represented by the constellation. Orion PO est. in 1848 (M. T. Stewart, *Pike Co.*, iii, 18).

ORRVILLE   Inc. town with PO at 321822NO871444W in Dallas Co. Developed around Orr's Mills, operated by James F. Orr, who had settled in the area in 1842 and was the first postmaster of Orrville PO, appointed in 1850. Inc. in 1854 (M. B. Owen 1:416).

OSANIPPA CREEK [ˌosə'nɪpə]   Stream rising at 325109NO852105W in Chambers Co. and flowing into Lake Harding at 324258NO850721W in Lee Co. OS-SUN-NUP-PAU in Hawkins's "A Sketch of the Creek Country in 1798 and 1799" (54). Name is derived from Creek *asunapi*, a compound of *asunwa* 'moss' and *api* 'stems' (Read 50).

OUYOUKAS CREEK   See WEOKA CREEK.

OVERBROOK   Community at 330720NO-

861322W in Talladega Co. that grew up around the terminus of a spur rail line built for the Kaul Lumber Co. Appears on the 1901 Central of Georgia RR map. Designation is a metathesis of the name of C. F. Brookover, a Kaul employee (McMillan).

OWASSA [o'wɑsə]   Settlement with PO at 312935NO865554W in Conecuh Co. Name is probably of Indian or of pseudo-Indian origin, but derivation is uncertain. PO est. in 1908 (G. R. Stewart 1970, 351).

OWENS   Community   at   340746NO-855101W in Etowah Co. Also known as OWENS CROSSROADS. Named for the Owens brothers, J. H., William, and Martin, who bought the land c. 1884–85 (Jolly).

OWENS CROSSROADS   Inc. town with PO at   343517NO862732W   in   Madison   Co. Named for Thomas P. Owens, the first postmaster, appointed in 1869. Inc. in 1967 ("Record of Appointment of Postmasters").

OWENS TANYARD   See IRONATON in Talladega Co.

OXFORD   Inc. town with PO at 333651NO-855006W in Calhoun Co. Originally known as LICKSKILLET, a humorous designation implying that the residents were so poor that they had to lick their frying pans to obtain enough food to survive. Renamed in the 1840s, probably for Oxford, England. The Oxford Furnace, which has been proposed as the source for this name, was not commissioned or built by the Confederate government until 1863. Oxford PO est. in 1848. Inc. in 1852 (Jolly).

OYSTER BAY   Bay at 301621NO874352W in Baldwin Co., south of the mouth of the Bon Secour River. A descriptive and environmental name, probably descriptive of the kind of mollusk found here (U.S.G.S., 1966 Base Maps).

OZARK   Inc. co. seat at 312732NO-853826W in Dale Co. First called MERRICKS in honor of John Merrick, a revolutionary war soldier who moved here and opened a grocery store. Then known as WOODSHOP for the woodworking plant located in a blacksmith shop here. Finally, named OZARK by E. T. Matthews, the postmaster appointed in 1859, for the Indians in AK and MO named by the French *Aux Arks*. This phrase means 'in the country of the Arkansa,' the latter being the tribal name of these Indians. Woodshop PO est. in 1843,

Ozark PO in 1859. Became co. seat in 1871. Inc. in 1873 (F. S. Watson 1949, 27–32).

PACKERS   BEND   Community   at 314633NO872922W in Monroe Co. Named for a bend in the Alabama River, which itself had been named for a river landing made by David Packer in the early 1800s (Harris 1982, 126).

PAINT   CREEK   Stream   rising   at 330405NO862038W in Coosa Co. and flowing into the Coosa River at 325845NO863022W. Name probably refers to the colorful rock bed of the creek (U.S.G.S., 1966 Base Maps).

PAINTER   Settlement with discontinued PO at 341846NO860439W in DeKalb Co. Named for Harold Painter, who came here from NC in 1855. PO est. in 1900 (Raughton 61).

PAINT ROCK   Inc. town with PO at 343938NO861944W in Jackson Co. First known as CAMDEN, probably for Camden, SC. Next called REDMAN for John Redman, an early settler and later one of the town's postmasters. Finally, named PAINT ROCK for the nearby river. Camden PO est. in 1831; Redman PO in 1846; Paint Rock PO in 1864. Inc. in 1894 (Kennamer 157).

PAINT ROCK RIVER   Stream formed by the confluence of Larkin and Estill forks at 345353NO861014W in Jackson Co. that flows into the Tennessee River at 342834NO-863804W between Madison Co. and Marshall Co. Named for a high perpendicular bluff rising at the mouth of the river that has been colored by the mineral waters (*Alabama: A Guide*, 346; U.S.G.S., 1966 Base Maps).

PALESTINE   Community with discontinued PO at 335629NO852701W in Cleburne Co. Probably named for the biblical Holy Land, the area between the Mediterranean Sea and the Jordan River that was divided among Israel, Jordan, and Egypt in 1948. PO est. in 1851.

PALMER   See PALMERDALE in Jefferson Co.

PALMERDALE   Settlement with PO at 334419NO863846W in Jefferson Co. Also known as PALMER and PALMER'S STATION. Named for the Palmer family from whom the Louisville and Nashville RR bought the right-of-way and the land for the station. PO est. in 1936 (Hagood 20).

PALMETTO   Settlement with discontinued PO at 332902NO875840W in Pickens Co.

Named by William P. Richardson, the first postmaster, appointed in 1855, for his former home, Palmetto, SC (N. F. Brown 48).

PANOLA [pə'nolə] Settlement with discontinued PO at 315817NO862320W in Crenshaw Co. Name may be derived from Choctaw *ponola* 'cotton.' PO est. in 1879 (Read 51).

PANOLA Settlement with PO at 325702NO881608W in Sumter Co. Founded in 1909 as a station on the Alabama, Tennessee and Northern RR from which the local planters could ship their cotton. Name is derived from Choctaw *ponola* 'cotton.' PO est. in 1909 (Foscue 51).

PANSEY Community with PO at 310830NO-850844W in Houston Co. Named for the daughter of John Crosby, the first postmaster, appointed in 1890 (F. S. Watson 1972, 97).

PANTHER CREEK The following streams have environmental names, possibly translations of Indian designations.
1. Stream rising at 310529NO861728W in Covington Co. and joining Flat Creek at 310702NO860912W in Geneva Co. (U.S.G.S., 1966 Base Maps).
2. Stream rising at 321008NO864919W in Lowndes Co. and joining Big Swamp Creek at 321515NO864145W (U.S.G.S., 1966 Base Maps).

PARAGON Community with discontinued PO at 315234NO882228W in Choctaw Co. In 1880 called DRAG for a well-liked lazy boy. Later given the inspirational and symbolic name PARAGON. Drag PO est. in 1902, Paragon PO in 1910 (Choctaw Co. Bicentennial Commission 19).

PARIS See GASTONBURG in Wilcox Co.

PARKDALE Settlement at 330552NO-860644W in Coosa Co. on the Central of Georgia RR. Probably a subjectively descriptive name (1907 AL RR Commission report).

PARKER MOUNTAIN Mountain whose summit is at 323323NO864925W in Autauga Co. Named for the Parker Peach Orchard on top of the mountain, planted by Lazarus B. Parker I (DeVaughn; U.S.G.S., 1966 Base Maps).

PARKER SPRINGS Community at 310317NO864835W in Escambia Co. Named for the family who owned this site where mineral springs are located (Harris 1982, 127; *Official 1959 Alabama Highway Map*).

PARRISH Inc. town with PO at 334350NO871704W in Walker Co. Originally called HEWITT for the PO est. here in 1878, itself probably named for a local family. Also known as JONESBORO in honor of William R. Jones, the first postmaster. Renamed PARRISH to honor Alfred Parrish, a Philadelphia RR promoter. Parrish PO est. in 1890. Inc. in 1921 (Dombhart 106–07).

PARTRIDGE TOWN See SKIRUM in DeKalb Co.

PATAGAHATCHE RIVER See BLACK WARRIOR RIVER.

PATSALIGA CREEK [,pætsə'lækə] Stream rising at 320255NO861309W in Montgomery Co. and flowing into the Conecuh River at 312202NO863116W in Covington Co. Its tributary Little Patsaliga Creek rises at 320045NO860151W in Crenshaw Co. and joins the larger stream at 315646NO860700W. PAD-GEE-LIGAU in Benjamin Hawkins's "A Sketch of the Creek Country in 1798 and 1799" (62). The name means 'Pigeon Roost,' from Creek *pachi* 'pigeon' and *laiki* 'roost' (McMillan in Read 100; Read 51).

PATSBURG Settlement with discontinued PO at 314711NO861342W in Crenshaw Co. Name is a combination of *Pats*, for nearby Patsaliga Creek, and -*burg* 'town.' PO est. in 1887 (Harris 1982, 127).

PATTON'S HILL See SUMTERVILLE in Sumter Co.

PAUL Settlement with PO at 311912NO-864438W in Conecuh Co. Origin of name is unknown, but it is a personal one, possibly that of the apostle. PO est. in 1908.

PAYTON'S CREEK See CYPRESS CREEK in Lauderdale Co.

PEACHBURG Community with discontinued PO at 320949NO853727W in Bullock Co. First called FLORA in honor of Flora Redd, the wife of L. W. Redd, the town's leading merchant. Later given the name PEACHBURG because of the peach orchard of D. C. Turnipseed. Flora PO est. in 1876, Peachburg PO in 1909 (Harris 1982, 127).

PEA CREEK Stream rising at 315616NO-852539W in Barbour Co. and flowing into the Pea River at 314708NO853944W between Barbour Co. and Pike Co. Probably named for the river (Ellis 48; U.S.G.S., 1966 Base Maps).

PEARCES MILL Community with discontinued PO at 340715NO875012W in Marion

Co. Named for the mill owned by James P. Pearce, the first postmaster, appointed in 1873 (Lawler; "Record of Appointment of Postmasters").

PEA RIDGE   Community at 330914NO-865532W in Shelby Co. Named for the wild pea plants growing on the ridge upon which it is located (Tamarin; U.S.G.S., 1966 Base Maps).

PEA RIVER   Stream rising at 320815NO-853524W in Bullock Co. and flowing into the Choctawhatchee River at 310117NO855130W in Geneva Co. Probably named for the wild pea plants that once grew along its banks (U.S.G.S., 1966 Base Maps).

PEARSON   Settlement with discontinued PO at 330129NO871906W in Tuscaloosa Co. Named for the family who owned the land. PO est. in 1898 (Rich 1979, 433).

PECKERWOOD CREEK   Stream rising at 330730NO861743W in Coosa Co. and flowing into the Coosa River at 330635NO862851W in Talladega Co. OCHOCCOLA CR. on La Tourette's 1844 map. PECKERWOOD OR OCHOCCOLA CR. on E. A. Smith's 1891 map in Berney. *Ochoccola*, the Indian name that is no longer used, is derived from Creek *wiwa* or *oi-wa* 'water' and *chakala* 'woodpecker' (Read 52).

PEEKS CORNER   Settlement at 342335NO-855223W in DeKalb Co. Probably named for a local Peek family (U.S.G.S., 1966 Base Maps).

PEETES CORNER   Community at 344349NO865239W in Limestone Co. Named for Benjamin and Nancy Peete, who moved here c. 1830 from Hanover Co., VA (Edwards and Axford 173).

PELHAM   Inc. town with PO at 331708NO864836W in Shelby Co. Site of SHELBY COURTHOUSE, soon SHELBY-VILLE, the first co. seat, 1818–26. Later town located here was named for John Pelham, a major in the Confederate army from Calhoun Co. who was killed at Kelly's Ford, VA, in 1863. PO est. in 1873. Inc. in 1964 (Tamarin).

PELICAN BAY   Bay at 301348NO880512W in Mobile Co. between Dauphin Island and Baldwin Co. Probably an environmental name (U.S.G.S., 1966 Base Maps).

PELICAN ISLAND   Island in Pelican Bay at 301315NO880625W in Mobile Co. Probably named for the bay (U.S.G.S., 1966 Base Maps).

PELICAN POINT   Cape at 301452NO-880429W in Mobile Co. on Dauphin Island. Probably named for the bay (U.S.G.S., 1966 Base Maps).

PELL CITY   Inc. co. seat with PO at 333510NO861710W in St. Clair Co. Named for George H. Pell, the original promoter of the Pell City Iron and Land Co. PO est. in 1887. Inc. in 1891. Chosen to be the co. seat for the Southern Judicial District in 1902, but this action was not officially approved until 1907 after the state constitution was amended to allow two seats of justice in the same co. (Rich).

PENITENTIARY MOUNTAIN   Mountain whose summit is at 342608NO872018W in Lawrence Co. Named for a stagecoach stop built on the mountain in 1734 that also served as a penitentiary building for prisoners being transported to Tuscaloosa (Gentry 116).

PENNINGTON   Inc. town with PO at 321225NO880322W in Choctaw Co. Named for John Wesley Pennington, co. representative in the state legislature (1855–58). PO est. in 1883. Inc. in 1964 (Choctaw Co. Bicentennial Commission 19).

PENSACOLA JUNCTION   See FLOMA-TON in Escambia Co.

PENTON   Settlement with discontinued PO at 330023NO852756W in Chambers Co. Named for the Penton family who lived nearby. PO est. in 1892 (Dugas [Chambers Co.] 58).

PEPPERELL   ['pɛpərəl]   Settlement with PO at 323807NO852514W in Lee Co. Named for the Pepperell Manufacturing Co., a textile manufacturer that built a plant here in 1925. PO est. in 1971 (Harris 1982, 128).

PERDIDO   [pər'didə]   Settlement with PO on the Louisville and Nashville RR at 310027NO873738W in Baldwin Co. Probably named for the nearby river. Perdido Station PO est. in 1871, Perdido PO in 1910.

PERDIDO BAY   Bay at 302000NO872713W between Baldwin Co. and FL. The bay is said to have been named c. 1512 by one of Ponce de Leon's groups of explorers. The designation is the past participle form of the Spanish verb *perder* 'to lose' (Bush 70).

PERDIDO BEACH   Settlement with discontinued PO at 302026NO873018W in Baldwin Co. The beach upon which the town is located was probably named for the nearby bay. PO est. in 1909.

PERDIDO RIVER   Stream rising at

310150NO873543W in Escambia Co. and flowing between Baldwin Co., AL, and FL into Perdido Bay at 302700NO872313W. Probably named for the bay (U.S.G.S., 1966 Base Maps).

PERDUE HILL   Settlement with PO at 313050NO872936W in Monroe Co. After Thomas Gaillard moved his family away from Claiborne in 1855 to escape the malaria epidemic, he built here, on a hill, his house, later a summer resort that he named for the two Perdue brothers, prominent citizens of Claiborne. PO est. in 1876 (Dugas [Monroe Co.] 96).

PEROTE   ['pirot]   Settlement with PO at 315651NO854219W in Bullock Co. First called FULFORD'S CROSSROADS for Daniel Fulford, who had settled here in 1835; next known as MISSOURI, probably for the state, when the PO was est. Later named PEROTE by returning Mexican War soldiers for a fortress in Mexico. Missouri PO est. in 1837, Perote PO in 1852 (Harris 1982, 129).

PERRY COUNTY   Created by act of the AL territorial general assembly on Dec. 13, 1819. Bounded on the north by Bibb Co., on the east by Chilton Co., on the east and south by Dallas Co., and on the west by Marengo Co. and Hale Co. Named for Oliver Hazard Perry (1785–1819), the American naval commander who defeated the British on Lake Erie in the War of 1812. The co. seat was Perry Ridge, 1819–22; then Muckle's Ridge, soon renamed MARION, was chosen to replace it (Harder 321, 421).

PERRY RIDGE   Dead town about 6 miles northeast of Marion in Perry Co. William Ford and his sons, its first settlers, built a cabin, sawmill, and gristmill on the high ground here. When the settlement was chosen co. seat, it was probably named for the co. Served as co. seat, 1819–22 (Harris 1977, 68).

PERRYVILLE   Settlement with discontinued PO at 323700NO870651W in Perry Co. Probably named for the co. PO est. in 1839.

PERSIMMON CREEK   Stream rising at 315658NO863655W in Butler Co. and flowing into the Sepulga River at 313058NO864933W in Conecuh Co. Probably an environmental name (U.S.G.S., 1966 Base Maps).

PETERMAN   Settlement with PO on the Louisville and Nashville RR at 313504NO871534W in Monroe Co. Named for Allison E. Peterman, an agent of the RR and a resident of the co. PO est. in 1900 (Dugas [Monroe Co.] 96).

PETERMAN CREEK   Stream rising at 313625NO850841W in Henry Co. and joining Sandy Creek at 312802NO850831W. Probably named for a local family (U.S.G.S., 1966 Base Maps).

PETERSON   Settlement with PO at 331357NO872525W in Tuscaloosa Co. First called PETERSON CITY in honor of Charles M. Peterson, who purchased the land in 1903. When the Tuscaloosa Mineral RR (Louisville and Nashville) reached here in 1911, the station was named SHIRAS for Peter Shiras of Ottawa, KS, the only non-Tuscaloosan who had bought stock in the line. For a short while, the town was identified with both names, but by the time its PO was est. in 1914, PETERSON was preferred (Rich 1979, 435, 502).

PETERSVILLE   Settlement at 345119NO874130W in Lauderdale Co. Named for the Peters family who moved here from St. Florian c. 1912 (Sockwell).

PETREY   Inc. town with PO at 315055NO861228W in Crenshaw Co. Named for George Petrey, a local citizen. PO est. in 1887. Inc. in 1914 (Harris 1982, 129).

PHELAN   ['filǝn]   Settlement at 340759NO864902W in Cullman Co. Origin unknown; possibly a family name (U.S.G.S., 1966 Base Maps).

PHENIX CITY   Inc. co. seat with PO at 322815NO850003W in Russell Co. The older part of the town was once in GIRARD, the original seat of justice for the co. The newer settlement, first named BROWNEVILLE in honor of John Brown, a local judge, was inc. under that name in 1883. The RR station, however, had been named KNIGHTS STATION, probably for a local family, in 1891 by the Columbus and Western RR (Central of Georgia). When a PO was est. in 1884, it and the RR station were given the subjectively descriptive name LIVELY. In 1889 the PO and the settlement surrounding it became known as PHOENIX CITY for the Phoenix Mills across the Chattahoochee River in GA. When this newer settlement merged with what had been the northern part of GIRARD in 1923, PHENIX CITY was its officially adopted name. Chosen co. seat in 1935 (*Alabama: A Guide*, 339).

PHIL CAMPBELL   Inc. town with PO at 342103NO874223W in Franklin Co. Named for Philip Campbell, the contractor who built the Birmingham, Sheffield and Tennessee River RR through this area in 1886. L. M. Allen, one of the first settlers, had promised to name the town for Campbell if the latter built a spur track and depot here. PO est. in 1892. Inc. in 1915 (Knight 30).

PHOENIX CITY   See PHENIX CITY in Russell Co.

PICKENS   See PICKENSVILLE in Pickens Co.

PICKENS COUNTY   Created by the state general assembly on Dec. 19, 1820. Bounded on the north by Fayette Co. and Lamar Co., on the east by Greene Co. and Tuscaloosa Co., on the south by Sumter Co., and on the west by MS. Probably named for Andrew Pickens (1739–1817) of SC, a revolutionary war general who served at the Battle of Eutaw Springs, though some local historians believe the co. honors Israel Pickens, an early settler who later served as governor of the state (1821–25). The first co. seat was called PICKENS COURTHOUSE, later PICKENS, then PICKENSVILLE, 1820–30. The present one is Carrollton (Griffith 207; N. F. Brown 3).

PICKENSVILLE   Inc. town with discontinued PO at 331338NO881559W in Pickens Co. First named PICKENS COURTHOUSE, then PICKENS, and finally PICKENSVILLE for the co. Co. seat, 1820–30. Pickens Courthouse PO est. in 1823; Pickens PO in 1831; Pickensville PO in 1835. Inc. as PICKENSVILLE in 1835 (N. F. Brown 49).

PICKENSVILLE LAKE   See ALICEVILLE LAKE.

PICKWICK LAKE   Artificial lake formed by the impoundment of the Tennessee River with Pickwick Dam at 350409NO881501W in TN that extends to Wilson Dam between Lauderdale Co. and Colbert Co. in AL. Named for the dam, which received its designation in 1938 from the postmaster of the dam's PO, who had been reading *Pickwick Papers* by Charles Dickens (Sockwell).

PIEDMONT   Inc. town with PO at 335528NO853641W in Calhoun Co. Founded and named CROSS PLAINS by James Price in 1846, because of its situation on the edge of a plain where two important stagecoach roads intersected. Inc. as CROSS PLAINS in 1887, then as PIEDMONT, the name of the plateau on which it is located, in 1888. PO est. in 1971 (Jolly).

PIEDMONT SPRINGS   Settlement with discontinued PO at 335401NO854016W in Calhoun Co. Named for the resort hotel near the springs in this area that was opened in 1890 and closed in 1920. PO est. in 1890 (Jolly).

PIGEON CREEK   Stream rising at 315730NO863636W in Butler Co. and flowing into the Sepulga River at 312042NO864213W between Covington Co. and Conecuh Co. The environmental name refers to the wild pigeons once abundant in the area (Dugas [Butler Co.] 79; U.S.G.S., 1966 Base Maps).

PIGEON CREEK   Community with discontinued PO at 313927NO863026W in Butler Co. Named for the nearby creek. PO est. in 1856 (Dugas [Butler Co.] 79).

PIKE COUNTY   Created by act of the state general assembly on Dec. 17, 1821. Bordered on the north by Montgomery Co. and Bullock Co., on the east by Barbour Co., on the south by Coffee Co. and Dale Co., and on the west by Crenshaw Co. Named in honor of Zebulon M. Pike (1779–1813), the discoverer of Pike's Peak and U.S. army general who was killed in Canada in 1813. The co. seats have been Louisville, 1821–27; Monticello, 1827–38; and Troy, the present one, chosen in 1838 (M. B. Owen 1:497).

PIKE ROAD   Settlement with PO at

321703NO860611W in Montgomery Co. Name refers to the toll road linking Montgomery Co. and Bullock Co. that once passed through this area. PO est. in 1871 (Harris 1982, 130–31).

PIKEVILLE   Community at 344437NO-860219W in Jackson Co. Received its name because of its location at the head of a turnpike (Chambless; *Official 1983–84 Alabama Highway Map*).

PIKEVILLE   Dead town with discontinued PO 7 miles north of Guin in Marion Co. Probably named for the famous soldier and explorer Zebulon M. Pike (1779–1813). Co. seat, 1819–82. Gradually abandoned after the removal of the co. seat to Hamilton. PO est. in 1820 (Harris 1977, 97–98).

PILGRIM'S REST   See SOUTHSIDE in Etowah Co.

PINCHONY CREEK   [pɪnˈtʃonɪ]   Stream rising at 320104NO863807W in Lowndes Co. and joining Pintlalla Creek at 321328NO-862309W in Montgomery Co. PINCHOMA on La Tourette's 1844 map; PINCHONY on 1934 Rand McNally map. The first element seems to be derived from Creek *pin(wa)* 'turkey,' and the second seems to be a shortened form of *chuninitkita* 'to stoop while running' (Read 52–53).

PINCKARD   [ˈpɪŋkərd]   Inc. town with PO at 311841NO853311W in Dale Co. Formerly known as CROSS ROADS because of its location at the intersection of roads between Ozark and Midland City and Daleville and Headland. Later named for J. O. Pinckard, the town's first schoolteacher. PO est. in 1892. Inc. in 1893 (F. S. Watson 1968, 133–35).

PINE APPLE   Inc. town with PO at 315221NO865928W in Wilcox Co. Probably named for the many pine cones to be found here. PO est. in 1856. Inc. in 1872.

PINE BARREN CREEK   See PINE LOG CREEK in Baldwin Co.

PINE BARREN CREEK   Stream rising at 313213NO881634W in Butler Co. and flowing into the Alabama River between Dallas Co. and Wilcox Co. at 313918NO881202W. Name is probably descriptive of the barren lands covered with pine trees through which the creek flows (U.S.G.S., 1966 Base Maps).

PINE BRANCH   Community at 301353NO-874855W in Baldwin Co. between Little Lagoon and the Gulf of Mexico. Name is descriptive and environmental (Bush 71; *Official 1983–84 Alabama Highway Map*).

PINE DALE   Settlement at 345744NO-864939W in Limestone Co. Probably a descriptive and environmental name (U.S.G.S., 1966 Base Maps).

PINEDALE   Community at 321742NO-861419W in Montgomery Co. Named for the plantation owned by the Patterson family (*Official 1959 Alabama Highway Map*; Sartwell).

PINE GROVE   Settlement at 320209NO-853520W in Bullock Co. Probably named for the pines that once covered the area but were cut down in the 1850s (Harris 1982, 131).

PINE HILL   Inc. town with PO at 315846NO873517W in Wilcox Co. Name is descriptive of original location. PO est. in 1839. Inc. in 1895 (Harris 1982, 131).

PINE LEVEL   Settlement at 323501NO-862756W in Autauga Co. Named for Pine Level Branch, a small stream nearby (Biggs 37; *Official 1959 Alabama Highway Map*).

PINE LEVEL   See JACKSON in Clarke Co.

PINE LEVEL   Settlement with PO at 320404NO860335W in Montgomery Co. First called PINE TUCKY, probably because of its location on poor sandy soil covered with pines. Then renamed PINE LEVEL because the area is also wide and flat. PO est. in 1839 (*Alabama: A Guide*, 315).

PINE LOG CREEK   Stream rising at 310552NO873823W in Baldwin Co. and flowing into the Alabama River at 310552NO-873823W. PINE BARREN CREEK, a descriptive and environmental name, on H. S. Tanner's 1823 map. PINE LOG CREEK in 1835–39 "Baldwin Co. Private Land Grants." This name is descriptive of the practice of loggers of floating timber down the stream (Bush 71).

PINE ORCHARD   Community with PO at 313826NO870811W in Monroe Co. and Conecuh Co. Name is descriptive of the pine trees in the locality that appear to have been planted in an orchard. PO est. in 1879 (Harris 1982, 132).

PINE TUCKY   See PINE LEVEL in Montgomery Co.

PINEVILLE   See PUTNAM in Marengo Co.

PINEY CREEK   Stream rising in TN and flowing through Limestone Co. into Wheeler Lake of the Tennessee River at 343559NO-

865308W between Limestone Co. and Morgan Co. Probably a descriptive name (U.S.G.S., 1966 Base Maps).

PINEY GROVE   Settlement at 341800NO-870653W in Lawrence Co. Name is descriptive and environmental (Harris 1982, 132; *Official 1959 Alabama Highway Map*).

PINK   See KINSTON in Coffee Co.

PINKNEY CITY   See BLOSSBURG in Jefferson Co.

PINNACLE   See SOUTH VINEMONT in Cullman Co.

PINSON   Settlement with PO at 334120NO864100W in Jefferson Co. First known as HAGOOD'S CROSSROADS for Zachariah Hagood and his family, who moved here from SC. Name was changed to MOUNT PINSON, probably by horse traders from Pinson, TN, who passed through here on their way to and from the southern part of the state. Mount Pinson PO est. in 1837, Pinson PO in 1895 (Hagood 19; Harris 1982, 132).

PINTHTHLOCKO CREEK   See SWAMP CREEK in Coosa Co.

PINTLALLA CREEK   [pɪntˈlɑlə]   Stream rising at 315838NO861742W in Montgomery Co. and flowing into the Alabama River at 322035NO862950W between this co. and Lowndes Co. PILTH-LAU-LE in Benjamin Hawkins's "A Sketch of the Creek Country in 1798 and 1799" (85). The name seems to have been derived from Creek *pithlo* 'canoe' and a form of the verb meaning 'to pull' or 'to seize' that occurs in *halatas* 'I pull' or 'I seize.' Also known as MANACK'S CREEK in honor of Sam Manack (or Moniac), a part-Indian landowner (Harris 1982, 132; Swanton 1937, 214).

PIPER   Dead town with discontinued PO at 330522NO870229W in Bibb Co. Named for O. H. R. Piper of Memphis, later of Birmingham, who founded the Little Cahaba Coal Co. here c. 1901. PO, 1905–45 (Ellison 177).

PISGAH   Inc. town with PO at 344051NO-855052W in Jackson Co. Named for Mount Pisgah Baptist Church, founded c. 1870 and itself named for the mountain from which Moses viewed the Promised Land. PO est. in 1878. Inc. in 1947 (Kennamer 180).

PITTMAN   Community with discontinued PO at 331258NO852013W in Randolph Co.

Named for James F. Pittman, the first postmaster, appointed in 1891 ("Record of Appointment of Postmasters").

PITTSBORO   See PITTSVIEW in Russell Co.

PITTSBOROUGH   See DUDLEYVILLE in Tallapoosa Co.

PITTSVIEW   Settlement with PO at 321117NO850948W in Russell Co. Originally PITTSBORO, but name changed to avoid confusion with HURTSBORO. Named for Richard Pitts, the founder. PO est. in 1903 (A. K. Walker 1950, 354, 356).

PLANO   ['pleno]   Settlement with PO at 340651NO854339W in Cherokee Co. If named for Plano, TX, the term is the Spanish masculine adjective meaning 'level'; if not, it might be the Spanish masculine noun meaning 'plan' or 'map.' PO est. in 1877 (Harris 1982, 132).

PLANTERSVILLE   Settlement with PO at 323924NO865528W in Dallas Co. Name refers to the cotton planters in the area. PO est. in 1867 (Nelms).

PLANTERSVILLE   Community at 332211NO-861409W in Talladega Co. that grew up around Planters Institute in the 1850s. Name occurs frequently in a cotton-growing area (McMillan).

PLATEAU   Settlement with discontinued PO at 304410NO880350W in Mobile Co. Name is descriptive of the town's location. PO est. in 1899 (*Alabama: A Guide*, 359).

PLEASANT GAP   Settlement with discontinued PO at 335916NO853112W in Cherokee Co. A descriptive and environmental name. PO est. in 1847 (M. T. Stewart 1958, 1:54).

PLEASANT GROVE   Community at 325518NO854741W in Chilton Co. A subjectively descriptive name (Harris 1982, 133; *Official 1959 Alabama Highway Map*).

PLEASANT GROVE   Inc. town with PO at 332927NO865813W in Jefferson Co. Earlier identified with the humorously descriptive name FROG POND. Renamed for the Pleasant Grove Baptist Church. Inc. in 1934. PO est. in 1949 (Hagood 41).

PLEASANT GROVE   Community with discontinued PO at 330825NO875529W in Pickens Co. Subjectively descriptive name. PO est. in 1836 (N. F. Brown 49).

PLEASANT HILL   Settlement with discontinued PO at 320955NO865443W in Dallas Co. Subjectively descriptive name. PO est. in 1828 (C. H. Stewart 35).

PLEASANT HILL Community at 342639NO854954W in DeKalb Co. Subjectively descriptive name (Raughton 64; U.S.G.S., 1966 Base Maps).

PLEASANT SITE Settlement with discontinued PO at 343231NO880355W in Franklin Co. Subjectively descriptive name. PO est. in 1843 (Knight 31).

PLETCHER Settlement with discontinued PO at 324210NO864706W in Chilton Co. Originally called BROOKSON c. 1890 for A. M. Brookson, who helped grade the Mobile and Ohio RR. Name changed to PLETCHER in honor of E. Pletcher, who operated a sawmill here. Pletcher PO est. in 1898 (B. D. Roberts).

PLEVNA Settlement with discontinued PO at 345742NO862500W in Madison Co. Named for a city in Russia where a fortress important during the Russo-Turkish War of 1877 was located. PO est. in 1878 (Harris 1982, 133).

POARCH [port/] Community with discontinued PO at 310702NO873146W on part of a land grant in Escambia Co. and Baldwin Co. bestowed upon Lynn (Leonard) McGhee, a friendly Creek who had served as a guide for Andrew Jackson's forces during the Creek Indian War of 1813–14. His son Richard founded the settlement here, which was later named for the branch of the Creek Indians to which the McGhee family belonged. PO est. in 1905 (J. E. Hudgins; Waters 199–200).

POINT A LAKE Artificial lake formed by the impoundment of the Conecuh River at 312110NO863213W in Covington Co. Its name probably refers to the fact that the dam is the first of two in this co. on the Conecuh River (U.S.G.S., 1966 Base Maps).

POINT CLEAR Settlement with PO at 302826NO875509W in Baldwin Co. Named for nearby Great Point Clear. PO est. in 1877 (Bush 91).

POLECAT CREEK Stream rising at 324435NO872328W in Perry Co. and joining Big Bush Creek at 324504NO873317W in Hale Co. The name, a Southern dialect term for skunk, is probably an environmental one (U.S.G.S., 1966 Base Maps).

POLK Community with discontinued PO at 321620NO865319W in Dallas Co. Named for James K. Polk (1795–1849), president of the U.S. (1845–49). PO est. in 1891 (Harris 1982, 133).

POLLARD Inc. town with discontinued PO at 310137NO871025W in Escambia Co. Founded c. 1860 and named for Charles T. Pollard, the president of the Montgomery and West Point RR. Though burned by Union troops in 1865, the settlement was rebuilt after the Civil War and served as the first co. seat, 1868–80. PO est. in 1865. Inc. in 1895 (Moore 312).

POND CREEK Stream rising at 311543NO882555W in Washington Co. and flowing into the Escatawpa River at 310855NO882051W. Probably a descriptive and environmental name (U.S.G.S., 1966 Base Maps).

PONDELASSA See ROCKFORD in Coosa Co.

PONDS, THE See BELLEVILLE in Conecuh Co.

PONDVILLE Settlement with discontinued PO at 325418NO871840W in Bibb Co. Named for the local pond where a sawmill was once in operation. PO est. in 1876 (Ellison 196).

POOR CREEK Stream rising at 313636NO851653W in Henry Co. and flowing into the East Fork of the Choctawhatchee River at 312859NO852201W. Probably a humorously descriptive name (U.S.G.S., 1966 Base Maps).

POPE Community with discontinued PO at 320346NO873728W in Marengo Co. Named for the first postmaster, Hubert C. Pope, appointed in 1938 ("Record of Appointment of Postmasters").

POPLAR HEAD See DOTHAN in Houston Co.

POPLAR SPRING See FORT DALE in Butler Co.

POPLAR SPRINGS Settlement at 340157NO872346W in Winston Co. Founded c. 1900. A descriptive and environmental name (Gant).

PORT BIRMINGHAM See BIRMINGPORT in Jefferson Co.

PORTERSVILLE Settlement with discontinued PO at 341916NO854915W in DeKalb Co. Originally PORTER TOWN, it was named for a local family. Co. seat, 1876–77. PO est. in 1852 (Raughton 64).

PORTERSVILLE   See CODEN in Mobile Co.

PORTERSVILLE BAY   Bay above Mississippi Sound at 322000NO881500W in Mobile Co. Probably named for the town Portersville, now known as CODEN (D'Anville, 1788 map).

PORTER TOWN   See PORTERSVILLE in DeKalb Co.

PORT SMITH   See RIVERTON in Colbert Co.

POTASH   Community with discontinued PO at 331638NO852107W in Randolph Co. Probably an environmental name referring to a potassium compound found in the area. PO est. in 1890.

POTATOE CREEK   See CHEAHA CREEK.

POWELL CREEK   Stream rising at 322711NO873543W in Marengo Co. and joining Chickasaw Bogue at 321937NO874543W. Named for a local family (Johnson and Alexander 23; U.S.G.S., 1966 Base Maps).

POWELLS CROSSROADS   Inc. town with discontinued PO at 341711NO854458W in DeKalb Co. Also known as POWELL. Named for D. W. Powell. PO est. in 1898. Inc. in 1962 (Raughton 65).

POWERS   Community with discontinued PO at 325756NO873921W in Hale Co. Probably named for a local family. PO est. in 1886.

POWHATAN   ['pauhətæn]   Settlement with PO at 333526NO870631W in Jefferson Co. Named for the famous Indian chief, whose name, according to Gannett, means 'at the falls.' PO est. in 1919 (Gannett 1905, 252; Hagood 12).

PRACO   ['preko]   Settlement with PO at 333649NO870645W in Jefferson Co. The designation is an acronym for *Pratt Co.*, an abbreviated form of the name of the Pratt Consolidated Coal Co. PO est. in 1931 (Hagood 10).

PRAIRIE   Settlement with PO at 320914NO872624W in Wilcox Co. Although the name is descriptive of this town's location, it may have been borrowed from the nearby river town Prairie Bluff. PO est. in 1838 (Harris 1982, 134).

PRAIRIEVILLE   Community with discontinued PO at 323036NO874140W in Hale Co. Named MACON by early settlers from NC,

either for Nathaniel Macon (1757–1837), U.S. senator from that state (1815–28), or for the local Macon family, who were probably related to the senator. Also known as PRAIRIEVILLE because of the black prairie land where it was located. Prairieville PO est. in 1832; Macon PO in 1833; Prairieville PO again in 1902 (W. Smith).

PRATTS   Community on the Central of Georgia RR at 314951NO853035W in Barbour Co. Founded as PRATTS STATION c. 1890. Named for the local Pratt family (Ellis 50).

PRATTVILLE   Inc. co. seat at 322750NO862735W in Autauga Co. Developed around Pratt's Mills, the cotton gin manufacturing plant (mill) of Daniel Pratt (1799–1873) built here in 1833. Named PRATTVILLE when the PO was est. in 1846. Became co. seat in 1868. Inc. in 1872 (Biggs 38).

PRESTWICK   Settlement with discontinued PO at 312710NO875758W in Washington Co. Named for Prestwick, England, by the British Tory families who moved here from VA in the 1770s. PO est. in 1904 (Matte 281).

PRICES   Settlement at 335325NO854145W in Calhoun Co. First called SAVAGES in 1893 for a local family. Renamed in 1899 for the family of James H. Price, an early settler in the area (Jolly).

PRICEVILLE   Inc. town with discontinued PO at 343130NO865341W in Morgan Co. Named for Thomas Price, who settled in AL in the 1820s and served as engrossing clerk of the state house of representatives (1837–39). PO est. in 1879 (Ackley 39).

PRICHARD   Inc. town with PO on the Gulf, Mobile and Ohio RR at 304419NO880444W in Mobile Co. Founded as PRICHARD STATION and named for Cleveland Prichard, who, in 1879, had bought the land on which the town was built and was the first postmaster, appointed in 1880. Inc. in 1925 (M. B. Owen 1:487).

PRINCETON   Settlement with PO at 345036NO861435W in Jackson Co. First called BIRMINGHAM for the city in England. Name was later changed to PRINCETON, probably for the city in NJ. Birmingham PO est. in 1845, Princeton PO in 1848 (Kennamer 136, 143).

PROPELL   See VINCENT in Shelby Co.

PROSPECT   Settlement with discontinued PO at 335557NO872645W in Walker Co.

Probably a descriptive and environmental name that also has inspirational connotations. PO est. in 1888.

PROSPECT RIDGE See ORION in Pike Co.

PROVIDENCE Settlement with discontinued PO at 341621NO864844W in Cullman Co. First named NEEDMORE, according to tradition, during a period of hard times. Later known as PROVIDENCE, an inspirational and symbolic designation. Providence PO est. in 1891 (Harris 1982, 120).

PROVIDENCE Inc. town at 322101NO874625W in Marengo Co. Named for Providence Baptist Church. Inc. in 1971 (Johnson and Alexander 23).

PULL TIGHT Settlement at 340116NO874705W in Marion Co. Although its origin is unknown, the name may be an inspirational one, referring to the industry and cooperation of the town's residents (U.S.G.S., 1966 Base Maps).

PUNTA CLARA See GREAT POINT CLEAR in Baldwin Co.

PUPPY CREEK Stream rising at 310245NO881503W in Mobile Co. and flowing into the Escatawpa River at 305917NO882427W. Origin unknown, but it might be an animal-incident name (U.S.G.S., 1966 Base Maps).

PURDY, LAKE Artificial lake formed by the impoundment of the Little Cahaba River at 332735NO864009W in Shelby Co. Named for a man from PA who headed the dam-building project in 1910 (Hagood 27).

PURSLEY CREEK Stream rising at 315405NO871354W in Wilcox Co. and flowing into the Alabama River at 315447NO872248W. Probably named for a local family (U.S.G.S., 1966 Base Maps).

PUSHMATAHA [ˌpuʃmə'tɔhɔ] Settlement with discontinued PO at 321136NO882112W in Choctaw Co. Named for the noted Choctaw chief who served under Andrew Jackson in the Creek Indian War of 1813–14. His name is derived from either Choctaw *apushi* 'sapling,' *im* 'for him,' and *alhtaha* 'ready' or *apushi* 'sapling' and *imalhtaha* 'prepared' or 'qualified.' PO est. in 1848 (Read 54).

PUSS CUSS CREEK ['puskəs] Stream rising at 314543NO882554W in Choctaw Co. and joining Okatuppa Creek at 315359NO882222W. POOSCOOS PANHA on Purcell's map, c. 1770. Name is derived from Choctaw

puskus 'child' plus *paya* 'crying' (Read 54–55).

PUTNAM Settlement with PO at 320121NO880153W in Marengo Co. Originally identified with the environmental name PINEVILLE, but because there was already a Pineville PO in the state in 1876 when this town applied for its PO, both settlement and PO were named PUTNAM for a local family said to be related to the revolutionary war general Israel Putnam (1718–1790) (Johnson and Alexander 24).

PUTNAM MOUNTAIN Mountain whose summit is at 345305NO861752W in Jackson Co. Named for a local family (Melancon; U.S.G.S., 1966 Base Maps).

PYRITON ['paɪrətən] Settlement with discontinued PO at 332147NO855002W in Clay Co. PYRITON is probably a combination of *pyrite*, the name of a mineral known as "fool's gold" that consists of iron disulfide, and *-ton* 'town.' PO est. in 1903.

QUINTON Settlement with PO at 334019NO870400W in Walker Co. Name may be a personal one or possibly a combination of the Spanish masculine modifier *quinto* 'fifth' and *-ton* 'town.' PO est in 1906 (Gant).

RABBIT CREEK Stream rising at 314029NO874717W in Clarke Co. and joining Bassett Creek at 313101NO875013W. Probably an environmental name (U.S.G.S., 1966 Base Maps).

RABBIT TOWN Settlement at 341647NO861530W in Marshall Co. Possibly an environmental name (U.S.G.S., 1966 Base Maps).

RABUN Settlement with discontinued PO at 310136NO874330W in Baldwin Co. Said to have honored an early family whose name was *Rabon*. PO est. in 1916 (Bush 73).

RADFORD Settlement with discontinued PO at 323521NO871200W in Perry Co. Originally RADFORDVILLE. Named for the family of William Radford, who settled here in 1820. Radfordville PO est. in 1846, Radford PO in 1880 (Harris 1982, 136).

RADFORDVILLE See RADFORD in Perry Co.

RAGGED POINT Cape on Mobile Bay at 303510NO875457W in Baldwin Co. Probably a descriptive name (U.S.G.S., 1966 Base Maps).

RAGLAND Inc. town with PO at 334440NO860921W in St. Clair Co. Settled in

1833 by families from TN. Originally called TROUT CREEK for the nearby stream named for the kind of fish seen in it. Renamed RAGLAND for one of the owners of the Sims and Ragland Mining Co. of Talladega. Trout Creek PO est. in 1849, Ragland PO in 1887. Inc. in 1899 (Rich).

RAINBOW CITY   Inc. town with PO at 335717NO860231W in Etowah Co. Area first called COOSA BEND because of its location on a bend in the Coosa River. Until it was inc. in 1950, the settlement was known as MORGAN'S CROSSROADS for a local family. Present name is probably a subjectively descriptive and symbolic one. PO est. in 1971 (Jolly).

RAINS   CREEK   Stream   rising   at 305900NO874546W in Baldwin Co. and flowing into the Tensaw River at 305747NO-875235W. RAINS is a misspelling of *Rane's*, the possessive form of the name of Cornelius and Prudence Rane, owners of the land during the early 1880s (Bush 73).

RAINSVILLE   Inc. town with PO at 342939NO855052W in DeKalb Co. Named for Will Rains, who built the first store here in 1907. PO est. in 1954. Inc. in 1956 (Landmarks 103).

RALEIGH   See KIRK in Pickens Co.

RALPH   Settlement with PO at 330231NO-874608W in Tuscaloosa Co. Originally called HICKMAN for William P. Hickman, the first postmaster, appointed in 1867. Renamed for either Ralph Stewart, the eldest son of William L. Stewart, the first postmaster of Ralph PO, appointed in 1900, or for William Stewart's wife, Kathleen Ralf Stewart (Rich 1979, 279, 455).

RAMER   Settlement with PO at 320301NO-861317W in Montgomery Co. Originally known as ATHENS, but when the town applied for its PO in 1851, there already being an Athens PO in the state, it was given the name of the nearby creek (Freeman).

RAMER   CREEK   Stream   rising   at 320333NO861132W in Montgomery Co. and joining Catoma Creek at 321552NO861506W. Probably named for John Ramer, an early settler (Harris 1982, 136; U.S.G.S., 1966 Base Maps).

RANBURNE   Inc. town with PO at 333122NO852041W in Cleburne Co. Originally called LOST CREEK for the nearby stream where an Indian child had been lost.

Name later changed to RANBURNE, a blend of the names of Randolph Co. and Cleburne Co. Ranburne PO est. in 1899. Inc. in 1957 (Harris 1982, 136).

RANDOLPH   Settlement with PO at 325358NO865439W in Bibb Co. Probably named for Randolph Co., NC, the former home of many of its early settlers. PO est. in 1839 (Abrams 191).

RANDOLPH COUNTY   Created by act of the state general assembly on Dec. 18, 1832. Bordered on the north by Cleburne Co., on the east by GA, on the south by Chambers Co. and Tallapoosa Co., and on the west by Clay Co. Named for John Randolph (1773–1833), the U.S. senator from VA (1825–27). The co. seat was Hedgeman Triplett's Ferry until 1835 when Wedowee, the present one, was chosen (Harder 451).

RANDONS   CREEK   Stream   rising   at 312919NO872227W in Monroe Co. and flowing into the Alabama River at 312540NO-873414W. Named for John Randon, who owned the land through which the creek flows and who operated a ferry across the Alabama River in 1813 (Dugas [Monroe Co.] 98).

RANGE   Settlement with PO at 311845NO-871408W in Conecuh Co. The station for the Louisville and Nashville RR was called DEER RANGE, probably descriptive of the surrounding hunting land. The town was probably   given   the   shortened   name, RANGE, for the station. PO est. in 1888 (U.S.G.S., 1966 Base Maps).

RASH   Community with discontinued PO at 345226NO855342W in Jackson Co. Named for William Rash, a local resident. Also the site of Coffey's Store, a business operated by a local family. PO est. in 1901 (Melancon).

RATTLESNAKE   MOUNTAIN   Mountain whose summit is at 334618NO853623W in Cleburne Co. Probably an environmental name (U.S.G.S., 1966 Base Maps).

RAWHIDE   See CLOVERDALE in Lauderdale Co.

RAWLINGSVILLE   See CRYSTAL LAKE in DeKalb Co.

READ'S LEVEL   See RED LEVEL in Covington Co.

REBECCA MOUNTAINS   See TALLA-DEGA MOUNTAINS in Talladega Co.

RED BANK   Settlement on the banks of the Tennessee River at 344602NO872212W in Lawrence Co. Probably a descriptive and en-vironmental name (*Official 1959 Alabama Highway Map*).

RED BAY   Inc. town with PO where state highways 19 and 24 intersect at 342623NO-880827W in Franklin Co. First called VIN-CENTS CROSSROADS for a local family. Renamed by Edward W. Waldrop and Billy Stamphill for the red berries of the bay bushes in the area. PO est. in 1888. Inc. in 1907 (Knight 33).

RED CREEK   Stream rising at 314526NO-882337W in Choctaw Co. and flowing out of the state at 313456NO882805W into MS. Name is probably descriptive of the clay bed of the creek (U.S.G.S., 1966 Base Maps).

REDEMPTION   See CULLOMBURG in Choctaw Co.

RED HILL   Settlement at 324106NO-855635W in Elmore Co. Probably a descrip-tive and environmental name (U.S.G.S., 1966 Base Maps).

RED LEVEL   Inc. town with PO at 312425NO863644W in Covington Co. Area settled in the 1820s. First called READ'S LEVEL for the narrow level tract of land once owned by James Read; now known as RED LEVEL. Read's Level PO est. in 1857, Red Level PO in 1876. Inc. in 1901 (W. D. Ward 160–61).

REDMAN   See PAINT ROCK in Jackson Co.

RED MOUNTAIN   Mountain whose sum-mit is at 335948NO861234W in Etowah Co. Probably a descriptive and environmental name, it has been in use since the 1850s (Jolly).

RED ROCK   Settlement at 344152NO-875150W in Colbert Co. On Bacon's 1895 map. Named for the large red sandstone ridge nearby (Sockwell).

RED VALLEY   See BROWNVILLE in Tuscaloosa Co.

REECE CITY   Inc. town with PO at 340420NO860200W in Etowah Co. Hill PO (origin of name unknown) est. here in 1884.

Both it and the settlement renamed REECE-VILLE for a local family in 1903. Inc. as REECE CITY in 1956 (Jolly).

REECEVILLE   See REECE CITY in Etowah Co.

REEDY CREEK   Stream   rising   at 312625NO874835W in Clarke Co. and flowing into the Alabama River at 312202NO-874459W. Name is probably descriptive of the reeds growing along its banks (U.S.G.S., 1966 Base Maps).

REELTOWN   Settlement with discon-tinued PO at 323613NO854819W in Tal-lapoosa Co. *Reel* is a misspelling of *Real*, the last name of James Patrick and Phillip O'Real from Ireland when they dropped the *O* shortly after settling near here. Reeltown PO est. in 1854. Thaddeus PO, named for Thad-deus P. Webster, the postmaster, was est. here in 1880. The town also was known as THAD-DEUS, 1880–1902. Name changed back to REELTOWN after 1902 (Dugas [Tallapoosa Co.] 87).

REFORM   ['ri,fɔrm; rɪ'fɔrm]   Inc. town with PO at 332242NO880055W in Pickens Co. The traditional explanation of the name is that an itinerant preacher refused to return to the town until its residents had reformed. PO est. in 1841. Inc. in 1898 (N. F. Brown 51).

REMBERT   Community with discontinued PO at 321304NO875211W in Marengo Co. Named for the family of Caleb Rembert, who settled here in the 1830s. Also known as REMBERT HILLS. Rembert PO est. in 1882 (W. Smith).

REMLAP   Settlement   with   PO   at 334900NO863603W in Blount Co. The first postmaster, James W. Palmer, appointed in 1882, wanted to name the town for himself, but because his brother Perry had already founded Palmer in Jefferson Co., James gave his town their last name spelled backwards (Sartwell).

RENDALIA   Community with discon-tinued PO on the Anniston and Atlantic RR (Louisville and Nashville) at 331903NO-860926W in Talladega Co. Originally known as REYNOLDS STATION in honor of O. M. Reynolds, local landowner and son of Walker Reynolds (1799–1871), an early settler. The name proposed to the PO Dept. was REYNOLDALIA, but this was shortened to RENDALIA when the PO was est. in 1884 (McMillan).

RENFROE Settlement with discontinued PO at 332552NO861206W in Talladega Co. Named by D. M. and D. W. Rogers, who built a sawmill here for J. J. D. Renfroe (1821–1888), a local Baptist minister. PO est in 1880 (McMillan).

REPTON Inc. town with PO on the Louisville and Nashville RR at 312432NO-871421W in Conecuh Co. Possibly named for a local family. PO est. in 1881. Inc. in 1899.

REPUBLIC Settlement with PO at 333604NO865327W in Jefferson Co. First called WARNER for the Warner Mines. Renamed for the Republic Steel Corporation. Warner Mines PO est. in 1900, Republic PO in 1903 (Hagood 10).

REPUBLICVILLE See JACKSON in Clarke Co.

REUTERSVILLE See FLOMATON in Escambia Co.

REYNOLDS SATION See RENDALIA in Talladega Co.

RICE CREEK Stream rising at 324102NO-871948W in Perry Co. and flowing into the Cahaba River at 323314NO871416W. Possibly named for the wild rice once growing on its banks (England; U.S.G.S., 1966 Base Maps).

RICHARDSON STATION See CORTELYOU in Washington Co.

RICHMOND Dead town once located 10 miles east of Newton in Dale Co. First known as WIGGINS SPRINGS for springs probably honoring a local family. Later named for the city in VA. First co. seat of Henry Co., 1819–24. When the area where it was located became a part of Dale Co. in 1824, it served as the seat of justice for this co. until 1827 (Harris 1977, 101).

RICHMOND Settlement with discontinued PO at 320650NO870318W in Dallas Co. During the latter 1820s known as WARRENTON, possibly in honor of the local Warr family. The name was changed to RICHMOND when the PO was est. in 1840 to avoid confusion with a Warrenton PO already in the state. The new name was chosen because a number of its early residents had come from Richmond Co. on Staten Island, NY (Nelms).

RIDERVILLE Community with discontinued PO at 324038NO865553W in Chilton Co. Formerly a large lumbering center, it was probably named for the first postmaster,

Noah Rider, appointed in 1897 ("Record of Appointment of Postmasters"; B. D. Roberts).

RIDERWOOD Settlement with discontinued PO at 315628NO864942W. Named for a Mr. Rider, the president of the E. E. Jackson Lumber Co., operating here during the 1840s (Choctaw Co. Bicentennial Commission 2, 19).

RIDGEVILLE Community with discontinued PO at 315628NO864942W. Ernest's Store, operated by James Ernest, was located here during the 1820s. The settlement was given a name descriptive of its site, an 8-mile stretch of high land. Ridgeville PO est. in 1834 (Dugas [Butler Co.] 139).

RIDGEVILLE Inc. town c. 2 miles north of Attalla in Etowah Co. An all-black settlement with a descriptive and environmental name, it was inc. in 1968 (Jolly).

RILEY Settlement with discontinued PO at 314334NO870734W in Monroe Co. Named for a family from SC who settled in this area. PO est. in 1882 (Dugas [Monroe Co.] 96).

RINGGOLD Settlement with discontinued PO at 342002NO853252W in Cherokee Co. Probably named in honor of Samuel Ringgold, the first American officer killed in the Mexican War, at Palo Alto in 1846. PO est. in 1848 (Harris 1982, 139).

RIO DEL ESPIRITU SANTO See MOBILE RIVER in Mobile Co.

RIPLEY Settlement with discontinued PO at 344543NO870715W in Limestone Co. Probably named for the first postmaster, Samuel G. Ripley, appointed in 1880 ("Record of Appointment of Postmasters").

RIVER FALLS Inc. town with PO at 312110NO863221W in Covington Co. This once-important lumber town was named for a nearby waterfall in the Conecuh River. PO est. in 1871. Inc. in 1901 (Harris 1982, 139).

RIVER HILL See SALITPA in Clarke Co.

RIVERSIDE Inc. town with PO at 333622NO861216W in St. Clair Co. Name is descriptive of the settlement's location on the west bank of the Coosa River. PO est. in 1883. Inc. in 1891 (Rich).

RIVERTON Settlement at 345250NO-880436W in Colbert Co. Community first called PORT SMITH because it was a landing on the Tennessee River operated by a Mr. Smith; then CHICKASAW for the Indian tribe in the region. Finally, Alfred Parrish of Philadelphia bought the land around the port and laid out the town, giving it the descriptive and environmental name RIVERTON. Port Smith PO est. in 1846; Chickasaw PO in 1851; and Riverton PO in 1890 (Sockwell).

RIVER VIEW Settlement with PO at 324720NO850842W in Chambers Co. Name is descriptive of the view of the Chattahoochee River from the hill where the town is located. PO est. in 1890 (Dugas [Chambers Co.] 58).

RIVERVIEW Inc. town at 310130NO-870415W in Escambia Co. Name is descriptive of town's location overlooking the Conecuh River. Inc. in 1967 (Waters 291).

RIVIÈRE DE L'ILE AUX OIES See FOWL RIVER in Mobile Co.

RIVIÈRE DES ALIBAMONS See ALABAMA RIVER.

ROANOKE Inc. town with PO at 330904NO852220W in Randolph Co. During the 1830s identified as HIGH PINE, a descriptive and environmental designation; next named ROANOKE for the home of John Randolph of VA, the statesman for whom the co. was named. Briefly during the 1840s known as CHULAFINEE, from Creek *chuli* 'pine' and *fina* 'footlog'; then renamed ROANOKE. Roanoke PO est. in 1839; Chulafinee PO in 1842; Roanoke PO again in 1845. Inc. in 1890 (M. B. Owen 1:499).

ROBA ['robə] Settlement with PO at 321438NO853539W in Macon Co. Origin of name unknown. PO est. in 1895.

ROBBINSVILLE See NIXBURG in Coosa Co.

ROBERTSDALE Inc. town with PO at 303313NO874243W in Baldwin Co. Named for B. F. Roberts, an official of the Southern Plantation Development Co., founder of the settlement. PO est. in 1905. Inc. in 1921 (Bush 75).

ROBINSON CREEK Stream rising at 314415NO870454W in Monroe Co. and joining Big Flat Creek at 314226NO871919W. Named for a local family (U.S.G.S., 1966 Base Maps; Waters 201).

ROBINSON SPRINGS Settlement with discontinued PO at 323042NO862236W in Elmore Co. Named for springs that probably honored a local family. PO est. in 1884.

ROBINSONVILLE Community with dis-

continued PO at 310340NO872618W in Escambia Co. Named for a family who moved here from Monroe Co. PO est. in 1904 (Waters 201).

ROBJOHN ['rɑb,dʒɑn] Settlement with discontinued PO at 321250NO880738W in Choctaw Co. Name is a blend of the first names of two local businessmen, Robert Edwards and John Hodges. PO est. in 1888 (Choctaw Co. Bicentennial Commission 12, 19).

ROCK CASTLE CREEK See DAVIS CREEK in Tuscaloosa Co.

ROCK CITY Settlement at 335904NO-874231W in Marion Co. Name is probably descriptive of town's location (*Official 1959 Alabama Highway Map*).

ROCK CREEK Descriptive and environmental name for the following streams.
1. Stream rising at 343619NO875352W in Colbert Co. and joining Bear Creek at 343935NO880534W. BIG ROCK CREEK on Tuomey's 1849 map (Sockwell).
2. Stream rising at 341748NO870441W in Cullman Co. and joining Long Branch at 335933NO870854W in Winston Co. (U.S.G.S., 1966 Base Maps).

ROCK CREEK Community at 343548NO-875500W in Colbert Co. On J. H. Colton's 1878 map. Named for the nearby creek (Sockwell).

ROCKDALE Settlement with discontinued PO at 332046NO865841W in Jefferson Co. Probably a descriptive and environmental name. PO est. in 1846.

ROCKFORD Inc. co. seat with PO at 325322NO861311W in Coosa Co. First named PONDELASSA for Ebenezer Pond, an early resident. Then given its present descriptive and environmental name. Pondelassa PO est. in 1834; eight months later, Rockford PO. Became co. seat in 1835. Inc. in 1860 (Brannon 1930, 3; Brannon 1932, 3).

ROCKLAND See HAYDEN in Blount Co.

ROCKLEDGE Community at 340521NO-860646W in Etowah Co. Its descriptive and environmental name has been in use since the 1940s (Jolly).

ROCK MILLS Settlement with PO at 330935NO851715W in Randolph Co. A lumbering center, it developed around Protho's Mills. The town's name, ROCK MILLS, is for nearby Rock Creek and the mills. PO est. in 1847 (Harris 1982, 140).

ROCK RUN Settlement with discontinued PO at 340140NO852943W in Cherokee Co. An iron foundry here was destroyed by the Union army during the Civil War but was rebuilt c. 1879. PO, est. in 1883, was first called BASS, probably for the operator of the foundry; two months later, name was changed to ROCK RUN for a nearby stream (Harris 1982, 140).

ROCK SPRINGS Community at 320442NO882159W in Choctaw Co. Probably a descriptive and environmental name (U.S.G.S., 1966 Base Maps).

ROCK SPRINGS See ROXANA in Lee Co.

ROCKVILLE Community with discontinued PO at 312512NO875033W in Clarke Co. Named for the Rockville Academy, founded in the 1830s and closed in 1938. PO est. in 1900 (Clarke Co. Historical Society 308).

ROCKWOOD Settlement at 342718NO874705W in Franklin Co. Given its descriptive and environmental name by T. L. Fossick, who came here from England and founded a limestone quarry (Knight 33).

ROCKY CREEK Stream rising at 314835NO864531W in Butler Co. and joining Persimmon Creek at 313505NO864258W. Probably a descriptive and environmental name (U.S.G.S., 1966 Base Maps).

ROCKY HEAD Settlement with discontinued PO at 313405NO854607W in Dale Co. Originally founded 3 miles south of its present location at the head of Claybank Creek. Moved here shortly after the Civil War. Name is descriptive of its former site. PO est. in 1855 (F. S. Watson 1968, 136).

RODENTOWN Settlement with discontinued PO at 341404NO860101W in DeKalb Co. Named for Billy Roden, a local store owner. PO est. in 1874 (Raughton 69).

ROETON ['rotən] Settlement at 313551NO855005W in Coffee Co. Possibly named for a local resident. PO est. in 1901.

ROGERS Settlement with PO at 342029NO860529W in DeKalb Co. Named for Joel E. Rogers, the first postmaster, appointed in 1891 ("Record of Appointment of Postmasters").

ROGERSVILLE Inc. town at 344932NO871741W in Lauderdale Co. Named for a trader, either John or Samuel Rogers, who settled in this area in 1820. Inc. in 1858 (Sockwell).

ROME Community with discontinued PO at 310830NO864008W in Covington Co. Probably named for the town in GA that took its designation from the city in Italy. PO est. in 1871 (Harder 466).

ROMULUS Community with discontinued PO at 330851NO874507W in Tuscaloosa Co. Probably named for the legendary founder and first king of Rome, Italy. PO est. in 1835 (Rich 1979, 473).

ROOSEVELT CITY Inc. town with PO at 332622NO865559W in Jefferson Co. Probably named for Franklin Delano Roosevelt (1882–1945), president of the U.S. (1933–45). Inc. in 1967. PO est. in 1971 (Whiting).

ROSA Inc. town with discontinued PO at 335926NO863048W in Blount Co. Named by Ellis Bynum, the first postmaster, appointed in 1898, for his friend Rosa Honey, who lived in the Mt. Moriah area. Inc. in 1969 (Blount Co. Historical Society 84–86).

ROSA HILL Settlement with discontinued PO at 312657NO862022W in Covington Co. Might be either a personal or a descriptive and environmental name. PO est. in 1853.

ROSALIE Settlement with discontinued PO at 344159NO854607W in Jackson Co. Said to have been named for a relative of the first postmaster, David R. Garrin, appointed in 1890 (Chambless).

ROSEBORO Community at 345903NO862409W in Madison Co. Name is a combination of *rose* and *-boro*, but whether *rose* is a personal name or the designation for a flower is unknown (U.S.G.S., 1966 Base Maps).

ROSEBUD See MALCOLM in Washington Co.

ROSEBUD Settlement with discontinued PO at 315628NO870813W in Wilcox Co. Probably a descriptive and environmental name. PO est. in 1876.

ROSEWOOD Community with discontinued PO at 334700NO852602W in Cleburne Co. Probably a descriptive and environmental name. PO est. in 1858.

ROSSER Community with discontinued PO at 321822NO882326W in Sumter Co. Named for Elijah Rosser and his family, who settled here in 1831. PO est. in 1880 (Foscue 56).

ROUGH LOG See NEEDMORE in Pike Co.

ROUND MOUNTAIN Settlement with discontinued PO at 341256NO854102W in Cherokee Co. located on a southeastern spur of

Lookout Mountain called ROUND MOUN-TAIN. The Round Mountain Iron Furnace, built by Moses Stroup, was in operation here during the 1850s. PO est. in 1873. Largely inundated by Weiss Lake in the 1960s (Cherokee Co. Historical Society 1:209).

ROUND MOUNTAIN Mountain whose summit is at 332156NO871601W in Tuscaloosa Co. Descriptive name (Rich 1979, 476; U.S.G.S. Topographic Maps, 1934 Searles Quad.).

ROWLAND See TANNER in Limestone Co.

ROXANA Settlement with discontinued PO at 324113NO854009W in Lee Co. First given the descriptive and environmental name ROCK SPRINGS. However, because a PO in the state already had this name when Samuel A. Burns, the first postmaster, submitted his application, he devised a combination of a "phonetic spelling" of the word *rocks* and *Anna*, the name of his wife, for its designation (Harris 1982, 141).

ROY See FRISCO CITY in Monroe Co.

ROYAL Settlement with discontinued PO at 340419NO863008W in Blount Co. Name refers to the "battle royal" that took place nearby during the Civil War between the Union troops under the command of A. D. Streight and the Confederate forces under the command of Nathan Bedford Forrest. PO est. in 1890 (Weaver).

RUHAMA See DOG TOWN in DeKalb Co.

RURAL HOME Settlement at 314959NO-860855W in Pike Co. Originally named WINGARD for William Wingard (1797–1872), an early property owner. The current name, a descriptive one with symbolic overtones, dates from the 1960s. Wingard PO, 1886–1909 (M. T. Stewart, *Pike Co.*, 27; U.S.G.S., 1966 Base Maps).

RUSSELL Settlement with discontinued PO at 310251NO881455W in Mobile Co. Probably named for a local family. PO est. in 1896.

RUSSELL COUNTY Created by act of the state general assembly on Dec. 18, 1832. Bounded on the north by Lee Co., on the east by the GA, on the south by Barbour Co., and on the west by Macon Co. and Bullock Co. Named for Gilbert Christian Russell, a colonel in the U.S. army stationed in AL in 1818. The co. seats have been Girard, 1832–37; Crawford, 1837–68; Seale, 1868–1935; and the present one, Phenix City (A. K. Walker 1950, 102).

RUSSELL CROSSROADS See THREET in Lauderdale Co.

RUSSELL SETTLEMENT See GREENSBORO in Hale Co.

RUSSELLVILLE Inc. co. seat with PO at 343028NO874343W in Franklin Co. Settled in 1815 by William Russell, chief scout for Andrew Jackson in the Creek Indian War of 1813–14. Area first known as *Russell's Valley*. In 1819 the town was inc. as RUSSELLVILLE. Co. seat, 1818–49, and again from 1881 till the present. PO est. in 1819 (Knight 34).

RUSSELLVILLE VALLEY See MOULTON VALLEY.

RUTHERFORD Settlement with discontinued PO at 321120NO851905W in Russell Co. Named for Homer M. Rutherford, the first postmaster, appointed in 1892 ("Record of Appointment of Postmasters").

RUTHVEN Community with discontinued PO at 315112NO870147W in Wilcox Co. A resident who came from Lincolnshire, England, wanted to name the settlement *Lincoln*, but after his neighbors objected, he called it, instead, RUTHVEN for a division in the English co. PO est. in 1921 (Sartwell).

RUTLEDGE Inc. town with PO at 314349NO861835W in Crenshaw Co. Formerly called BARBER'S CROSSROADS for a local family. Named for Henry Rutledge, a Confederate captain from Butler Co. killed in action. Co. seat, 1866–93. PO est. in 1867. Inc. in 1871 (Harris 1982, 142).

RYAN CREEK Stream rising at 340819NO-864928W in Cullman Co. and flowing into the backwaters of Lewis Smith Lake at 340952NO864831W. Probably named for a local family (U.S.G.S., 1966 Base Maps).

RYLAND Settlement with PO at 344611NO862851W in Madison Co. Named for the first postmaster, Virgil H. Ryland, appointed in 1895 ("Record of Appointment of Postmasters").

SACO ['seko] Settlement with discontinued PO at 315718NO854915W in Pike Co. Although its origin is unknown, the designation for the town may be an acronym of the name of a business. PO est. in 1905.

SAFFORD Settlement with PO at 321716NO872217W in Dallas Co. Originally SAFFORD STATION, named for the chief engineer of the Mobile and Birmingham RR (Southern), which reached this point c. 1888. PO est. in 1890 (Nelms).

SAGE TOWN See SCOTTSBORO in Jackson Co.

SAGINAW Settlement with PO at 331258NO864731W in Shelby Co. A lumber town on the Louisville and Nashville RR, it was named for the older lumber town in MI. PO est. in 1903 (Harris 1982, 143).

SAINT CLAIR Settlement with PO on the Western RR of Alabama at 321924NO-863700W in Lowndes Co. Possibly named for St. Clair Tennille from Troy, AL, a promoter of rail transportation. PO est. in 1878 (Farmer 1973, 408).

ST. CLAIR COUNTY Created by act of the AL territorial general assembly on Nov. 20, 1818. Bordered on the north by Etowah Co., on the east by Calhoun Co., on the southeast by Talladega Co., on the south by Shelby Co., on the west by Jefferson Co., and on the northwest by Blount Co. Named for Arthur St. Clair (1734–1818), revolutionary war general and later an Indian fighter. This co. is the only one in AL to have two seats of justice. Since 1907 the Northern Judicial District co. seat has been Ashville, the original one, and the Southern Judicial District co. seat has been Pell City (Rich 1973, 3).

ST. CLAIR SPRINGS Settlement with discontinued PO at 334547NO862411W in St. Clair Co. John I. Thomason, owner of land near the sulphur springs where Ryland Randolph built a small hotel and seven cottages during the 1850s, managed the resort known as ST. CLAIR SPRINGS until his son-in-law Francis M. Goodwin replaced him during the

1880s. During the latter period, the resort was called CORNELIA for Goodwin's daughter. St. Clair Springs PO est. in 1853, Cornelia PO in 1880 (Sulzby 218–20).

ST. CLAIRSVILLE See ASHVILLE in St. Clair Co.

ST. ELMO Settlement with PO at 303012NO881515W in Mobile Co. Named for the novel by Augusta Evans Wilson (1835–1909), who was a resident of Mobile and nearby Spring Hill, now part of Mobile, most of her life. PO est. in 1871 (Harris 1982, 143).

ST. FLORIAN Inc. town with discontinued PO at 345224NO873724W in Lauderdale Co. Originally called WILSON STAND because it was located on the plantation owned by John and Matthew Wilson. After J. H. Heuser, a Roman Catholic priest, purchased the land to found a colony of German Catholics under the articles of the German Catholic Homestead Association of Cincinnati, the settlement was named for the patron saint of fire, for whom the man who donated the church bell, Florian Rasch, was also named. PO est. in 1879. Inc. in 1970 (Sockwell).

SAINTS CROSSROADS Settlement at 343256NO873520W in Franklin Co. Named for the family of James Saint, owner during the middle 1800s of the land where two roads intersected (1965 General Highway Map of Franklin Co.; Knight).

ST. STEPHENS Two settlements in Washington Co. have had this name.

1. Dead town once located 2 miles north of the present settlement with this name. A fort was erected on this site by the Spaniards in 1789 and was named for the first Christian martyr. Turned over in 1799 to the U.S. government, which founded the Choctaw Trading House here in 1803. Co. seat, 1815–25. Capital of the AL Territory, 1817–19. PO est. in 1818. When Cahaba in Dallas Co. was chosen to be the first state capital in 1819, many residents moved away. By 1899 the area had become a deserted wilderness. Now usually known as OLD ST. STEPHENS (Matte 50).

2. Settlement with PO at 313225NO880319W. Originally founded to serve as the RR station for the nearby older town for which it was named. Co. seat, 1848–1907. St. Stephens PO relocated here in 1848. Now often called NEW ST. STEPHENS (Harris 1982, 143).

SALEM Settlement with discontinued PO

at 323548NO851419W in Lee Co. Named for the Salem Methodist Church, organized in 1835. *Salem*, a shortened form of *Jerusalem*, is a name reminiscent of that of Salem, MA, once thought to be derived from a Hebrew word meaning 'peace.' PO est. in 1839 (Nunn 102–06; G. R. Stewart 1970, 419).

SALEM   Settlement at 345620NO870653W in Limestone Co. Possibly named for the nearby Salem Springs Church (1974 General Highway Map of Limestone Co.).

SALITPA [sə'lɪtpə]   Settlement with PO at 313746NO880112W in Clarke Co. Originally located about 3 miles from its present location. Before Salitpa was moved to this site, the community here was known as RIVER HILL because it was on a hill overlooking the Tombigbee River. The settlement that was moved to this place was to have been named for the Satilpa River, but when the first postmaster, George Cox, made his application to the PO Dept. in 1855, he crossed the *l* rather than the *t* (Clarke Co. Historical Society 312–13).

SAMANTHA   Settlement with PO at 332841NO873616W in Tuscaloosa Co. Originally located a short distance to the south and named COWDEN for Sylvester Monroe Cowden, merchant and landowner. When the PO was est. at the new site, Cowden, the first postmaster, appointed in 1884, named it SAMANTHA for his wife. Called CRUMP, 1890–1907, for William M. Crump, who settled in the area in 1818 (Rich 1979, 177, 183, 486–87).

SAMPLES   See HOLLYWOOD in Jackson Co.

SAMSON   Inc. town with PO at 310646NO-860246W in Geneva Co. Named for the biblical hero. PO est. in 1903. Inc. in 1905 (Harris 1982, 143).

SANDERSON TOWN   See HATTON in Lawrence Co.

SAND ISLAND   Island in Pelican Bay at 301147NO880312W in Mobile Co. Probably a descriptive and environmental name (U.S.G.S., 1966 Base Maps).

SAND MOUNTAIN   Extensive plateau approximately 25 miles wide and 75 miles long that includes large portions of Jackson Co., DeKalb Co., Marshall Co., Etowah Co., and Blount Co. Its name, descriptive of its soil, dates from at least the 1830s (Roden 53).

SAND ROCK   Settlement with discon-tinued PO at 341434NO854607W in Cherokee Co. Name is probably descriptive and environmental. PO est. in 1855.

SANDTOWN   See WHITE HALL in Lowndes Co.

SANDY   See VICK in Bibb Co.

SANDY CREEK   Both streams probably have descriptive and environmental names.
1. Stream rising at 330031NO852807W in Chambers Co. and joining Chattasofka Creek at 330235NO853130W in Tallapoosa Co. (U.S.G.S., 1966 Base Maps).
2. Stream rising at 314204NO851259W in Henry Co. and flowing into the Chattahoochee River at 314615NO850936W (U.S.G.S., 1966 Base Maps).

SANDY RIDGE   Settlement with discontinued PO at 320128NO862707W in Lowndes Co. Area first known as *Payne's Precinct* in honor of William Payne, who settled here in 1818. The town was given its descriptive and environmental name when the PO was est. in 1838 (Harris 1982, 144).

SANFORD   Inc. town with discontinued PO on the Louisville and Nashville RR at 311753NO862321W in Covington Co. Probably a personal name, but identity of individual or family unknown. PO est. in 1879. Inc. in 1867.

SANFORD COUNTY   See LAMAR CO.

SANTA BOGUE CREEK   See SINTA BOGUE CREEK in Washington Co.

SANTAFEE   See SUMMIT in Blount Co.

SANTUCK   Settlement with discontinued PO at 323758NO860747W in Elmore Co. Formerly identified with the humorous designation FLEA HOP. When the PO was est. in 1873, it was given the descriptive and environmental name SANDTUCK. The origin of the second element of this name is uncertain. It may be the SC regional term meaning 'nook' or 'cove.' A second possibility is that it may be the shortened form of *tuckahoe*, an Algonquian word meaning 'round,' referring to roots such as the VA truffle that was often applied to the poor people or land in southern VA (Brannon 1930, 3; Foscue 57; G. R. Stewart 1970, 496).

SARAGOSSA   [ˌserə'gɑsə]   Settlement with discontinued PO at 335336NO872357W in Walker Co. Perhaps named for the major city in the Aragon region of northeastern Spain. PO est. in 1920.

SARALAND   ['serələnd]   Inc. town with

PO at 304914NO880414W in Mobile Co. During the 1880s called CLEVELAND, probably in honor of Grover Cleveland (1837–1908), president of the U.S. (1885–89, 1893–97); in the 1890s known as ALVAREZ STATION in honor of an early local family; in 1900 Clark J. DeWitt, the postmaster, named the PO and the settlement SARALAND for his wife and also for nearby Sara Creek, which had honored Sara Alvarez years before. Alvarez PO est. in 1896, Saraland PO in 1900 (Boudousquie, 1889 map; Harris 1982, 144).

SARDINE See STANLEYS CROSSROADS in Escambia Co.

SARDIS Settlement with PO at 321715NO865909W in Dallas Co. Probably named for the ancient capital of Lydia in Asia Minor. PO est. in 1856 (G. R. Stewart 1958, 424).

SARDIS CITY Inc. town at 341027NO860722W in Etowah Co. Probably named for Sardis Baptist Church, which was founded c. 1882. Inc. in 1963 (Jolly).

SATILPA CREEK [sə'tɪlpə] Stream rising at 315306NO874941W in Clarke Co. and flowing into the Tombigbee River at 314010NO880439W. SATILPA CR. on E. A. Smith's 1891 map in Berney. Name is probably derived from Choctaw *isito* 'pumpkin' and *ilhpa* 'provisions' (Read 56).

SATSUMA Inc. town with PO at 305111NO880322W in Mobile Co. Probably named for the tree that bears citrus fruit also known as tangerines or mandarin oranges. PO est. in 1912. Inc. in 1959.

SAUTA COVE ['sɔtə] Dead town located about 4 miles south of Larkinsville in a small valley near North Sauta Creek in Jackson Co. *Sauta* is derived from Cherokee *itsati*, whose meaning is unknown. Temporary co. seat, 1819–21 (Kennamer 18; Read 56).

SAVAGES See PRICES in Calhoun Co.

SAVILLE ['sevəl] Community with discontinued PO at 315238NO861952W in Crenshaw Co. Origin of name unknown. PO est. in 1872.

SAWMILL TOWN See HUNNICUT in Shelby Co.

SAWYERVILLE Settlement with PO at 324506NO874346W in Hale Co. Named for the family of the first postmaster, Enoch Sawyer, appointed in 1871 (Holliman).

SAYRE Settlement with PO at 334244NO865828W in Jefferson Co. Named for Robert H. Sayre, owner of land here who organized the Sayre Mines and Manufacturing Co. in 1903. PO est. in 1971 (Hagood 30).

SCANT CITY Settlement at 342144NO862525W in Marshall Co. The most believable of the traditional explanations of the name is that whiskey made by mountain distillers during Prohibition was sold here in twelve-ounce bottles known as "scant pints" (Harris 1982, 144–45).

SCARHAM CREEK ['skɜrəm] Stream rising at 342126NO855624W in DeKalb Co. and flowing into Guntersville Lake at 341956NO861114W in Marshall Co. Probably named for an early local individual or family. Name approved by U.S. Board on Geographic Names in 1895.

SCHULTZ CREEK Stream rising at 330710NO871629W in Bibb Co. and flowing into the Cahaba River at 325931NO870801W. Named for a man who operated a mill on the creek (Hubbs; U.S.G.S., 1966 Base Maps).

SCHUSTER Community with discontinued PO at 315150NO870249W in Wilcox Co. Probably named for a local family. PO est. in 1901.

SCOTTSBORO Inc. co. seat at 344020NO860203W in Jackson Co. Community originally identified with the descriptive and environmental name SAGE TOWN. The town was named for Robert T. Scott from NC, who owned the land on which it was founded. First called SCOTTSVILLE, then SCOTT'S MILL, finally SCOTTSBORO. Chosen co. seat in 1859, but courthouse not finished until after the Civil War. Scott's Mill PO est. in 1854, Scottsboro PO in 1859. Inc. in 1869 (Kennamer 58, 165).

SCOTT'S MILL See SCOTTSBORO in Jackson Co.

SCOTTSVILLE See SCOTTSBORO in Jackson Co.

SCYRENE ['saɪˌrin] Community with discontinued PO at 314520NO873852W in Clarke Co. Settled by the early 1830s. Origin of name unknown. PO est. in 1901 (Clarke Co. Historical Society 340).

SEABOARD Settlement with discontinued PO at 311916NO881119W in Washington Co. Settled in 1880 and named for the Seaboard Cotton and Lumber Co. PO est. in 1893 (Matte 351).

SEABURY CREEK Stream rising at 304918NO881453W in Mobile Co. and flowing into Mobile Bay at 304727NO880832W.

Perhaps a descriptive and environmental name (Boudousquie, 1889 map).

SEALE   Settlement with PO at 321750NO-851008W in Russell Co. First called SILVER RUN for a nearby stream. When the Mobile and Girard RR (Central of Georgia) reached here, name changed to SEAL STATION for Arnold Seale of Chambers Co., a director of the rail line, because there was already a Silver Run in the state. Seal Station PO est. in 1856, Seale PO in 1880. Co. seat, 1868–1935 (M. B. Owen 1:502).

SEALY SPRINGS   Settlement with discontinued PO at 310212NO851832W in Houston Co. Probably named for springs on land owned by the family of Susie W. B. Sealy, the first postmaster, appointed in 1937 ("Record of Appointment of Postmasters").

SEARIGHT   Settlement with discontinued PO on the Central of Georgia RR at 312815NO862336W in Crenshaw Co. Named for an employee of the RR. PO est. in 1892 (Harris 1982, 145).

SEARLES   Settlement with discontinued PO at 331927NO871918W in Tuscaloosa Co. Named for John E. Searles, an officer of the Alabama Consolidated Coal and Iron Co. PO est. in 1900 (Rich 1979, 494).

SECOND CREEK   Stream rising in TN that enters AL at 350605NO872011W in Lauderdale Co. and flows into Wheeler Lake at 344854NO872237W. Mentioned in the original government survey of 1817. Name refers to the fact that this is the second creek west of the confluence of the Elk and Tennessee rivers (Sockwell).

SECTION   Inc. town with PO at 343444NO855912W in Jackson Co. The community and PO were first known as MOUNT ZION for a local Baptist church; the PO was next known as KIRBY CREEK for a nearby creek; finally the town and PO were named SECTION for the sixteenth section of land that was set aside by the legislature for public schools. Mount Zion PO est. in 1875; Kirby Creek PO in 1876; and Section PO in 1892. Inc. in 1910 (Kennamer 177–79).

SEDGEFIELD   Settlement at 321101NO-854217W in Bullock Co. Named for Sedgefields, the plantation of the Maytag family that was itself named for the sedge plant growing in the area (1968 General Highway Map of Bullock Co.; Harris 1982, 146).

SELFVILLE   Settlement with discontinued

PO at 334949NO864005W in Blount Co. Named for the pioneering family of Elijah Self, the first postmaster, appointed in 1889 (Blount Co. Historical Society 89).

SELLERS   Settlement with discontinued PO at 320322NO861811W in Montgomery Co. Named for the family of William Sellers, the first postmaster, appointed in 1890 (Harris 1982, 146).

SELLERSVILLE   Settlement with discontinued PO at 310747NO860015W in Geneva Co. Probably named for a local Sellers family. PO est. in 1902.

SELMA   Inc. co. seat with PO on the north bank of the Alabama River at 322426NO-870116W in Dallas Co. Site called *Ecor Bienville* 'Bienville's Bluff' on D'Anville's 1732 map. This name commemorates a battle in this locality between Bienville (1680–1765), founder of Mobile, and the Alabama Indians. Between 1805 and 1810 identified with the descriptive and environmental name *High Soap Stone Bluff*; finally called *Moore's Bluff* for Thomas Moore, who settled here c. 1815. The Selma Land Co., organized by William Rufus King and others, founded c. 1819 the town of SELMA, whose name King had selected from one of *The Poems of Ossian* by James Macpherson. Selma PO est. in 1819. Inc. in 1820. Chosen co. seat in 1865 (Nelms).

SEMAN   Settlement with discontinued PO at 324357NO860644W in Elmore Co. Probably a family name. PO est. in 1902.

SEMINOLE   Settlement with PO at 303054NO872826W in Baldwin Co. In 1899 *Century Atlas*. The name, a Creek term meaning 'separatist,' was that of a Muskhogean tribe of FL. PO est. in 1928 (Read 57).

SEMMES   Settlement with PO on the Gulf, Mobile and Ohio RR at 304641NO881533W in Mobile Co. Named for Raphael Semmes (1809–1877), Confederate admiral who commanded the battleship *Alabama* and then lived in Mobile following the Civil War. PO est. in 1890 (Harris 1982, 146).

SEPULGA RIVER   [sə'pʌlgə]   Stream that rises at 313553NO865712W in Conecuh Co., forms part of the boundary between Conecuh Co. and Butler Co., and flows into the Conecuh River at 313056NO864558W in Escambia Co. SUPPULGAWS in Benjamin Hawkins's Feb. 10, 1797, letter. If of Creek origin, the name may be derived from *asi* 'yaupon,' *api* 'tree,' and *algi* 'grove' (Read 57).

SEVEN HILLS Settlement at 303914NO-881811W in Mobile Co. Name is probably environmental, but it may also be reminiscent of the Seven Hills of Rome (Harris 1982, 147; *Official 1959 Alabama Highway Map*).

SHADES MOUNTAIN Mountain whose summit is at 332501NO865104W in Jefferson Co. Named for the dark valley called *Shades of Death* by both the Chickasaw Indians and the white traders. It was the place where a number of persons were killed when the area was part of the MS Territory (Hagood 12).

SHADY GROVE Settlement at 331008NO-860022W in Clay Co. Name is probably subjectively descriptive (U.S.G.S., 1966 Base Maps).

SHADY GROVE Settlement with discontinued PO at 315434NO860945W in Pike Co. First called CHESSER for Jim Chesser, an early settler. Renamed for the Shady Grove Methodist Church, founded in 1866. Chesser PO est. in 1880, Shady Grove PO in 1890 (Farmer 1973, 398–99).

SHANNON Settlement with PO at 332419NO865219W in Jefferson Co. Named for John James Shannon, who operated a mine here in 1912. PO est. in 1915 (Brown and Nabers 192).

SHANTY See SUMMIT in Blount Co.

SHARON See DORA in Walker Co.

SHAWMUT Settlement with PO at 325025NO851100W in Chambers Co. Founded c. 1907 by the West Point Manufacturing Co., it was named for the Shawmut National Bank of Boston, MA, from which the money had been borrowed to erect the textile mill here. *Shawmut* is the Indian name for the peninsula on which the city of Boston is located. PO est. in 1876 (Harris 1982, 147).

SHEFFIELD Inc. town with PO at 344554NO874155W in Colbert Co. Named for the iron-manufacturing city in Yorkshire, England. Inc. in 1885. PO est. in 1884 (Sockwell).

SHELBY Settlement with PO at 330637NO863503W in Shelby Co. Named for the Shelby Iron Works, founded here by Horace Ware in the latter 1840s and destroyed by Union troops during the Civil War. PO est. in 1888 (Tamarin).

SHELBY COUNTY Created by act of the MS territorial general assembly on Feb. 7, 1817. Bounded on the north by St. Clair Co., on the east by Talladega Co. and Coosa Co., on the south by Chilton Co., on the southwest by Bibb Co., and on the northwest by Jefferson Co. Named for Isaac Shelby (1750–1826), a revolutionary war soldier and a governor of KY (1792–96, 1812–16). The co. seat, first called SHELBY COURTHOUSE, was at Shelbyville until 1826 when it was relocated at Columbia, whose name was later changed to COLUMBIANA (Tamarin).

SHELBY COURTHOUSE See PELHAM in Shelby Co.

SHELBYVILLE See PELHAM in Shelby Co.

SHELBYVILLE See TUSCALOOSA in Tuscaloosa Co.

SHELLEYVILLE See TUSCALOOSA in Tuscaloosa Co.

SHELLHORN Settlement with discontinued PO at 315233NO860447W in Pike Co. Name is derived from "shell corn." PO est. in 1904 (Farmer 1973, 96).

SHELLYTOWN See TUSCALOOSA in Tuscaloosa Co.

SHEPARDVILLE Community at 320808NO-870458W in Dallas Co. Probably named for a local Shepard family (1968 General Highway Map of Dallas Co.).

SHILOH Community at 330115NO-853212W in Chambers Co. Named for the Shiloh Baptist Church, a mission organized here c. 1865 by the nearby Milltown Baptist Church (Harris 1982, 148).

SHILOH Inc. town at 342745NO855247W in DeKalb Co. A biblical name, that of a place where the Israelites built a tabernacle. The Hebrew word means 'place of rest.' Inc. in 1962 (Landmarks 119).

SHILOH Community with discontinued PO at 320738NO874407W in Marengo Co. Named for Shiloh Baptist Church, founded in 1827 and used as a union church by Baptists and Presbyterians until 1840 when the Baptist congregation was admitted into the Bethel Association. PO est. in 1829 (W. Smith).

SHILOH   Settlement   at   314652NO-854439W in Pike Co. Named for a local Baptist church (Harris 1982, 148; *Official 1959 Alabama Highway Map*).

SHIRAS   See PETERSON in Tuscaloosa Co.

SHOAL CREEK   The names of the following four streams are probably descriptive and environmental.

1. Stream rising at 324150NO862930W in Autauga Co. and flowing into the Coosa River at 323926NO861925W in Elmore Co. (Biggs 39; 1965 General Highway Map of Autauga Co.).

2. Stream rising in TN and flowing across Lauderdale Co. into the Tennessee River at 345017NO873312W. SHOAL CREEK on Gardiner's map, c. 1817. CLEAR CREEK, another descriptive name, in Tuomey's 1858 report (Sockwell).

3. Stream rising at 333922NO862232W in St. Clair Co. and flowing into Neely Henry Lake at 334838NO860357W (Rich; U.S.G.S., 1966 Base Maps).

4. Stream rising at 331054NO865256W in Shelby Co. and flowing into the Little Cahaba River at 330336NO865625W in Bibb Co. Formerly called WILSON'S CREEK for an early settler (Abrams 16; U.S.G.S., 1966 Base Maps).

SHOPTON   Settlement with discontinued PO at 320701NO855632W in Bullock Co. Although its origin is unknown, the name might be a descriptive combination of *shop* and *-ton* 'town.' PO est. in 1886.

SHORT   CREEK   Stream   rising   at 340703NO860650W in Etowah Co. and flowing into Guntersville Lake at 342229NO-861434W in Marshall Co. Probably a descriptive name (U.S.G.S., 1966 Base Maps).

SHORT CREEK   Settlement at 333304NO-870605W in Jefferson Co. Named for a nearby creek whose designation is descriptive of its length (Hagood 47; *Official 1959 Alabama Highway Map*).

SHORTER   Settlement   with   PO   at 322341NO855501W in Macon Co. Site of Simmon's Grocery. Town first called CROSS KEYS for the birthplace in SC of an early settler, J. H. Howard; then named SHORTER

for a family prominent in AL politics. Cross Keys PO est. in 1837, Shorter's Depot PO in 1869, the possessive and the word *depot* being dropped in 1893 (Harris 1982, 149).

SHORTERVILLE   Settlement with PO at 313412NO850605W in Henry Co. Named for a local resident. PO est. in 1858 (Warren, *Henry's Heritage*, 86).

SHOTTSVILLE   Settlement with discontinued PO at 341539NO880738W in Marion Co. Named for the family of John Shotts, who moved here in 1839. PO est. in 1874 (Harris 1982, 149).

SHREVE   Community   at   313034NO-864225W in Conecuh Co. Probably a family name (U.S.G.S., 1966 Base Maps).

SHUFF, LAKE   See HIGHLAND, LAKE in Blount Co.

SIBLEY CITY   See MONTROSE in Baldwin Co.

SIKES   Community at 325319NO853331W in Chambers Co. Named for a family who owned a plantation in the area (Crump; *Official 1959 Alabama Highway Map*).

SILAS   Settlement with PO at 314555NO-881945W in Choctaw Co. Named for Silas Shoemaker, the first postmaster, appointed in 1881 (Choctaw Co. Bicentennial Commission 20).

SILURIA   Formerly inc. town with PO at 331345NO864930W in Shelby Co., now part of Alabaster. Named for a geologic age because rocks dating from that period were found in this area. PO est. in 1872. Inc. in 1954. Merged with Alabaster in 1971 (Tamarin).

SILVER   CREEK   Stream   rising   at 314749NO873721W in Clarke Co. and flowing into the Alabama River at 313945NO-873409W. Probably a descriptive name (U.S.G.S., 1966 Base Maps).

SILVERHILL   Inc. town with PO at 303243NO874506W in Baldwin Co. Founded in 1897 by emigrants from Scandinavia and Bohemia. Origin of name unknown. The designation for the hill where the town is located might refer to the original owner of the land, to silver deposits supposedly discovered here, or even to a buried treasure. PO est. in 1899. Inc. in 1926 (Bush 80).

SILVER RUN   See SEALE in Russell Co.

SILVER RUN   Settlement on the Southern RR at 333354NO855429W in Talladega Co.

Named by Sterling Jenkins (1808–1880) for the clear run (brook) whose current name, *Silver Run Creek*, is descriptive of its silvery appearance (McMillan).

SIMCOE   Settlement with discontinued PO at 341327NO864404W in Cullman Co. Starling Austin, refusing to have the town called *Austinville* for himself, named it instead for Lake Simcoe in Ontario, Canada. PO est. in 1884 (Whitehead 15).

SIMMON TOWN   See HIGHTOGY in Lamar Co.

SIMMSVILLE   Community with discontinued PO at 331928NO864232W in Shelby Co. Named for the first postmaster, William D. Simms ("Record of Appointment of Postmasters").

SIMPKINSVILLE   See OLD TEXAS in Monroe Co.

SIMS CHAPEL   Community with discontinued PO at 311308NO880848W in Washington Co. Named for James Sims, who moved here from near Mobile in 1848. PO est. in 1879 (Harris 1982, 149).

SINKING CREEK   Stream rising at 345129NO874534W in Lauderdale Co. and flowing into the Tennessee River at 344450NO874946W. Mentioned in the original 1817 government surveys. Name is descriptive of the creek's sinking into the ground, then emerging farther south (Sockwell).

SINTA BOGUE CREEK   ['sɪntə,bog] Stream rising at 313612NO881639W in Washington Co. and flowing into the Tombigbee River at 314119NO880518W. Also known as SANTA BOGUE CREEK. CENTE BONEK in the 1765 British-Choctaw treaty. Name is derived from Choctaw *sinti* 'snake' and *bok* 'creek' (McMillan in Read 96; Read 56).

SIPSEY   ['sɪpsɪ]   Inc. town with PO at 334929NO870510W in Walker Co. Coal-mining town founded in 1912 by Milton H. Fies, the first postmaster, appointed in 1913. Named for nearby Sipsey Fork of the Black Warrior River. Inc. in 1965 (Gant).

SIPSEY CREEK   Stream rising at 341033NO880843W in Marion Co. and flowing into the Buttahatchee River in Monroe Co., MS. *Sipsi* is the Chickasaw-Choctaw name of the poplar or cottonwood tree (Read 59).

SIPSEY FORK OF THE BLACK WARRIOR RIVER   Stream rising at 341921NO872820W in Winston Co. and flowing between Cullman Co. and Walker Co. into Lewis

Smith Lake at 334856NO870326W. Name is the Chickasaw-Choctaw word meaning 'poplar' or 'cottonwood' (Read 59).

SIPSEY RIVER   Stream formed by various tributaries at 335451NO874114W in Fayette Co. that flows into the Tombigbee River at 330014NO881019W between Pickens Co. and Greene Co. Its main source, rising at 340702NO873728W in Winston Co., is known as NEW RIVER (probably a reference to its discovery); earlier this shorter stream had the descriptive name NINE ISLAND CREEK. SIPSEY R. on La Tourette's 1844 map. The name is the Chickasaw-Choctaw word meaning 'poplar' or 'cottonwood' (Read 59).

SIPSEY TURNPIKE   See ELROD in Tuscaloosa Co.

SIX MILE   Settlement with discontinued PO at 330028NO870020W in Bibb Co. Founded in the 1830s and named for the nearby creek. PO est. in 1857 (Ellison 79–80).

SIX MILE CREEK   Stream rising at 325412NO864851W in Chilton Co. and flowing into the Little Cahaba River at 330254NO870304W in Bibb Co. The explanation of the name, dating from the 1820s, is that its bed is 6 miles long before the creek enters the Little Cahaba River (Ellison 79–80).

SIZEMORE CREEK   Stream rising at 310718NO873303W in Escambia Co. and joining Big Escambia Creek at 310535NO872141W. Named for a family living near the creek before 1868, while this area was still part of Baldwin Co. (Waters 202).

SKEGGS CROSSROADS   Community at 330655NO860646W in Coosa Co. Probably named for a local family (U.S.G.S., 1966 Base Maps).

SKINNERTON   Settlement with discontinued PO at 314011NO870354W in Monroe Co. Named for William M. Skinner, the first postmaster, appointed in 1887 ("Record of Appointment of Postmasters").

SKIPPERVILLE   Settlement with discontinued PO at 313327NO853244W in Dale Co. Probably named for the local Skipper family. PO est. in 1853 (F. S. Watson 1949, 46–50).

SKIRUM   ['skɜrəm]   Settlement with discontinued PO at 341925NO855802W in DeKalb Co. Originally called PARTRIDGE TOWN for a local family. After the Partridges moved away, the town was given for its name what is probably a variant of *Scarham*, the designation for a nearby creek. PO est. in 1883 (Landmarks 121).

SKYLINE Community at 344922NO-860651W in Jackson Co. Name is descriptive of its mountainous location (Melancon 7; U.S.G.S., 1966 Base Maps).

SLAB CREEK Stream rising at 341242NO-860850W in Marshall Co. and flowing into Locust Fork of the Black Warrior River at 340905NO862411W in Blount Co. Name is probably descriptive of the rocky area through which the creek flows (U.S.G.S., 1966 Base Maps).

SLEDGE Community on the Alabama, Tennessee and Northern RR at 324158NO-881826W in Sumter Co. Named for Simms Sledge, one of the men who killed the northern attorney W. P. Billings, blamed for encouraging dissatisfaction among blacks following the Civil War (Foscue 21, 59).

SLOAN Community with discontinued PO at 335051NO865721W in Blount Co. Probably named for a local family. PO est. in 1890.

SLOCOMB Inc. town with PO at 310629NO853540W in Geneva Co. Named for Frank W. Slocomb, who operated a turpentine still here and was also the first postmaster, appointed in 1900. Inc. in 1901 (M. B. Owen 1:431).

SMALLWOOD See VANCE in Tuscaloosa Co.

SMITH HILL Settlement at 330720NO-870607W in Bibb Co. A mining community located on a hill, probably named for a local family (Ellison 177; U.S.G.S., 1966 Base Maps).

SMITHS Settlement with PO on the Columbus and Western RR (Central of Georgia) at 323224NO850555W in Lee Co. Also known as SMITHS STATION. Named for Broadus Smith, who donated land for the station. PO est. in 1866 (Harris 1982, 150).

SMITHSONIA Community with discontinued PO at 344739NO875245W in Lauderdale Co. Once called CAVE SPRINGS because of the topographical features here. Named SMITHSONIA for Columbus Smith, a merchant and landowner in the area following the Civil War. PO est. in 1886 (Sockwell).

SMITHVILLE See GROVE HILL in Clarke Co.

SMITHVILLE See TOADVINE in Jefferson Co.

SMOKE NECK See SOUTHSIDE in Etowah Co.

SMUT EYE Community at 315840NO-853901W in Bullock Co. Humorous name usually explained with traditional stories about smut from fires blackening the faces or getting into the eyes of persons working over them or passing near them (Harris 1982, 150–51; *Official 1959 Alabama Highway Map*).

SMUT EYE See VICTORIA in Coffee Co.

SNEAD Inc. town with PO at 340710NO-862344W in Blount Co. Founded by G. W. White, a merchant who moved here in 1853. Named for a local family, probably that of the first postmaster, John H. Snead, appointed in 1883. Inc. in 1966 (Blount Co. Historical Society 27, 92–93).

SNOWDOUN ['snodən] Settlement with discontinued PO at 321429NO861747W in Montgomery Co. Named by William Falconer for Mount Snowdoun in Wales. PO est. in 1859 (Robertson 71).

SNOW HILL Settlement with PO at 320016NO870026W in Wilcox Co. First located about 4 miles to the northeast, it was moved here after the Civil War to be located on the Louisville and Nashville RR. Named for William Snow, the first settler of the original town. PO est. in 1833 (Harris 1982, 151).

SNOWTOWN Settlement with discontinued PO at 333947NO870218W in Jefferson Co. Also called SNOWVILLE. Named for J. W. Snow, a physician who operated a clinic here. Snowtown PO est. in 1897 (Hagood 25).

SNOWVILLE See SNOWTOWN in Jefferson Co.

SOAPSTONE CREEK Stream rising at 321326NO865115W in Lowndes Co. and flowing into the Alabama River at 322152NO-865352W in Dallas Co. Formerly named TARVER'S MILL CREEK for a mill owned by a local family. Current name is descriptive and environmental (Harris 1982, 151; U.S.G.S., 1966 Base Maps).

SOCIETY HILL Settlement with discontinued PO at 322535NO852643W in Macon Co. Probably named for the town in SC that received its designation because the St. David's Society of Welch Baptists had founded an academy there in 1778. PO est. in 1837 (G. R. Stewart 1970, 451).

SOMERVILLE Inc. town with PO at 342823NO864755W in Morgan Co. Named for Robert M. Summerville, an army officer killed at the Battle of Horseshoe Bend fighting against hostile Creek Indians on March 27, 1814. Co. seat, 1818–91. PO est. in 1824. Inc. in 1839 (Ackley 44).

SOUGAHATCHEE CREEK [ˌsɔgə'hæt/ɪ] Stream rising at 324314NO852221W in Chambers Co. and flowing into the Tallapoosa River at 323620NO855330W. SOU-GO-HAT-CHE in Benjamin Hawkins's "A Sketch of the Creek Country in 1798 and 1799" (49). Name means 'Rattle Creek,' from Creek *saugu* 'a rattle [gourd]' and *hachi* 'creek' (Read 60).

SOUTH Community with discontinued PO at 312639NO863647W in Covington Co. Name might be a personal one or it might refer to town's location in the southern part of the state. PO est. in 1900.

SOUTH CALERA Community with discontinued PO at 330428NO864458W in Shelby Co. Named for the town Calera, located to its north. PO est. in 1888 (Tamarin).

SOUTH ORCHARD Settlement at 302753NO-880902W in Mobile Co. Name refers to orange orchards that once covered the area and to the location of this town in relation to the settlement Orchard to its north (Pipes; U.S.G.S., 1966 Base Maps).

SOUTH SAUTY CREEK ['sɔtɪ] Stream rising at 343811NO854331W in DeKalb Co. and flowing into Guntersville Lake at 343235NO860717W in Marshall Co. The northern branch of this stream, North Sauty Creek, rises at 344343NO861253W in Jackson Co. and joins the southern branch at 343417NO860530W on the border between Jackson Co. and DeKalb Co. SAUTA C. on La Tourette's 1844 map. The name is derived from Cherokee *itsati*, whose meaning is unknown (Read 56).

SOUTHSIDE Inc. town at 335528NO-860121W in Etowah Co. Area has also been identified with the descriptive and environmental names: SMOKE NECK, CEDAR BEND, and BRANNON SPRINGS, *Brannon* being the name of the owner of the mineral springs here. For a while also called PILGRIM'S REST for the Baptist church founded in 1856. The present name, SOUTH-SIDE, probably refers to the settlement's location on the south bank of the river. Inc. in 1957 (Jolly).

SOUTH VINEMONT Inc. town at 341508NO865145W in Cullman Co. First called PINNACLE because of its location on a mountain. Name changed to VINEMONT in 1898 because the founders thought the soil in the area suited to the cultivation of grapes. Inc. in 1912 as VINEMONT; inc. again in 1961 as SOUTH VINEMONT. Pinnacle PO

130

est. in 1887, Vinemont PO in 1898 (Whitehead 16).

SPANISH FORT Community with PO at 304021NO875245W in Baldwin Co. Named for the military fortification built in 1780 by the Spanish to guard Mobile from the British, who were trying to recapture the city. PO est. in 1971 (Comminge and Albers 45).

SPARKS CREEK Stream rising at 324940NO872709W in Perry Co. and joining Big Brush Creek at 324505NO873314W in Hale Co. Probably named for an early settler (U.S.G.S., 1966 Base Maps).

SPARTA Dead town with discontinued PO located just east of Murder Creek 10 miles southeast of Belleville in Conecuh Co. Founded in 1818, it was named by Thomas Watts, an attorney, for his former home in Sparta, GA. PO est. in 1820. Co. seat, 1820–66. After the courthouse was burned by Union troops and the seat of justice was moved to Evergreen, the town was gradually abandoned (Harris 1977, 105–06).

SPEIGNER ['spaɪgnər] Settlement with discontinued PO on the Louisville and Nashville RR at 323502NO862041W in Elmore Co. Named for a pioneering family from SC. PO est. in 1890 (Harris 1982, 152).

SPEIGNER LAKE Artificial lake formed by the impoundment of Mortar Creek at 323407NO862033W in Elmore Co. Probably named for the town (U.S.G.S., 1966 Base Maps).

SPLUNGE CREEK Stream rising at 340904NO873602W in Winston Co. and joining Blackwater Creek at 340035NO872809W. Although its origin is unknown, perhaps the name is intended to suggest the sound made by the moving water (U.S.G.S., 1966 Base Maps).

SPRAGUE Settlement with PO at 320758NO861612W in Montgomery Co. Named for a conductor on the Atlantic Coast Line. PO est. in 1892 (Harris 1982, 152).

SPRING CREEK Both streams are probably named for the source of their water.
1. Stream rising at 343113NO874110W in Franklin Co. and flowing into the Tennessee River at 344455NO874336W in Colbert Co. On Gardiner's map, c. 1817 (Sockwell).
2. Stream rising at 310301NO854052W in Geneva Co. and flowing into the Choctawhatchee River at 310043NO855006W (U.S.G.S., 1966 Base Maps).

SPRING GARDEN Settlement with PO at

335822NO853314W in Cherokee Co. Subjectively descriptive name. PO est. in 1843 (M. T. Stewart 1958, 1:33).

SPRING HILL   Settlement at 320445NO-852013W in Barbour Co. Founded during the 1830s. Descriptive and environmental name (Ellis 54).

SPRING HILL   Community at 315221NO-863427W in Butler Co. Probably a descriptive and environmental name (1968 General Highway Map of Butler Co.).

SPRING HILL   See OLD SPRING HILL in Marengo Co.

SPRING HILL   Settlement at 314127NO-855738W in Pike Co. Before 1860 the town surrounded a school with the descriptive and environmental name *Spring Hill* located 2 miles north of its present site. After being moved, the town retained this name (M. T. Stewart, *Pike Co.*, 17).

SPRING VALLEY   Settlement at 393924NO-873700W in Colbert Co. Named for the valley where it is located, the valley having the designation of a nearby creek (Sockwell; General Land Office, 1878 map).

SPRINGVILLE   Inc. town with PO at 334630NO862818W in St. Clair Co. Settled c. 1817 and called BIG SPRINGS because of the numerous springs in the area. Renamed SPRINGVILLE in 1834 when the PO was est. Inc. in 1873 (Rich).

SPROTT   Settlement with PO at 324036NO-871317W in Perry Co. Named for Thomas W. Sprott, the first postmaster, appointed in 1881 ("Record of Appointment of Postmasters").

SPRUCE PINE   Settlement with PO at 342331NO874335W in Franklin Co. Named by C. F. and A. M. Rauschenburg, who settled here in 1892, for the eastern hemlock trees growing in the area. PO est. in 1857 (Knight 36).

STAFFORD   Community with discontinued PO at 332648NO881442W in Pickens Co. Probably named for a local family. PO est. in 1881 (N. F. Brown 54).

STANDING ROCK   Settlement with PO at 330447NO851511W in Chambers Co. Name refers to a large rock in the area. The traditional story is that the Creek Indians placed the rock here before they left the state for OK, warning they would return to haunt the white settlers if the latter group ever moved the rock. PO est. in 1837 (Harris 1982, 153).

STANLEYS CROSSROADS   Community at 310804NO872025W in Escambia Co. An earlier name, SARDINE, was borrowed from a bridge over Big Escambia Creek. Later, the settlement was called MAGNOLIA for the Magnolia Baptist Church, organized in 1879. When co. highways 17 and 27 intersected near the home of A. S. Stanley during the early part of this century, the community became known as STANLEY'S CROSSROADS (Waters 201–02).

STANTON   Settlement with PO at 324408NO865359W in Chilton Co. Founded as a station on the Selma, Rome and Dalton RR and named for Myron Stanton (1833–1879), the assistant superintendent of the rail line. PO est. in 1883 (B. D. Roberts).

STAPLETON   Settlement with PO at 304433NO874736W in Baldwin Co. Named for the Stapleton family, prominent landowners. PO est. in 1929 (Bush 83).

STAR   Community with discontinued PO at 334120NO880932W in Lamar Co. Named for a now closed school. PO est. in 1888 (Harris 1982, 154).

STATESVILLE   Settlement at 330703NO-870900W in Bibb Co. Named for a discontinued school built here by the state about 1914. The local residents, however, have always preferred to call their community LOWREYTOWN for the local Lowrey family (Cottingham; *Official 1959 Alabama Highway Map*).

STEELE   Inc. town with PO on the Alabama Great Southern RR at 335623NO-861206W in St. Clair Co. First named STEELE'S DEPOT for J. Toliver Steele, who moved here in 1863. PO est. in 1871. Inc. in 1952 (Rich).

STEELWOOD   Settlement with discontinued PO at 304256NO874705W in Baldwin Co. Although its origin is unknown, the town's designation might be a combination of the personal name *Steele* and the descriptive and environmental term *wood*. PO est. in 1948 (Bush 83).

STEEP CREEK   Stream rising at 320818NO-862920W in Lowndes Co. and joining Pintlalla Creek at 321610NO862816W. Probably a descriptive and environmental name (U.S.G.S., 1966 Base Maps).

STEEP HEAD CREEK   Stream rising at 312318NO855337W in Coffee Co. and joining Claybank Creek at 312147NO854412W in Dale Co. Probably a descriptive and environmental name (U.S.G.S., 1966 Base Maps).

STERRETT Settlement with PO at 332655NO862848W in Shelby Co. Named for a prominent local family, one of whose members was Alphonso Anderson Sterrett (1816–c. 1880), a member of the state legislature. PO est. in 1857 (Tamarin).

STEVENSON Inc. town with PO at 345207NO855022W in Jackson Co. Founded in 1853 on the Nashville and Chattanooga RR (Louisville and Nashville). Named for Vernon King Stevenson, cofounder with John F. Anderson of the town. PO est. in 1856. Inc. in 1866 (Kennamer 169).

STEWART Settlement with discontinued PO at 325440NO874222W in Hale Co. Founded in 1844 as STEWART'S STATION on the Alabama Great Southern RR. Named for Charlie Stewart, an early settler. PO est. in 1871 (Harris 1982, 154).

STEWART'S GAP See GLEN ALLEN in Fayette Co.

STEWARTVILLE Settlement with discontinued PO at 330445NO861440W in Coosa Co. Named for H. C. Stewart, the first postmaster, appointed in 1872 ("Record of Appointment of Postmasters").

STITH See ALDRIDGE in Walker Co.

STOCKTON Settlement with PO at 305937NO875129W in Baldwin Co. on Tensaw Bluff, where the Tensas Indians had lived in 1744. The town is said to have been founded by Tory refugees during the latter 1700s. Probably named for the family of Francis B. Stockton, one of the commissioners appointed in 1809 to select a site for the first co. courthouse. PO est. in 1833 (Bush 84; T. M. Owen 1:85).

STRAIGHT MOUNTAIN Mountain whose summit is at 340043NO862033W in Etowah Co. It is said to have been named for A. D. Streight, the colonel commanding the Union troops in their encounter in Blount Co. during the Civil War with the Confederate forces under Nathan Bedford Forrest (U.S.G.S., 1966 Base Maps; Weaver).

STRATA Settlement with discontinued PO at 320204NO861739W in Montgomery Co. The name is the geological term for a bed formed of layers of sedimentary rock. PO est. in 1849 (Freeman).

STROUD Settlement with discontinued PO at 330317NO851951W in Chambers Co. Probably named for a local family. PO est. in 1925.

STUDDARD'S CROSSROADS Settlement at 334830NO873515W in Fayette Co. Probably named for Andrew Studdard, who received a land grant in this area in 1860 (Peoples 17).

STYX RIVER Stream rising at 305204NO874628W in Baldwin Co. and flowing into the Perdido River at 303052NO872701W. Probably named for the mythical river in Hades (U.S.G.S., 1966 Base Maps).

SUCARNOCHEE RIVER [ˌsʊkəˈnɑtʃɪ] Stream rising in Kemper Co., MS, and flowing into the Tombigbee River at 322459NO880231W between Sumter Co. and Marengo Co. SOOK HANATCHA on Romans's 1772 map. The name means 'hog river,' from Choctaw *shuka* 'hog,' *in* 'its,' and *hacha* 'river.' *Shuka* was the Choctaw word for 'opossum,' but when hogs were introduced among the Indians, the similarity of these animals to the opossum led to the transference of the name (T. M. Owen 2:1276; Read 60–61).

SUGAR CREEK Stream rising in TN that crosses the state boundary at 350159NO871325W in Limestone Co. and flows into the Elk River at 345212NO870648W. Probably a subjectively descriptive name (U.S.G.S., 1966 Base Maps).

SUGGSVILLE Settlement with discontinued PO at 313522NO874135W in Clarke Co. Named for William Suggs, who opened a general store here in 1814. PO est. in 1824 (Clarke Co. Historical Society 352).

SUGGSVILLE STATION See ALLEN in Clarke Co.

SULLIGENT Inc. town with PO at 335406NO880804W in Lamar Co. The name is a blend of those of two St. Louis and San Francisco RR officials, *Sullivan* and *Sargent*. PO est. in 1887. Inc. in 1897 (Acee 12).

SULPHUR SPRINGS See GAYLESVILLE in Cherokee Co.

SULPHUR SPRINGS Community with discontinued PO at 344151NO853449W in DeKalb Co. A resort named for the springs in the area was in operation here, 1885–c. 1918. PO est. in 1883 (Raughton 75).

SULPHUR SPRINGS See TALLADEGA SPRINGS in Talladega Co.

SULPHUR SPRINGS See BROWNVILLE in Tuscaloosa Co.

SUMITON [ˈsʌmətən] Inc. town with PO at 334520NO870300W in Walker Co. Originally known as SUMMIT, but the name was changed to SUMMITON, *summit* plus *-ton* 'town,' because of an already existing Summit PO in the state, when a PO was est. here in 1924. Both names are descriptive and environmental. Inc. in 1952 (Gant).

SUMMERDALE   Inc. town with PO at 302915NO874159W in Baldwin Co. Named for Eli Summers, who founded the settlement in 1904 to serve as a center for the cultivation of tobacco, a hope that was never realized. PO est. in 1905. Inc. in 1929 (Bush 84).

SUMMERFIELD   See VERBENA in Chilton Co.

SUMMERFIELD   Settlement with discontinued PO at 323114NO870230W in Dallas Co. VALLEY CREEK, named for a nearby stream, was the first settlement by white people in this co.; it was made here c. 1819 under the direction of James Russell. Name changed to SUMMERFIELD for John Summerfield, a prominent Methodist minister, when PO was est. in 1845 (C. H. Stewart 1, 7, 35).

SUMMERHOUSE MOUNTAIN   Mountain whose summit is at 345743NO854625W in Jackson Co. Name refers to the rustic cabins built on its slopes where nearby residents lived during the summers of the first third of this century to escape the heat (Chambless).

SUMMIT   Settlement with discontinued PO at 341216NO862939W in Blount Co. Originally called SHANTY, probably because of the small cabins first built here; then known as MARTIN'S STAND because the PO was est. in the store of James Martin, the first postmaster, appointed in 1841; name changed to SUMMIT in 1845 because of the location of the settlement on a mountain; during 1846 called SANTAFEE, possibly for Santa Fe, NM; then in 1847 renamed SUMMIT (Blount Co. Historical Society 93–98).

SUMMIT   See SUMITON in Walker Co.

SUMMIT CUT   See FRUITHURST in Cleburne Co.

SUMTER COUNTY   Created by act of the state general assembly on Dec. 18, 1832. Bounded on the north by Pickens Co., on the east by Greene Co. and Marengo Co., on the south by Choctaw Co., and on the west by MS. Named for Thomas Sumter (1734–1832), revolutionary war general known as the "Gamecock of the Revolution," who, although born in VA, is usually associated with SC. The co. seat is Livingston (Foscue 61).

SUMTERVILLE   Settlement with discontinued PO at 324242NO881420W in Sumter Co. Founded before 1830 and locally called PATTON'S HILL in honor of James W. Patton, who had moved here from MS and purchased the land. Named SUMTERVILLE for the co. Sumterville PO est. in 1834 (Foscue 61–62, 65).

SUNDAY CREEK   See BRUSH CREEK in Lauderdale Co.

SUNFLOWER   Settlement with discontinued PO at 312256NO880030W in Washington Co. Origin of name is uncertain. A Spanish land grant was made to a man named *San Fleur*. Possibly this name became, through folk etymology, *Sunflower*, or the community may have been given the designation for a nearby stream appearing on early maps of the area. PO est. in 1892 (Matte 369).

SUNNY SOUTH   Settlement with PO at 315753NO873824W in Wilcox Co. Named for the *Sunny South*, a steamboat destroyed by fire in 1867 at Portland, a dead town once located on the banks of the Alabama River in Dallas Co. PO est. in 1888 (Harris 1982, 56–57).

SURGINER   ['sɜrdʒənər]   Settlement with discontinued PO at 320319NO874233W in Marengo Co. Named for Earl P. Surginer, the first postmaster, appointed in 1914 ("Record of Appointment of Postmasters").

SURVEYORS CREEK   Stream rising at 320131NO881624W in Choctaw Co. and flowing into the Tombigbee River at 315036NO881340W. Name probably refers to an early surveyor who worked in the area (U.S.G.S., 1966 Base Maps).

SUSAN MOORE   Settlement at 340501NO862542W in Blount Co. Named for the school financed by David and Joseph Moore, Birmingham physicians who gave the school the name of their mother. Also known as CLARENCE for Clarence Moore, the grandson of Robert M. Moore, the founder of the community in 1865 (Blount Co. Historical Society 54–56).

SUTTLE   Settlement with discontinued PO at 323210NO871047W in Perry Co. Probably named for the family of Joseph F. Suttle, the first postmaster, appointed in 1933 ("Record of Appointment of Postmasters").

SUTTLETON   See WEST BLOCTON in Bibb Co.

SWAIM [swem]   Settlement with discontinued PO at 345210NO861154W in Jackson Co. Probably named for the family of Moses Swaim, who moved here in 1823. PO est. in 1910 (Melancon).

SWAMP CREEK   Stream rising at 325217NO860631W in Coosa Co. and joining Hatchet Creek at 325139NO862019W. The former Indian name was PINTHTHLOCKO (La Tourette, 1833, 1844 maps), from Creek *opilwa* 'swamp' and *lako* 'big' (Read 50, 61).

SWAN CREEK   Stream rising at 345320NO865709W in Limestone Co. and flowing into Wheeler Lake of the Tennessee River at 344040NO865936W. The name probably refers to some of the abundant waterfowl found here by settlers during the early 1800s (U.S.G.S., 1966 Base Maps).

SWAYNE COURTHOUSE   See VERNON in Lamar Co.

SWEET WATER   Inc. town with PO at 320550NO875203W in Marengo Co. Originally located about 2 miles to the south; then moved here c. 1870. Named for the nearby creek, which had probably been given a designation suggesting the smooth, sweet taste of its water. PO est. in 1848. Inc. in 1963 (W. Smith).

SWIFT CREEK   Stream rising at 324659NO863753W in Chilton Co. and flowing into the Alabama River at 322410NO863807W in Autauga Co. On La Tourette's 1838 map. Descriptive name (Biggs 40).

SYCAMORE   Settlement with PO at 331504NO861209W in Talladega Co. Originally named SYCAMORE GROVE for the trees at the site. Sycamore PO est. in 1876 (McMillan).

SYLACAUGA [sɪlə'kɑgə]   Inc. town with PO at 331023NO861506W in Talladega Co. Name is derived from Creek *suli* 'buzzards' and *kagi* 'roost,' from *kakita* 'to sit.' PO est. in 1837. Inc. in 1867 (McMillan; Read 61).

SYLVANIA   Inc. town with PO at 343344NO854845W in DeKalb Co. Named by Jim Duncan, an early settler, for his home in GA. PO est. in 1893. Inc. in 1967 (Raughton 76).

SYLVAN SPRINGS   Inc. town at 333056NO870054W in Jefferson Co. The name is probably reminiscent of those of older places derived from the Latin noun *silva* 'forest,' but it is also descriptive of the site. Inc. in 1957.

TAIT'S GAP   Community in a small valley at 335753NO862358W in Blount Co. Named for the Tait family who made surveys of the area in the 1790s when the land was still part of GA (Weaver).

TALLADEGA [,tælə'dɪgə]   Inc. co. seat with PO at 332609NO860621W in Talladega Co. The name was that of a Creek village, derived from *tal(wa)* 'town' and *atigi* 'border.' It was an Upper Creek border town on the edge of the Cherokee and Chickasaw lands. In 1813 during the war with the hostile Creeks, the fortified place for the town was called FORT LESLIE for Andrew Leslie, a local trader. FORT TALLADEGA was another designation; TALLADEGA BATTLE GROUND refers to the battle fought here during that war. The town was called TALLADEGA COURT HOUSE in 1832 when it was chosen to be the seat of justice for Talladega Co. PO est. in 1833. Inc. in 1835 (McMillan; Read 62).

TALLADEGA COUNTY   Created by act of the state general assembly on Dec. 18, 1832. Bordered on the north by Calhoun Co., on the east by Clay Co. and Cleburne Co., on the south by Coosa Co., and on the west by Shelby Co. and St. Clair Co. Named for the town Talladega, which was chosen to be its co. seat (McMillan).

TALLADEGA CREEK   Stream rising at 332442NO855000W in Clay Co. and flowing into the Coosa River at 331826NO862137W in Talladega Co. Earliest recorded name, KYMULGA C., on Purcell's map, c. 1770, is that of a Creek Indian town on the lower part of the Coosa River. EUFAULA-HATCHIE

CR. in "Letters of Benjamin Hawkins, 1796–1806" (169). EUFAULA was the name of a Creek town on this stream. TALLADEGA CR. on Melish's 1818 map. Named for the town Talladega (McMillan).

TALLADEGA MOUNTAINS Mountain range straddling Talladega Co. and Clay Co., the western end of the Appalachians. TALLADEGA MOUNTAINS in the 1832 "Field Notes." Named for the town. REBECCA MOUNTAINS on La Tourette's 1856 map. Origin of this name unknown. BLUE (RIDGE) MOUNTAINS in E. A. Smith's 1874 *Report of Progress* (37), probably for the mountains in VA. Usually called TALLADEGA MOUNTAINS now (McMillan).

TALLADEGA SPRINGS Inc. town with discontinued PO at 330717NO862636W in Talladega Co. Formerly a resort village named for the co. and for the sulphur and chalybeate springs at the site. Also known as SULPHUR SPRINGS. Talladega Springs PO est. in 1885. Inc. in 1913 (McMillan).

TALLAHATTA SPRINGS [ˌtælə'hætə] Community with discontinued PO at 315434NO875236W in Clarke Co. Known as LOWDER SPRINGS for George Lowder, the owner of the land c. 1830. Named TALLAHATTA SPRINGS by Benjamin C. Foster, who opened a health resort here in the 1840s. This name comes from Choctaw *tali* 'rock' or 'metal' and *hata* 'white.' Tallahatta Springs PO est. in 1876 (Clarke Co. Historical Society 369; Read 62).

TALLAPOOSA COUNTY [ˌtælə'pusə] Created by act of the state general assembly on Dec. 18, 1832. Bordered on the north by Clay Co. and Randolph Co., on the east by Chambers Co., on the southeast by Lee Co., on the south by Macon Co., and on the west by Elmore Co. and Coosa Co. Named for the river. The co. seats have been Okfuskee, 1832–38, and Dadeville, the present one (Dugas [Tallapoosa Co.] 86–88).

TALLAPOOSA RIVER Stream rising in western GA, entering AL at 335048NO-850044W in Cleburne Co., and joining the Coosa River at 323021NO861600W between Elmore Co. and Montgomery Co. Named for an ancient Upper Creek Indian town whose designation comes from Choctaw or Alabama *tali* 'rock' and *pushi* 'pulverized' (Read 62–63).

TALLASEEHATCHEE CREEK [ˌtæləsə'hætʃɪ] Stream rising at 331148NO860411W in Clay Co. and flowing into the Coosa River at 331740NO862127W in Talladega Co. TALLASIHATCHIE in 1772 "Journal of David Taitt." NATCHEW CREEK in "Letters of Benjamin Hawkins, 1796–1806" (34). The former name, the one now used, is derived from Creek *tallasi hatchi* 'old town creek' or 'captured town creek.' The latter designation is a variant of the name of the Natchez Indians (McMillan; Read 28–29, 63).

TALLASSEE ['tæləsɪ] Inc. town with PO at 323209NO855336W in Elmore Co. Named by Thomas Barnett, who built a small cotton mill here c. 1838 and named the settlement for an ancient Indian town. The name of the Upper Creek town *Talase* is probably derived from Creek *talofa* 'town' and *isi* 'taken.' PO est. in 1880. Inc. in 1908 (M. B. Owen 1:421–22; Read 29, 63).

TALLAWAMPA CREEK [ˌtælə'wampə] Stream rising at 315157NO880946W in Choctaw Co. and flowing into the Tombigbee River at 315115NO880932W. Also known as BIG TALLAWAMPA CREEK. TALLAWAPPA C. on La Tourette's 1844 map. The name is probably derived from Choctaw *taloa* 'to sing' and *ampa* 'to eat' or from *taloa* 'to sing' and *abi* or *ambi* 'to kill' (Read 64).

TALLULA See COVIN in Fayette Co.

TANNER Settlement with PO on the Louisville and Nashville RR at 344353NO-865814W in Limestone Co. Named for Samuel Tanner, the first mayor of Athens. Earlier called MCDONALD'S STATION and ROWLAND, both probably for local families. Rowland PO est. in 1878, Tanner PO in 1913 (Wellden).

TANNER WILLIAMS Settlement at 304326NO882212W in Mobile Co. Named for the two principal landowners in the area (Harris 1982, 159; *Official 1959 Alabama Highway Map*).

TARENTUM ['tærəntəm] Settlement with discontinued PO at 313821NO855244W in Pike Co. The name is probably reminiscent of the ancient form of the designation for Tarento, a city in southeastern Italy. PO est. in 1893.

TARRANT ['tærənt] Inc. town with PO at 333500NO864622W in Jefferson Co. Named in honor of Felix Isham Tarrant, a former president of the National Cast Iron Pipe Co., around whose plant the settlement developed. PO est. in 1819. Inc. as TARRANT CITY in 1918, the word *city* being dropped following an election held in 1984 (Hagood 34).

TARVER'S MILL CREEK See SOAPSTONE CREEK.

TASCALOUSSA RIVER See BLACK WARRIOR RIVER.

TATTILABA CREEK [ˌtætə'ebə] Stream rising at 314349NO874919W in Clarke Co. and joining Jackson Co. at 313531NO875835W. Name probably means 'Dead Tree on a High Point,' from Choctaw *iti hata* 'whitewood,' *illi* 'dead,' and *aba* 'above' (McMillan in Read 100; Read 65; U.S.G.S., 1966 Base Maps).

TAYLOR Inc. town with discontinued PO at 310953NO852806W in Houston Co. Named for James Taylor, an early settler. PO est. in 1885. Inc. in 1967 (F. S. Watson 1972, 106–07).

TAYLOR CREEK Stream rising at 324735NO875613W in Greene Co. and flowing into the Tombigbee River. Probably named for Robert Taylor, a planter in the area in the 1850s (Rich 1979, 536).

TECUMSEH [tɪ'kʌmsɪ] Community with discontinued PO at 335956NO852527W in Cherokee Co. Developed around the furnace of the Tecumseh Iron Co. built here in 1873. The name was chosen to honor the Shawnee chief Tecumseh (1768–1813), who visited the southern Indians in 1811. His name is derived from Shawnee *Tikamthi* or *Tecumtha* 'one who springs.' PO est. in 1873 (Harris 1982, 159; Read 66).

TEKETANOAH CREEK See CYPRESS CREEK in Lauderdale Co.

TENNANT Community with discontinued PO at 331605NO852725W in Randolph Co. Named for Rachel L. Tennant, the first postmaster, appointed in 1898 ("Record of Appointment of Postmasters").

TENNESSEE RIVER [ˌtɛnə'si] Stream formed by the confluence in east TN of the Holston and French Broad rivers that enters AL in Jackson Co. and flows across the northern part of this state back into TN at the northwestern border of Lauderdale Co. After reentering TN, it flows north through that state and through KY until it empties into the Ohio River. Its name, that of several Indian towns in TN and NC, in Cherokee is *Tenasi* and has no specific meaning. First applied to a watercourse near one of these towns in TN and carried downstream by the English settlers, who used it to identify the entire river (Read 66; G. R. Stewart 1970, 477–78).

TENNILLE ['tɛnəl] Settlement with discontinued PO at 313723NO854607W in Pike Co. Named for St. Clair Tennille from Troy, AL, a promoter of rail transportation. PO est. in 1890 (Farmer 1973, 408).

TENSAW ['tɛnsɔ] Community with discontinued PO at 310924NO874757W in Baldwin Co. Area settled in the 1790s by, among others, John and William Pierce, who founded a cotton gin and a school here. Named for the river. PO est. in 1808 (Bush 85–86).

TENSAW RIVER Stream rising at 310404NO875747W in Baldwin Co. and flowing into Mobile Bay at 304106NO880025W. Named for the Tensas Indians who had been first brought to Mobile from LA before 1709. By 1744 they had left Mobile and were living in Baldwin Co. In "A Sketch of the Creek Country in 1798 and 1799," Benjamin Hawkins says, "The settlement of Ta-en-sau borders on the Mobile and Alabama, on the left side" (23). The meaning of the name is unknown (Read 66).

TERESE [tə'ris] Settlement with discontinued PO at 314817NO850950W in Barbour Co. Named for Teresa McTyer, a relative of Robert A. McTyer, the first postmaster, appointed in 1882 (Ellis 57).

TERRAPIN CREEK Stream rising in GA, entering AL in Cleburne Co., and flowing into Weiss Lake at 340750NO854116W in Cherokee Co. This name, probably a descriptive and environmental one, has been in use since the 1830s. COOSAHATCHIE appears in Tuomey's 1858 *Report* (90). *Coosa* might have been borrowed from the name of the Coosa River and the second element might be *hachi*, the Creek word for 'creek' (Jolly).

TERRAPIN MOUNTAIN See DUGGAR MOUNTAIN in Calhoun Co.

TEXAS Settlement with discontinued PO at 335547NO874043W in Marion Co. Designation probably borrowed from that of the state, whose name, an Indian variant of *tejas* 'allies,' was applied by Spanish explorers to a group of Indian tribes living in the territory east of NM. PO est. in 1876 (G. R. Stewart 1970, 480).

TEXASVILLE Settlement with discontinued PO at 314254NO852528W in Barbour Co. While many Alabamians were moving westward to TX, named for that state. Texasville PO est. in 1857; Alston PO, 1892–1906; Texasville PO again in 1906. ALSTON, a temporary designation for both the town and PO, honored A. H. Alston, a local judge (Ellis 16, 57–58).

THACH [θæt∫] Settlement with discontinued PO at 345511NO865334W. Probably named for the prominent Thach family. PO est. in 1921 (Edwards and Axford 219).

THADDEUS See REELTOWN in Tallapoosa Co.

THARPTOWN Settlement at 343120NO873743W. Named for John Bull Tharp, who passed through this area in 1814 with Andrew Jackson while they were on their way to participate in the Battle of New Orleans and who later returned to settle here (Knight 37).

THEODORE Settlement with PO at 303251NO881031W in Mobile Co. When the Mobile and New Orleans RR (Louisville and Nashville) reached this point c. 1880, the town was called FOWL RIVER STATION for the nearby river. Renamed for William Theodore Hieronymous, operator of the local sawmill and the first postmaster, appointed in 1886 (Harris 1982, 160).

THOLOCCO, LAKE [θə'lɑkə] Artificial lake formed by the impoundment of Claybank Creek at 312313NO854322W in Dale Co. In the late 1930s a prize of $10 was awarded to Fanny Hutchinson of Enterprise for suggesting the name. According to legend, it was a title of respect meaning something like 'Big Chief' given to Samuel Dale, the hero honored with the naming of Dale Co., by his Indian opponents in the Creek War of 1813–14 (F. S. Watson 1968, 82).

THOMAS CROSSROADS See WALNUT GROVE in Etowah Co.

THOMAS STATION See INVERNESS in Bullock Co.

THOMASTON Inc. town with PO at 321559NO873731W in Marengo Co. Named for Charles Brooks Thomas, who bought the land c. 1890 and became the first postmaster of Thomaston PO, appointed in 1892. Inc. in 1901 (W. Smith).

THOMASVILLE Inc. town with PO at 315448NO874409W in Clarke Co. Located in the area known as *Choctaw Corners* on the border between the lands of the Choctaw and Creek nations. Named for Samuel Thomas, a financier of the rail line later known as the Southern RR. PO est. in 1888. Inc. in 1899 (D. S. Akens 7, 42).

THORNTON Settlement with discontinued PO at 324207NO854453W in Tallapoosa Co. Named for the local Thornton family. PO est. in 1882 (Dugas [Tallapoosa Co.] 88).

THORTONTOWN Settlement at 345022NO872120W in Lauderdale Co. Named for the local Thornton family (Sockwell; U.S.G.S. Topographical Maps, 1936 Thortontown Quad.).

THORSBY Inc. town with PO at 325456NO864257W in Chilton Co. Founded in 1896 by Thomas Thorsen and others from Scandinavia. Said to have been named for Thorsen's former hometown. PO est. in 1896. Inc. in 1901 (Covington 29).

THREE NOTCH Settlement at 320622NO853445W in Bullock Co. Named for the military road built in 1824 whose route had been marked by three blazes (notches) on the trees along the way. PO est. in 1871 (Farmer 1952, 34–35).

THREE RUNS CREEK Stream rising at 315810NO862430W in Lowndes Co. and joining Pigeon Creek at 315021NO862917W in Butler Co. Name is descriptive of the three smaller streams feeding this one (J. Taylor; U.S.G.S., 1966 Base Maps).

THREET Community with discontinued PO at 345702NO874944W in Lauderdale Co. Originally called RUSSELL CROSSROADS for Alexander Russell, who bought land here in 1836 and 1856. Renamed for John Threet, who had purchased land here in 1831. Threet PO est. in 1893 (Sockwell).

TIBBIE Settlement with PO at 312143NO881455W in Washington Co. TIBBIE probably is a shortened form of *Okatibbee*, the name of a creek in MS. *Okatibbee* seems to have been derived from *Oakibbeha* 'blocks of ice therein,' from Choctaw *okti* 'ice' and the plural form *abeha* 'to be in.' PO est. in 1910 (Read 67).

TICKABUM CREEK See TUCKABUM CREEK in Choctaw Co.

TIDMORE See NECTAR in Blount Co.

TIGHT EYE CREEK Stream rising at 311943NO860109W in Coffee Co. and joining Double Bridges Creek at 310832NO855915W in Geneva Co. Though its origin is unknown, the name might have been derived through folk etymology from an Indian designation (U.S.G.S., 1966 Base Maps).

TITUS Settlement with PO at 324244NO-861906W in Elmore Co. A personal name, probably either that of a local resident or of the Roman emperor (AD 79–81). PO est. in 1887.

TOADVINE Community with discontinued PO at 332958NO870924W in Jefferson Co. First called SMITHVILLE in honor of Cape Smith, a Confederate veteran and postmaster who named the PO est. in 1873 TOAD VINES, later TOADVINE, for a Confederate soldier from GA who had befriended him while both were Union prisoners. Later the town was named for the PO (Hagood 28).

TOLL GATE See HAMILTON in Marion Co.

TOMBIGBEE RIVER [tɑmˈbɪgbɪ] Stream rising in northeastern MS, flowing into AL between Pickens Co. and Sumter Co., and joining with the Alabama River at 310810NO-875639W near the southeastern corner of Washington Co. to form the Mobile River. TOMBECKBAY RIVER on Romans's 1772 map. The name, derived from Choctaw *itombi* 'box, coffin' and *ikbi* 'makers,' refers to old men who cleaned the bones of the dead before placing these in boxes for burial (Read 69).

TONEY Settlement with PO at 345353NO-864401W in Madison Co. Probably named for the family of the first postmaster, Blanche R. Toney, appointed in 1898 ("Record of Appointment of Postmasters").

TOWN CREEK The designations for both streams probably refer to Indian villages once located nearby.

1. Stream rising at 344317NO853548W in De-Kalb Co. and flowing into Guntersville Lake at 342415NO861317W in Marshall Co. (U.S.G.S., 1966 Base Maps).

2. Stream rising at 342653NO872111W in Lawrence Co. and flowing between that co. and Colbert Co. into the Tennessee River at 344730NO872540W. In 1817 also designated with the environmental name BEAVER CREEK (Sockwell).

TOWN CREEK Inc. town with PO at 342812NO872525W in Lawrence Co. First called JONESBORO, probably for a local Jones family. Renamed for the nearby creek. PO est. in 1854. Inc. in 1875 (Gentry 11, 66, 82).

TOWNLEY Settlement with PO at 334944NO872554W in Walker Co. Probably named for the family of Daniel Townley, who settled here in 1882. PO est. in 1887 (Gant).

TOXEY Inc. town with PO at 315446NO-881834W in Choctaw Co. Named by John T. Cochrane for a backer of his RR, the Tusca-loosa Belt Line (Alabama, Tennessee and Northern), who lived in NY. PO est. in 1847. Inc. in 1949 (Choctaw Co. Bicentennial Commission 20).

TRAFFORD Inc. town with discontinued PO at 334905NO864434W in Jefferson Co. First called UNION CITY, but when the Louisville and Nashville RR reached here, to avoid confusion with another station on the line, its name was changed to honor C. R. Trafford, a local landowner. PO est. in 1915. Inc. in 1948 (Hagood 19).

TRAVELER'S REST See KELLY'S CROSSROADS in Coosa Co.

TRENTON Settlement with PO at 344441NO861506W in Jackson Co. Probably named for the city in NJ where a battle of the revolutionary war occurred. PO est. in 1834 (Kennamer 142).

TRIANA [traɪˈænə] Inc. town with discontinued PO on the Tennessee River at 343510NO864400W in Madison Co. Once an important river port, it is said to have been named for a soldier who accompanied Columbus to the New World in 1492. Inc. in 1819. PO est. in 1821 (Harris 1982, 162).

TRICKEM [ˈtrɪkəm] Community with discontinued PO at 333322NO852440W in Cleburne Co. It received its name when three communities in the area chose this place to be the site of their Mt. Giliard Church, familiarly known as *Tri-Com*, a reduced form of *Three (Tri) Communities Church*. PO est. in 1891 (Harris 1982, 162–63).

TRIMBLE Settlement with discontinued PO at 340536NO865655W in Cullman Co. Named for William S. Trimble, the first postmaster, appointed in 1886 (Whitehead 16).

TRINITY Inc. town with PO at 343624NO-870518W in Morgan Co. In 1810 named FENNEL'S TURNOUT for the family of Willie Fennel, who had moved here from VA. In the 1820s the name was changed to TRINITY for Trinity Methodist Church. PO est. in 1848. Inc. in 1901 (Ackley 47).

TRION See VANCE in Tuscaloosa Co.

TROUT CREEK See RAGLAND in St. Clair Co.

TROY See GREENSBORO in Hale Co.

TROY Inc. co. seat with PO at 314831NO-855812W in Pike Co. Indians called the area *Deer Stand Hill*. The first white settlers called the place ZEBULON for Zebulon Pike, for whom the co. is named, later renaming it CENTREVILLE because of its central location. In 1838 Luke R. Simmons named the town TROY, either for Troy, NY, or in honor of Alexander Troy, the father of D. S. Troy of Montgomery. Became co. seat and received its PO in 1838. Inc. in 1843 (Farmer 1973, 35–36).

TRUSS See TRUSSVILLE in Jefferson Co.

TRUSSELLS CREEK Stream rising at 325815NO875239W in Greene Co. and flowing into the Tombigbee River at 324817NO-880445W. Named for James Trussell, purchaser of nearby land in 1823 (Rich 1979, 552–53).

TRUSSVILLE Inc. town with PO at 333711NO863632W in Jefferson Co. First called TRUSS. Named for Warren Truss (1772–1837), who settled here in 1821. Trussville PO est. in 1833. Inc. in 1947 (Hagood 20).

TUCKABUM CREEK ['tʌkəbʌm] Stream rising at 321548NO882713W in Choctaw Co. and flowing into the Tombigbee River at 320917NO880102W. Also known as TICKABUM CREEK. TUCKABURNE on La Tourette's 1844 map. According to Brannon (1925, 12), the name probably means 'fired' or 'an explosion,' from Choctaw *tukafa* 'to fire.' Read (67) suggests that the name may be derived from Choctaw *iti* 'wood' plus *hakbona* 'moldy' or from Choctaw *tikpi* 'knob, bend in a stream' plus *buna* 'double' or even from Choctaw *hatakabi* 'murderer, man killer.'

TUMBLETON Settlement at 312423NO-851524W in Henry Co. Although its origin is unknown, the name might be a humorously descriptive combination of *tumble* and *-ton*

'town' (*Official 1959 Alabama Highway Map*).

TUMKEEHATCHEE CREEK [ˌtʌmki'hæt/ɪ] Stream rising at 323809NO860113W in Elmore Co. and flowing into the Tallapoosa River at 322658NO855623W. TOMGAHATCHEE C. on La Tourette's 1833 map. The name is a reduced form of *Wetumkeehatchee* 'sounding water creek,' from Creek *wi* 'water' plus *tamka* 'sounding' plus *hachi* 'creek' (Read 71).

TUNNEL SPRINGS Settlement with discontinued PO at 313833NO871424W in Monroe Co. Originally called LONG STREET, probably a descriptive name; then KEMPVILLE for Bill Kemp, a prominent businessman of the time. East's Store was located here. The tunnel built by the Louisville and Nashville RR near the town's spring is the source of the current name. PO est. in 1902 (Dugas [Monroe Co.] 97).

TURKEY CREEK The following streams have environmental names, all possibly translations of Indian designations.

1. Stream rising at 310847NO873759W in Baldwin Co. and flowing into Holley Creek at 311503NO874623W (U.S.G.S., 1966 Base Maps).

2. Stream rising at 314346NO882051W in Choctaw Co. and flowing into the Tombigbee River at 314721NO881000W. Its Indian name FAKITCHIPUNTA is Choctaw for 'Little Turkeys,' from *fakit* 'turkeys' and *chipunta* 'little' (Read 32; U.S.G.S., 1966 Base Maps).

3. Stream rising at 334207NO863637W in Jefferson Co. and flowing into Locust Fork of the Black Warrior River at 334612NO-864931W. The name is said to be a translation of its Creek Indian designation (Brown and Nabers 179).

4. Stream rising at 314743NO865942W in Monroe Co. and joining Pine Barren Creek at 315701NO865914W in Wilcox Co. (U.S.G.S., 1966 Base Maps).

TURKEY HEAVEN MOUNTAIN Mountain whose summit is at 333250NO852801W in Cleburne Co. Probably a humorously descriptive environmental name (U.S.G.S., 1966 Base Maps).

TUSCALOOSA [ˌtʌskə'lusə] Inc. co. seat with PO near falls on the Black Warrior River at 331235NO873409W in Tuscaloosa Co. TASCALUCA, among other spellings, first appeared in the journals of de Soto's secretaries in 1540, referring to a province and a chief. After the arrival of the first English-speaking settlers in 1816, the site was called TUSCALOOSA FALLS or FALLS OF TUS-CALOOSA, BLACK WARRIOR FALLS or FALLS OF THE BLACK WARRIOR, all making reference to the river falls and using the Indian or translated name of the river. The settlement was known during 1816–17 as SHELLEYVILLE, SHELBYVILLE, or SHELLYTOWN, probably all referring to the mussel shells found on the site, and as MATHILDAVILLE for the wife of Joshua Halbert, a pioneer settler, 1816–19. By 1818 the name TUSCALOOSA was preferred, though it was spelled with a *k* rather than a *c* until the late 1900s. This name, which spread from a Choctaw tribe to a province, to the chief or class of chieftains, to the river or the falls, and finally to the settlement, is derived from Choctaw *tashka* 'warrior' and *lusa* 'black.' Co. seat, 1818–22, and 1826–. Inc. in 1819. Black Warrior Falls PO est. in 1818, re-named TUSCALOOSA PO in 1825. State capital, 1826–46 (Rich 1979, 364, 499).

TUSCALOOSA COUNTY   Created by act of the AL territorial general assembly on Feb. 7, 1818. Bounded on the north by Fayette Co. and Walker Co., on the east by Jefferson Co. and Bibb Co., on the south by Hale Co. and Greene Co., and on the west by Pickens Co. Named for the river and settlement. Tusca-loosa has served as the co. seat since 1818, except for the period 1822–26, when New-town held the courthouse (Rich 1979, 560).
TUSCALOOSA FALLS   See TUSCA-LOOSA in Tuscaloosa Co.
TUSCUMBIA [tʌsˈkʌmbiə]   Inc. co. seat with PO at 344352NO874209W in Colbert Co. Town inc. in 1820 as OCOCOPOSO, derived from *Oka Kapassa* 'cold water' in the Choc-taw and Chickasaw dialects. Also sometimes designated with the translation of this name. Because of the big nearby spring that provides the cold water, the name of the town was changed to BIG SPRING in 1821. In 1822

became known as TUSCUMBIA, the name of a famous Cherokee chief that is derived from Choctaw or Chickasaw *tashka* 'warrior' and *abi* or *ambi* 'killer' or from *tashka* 'war-rior' and *umbachi* 'rainmaker' or *taska umba ikbi* 'warrior rainmaker.' Big Spring PO est. in 1814, Tuscumbia PO in 1822. Chosen co. seat in 1867 (Sockwell).
TUSKEGEE [tʌsˈkigɪ]   Inc. co. seat at 322526NO854130W in Macon Co. Founded in 1833 and named for a Creek Indian town once located in the fork of the Coosa and Talla-poosa rivers. Name is probably that of a Muskhogean tribe meaning 'warrior' in vari-ous Muskhogean dialects or, specifically in Creek, 'warriors' from *taskialgi*. Became co. seat in 1833. PO est. in 1834. Inc. in 1843 (Read 73).
TWICKENHAM   See HUNTSVILLE in Madison Co.
TWIN   Settlement at 340019NO875123W in Marion Co. Location of Burleson's Store. TWIN may have resulted from the practice of calling this community and a nearby one, Yampertown (origin of name unknown), "Twin Towns" (Lawler; *Official 1959 Ala-bama Highway Map*).
TYLER   Settlement with PO at 322021NO-865247W in Dallas Co. Possibly named for John Tyler (1790–1862), tenth president of the U.S. (1841–45). PO est. in 1891 (Harris 1982, 165).
UCHEE [ˈutʃɪ]   Community with discon-tinued PO at 322102NO852153W in Russell Co. Named for the creek. PO est. in 1835 (Brannon 1959, 102; McMillan in Read 100).
UCHEE CREEK   Stream, also known as BIG UCHEE CREEK, rising at 322747NO-852317W in Lee Co. and flowing into the Chattahoochee River at 321822NO845722W in Russell Co. Its tributary Little Uchee Creek, also called WETUMPKA CREEK (for meaning see WETUMPKA), rises at 323646NO851938W in Lee Co. and joins (Big) Uchee Creek at 322106NO850421W in Rus-sell Co. According to Read, *Uchee* or *Yuchi* is the name of an Indian tribe belonging to the Creek confederacy, probably meaning 'at a distance,' from *yu* 'at a distance' and *chi* 'sit-ting down.' Swanton, however, says that the name may be derived "from Hitchiti *Ochesee* 'people of a different speech,' a name also ap-plied to the Lower Creek Indians" (McMillan in Read 98; Read 73–74).

UNDERWOOD Community with discontinued PO at 330848NO865036W in Shelby Co. Named for a family who settled in the area in the 1830s. PO est. in 1916 (Tamarin).

UNDERWOOD CROSSROADS Settlement at 344523NO873145W in Colbert Co. Known as ALEXANDER CROSSROADS for a local family, c. 1908–55; then renamed UNDERWOOD CROSSROADS for another local family (Sockwell).

UNION Inc. town with discontinued PO at 325917NO875454W in Greene Co. Named in 1821 for the town in SC by settlers from that state. PO est. in 1836. Inc. in 1979 (Rich 1979, 566).

UNION CHURCH COMMUNITY See DEES in Mobile Co.

UNION CITY See TRAFFORD in Jefferson Co.

UNION GROVE Settlement at 325857NO864051W in Chilton Co. Named for the union church of several denominations that was formed to hold services in a grove of trees because there were no churches in the area. Some years later, in 1898, the Union Grove Baptist Church was organized at this site (Harris 1982, 165).

UNION GROVE Inc. town with PO at 342406NO862657W in Marshall Co. Probably an inspirational and descriptive name. PO est. in 1889. Inc. in 1962.

UNION HILL Settlement at 342825NO863719W in Morgan Co. Known as WOLFF for an early family until the 1860s. It received its current name when the residents formed a union to organize a church and a school (Ackley 48).

UNION SPRINGS Inc. co. seat with PO at 320839NO854254W in Bullock Co. Named for the large springs that come together on Chunnennuggee Ridge where the settlement is located to form the Conecuh River. PO est. in 1837. Inc. in 1844. Became the co. seat in 1867 (T. M. Owen 2:1348).

UNIONTOWN Inc. town with PO at 322658NO873051W in Perry Co. Settled in 1818 by the Wood brothers, who were honored with the town's original name, WOODVILLE. Because there was already a Woodville PO in the state when the PO was est. here in 1833, Philip J. Weaver suggested the name be changed to UNIONTOWN for his father's PO in MD. Inc. in 1836 (T. M. Owen 2:1348).

UNITY Settlement at 330019NO862133W in Coosa Co. An inspirational and symbolic name (Harris 1982, 165; *Official 1983–84 Alabama Highway Map*).

UPHAPEE CREEK [juˈfɔbɪ] Stream rising at 322533NO853720W in Macon Co. and flowing into the Tallapoosa River at 322834NO855112W. EUPHAUBE in Benjamin Hawkins's "A Sketch of the Creek Country in 1798 and 1799" (26). Although the meaning of the name is uncertain, Read thinks it is a variant of *Naufaba*, from Hitchiti *nofapi*, a compound of *nofi* 'beech' and *api* 'tree' (32).

UPSHAW Settlement with discontinued PO at 341653NO870921W in Winston Co. Probably named for a local family. PO est. in 1889.

URIAH Settlement with PO at 311818NO873008W in Monroe Co. Area first called *Butterfork*, possibly a humorously descriptive name. The brothers David and Uriah Blackshear first leased, then bought, the land for their logging business, founding a town that they first called MAROS, possibly for the river in Hungary. It was later renamed URIAH, probably for Uriah Blackshear. Uriah PO est. in 1914 (Dugas [Monroe Co.] 97).

VALHERMOSO SPRINGS [vælhərˈmoso] Settlement with PO at 343004NO864109W in Morgan Co. Lancelot Chunn discovered the springs at this site c. 1813; later they were named for him. James Manning of Madison Co. operated a hotel at the springs then named for him, 1818–23. In 1834 the PO opened here was called WHITE SULPHUR SPRINGS. Finally, in 1856 Jean J. Giers, a native of the Rhineland, bought the hotel and gave it a national reputation as a resort and health spa. He named the springs, the resort, and the settlement surrounding it VALHERMOSO, a Spanish form meaning 'beautiful valley.' In 1857 the name of the PO was changed to VALHERMOSO SPRINGS. In 1950 a tornado and fire destroyed most of the hotel, which was then closed (Ackley 48).

VALLEY Inc. town at 323746NO850818W in Lee Co. The name is descriptive of the settlement's location in the Wacoochee Valley. Inc. in 1980 (Harris 1982, 166; *Official 1959 Alabama Highway Map*).

VALLEY CREEK Both streams probably have descriptive names.

1. Stream rising at 324101NO865809W in Dallas Co. and flowing into the Alabama River at 323451NO870216W. Name in use as early as 1894 (Griffith 514–15).

2. Stream rising at 333034NO864934W in Jefferson Co. and flowing into the Black Warrior River at 333213NO871348W. Formerly CUTTACOOCHEE CREEK. CUTOCACHE on La Tourette's 1844 map. The present name is a translation of either Chickasaw *okkattahaka* 'hillside' and *hutche* (*hacha*) 'stream' or Chickasaw *okhoatakachi* 'crosswise,' with an implied *bok* 'creek' (Read 74).

VALLEY CREEK   See SUMMERFIELD in Dallas Co.

VALLEY CREEK   Settlement at 332315NO870420W in Jefferson Co. Named for the creek (*Official 1959 Alabama Highway Map*; Sartwell).

VALLEY HEAD   Inc. town with PO at 343408NO853654W in DeKalb Co. Name is descriptive of settlement's location where Will's Creek rises in Will's Valley. PO est. in 1837. Inc. in 1923 (Raughton 78).

VANCE   Inc. town with PO at 331027NO871401W in Tuscaloosa Co. Settled prior to 1830 and known as TRION, probably a name transferred from GA, or possibly a respelling of *Tryon*, the name of a town in NC honoring William Tryon (1725–1788), a colonial governor. In the early 1870s called SMALLWOOD for Charles Smallwood, a local sawmill owner. In the late 1870s named VANCE for a local family, especially for William Vance. Trion PO est. in 1849; Smallwood PO in 1872; Vance PO in 1879. Inc. in 1970 (Rich 509, 551–52, 573).

VANDIVER ['vændəvər]   Settlement with PO at 332814NO863048W in Shelby Co. Named for James L. Vandiver, the first postmaster, appointed in 1888 (Tamarin).

VAUGHN   Settlement at 310147NO875140W in Baldwin Co. Probably named for the Vaughn family who owned land in this area c. 1830 (Bush 87).

VEASEY CREEK   Stream rising at 330103NO852052W in Chambers Co. and flowing into GA at 330001NO851211W. Named for an early local family (Crump; U.S.G.S., 1966 Base Maps).

VERBENA   Settlement with PO at 324459NO863041W in Chilton Co. Once a popular health resort, it was first called SUMMERFIELD, possibly a descriptive and environmental name, but because of the existence of another town in AL with that name when the PO was est. in 1871, Kate Norton, a relative of an early settler, suggested that it be named VERBENA for the wild flowers growing in the area (B. D. Roberts).

VERNON   Inc. co. seat with PO at 334525NO880632W in Lamar Co. Formerly called SWAYNE COURTHOUSE in honor of Wager Swayne, military governor of the Chattahoochee District of the state, 1866–67. In 1868 when it was chosen to be the co. seat, it was renamed for Edmund Vernon, an immigrant from Vernon, England. PO est. in 1869. Inc. in 1870 (Acee 2, 11).

VESTAVIA HILLS   Inc. town with PO at 332655NO84716W in Jefferson Co. Also known as VESTAVIA, it was named for a now razed mansion built by George Ward, an early mayor of Birmingham, to resemble the temple of the Vestal Virgins of Rome. Inc. in 1950. PO est. in 1971 (Hagood 53).

VICK   Settlement with discontinued PO at 325627NO870500W in Bibb Co. Named for Gertrude Victoria Brown, wife of James Brown, member of a prominent local family. Vick PO, 1899–1912. Now, most residents call their community SANDY for nearby Sandy Chapel, a Methodist church organized in 1828 (Abrams 74–75; Cottingham).

VICTORIA   Settlement with discontinued PO at 313147NO855618W in Coffee Co. First called SMUT EYE, supposedly because the faces of the men standing around a fire outside J. C. Brown's store would become coated with soot. Next, known as BUZBEEVILLE for William H. Buzbee, the postmaster. Finally, named for Victoria Winslow, a local beauty. Smut Eye PO est. in 1850; Buzbeeville PO in 1853; and Victoria PO in 1868 (F. S. Watson 1970, 74).

VIDETTE ['vaɪdɛt]   Community with discontinued PO at 314358NO861142W in Crenshaw Co. Possibly named for a local woman. PO est. in 1882.

VILLAGE POINT   Cape on Mobile Bay at 303740NO875509W in Baldwin Co. Named for Village, a French settlement that was located near here, c. 1704–64 (Bush 87).

VILLAGE SPRINGS   Settlement with discontinued PO at 334530NO863819W in Blount Co. Descriptive and environmental name. PO est. in 1832 (Harris 1982, 167).

VILLULA [vəˈlulə]   Settlement with discontinued PO at 321557NO850953W in Russell Co. The name probably alludes to an early description of the town as "a settlement of villas." PO est. in 1847 (A. K. Walker 1950, 218–19).

VINA [ˈvaɪnə]   Inc. town with PO where co. Highway 23 crosses state Highway 19 at 342235NO880331W in Franklin Co. Originally called JONES CROSSROADS for a local family. Later known as NEW BURLESON because it is near the dead town BURLESON, also named for a local family. Finally named VINA by an engineer for the Illinois Central RR for his wife. Vina PO est. in 1907. Inc. in 1909 (Knight 38).

VINCENT   Inc. town with PO at 332304NO862443W in Shelby Co. The PO located here, 1871–88, was known as PROPELL (origin unknown). The town and later the PO were named for the Vincent family, who were among the earliest settlers. Inc. in 1897 (M. B. Owen 1:506).

VINCENTS CROSSROADS   See RED BAY in Franklin Co.

VINE HILL   Settlement with discontinued PO at 323644NO865408W in Autauga Co. Descriptive and environmental name. PO est. in 1886 (Biggs 42).

VINEGAR BEND   Settlement with PO located on the Mobile and Ohio RR in a bend of Escatawpa Creek at 311549NO882041W in Washington Co. Origin of the name is unknown. Among the traditional explanations is the one that a train car filled with vinegar overturned here spilling vinegar over the ground. Another is that convicts released to work for the lumber companies in the area were caught with whiskey jugs, which they claimed contained vinegar. PO est. in 1889 (Matte 375–83).

VINELAND   Settlement with discontinued PO at 320208NO873934W in Marengo Co. The name might be an allusion to the attempt by French Napoleonic refugees to grow grapes in this co., or it might be descriptive of the wild vines once growing in the area. PO est. in 1887 (W. Smith).

VINEMONT   See SOUTH VINEMONT in Cullman Co.

VIRGINIA   Settlement at 332432NO870302W in Jefferson Co. It is said to have been named for Virginia City, NV, by two brothers, George and E. T. Shuler, who had moved from there to AL c. 1860 hoping to find gold here (Hagood 8–9).

VREDENBURG   Inc. town with PO at 314942NO871918W in Monroe Co. Founded by and named for Peter Vredenburg II of Springfield, IL, who built a sawmill here in 1912. PO est. in 1911. Inc. in 1913 (Dugas [Monroe Co.] 97).

WACOOCHEE CREEK [wəˈkutʃi]   Stream rising at 323750NO851634W in Lee Co. and flowing into the Chattahoochee River at 323804NO850555W. WOC-COO-CHE in Benjamin Hawkins's "A Sketch of the Creek Country in 1798 and 1799" (54). The name, meaning 'calf,' is a combination of *waka* 'cow' and *-uchi* 'little' (Read 74).

WADE MOUNTAIN   Mountain whose summit is at 344900NO863659W in Madison Co. Probably named for an early settler (U.S.G.S., 1966 Base Maps).

WADE'S STATION   See FULTON in Clarke Co.

WADLEY   Inc. town with PO on the Atlanta, Birmingham and Atlantic RR at 330717NO853359W in Randolph Co. Named for George Dale Wadley, the vice-president and general manager for construction of the RR. Inc. in 1970. PO est. in 1907 (Harris 1982, 168).

WADSWORTH   Settlement with discontinued PO at 322351NO863142W in Autauga Co. Named for William W. Wadsworth, the first postmaster, appointed in 1887, who settled here in 1880 (Biggs 42).

WAGER [ˈwægər]   Community with discontinued PO at 312630NO875937W in Washington Co. Named for Fred Wager, who, with his brother Ernest, founded a large sawmill here. PO est. in 1890. Most of the town moved 2 miles west and was called WAGERVILLE after a new school was built there (Matte 384–85).

WAGERVILLE   Community with discontinued PO at 312610NO880142W in Washington Co. Named for the older settlement WAGER located 2 miles to the east. PO est. in 1957 (Matte 384–85).

WAGNON MOUNTAIN   Mountain whose summit is at 343754NO874957W in Colbert Co. Named for the Wagnon families, who owned land in this area c. 1908 (Sockwell).

WAHALAK CREEK [ˈwɔhəlɑk]   Stream rising at 320346NO881843W in Choctaw Co. and flowing into the Tombigbee River at

320117NO880704W. WAHLOH, WAHLOK in *American State Papers*, Indian Affairs, vol. 2 (1834): 84. The Choctaw name *Wahhaloha* 'pronged' refers to the two branches of the stream (Read 74–75).

WAIT   See DREWERY in Monroe Co.

WAKEFIELD   Dead town that was located 15 miles south of St. Stephens in the bend of the Tombigbee River near McIntosh in Washington Co. Second co. seat, 1805–09, while Washington Co. was still a part of the MS Territory. Named by Harry Toulmin, a territorial judge in the Tombigbee District in 1804 and later a member of the AL general assembly, for the English town in Oliver Goldsmith's novel *The Vicar of Wakefield* (Harris 1977, 109; Harris 1982, 168).

WALDO   Inc. town with discontinued PO at 332249NO860137W in Talladega Co. During the 1850s Riddle's Iron Works and Riddle's Mill were operated here by the Riddle brothers, Walter, Samuel, and John, from Hollidaysburg, PA. When PO was est. in 1870, it and town were named WALDO for Ralph Waldo Emerson (1803–1882), American essayist, a relative of the Riddle family. Inc. in 1972 (McMillan).

WALKER COUNTY   Created by act of the state general assembly on Dec. 20, 1824. Bordered on the north by Winston Co., on the northeast by Cullman Co., on the east by Blount Co., on the southeast by Jefferson Co., on the south by Tuscaloosa Co., and on the west by Fayette Co. and Marion Co. Named for John Williams Walker of Madison Co. (1783–1823), U.S. senator (1819–23). Jasper is the co. seat (M. B. Owen 1:517).

WALKER SPRINGS   Settlement with PO at 313226NO874728W in Clarke Co. Named for William Walker, who operated a tavern here c. 1811. PO est. in 1887 (Clarke Co. Historical Society 382–83).

WALLACE   Settlement with discontinued PO at 311234NO871306W in Escambia Co. Originally called FLORENCE, but there already being a town with this name in the state, the PO was est. in 1880 as MIRIAMVILLE, probably to honor a local woman. The next year both it and the town were renamed WALLACE for William Wallace, a local sawmill owner (Waters 204–06).

WALLERS CREEK   Stream rising at 311756NO873310W in Monroe Co. and flowing into the Alabama River at 312414NO874132W. According to tradition, named for Thomas Waller, of Selma, who built the first sawmill in the co. in 1820 on this creek (Dugas [Monroe Co.] 98).

WALLSBORO   Settlement at 323512NO861233W in Elmore Co. Possibly named for a local Wall family (U.S.G.S., 1966 Base Maps).

WALNUT CREEK   Both streams probably have environmental names.
1. Stream rising at 325040NO863702W in Chilton Co. and flowing into the Coosa River at 325206NO862753W (U.S.G.S., 1966 Base Maps).
2. Stream rising at 314908NO855333W in Pike Co. and joining Whitewater Creek at 314054NO855429W (U.S.G.S., 1966 Base Maps).

WALNUT GROVE   Inc. town with PO at 340356NO861823W in Etowah Co. Named THOMAS CROSSROADS for a local family c. 1825; then CORNELIUS in honor of Harvey Cornelius, the first postmaster, appointed in 1848. Both the town and the PO were given the descriptive and environmental name WALNUT GROVE on Sept. 19, 1849. Inc. in 1886 (Jolly).

WALNUT HILL   Settlement with discontinued PO at 324236NO854708W in Tallapoosa Co. Name is descriptive of the abundant walnut trees in the area (Dugas [Tallapoosa Co.] 88).

WALTER   Settlement with discontinued PO at 340707NO864037W in Cullman Co. Named for the son of Elijah W. Harper, the first postmaster, appointed in 1888 (Whitehead 16).

WALTER F. GEORGE RESERVOIR   Artificial lake formed by the impoundment of the Chattahoochee River at 313705NO850423W in Henry Co. with Fort Gaines Lock and Dam, now the Walter F. George Lock and Dam. Briefly called FORT GAINES LAKE for the dam; then renamed in 1962 for Walter

F. George (1878–1957), U.S. senator from GA (1922–57). Also called LAKE EUFAULA for the nearby town in Barbour Co. (Harder 583; U.S.G.S., 1966 Base Maps).

WARD Settlement with PO at 322143NO-881641W in Sumter Co. Named c. 1910 for H. B. Ward, a prominent local physician. PO est. in 1912 (Foscue 64).

WARNER See REPUBLIC in Jefferson Co.

WARRENTON See RICHMOND in Dallas Co.

WARRENTON Settlement with discontinued PO at 342124NO862134W in Marshall Co. Named by the pioneering Smith family for their former home, Warren Co., VA. PO est. in 1836. Co. seat, 1841–48 (Roden 53).

WARRIOR Inc. town with PO on a spur of the Louisville and Nashville RR at 334851NO864834W in Jefferson Co. Also known as WARRIOR STATION. Named for the Warrior Coal Fields, opened here in 1872 by J. T. Pierce. PO est. in 1872. Inc. in 1899 (Harris 1982, 169).

WARRIOR BRIDGE See BLADON SPRINGS in Choctaw Co.

WARRIOR RIVER See BLACK WARRIOR RIVER.

WARRIOR STAND Settlement with discontinued PO at 321842NO853312W in Macon Co. A probable explanation for the name is that an Indian village was once located here. PO est. in 1846 (Harris 1982, 169).

WARSAW Settlement with discontinued PO at 325615NO881211W in Sumter Co. First called JAMESTOWN, probably for the first permanent English colony in this country in VA. Later named WARSAW, probably for Warsaw, VA, the former home of some of the town's early settlers. Jamestown PO est. in 1832, Warsaw PO in 1842 (Foscue 39, 64).

WASHINGTON Dead town with discontinued PO once located on the north bank of the Alabama River just west of the mouth of Autauga Creek in the southern part of Autauga Co. Founded in 1817, it was probably named for George Washington (1732–1799), first president of the U.S. (1789–97). Co. seat, 1829–30. PO, 1819–35. Inc. in 1820. By 1879 all but deserted (Harris 1977, 110).

WASHINGTON COUNTY Created on June 4, 1800, by the MS territorial legislature. Bordered on the north by Choctaw Co., on the east by Clarke Co., on the south by Mobile Co., and on the west by MS. The oldest co. in the state, it was named for George Washington (1732–1799), first president of the U.S. (1789–97). Its co. seats have been McIntosh Bluff, 1800–1805; Wakefield, 1805–09; Franklin, 1809–15; Old St. Stephens, 1815–25; Washington Courthouse, 1825–42; Barrytown, 1842–47; New St. Stephens, 1848–1907; and the current one, Chatom (Matte 1–62).

WASHINGTON COURTHOUSE Dead town with discontinued PO once located 6 miles southeast of Millry in Washington Co. Name is descriptive, because the settlement served as the Washington Co. seat of justice, 1825–42. PO, 1825–42 (Matte 50).

WASHINGTON CREEK Stream rising at 324019NO872521W in Perry Co. and joining Boguechitto Creek at 322843NO871947W in Dallas Co. Probably named for George Washington (1732–1799), first president of the U.S. (1789–97) (U.S.G.S., 1966 Base Maps).

WATERFORD Community at 312109NO-853605W in Dale Co. First called DEMMICK, probably in honor of a local resident. Name changed c. 1907 to WATERFORD by the Alabama Midland RR Co. because of the large water tank erected beside the tracks here where trains stopped for water (F. S. Watson 1968, 138).

WATERLOO Inc. town with PO at 345505NO880351W in Lauderdale Co. Laid out in 1819 and named for the town in Belgium near which the duke of Wellington had defeated Napoleon four years earlier. PO est. in 1827. Inc. in 1832 (Sockwell).

WATTERS CREEK Stream rising at 324050NO870819W in Perry Co. and flowing into the Cahaba River. Named for a family living in the eastern part of the co. (England; U.S.G.S., 1966 Base Maps).

WATTSVILLE Community with PO at 334053NO861647W in St. Clair Co. In 1839 called BOLTON'S CROSSROADS for a local family. In 1890 John Postell, who had purchased the mineral rights here and built a rail line to connect the town to GA, called the settlement COAL CITY. Later, named WATTSVILLE for Watt T. Brown, a local resident who owned and operated the mines during the 1880s. Wattsville PO est. in 1929 (Rich).

WATULA CREEK [wə'tulə] Stream rising at 323236NO852053W in Lee Co. and joining Uchee Creek at 322322NO851846W in Russell Co. WATOOLEE on the U.S.G.S. Topographic Maps, 1903 Opelika Quad. The current name is a reduced form of Creek *watula* 'crane,' *haki* 'whooping,' and *hachi* 'creek' (Read 75).

WAVELAND See CLOVERDALE in Lauderdale Co.

WAVERLY Inc. town with PO at 324407NO853445W in Chambers Co. Named for the Waverly novels of Sir Walter Scott. PO est. in 1851. Inc. in 1911 (Dugas [Chambers Co.] 58).

WAYSIDE Community with discontinued PO at 335154NO875326W in Fayette Co. Name suggested by the wife of Terrell M. Reese, the first postmaster, appointed in 1878. She thought it appropriate because the settlement was located by "the wayside of the road" to Guin (Newell and Newell 33).

WEAVER Inc. town with PO on the Southern RR at 334507NO854841W in Calhoun Co. Named WEAVER'S STATION in 1871 for Daniel F. Weaver, RR and express agent and later postmaster. Weaver Station PO est. in 1871, *station* being dropped in 1903. Inc. in 1945 (Jolly).

WEBB Inc. town with PO at 311537NO-851624W in Houston Co. Named for B. F. Webb, the founder of the settlement. PO est. in 1900. Inc. in 1910 (F. S. Watson 1972, 13, 110).

WEBB See HENSON SPRINGS in Lamar Co.

WEDGWORTH Settlement with discontinued PO at 324829NO874545W in Hale Co. Named for the pioneering family of John Wedgworth, who died in this area in 1824. PO est. in 1904 (W. Smith).

WEDOWEE [wi'dauɪ] Inc. co. seat with PO at 331832NO852905W in Randolph Co. Laid out in Dec. 1835 by Hedgeman Triplett, the first co. surveyor, and named for an Indian called "Wahdowwee," who lived in a nearby village. Between 1840 and 1844 called MCDONALD, probably for a local family. Renamed WEDOWEE in 1844. *Wahdowwee* may be derived from Creek *wiwa* 'water' and *tawa* 'sumac' or from *wiwa* and *towi* 'old,' thus meaning either 'sumac water' or 'old water.' Chosen co. seat in 1835. Wedowee PO est. in 1837; McDonald PO in 1840; Wedowee PO again in 1844 (Read 76).

WEDOWEE CREEK Stream rising at 332116NO851828W in Randolph Co. and flowing into the Little Tallapoosa River at 332047NO853050W. Probably named for the town (U.S.G.S., 1966 Base Maps).

WEEKS BAY Bay with an outlet into Mobile Bay at 302351NO875001W in Baldwin Co. Earlier known as FISH BAY because of the abundant fish, but renamed for N. Weeks, who bought the bay and the surrounding area in 1809 for $100 (Bush 88).

WEISNER MOUNTAIN ['waɪsnər] Mountain whose summit is at 340135NO854028W in Cherokee Co. Named for a local family reputed to be Cherokee Indians (Cherokee Co. Historical Society 3:181; U.S.G.S., 1966 Base Maps).

WEISS LAKE [waɪs] Artificial lake formed by the impoundment of the Coosa River at 341021NO854513W in Cherokee Co. by Weiss Dam. Originally known as WEISS RESERVOIR, it was named in 1961 for F. C. Weiss, the vice-president in charge of construction of the Alabama Power Co. dam. Present designation approved by the U.S. Board on Geographic Names in 1978 (Harris 1982, 171).

WELCH Settlement with discontinued PO at 330517NO852022W in Chambers Co. Probably named for a local family. PO est. in 1888 (Dugas [Chambers Co.] 58).

WELLBORN Dead town with discontinued PO once located 12 miles east of Enterprise in Coffee Co. Named for William Wellborn, a general in the Creek Indian War of 1836–37. Co. seat, 1841–52. After the PO, est. in 1846, was closed in 1866, the town was gradually abandoned (Harris 1982, 170).

WELLINGTON Settlement with PO at 334921NO855334W in Calhoun Co. Named by O. M. Alexander, who settled here before 1900, for his former home in OH. PO est. in 1904 (Lindsey 75).

WELLS STATION See NEWVILLE in Henry Co.

WEOGUFKA [ˌwiəˈgʌfkə] Settlement with PO at 330059NO861844W in Coosa Co. Named for an Upper Creek town that was itself named for the nearby creek. PO est. in 1837 (Hopkins; McMillan in Read 100).

WEOGUFKA CREEK Stream rising at 330810NO860849W in Clay Co. and flowing into the Coosa River at 325208NO862432W in Coosa Co. On La Tourette's 1844 map. Name is derived from Creek *wi* 'water' and *ogufki* 'muddy' (Read 77).

WEOKA [wiˈokə] Settlement with discontinued PO at 324303NO861103W in Elmore Co. Named for the Upper Creek town that was itself named for the nearby creek. PO est. in 1880 (Read 78).

WEOKA CREEK Stream rising at 323919NO861805W in Elmore Co., flowing into Coosa Co., then back into Elmore Co. where it empties into Jordan Lake at 323919NO861805W. OUYOUKAS on De Crenay's 1733 map. WEWOKA, an Upper Creek town on a creek with the same name, in Benjamin Hawkins's "A Sketch of the Creek Country in 1798 and 1799" (40). Name comes from Creek *wi* 'water' and *wohka* 'barking' or 'roaring' (Read 78).

WEST BEND Settlement with discontinued PO on the east bank of the Tombigbee River at 314927NO880756W in Clarke Co. Name is descriptive of the nearby bend in the Tombigbee. PO est. in 1888 (D. S. Akens 43).

WEST BLOCTON Inc. town with PO at 330705NO870730W in Bibb Co. First called SUTTLETON for Julian LaFayette Suttle, a local businessman. Renamed for Blocton, a town less than 1/2 mile to the east, c. 1901. The older settlement, founded c. 1833 by the Cahaba Coal Mining Co., was named by Thomas H. Aldrich, one of its mining engineers. *Blocton* is said to refer to a block of coal weighing over a ton removed from the mine. Inc. in 1901. PO est. in 1904 (Ellison 178–84).

WEST END Settlement approximately 1 mile west of Anniston at 333717NO855159W in Calhoun Co. Formerly known as COBB TOWN, probably for a local family. In recent years, the directional and generic name has been used (Jolly; *Official 1983–84 Alabama Highway Map*).

WEST GREENE Community with PO at 325525NO880507W in Greene Co. First designated with the inspirational and symbolic name HOPEWELL, but after the Civil War, to avoid confusion with another town, the name of the PO and later the settlement was changed to one descriptive of the town's location in northwest Greene Co. Hopewell PO est. in 1824, West Greene PO in 1879 (Rich 1979, 288–89, 588–89).

WEST JEFFERSON Inc. town at 333857NO870407W in Jefferson Co. Name is probably descriptive of the settlement's location in the western part of the co. Inc. in 1964.

WESTON Inc. town at 340935NO880155W in Marion Co. Name, a combination of *west* plus *-ton* 'town,' is descriptive of the settlement's location in the western part of the co. Inc. in 1960 (Lawler).

WESTOVER Community with PO at 332058NO863209W in Shelby Co. A borrowed name, possibly from the plantation home of William Byrd in VA. PO est. in 1909 (Harris 1982, 172).

WEST POINT Inc. town at 341419NO865733W in Cullman Co. The town was given this descriptive and locational name c. 1910 by Jim Lamb because several roads meet at this point c. 8 miles northwest of Cullman, the co. seat. Inc. in 1978 (Whitehead 17).

WEST SELMONT Settlement at 322328NO870102W in Dallas Co. Name is a combination of the first syllables of *Selma* and *Montgomery* that is descriptive of the town's location west of Montgomery on old U.S. Highway 80 between that city and Selma (Nelms; U.S.G.S., 1966 Base Maps).

WEST WELLINGTON Settlement at 334929NO855436W in Calhoun Co. Name is descriptive of this town's location west of the settlement Wellington (Jolly; U.S.G.S. Topographic Maps, 1947 Wellington Quad.).

WETUMPKA [wiˈtʌmpkə] Inc. co. seat with PO at 323237NO861243W in Elmore Co. The name means 'sounding or tumbling water,' from Creek *wi* 'water' and *tamka* 'sounding.' Settled in the early 1830s when the site was still a part of Coosa Co. PO est. in 1833. Inc. in 1839. Chosen co. seat when Elmore Co. was created in 1866 (Read 78–79).

WETUMPKA CREEK See (LITTLE) UCHEE CREEK in Russell Co.

WHATLEY Settlement with PO at 313902NO874218W in Clarke Co. Named for Franklyn Benjamin Whatley (1826–1896), who deeded land for a station to the Southern RR c. 1886. PO est. in 1890 (Clarke Co. Historical Society 410–11).

WHEELER Settlement with discontinued PO on the Memphis and Charleston RR (Southern) at 343909NO871459W in Lawrence Co. Named for Joseph Wheeler (1836–1906), a general in the Confederate cavalry and the Spanish-American War who lived here. Wheeler Station PO est. in 1870, *station* being dropped in 1895 (Harris 1982, 173).

WHEELER LAKE Artificial lake formed by the impoundment of the Tennessee River with Wheeler Dam at 344830NO872300W between Lawrence Co. and Lauderdale Co. that extends 74 miles east to Guntersville Dam in Marshall Co. Wheeler Dam was completed in 1936, at which time it and the lake were named for Joseph Wheeler (1836–1906), the Confederate and Spanish-American War general (Sockwell).

WHEELERVILLE See CRAGFORD in Clay Co.

WHITE CITY Community at 323854NO863558W in Autauga Co. Named for a nearby pond whose designation is descriptive of its bed of white sand (DeVaughn; *Official 1983–84 Alabama Highway Map*).

WHITE HALL Inc. town with discontinued PO at 321937NO864243W in Lowndes Co. Settled c. 1819, its first designation was the descriptive and environmental SANDTOWN. Later named for the plantation home of Reubin White destroyed by a tornado in 1882. PO est. in 1874. Inc. in 1979 (Harris 1982, 173).

WHITEHEAD Settlement with discontinued PO at 345317NO871938W in Lauderdale Co. Settled between 1847 and 1850 and named for an early family. PO est. in 1891 (Sockwell).

WHITEOAK ' Settlement at 343911NO873143W in Franklin Co. Name is probably descriptive and environmental (1965 General Highway Map of Franklin Co.).

WHITE PLAINS Settlement with discontinued PO at 334450NO854121W in Calhoun Co. Known as CHOCCOLOCCO for the nearby creek in 1828. An early settler renamed the town for his former home in GA. PO est. in 1837 (Jolly).

WHITE PLAINS Community at 325932NO852357W in Chambers Co. Name is descriptive of the effect of the sun shining upon the relatively flat land in the area (Dugas [Chambers Co.] 58; U.S.G.S., 1966 Base Maps).

WHITESBURG Settlement with discontinued PO at 343435NO863349W in Madison Co. Various ferries across the Tennessee River such as those operated by a Mr. Hobbs and by a Mr. Black were located here first. For a while known as DITTO'S LANDING for John Ditto, a trader with the Indians. In 1824 renamed WHITESBURG for James White, a member of the firm of Read and White, in business here from 1820. Ditto's Landing PO est. in 1820, Whitesburg PO in 1827 (Green; Record 1:67, 72).

WHITES CHAPEL Inc. town at 333556NO863223W in St. Clair Co. Named for the church for which W. L. White, an early Baptist minister, donated the land. Inc. in 1962 (Rich).

WHITESIDE Community on the north bank of the Tennessee River at 343742NO865818W in Limestone Co. Named for James White, the merchant from VA who traded salt for land along the river in Limestone Co. and Madison Co. before 1820 (Harris 1982, 173).

WHITE SULPHUR SPRINGS See VAL-HERMOSO SPRINGS in Morgan Co.

WHITEWATER CREEK Stream rising at 314917NO855143W in Pike Co. and flowing into the Pea River at 312454NO860346W in Coffee Co. Probably a descriptive name (U.S.G.S., 1966 Base Maps).

WHITFIELD Settlement with discontinued PO at 323155NO880525W in Sumter Co. First known as BLACK BLUFF, the translation of *sakti* 'bluff' and *lusa* 'black,' the Indian name of the Tombigbee River bluff on which it is located. Renamed for the family of J. G. Whitfield, an early settler. PO est. in 1885 (Foscue 65).

WHITING See FLOMATON in Escambia Co.

WHITNEY Settlement with PO at 335204NO861729W in St. Clair Co. Named for Charley Whitney, a member of the state legislature during Reconstruction following the Civil War. PO est. in 1875 (Rich).

WHITON ['hwaɪtən] Settlement with

discontinued PO at 342120NO860445W in DeKalb Co. Name is a combination of *White* and *-ton* 'town,' in honor of P. White, the first postmaster, appointed in 1878 (Raughton 81).

WHITSON Community at 333407NO872428W in Tuscaloosa Co. Named for the Whitson family who settled here by 1818 (Rich 1979, 594).

WICKSBURG Settlement with discontinued PO at 311229NO853721W in Houston Co. Name consists of the last syllable of the last name of Elijah A. Trawick, the first postmaster, plus the possessive suffix *-s* and *-burg*. PO est. in 1878 (F. S. Watson 1972, 114).

WIGGINS SPRINGS See RICHMOND in Dale Co.

WILBURN Settlement with discontinued PO at 335706NO870203W in Cullman Co. Named by Charles Sandlin, the first postmaster, possibly for a local individual. Better known now as BUG TUSSLE, a humorous name generally assumed to imply that one is likely to encounter bugs in this place. Wilburn PO, 1903–06 (G. R. Stewart 1970, 64; Whitehead 13).

WILCOX COUNTY Created by act of the AL territorial general assembly on Dec. 13, 1819. Bordered on the north by Dallas Co., on the east by Lowndes Co. and Butler Co., on the south by Monroe Co., on the southwest by Clarke Co., and on the northwest by Marengo Co. Named for Joseph M. Wilcox, an army lieutenant killed by hostile Creeks on Jan. 15, 1814. Canton Bluff was the temporary co. seat until 1832 when Barboursville, later renamed CAMDEN, became the permanent one (Harris 1982, 174).

WILLIAM "BILL" DANNELLY RESERVOIR ['dænlɪ] Artificial lake formed by the impoundment of the Alabama River at 320527NO872353W between Wilcox Co. and Dallas Co. Named in 1970 for William, "Bill," Dannelly, probate judge of Wilcox Co., c. 1950–69 (Sartwell).

WILLIAMS CREEK Stream rising at 341549NO880033W in Marion Co. and flowing into the Buttahatchee River at 340856NO875814W. Named for Stephen Williams, who settled here in 1820 and operated a mill on the creek (Lawler).

WILLIAMS STATION See ATMORE in Escambia Co.

WILMER Inc. town with PO at 304923NO882141W in Mobile Co. Named for Richard H. Wilmer (1816–1900), a bishop of the Episcopal Church of Alabama. PO est. in 1894. Inc. in 1970 (Harris 1982, 174–75).

WILSON CREEK Stream rising at 335058NO880826W in Lamar Co. and joining Yellow Creek at 334020NO881430W. Probably named for a local family (U.S.G.S., 1966 Base Maps).

WILSONIA Community at 340559NO855415W in Etowah Co. Probably named for a local Wilson family (Rand McNally, 1899 map).

WILSON LAKE Artificial lake formed by the impoundment of the Tennessee River with Wilson Dam at 344803NO873733W between Lauderdale Co. and Colbert Co. The dam, named for Woodrow Wilson (1856–1924), president of the U.S. (1913–21), was completed in 1925 (Sockwell).

WILSON'S CREEK See SHOAL CREEK.

WILSON'S HILL See MONTEVALLO in Shelby Co.

WILSON STAND See ST. FLORIAN in Lauderdale Co.

WILSONVILLE Inc. town with PO at 331403NO862901W in Shelby Co. Named for its earliest settler, Elisha Wilson. PO est. in 1822. Inc. in 1897 (Tamarin).

WILTON Inc. town with PO at 330443NO865254W in Shelby Co. First called BIRMINGHAM JUNCTION when the Southern RR was connected here with the Alabama and Tennessee Rivers RR (Southern) in 1890; next known as BISMARCK for Otto Eduard Leopold von Bismarck (1815–1898), first chancellor of the German Empire (1871–90); then CATOOSA for a town in GA; and finally WILTON, probably for Wilton, England. Bismarck PO est. in 1892; Catoosa PO in 1899; and Wilton PO in 1907. Inc. in 1918 (Tamarin).

WIND CREEK Stream rising at 324144NO853916W in Lee Co. and flowing into the Tallapoosa River at 324029NO-

855421W in Tallapoosa Co. Said to be named for the Wind Indians, who once lived in this area (Dugas [Tallapoosa Co.] 88).

WINDHAM SPRINGS Settlement at 332929NO872955W in Tuscaloosa Co. Named for the resort at the sulphur springs founded by Levi Windham in 1850. The resort closed after a storm destroyed the hotel in 1917 (Rich 1979, 600).

WINFIELD Inc. town with PO at 335544NO874902W in Marion Co. First called LUXAPALLILA for a nearby creek, then NEEDMORE, a humorously descriptive compound. Later named WINFIELD in honor of Winfield Scott (1786–1866), commanding general of U.S. forces in the Mexican War (1846–48). PO est. in 1888. Inc. in 1898 (Harris 1982, 175).

WING Settlement with PO at 310139NO-863638W in Covington Co. Although its origin is unknown, the name might be a translation of an Indian designation for a nearby natural feature. PO est. in 1955.

WINGARD See RURAL HOME in Pike Co.

WINN Settlement with discontinued PO at 313906NO875502W in Clay Co. Named for the family of Frank Winn, the first postmaster, appointed in 1881 (Clarke Co. Historical Society 414–19).

WINSTON COUNTY Created by act of the state general assembly as HANCOCK COUNTY on Feb. 12, 1850. Bordered on the north by Franklin Co. and Lawrence Co., on the east by Cullman Co., on the south by Walker Co., and on the west by Marion Co. First named for John Hancock (1737–1793), the MA statesman. On Jan. 22, 1858, name changed to WINSTON in honor of John Anthony Winston (1812–1871), governor of AL (1853–57). The co. seat was Houston until 1882 when Double Springs, the present one, was chosen (Gant).

WINTERBORO Settlement with discontinued PO at 331917NO861149W in Talladega Co. Named for Joseph Winter, who had

planned a plank toll road from Wetumpka to Talladega in the 1850s. When the residents of Talladega failed to give him the expected financial support, he ended the road at this point, naming the settlement here for himself. PO est. in 1853 (McMillan).

WOLF BAY Bay opening into Perdido Bay at 301934NO873537W in Baldwin Co. WOLF is either the name of an early settler or a translation of an Indian designation (Bush 90; U.S.G.S., 1966 Base Maps).

WOLF CREEK The names of the following streams are probably environmental ones that may be translations of Indian designations.
1. Stream rising at 315127NO864325W in Butler Co. and joining Cedar Creek at 315943NO865353W in Wilcox Co. Probably named by Thomas Hill, who settled in the area c. 1816–17 (J. Taylor; U.S.G.S., 1966 Base Maps).
2. Stream rising at 333818NO873253W in Fayette Co. and joining Lost Creek at 333818NO871641W in Walker Co. Nathias Turner, one of Andrew Jackson's TN volunteers in the Creek Indian War of 1813–14, gave the creek its name (Gant).
3. Stream rising at 333854NO861840W in St. Clair Co. and joining Kelly Creek in Shelby Co. (Rich).

WOLF CREEK Settlement with PO at 333145NO862255W in St. Clair Co. Named for the nearby creek. PO est. in 1857 (Rich).

WOLFF See UNION HILL in Morgan Co.

WOMACK HILL Settlement with PO at 315111NO881119W in Choctaw Co. Named for a Mr. Womack, who operated a tanyard. PO est. in 1878 (Choctaw Co. Bicentennial Commission 20).

WOODLAND Settlement with PO at 332227NO852329W in Randolph Co. First known as LAMAR, possibly for a local family; later given its current descriptive and environmental name. Lamar PO est. in 1844, Woodland PO in 1934 (Harris 1982, 176).

WOODLAWN See OAKBOWERY in Chambers Co.

WOODS BLUFF Community with discontinued PO on a bluff overlooking the Tombigbee River at 315608NO880342W in Clarke Co. The designation of the bluff is the possessive form of the name of the former owner of the land, who had served as a major in the Creek Indian War of 1813–14. PO est. in 1835

(Clarke Co. Historical Commission 422–24).

WOODSHOP   See OZARK in Dale Co.

WOODSTOCK   Settlement with PO at 331224NO870900W in Bibb Co. A sawmill town named by the first postmaster, appointed in 1855, James W. Ray, for the home in England of his grandfather, Ansil Ray (Ellison 165–69).

WOODSTOCK   See ANNISTON in Calhoun Co.

WOODVILLE   See MILLTOWN in Chambers Co.

WOODVILLE   See GORDON in Houston Co.

WOODVILLE   See OLD WOODVILLE in Jackson Co.

WOODVILLE   Inc. town with PO at 343740NO861628W in Jackson Co. First located, c. 1815, 3/4 mile to the east of its present location. It served as the seat of justice for Decatur Co., 1821–24. A few years later, moved to its present site to be on the Southern RR. Named for Richard Wood, an early settler. PO est. in 1829. Inc. in 1880 (M. B. Owen 1:441).

WOODVILLE   See UNIONTOWN in Perry Co.

WOODWARD CROSSING   See BRIGHTON in Jefferson Co.

WOOTEN   See LIBERTY in Blount Co.

WREN   Settlement with PO at 342603NO871737W in Lawrence Co. Probably named for the local Wren family. PO est. in 1896 (Gentry 61).

WRIGHT   Settlement with discontinued PO at 345431NO875924W in Lauderdale Co. Probably named for Moses Wright (1749–1876), once a post rider on the Natchez Trace, who settled here c. 1832 and operated a general store. PO est. in 1891 (Sockwell).

YANTLEY ['jæntlɪ]   Settlement with PO at 321445NO882246W in Choctaw Co. Named for the nearby creek. PO est. in 1845 (Choctaw Co. Bicentennial Commission 5–6, 20).

YANTLEY CREEK   Stream rising at 321747NO882714W in Choctaw Co. and joining Tuckabum Creek at 321200NO880803W. YANILLO CREEK or 'Running Water' in *American State Papers*, Indian Affairs, vol. 2 (1834): 67, 73. Name is derived from Choctaw *oka yanalli* 'running water' (Read 79).

YARBO   Settlement with discontinued PO at 313237NO881640W in Washington Co.

Designation is probably a clipped form of the name of the first postmaster, Robert E. Yarborough, appointed in 1917 ("Record of Appointment of Postmasters").

YARBOROUGH   See BATTLES WHARF in Baldwin Co.

YELLOW BLUFF   Community with discontinued PO on the St. Louis and San Francisco RR at 315803NO872805W in Wilcox Co. Formerly located a few miles to the east on a bluff overlooking the Alabama River. *Yellow* is descriptive of the soil at this earlier site. PO est. in 1878 (Harris 1982, 177).

YELLOW CREEK   The names of the following streams, which may be translations of Indian designations, are probably descriptive of the muddy waters of these creeks.
1. Stream rising at 335309NO875706W in Fayette Co. and flowing across Lamar Co. into MS at 333400NO881945W (U.S.G.S., 1966 Base Maps).
2. Stream rising at 332558NO872745W in Fayette Co. and flowing into the Black Warrior River at 331518NO872705W in Tuscaloosa Co. On H. S. Tanner's 1825 map. Also known as BIG YELLOW CREEK (Rich 1979, 604).

YELLOWLEAF CREEK   Stream formed by the confluence at 331754NO863455W in Shelby Co. of the North Fork of Yellowleaf Creek, rising at 332530NO863757W, and the South Fork of Yellowleaf Creek, rising at 331544NO864545W. The combined streams flow into the Coosa River at 331436NO862649W. The designation is a translation of the Creek name *Asilanapi* 'Yellow Leaf Tree,' from *asi* 'leaf,' *lani* 'yellow,' and *api* 'tree' (Read 79).

YELLOW PINE   Settlement with PO at 312420NO882547W in Washington Co. Named for the Yellow Pine Lumber Co., which operated in the area. PO est. in 1888 (Matte 385–86).

YELLOW RIVER   Stream rising at 312723NO862005W in Covington Co. and flowing into FL at 303326NO865943W. Name is probably descriptive of the muddy water (U.S.G.S., 1966 Base Maps).

YORK   Inc. town with PO where the Alabama, Tennessee and Northern RR crosses the Southern RR at 322910NO881747W in Sumter Co. Settled c. 1866 by Middleton Praytor. Probably named for the dead town New York once located across Alamuchee

Creek from the present settlement. York Station PO est. in 1866, *station* being dropped in 1902 (Foscue 66).

YORK　　See OAKMAN in Walker Co.

YOUNGBLOOD　　Settlement with discontinued PO at 315042NO860410W in Pike Co. Probably named for Marshall J. Youngblood, the first postmaster, appointed in 1894 ("Record of Appointment of Postmasters").

YOUNGSVILLE　　See ALEXANDER CITY in Tallapoosa Co.

ZEBULON　　See TROY in Pike Co.

ZIDONIA　　See FRUITHURST in Cleburne Co.

ZIMCO　　Community at 314210NO875241W in Clarke Co. The name is an acronym for the [C. W.] Zimmerman Manufacturing Co., which had a logging operation here in the latter 1890s (Clarke Co. Historical Society 245–51).

ZIP CITY　　Community at 345717NO874012W in Lauderdale Co. Settled c. 1815 but had no name until the 1920s when Alonzo Parker gave it the humorous one ZIP CITY because of the speed of cars "zipping" through here on their way to TN where liquor could be purchased legally (Sockwell).

Sources

The sources listed below include place-name references used as models, published and unpublished works containing facts about Alabama geographic names, and informants. Unless otherwise stated, all the documents are in the main library of The University of Alabama in Tuscaloosa.

I. Published Monographs, Articles, and Maps

Abernethy, Thomas P. *The Formative Period in Alabama, 1815–1828*. Montgomery: Brown Printing Co., 1922.

Abrams, Ulysses H. *A History of Early Bibb County, Alabama, 1820–1870*. Ed. Mattie S. Johnson. Privately printed, c. 1981.

Acee, Joe G. *Lamar County History and Events*. Vernon: *Lamar Democrat*, 1976.

Acts of the General Assembly of the Alabama Territory. St. Stephens: Thomas Eastin, 1818.

Acts of the General Assembly of the State of Alabama. Huntsville, Cahaba, Tuscaloosa, Montgomery, 1819–67.

Acts of the Legislature of Alabama. Montgomery, 1868–1981.

Adams, John D. "Coosa County: Present Day Place Names Showing Aboriginal Influence." *Arrow Points* 2 (1921): 73–75.

Adelman, Bob. *Down Home: Camden, Alabama*. Ed. Susan Hall. New York: McGraw-Hill, 1972.

Alabama: A Guide to the Deep South. Comp. Works Progress Administration. New York: R. R. Smith, 1941.

Alabama Anthropological Society. *Handbook*. Montgomery: Brown Printing Co., 1920.

Alabama Blast Furnaces. Woodward: Woodward Iron Co., 1940.

"Alabama County Names." *Magazine of History* (Aug. 1917): 54–59.

Alabama. Department of Agriculture and Industries. *Alabama*. Bull. 27. Montgomery, 1907.

Alabama. Department of Agriculture and Industries. *Alabama*. Map. Montgomery, 1919.

Alabama. Department of Agriculture and Industries. *Alabama: Agricultural and Industrial Resources and Opportunities Handbook*. Montgomery, 1919.

Alabama. Department of Agriculture and Industries. *A General Description of the State of Alabama*. Montgomery, 1884.

Alabama. Department of Agriculture and Industries. *Home Seekers' and Capitalists' Guide to Alabama*. Chicago: Rand McNally, 1904.

Alabama. Department of Agriculture and Industries. *State of Alabama Elevations Map*. Montgomery, 1953.

Alabama. Department of Archives and History. *Alabama Official and Statistical Register* [biennial]. Montgomery, 1903–.

Alabama. Geological Survey. *Geologic Map of Alabama*. Tuscaloosa, 1858, 1894, 1926. Geological Survey of Alabama Library, Tuscaloosa.

Alabama Historical Records Survey. *Guide to the Vital Statistics Records in Alabama: Church Archives*. Birmingham, 1942.

Alabama Historical Records Survey. *Inventory of the Church Archives of Alabama*. Birmingham, various dates.

Alabama Historical Records Survey. *Inventory of the County Archives*. Birmingham, various dates.

Alabama History Commission. *Alabama's Tapestry of Historic Places*. Montgomery, 1978.

Alabama Mineral Lands Company Map. N.p., 1890. Geological Survey of Alabama Library, Tuscaloosa.

Alabama. Office of State Planning and Federal Programs. *Alabama Municipal Data Book*. Montgomery, 1980.

Alabama Power Co. *Annual Report*. Birmingham, various dates.

Alabama Power Co. Lake Recreational Maps. Birmingham, various dates.

Alabama Railroad Commission. *Report of the Railroad Commission* [biennial]. Montgomery, 1882–1912. Maps, 1882–1904, by Rand McNally.

Alabama. State Commission of Forestry. *Map of Alabama*. Montgomery, 1938.

Alabama. State Highway Commission. *Annual Report*. Montgomery, 1912–.

Alabama. State Highway Commission. General Highway Maps of Alabama Counties. Montgomery, various dates.

Alabama. State Highway Commission. Official Alabama Highway Maps. Montgomery, various dates.

Alabama. State Planning Commission. *Map of Alabama*. Montgomery, 1937.

Alabama. State Planning Commission. *State of Alabama Land Capability Map*. Montgomery, 1948.

Alabama: The Sesquicentennial of Statehood. Washington, D.C.: Library of Congress, 1969.

Albaugh, June M. *Collirene: the Queen Hill*. Montgomery: Paragon Press, c. 1977.

American State Papers. Indian Affairs. Vol. 1 (Washington, D.C.: GPO, 1832). Vol. 2 (Washington, D.C.: GPO, 1834).

American State Papers. Public Lands. Washington, D.C.: GPO, 1860–.

Anders, James M. *The Political History of Marengo County, Alabama, 1890–1910*. University: University of Alabama Press, 1940.

[Anderson, Neal L.]. *A Handbook of Presbyterian Missions in the Synod of Alabama*. Montgomery: Alabama Printing Co., 1898.

Andrews, W. L. "Early History of Southeast Alabama." *Alabama Historical Quarterly* 10 (1948): 99–132.

Andrews, W. T. *Memorial Sketches of the Lives and Labors of the Deceased Ministers of the North Alabama Conference, Methodist Episcopal Church, South, 1870–1912*. Nashville: Publishing House of the Methodist Episcopal Church, South, 1912.

Annual of the Alabama Baptist State Convention. Montgomery, 1912.

Anthony, J. D. "Cherokee County, Alabama: Reminiscences of Its Early Settlements." *Alabama Historical Quarterly* 8 (1946): 319–42.

Armes, Ethel M. *The Story of Coal and Iron in Alabama*. Birmingham: Birmingham Chamber of Commerce, 1910.

Asher and Adams. *Georgia and Alabama*. Map. N.p., 1872.

Atlas to Accompany the Official Records of the Union and Confederate Armies. Washington, D.C.: GPO, 1891–95.

"Autauga County." *Alabama Historical Quarterly* 14 (1952): 77.

Bacon, Delos H. *Map of Colbert County, Alabama*. N.p., 1895. Geological Survey of Alabama Library, Tuscaloosa.

———. *Map of Lauderdale County, Alabama*. N.p., 1896. Geological Survey of Alabama Library, Tuscaloosa.

Ball, T. H. *A Glance into the Great Southeast: Or Clarke County and Its Surroundings, from 1540 to 1877*. Grove Hill, 1882.

Bartholomew, John. *Map of Alabama*. Edinburgh: A. and C. Black, 1856.

———. *Map of Tennessee, Georgia, Mississippi, Louisiana, Alabama, Arkansas, and Northern Part of Florida*. Philadelphia: T. Elwood Zell, c. 1873.

Berney, Saffold. *Handbook of Alabama: A Complete Index to the State*. 2d ed. Birmingham: Roberts and Sons, 1892. Map, 1891, by Eugene A. Smith.

Besson, J. A. B. *History of Eufaula, Alabama: The Bluff City of the Chattahoochee*. Atlanta: Franklin Steam Printing House, 1875.

Betts, Edward Chambers. *Early History of Huntsville, Alabama, 1804 to 1870*. Montgomery: Brown Printing Co., 1916.

Bibb, J. Porter. "Montgomery County Present Day Place Names Showing Aboriginal Influence." *Arrow Points* 2 (1921): 1–3.

Blackford, Randolph F. *Fascinating Talladega County: Rich in History and in Legends*. Talladega: Randolph Brannon Printing Co., 1957.

Blount County Historical Society. *Bicentennial Edition of the Heritage of Blount County*. Privately printed, 1977.

Blue, M. P. *City Directory and History of Montgomery, Alabama*. Montgomery: T. C. Bingham, 1878.

Bond, Horace M. *Negro Education in Alabama: A Study in Cotton and Steel*. Washington, D.C.: Associated Publishers, 1939.

Boothe, Charles O. *The Cyclopedia of the Colored Baptists of Alabama: Their Leaders and Their Work*. Birmingham: Alabama Publishing Co., 1895.

Boudousquie, Paul C. *Reference Map of Mobile and Vicinity*. N.p., 1889. Library of Congress, Washington, D.C. Photocopy.

Bourne, Edward G. *Narratives of the Career of Hernando de Soto*. New York: A. S. Barnes, 1904.

Boyd, Minnie C. *Alabama in the Fifties*. New York: Arm Press, 1966.

Bradford, Thomas G. *An Illustrated Atlas: Geographical, Statistical, and Historical of the United States*. Philadelphia: E. S. Grant and Co., 1838.

———. *Map of Alabama*. Boston: C. S. Strong, 1841.

Brannon, Peter A. "Aboriginal Towns in Alabama: Showing Locations by Present County Boundary Lines." *Arrow Points* 4 (1922): 26–28.

———. "Alabama Post Office and Stream Names, 1922: A Study of the Etymology of the Names of the State's Present Post Offices and Streams." *Arrow Points* 6 (1923): 3–7.

———. "Barbour County Place Names." *Arrow Points* 5 (1922): 32–37.

———. "The Central Plank Road." *Alabama Highways* 2 (Dec. 1928): 3.

———. "Certain Place Names in Choctaw County." *Arrow Points* 11 (1925): 8–12.

———. "Clay County Present Day Place Names Suggesting Aboriginal Influence." *Arrow Points* 4 (1922): 96–98.

———. "County Names in Alabama History." *Arrow Points* 4 (1922): 33–34.

———. "Early Settlements in Autauga County." *Alabama Highways* 7 (Apr. 1933): 1.

———. "Elmore County Present Day Place Names Suggesting Aboriginal Influence." *Arrow Points* 4 (1922): 46–50.

———. "Jackson County Place Names." *Arrow Points* 13 (1928): 9–11.

———. "The Jackson Trace." *Alabama Highways* 3 (Apr. 1929): 3.

———. "Little Journeys Through Alabama from Aberfoil to Chunnenuggee by Clayton and Midway." *Arrow Points* 14 (1930): 1–6.

———. "Mooresville in Limestone: Some References to Early Tennessee Valley History." *Alabama Highways* 5 (June 1931): 3, 5, 8.

———. "Name Places Affected by the Indian War of 1813–14." *Alabama Historical Quarterly* 13 (1951): 132–35.

———. "Russell County Place Names." *Arrow Points* 8 (1924): 5–11.

———. "Russell County Place Names: Present Day Names Perpetuating Aboriginal and Early Historic Points in the Country." *Alabama Historical Quarterly* 21 (1959): 96–103.

———. "Some Early Taverns in Alabama." *Arrow Points* 5 (1922): 52–58.

———. "Some Peculiarities in Alabama Names." *Arrow Points* 12 (1926): 52–61.

———. "Tallapoosa County Present Day Place Names Suggesting Aboriginal Influence." *Arrow Points* 3 (1921): 46–49.

———. "Up the Pike to Rockford." *Alabama Highways* 6 (Sept. 1932): 1–5.

———. "Western Barbour." *Alabama Highways* 8 (May–June 1934): 3–12.

Brantley, Mary E. *Early Settlers Along the*

Old Federal Road in Monroe and Conecuh Counties, Alabama. Baltimore: Gateway Press, 1976.

Brewer, George E. *History of Coosa County*. Alabama Historical Quarterly 4 (Spring–Summer 1942).

Brewer, William M. *The Upper Gold Belt of Alabama*. Geological Survey of Alabama. Bull. 5. Montgomery, 1896.

Brewer, Willis. *Alabama: Her History, Resources, War Record, and Public Men, from 1840 to 1872*. Tuscaloosa: Willo Co., 1872.

Brown, Virginia P., and Helen M. Akens. *Alabama Heritage*. Huntsville: Strode Publishers, 1967.

Brown, Virginia P., and Jane P. Nabers. "The Origin of Certain Place Names in Jefferson County, Alabama." *Alabama Review* 5 (1952): 177–202.

Brunson, Marion B. *Pea River Reflections*. Birmingham: Portals Press, 1975.

Burroughs, H. N. *A New Map of Alabama with Its Roads and Distances from Place to Place Along the Stage and Steam Boat Routes*. N.p., 1846.

Butler County Historical Society. *Publications of the Butler County Historical Society*. Privately printed, 1965–80.

Carey, H. C., and I. Lea. *A Complete Historical, Chronological, and Geographical American Atlas*. Philadelphia, 1822.

Carey, John. *Mississippi Territory*. Map. N.p., 1814.

Cassidy, Frederic G. *The Place Names of Dane County, Wisconsin*. Publication of the American Dialect Society, no. 7 (April 1947).

Central of Georgia Railroad. *County Map of Georgia and Alabama*. Chicago: Poole Brothers, 1901.

Century Atlas of the World. New York: Century Co., 1899.

Chalmers, B. *New Map of the State of Alabama*. Washington, D.C., c. 1837. Photocopy.

Chambers, Nella J. "Early Days in East Alabama." *Alabama Review* 13 (1960): 177–84.

Cherokee County Historical Society. *Cherokee County Heritage*. 7 vols. Cedar Bluff, 1972–78.

Cherry, F. L. "The History of Opelika and Her Agricultural Tributary Territory." *Alabama Historical Quarterly* 15 (1953): 176–237.

Choctaw County Bicentennial Commission. *Alokoli: The Choctaw County Bicentennial Book*. Butler, 1976.

Clanahan, James F. *The History of Pickens County, Alabama, 1540–1920*. Carrollton: Clanahan Publications, 1964.

Clark, Willis G. *A History of Education in Alabama, 1702–1889*. Washington, D.C.: U.S. Bureau of Education, 1889.

Clarke County Historical Society. *Historical Sketches of Clarke County, Alabama: A Story of the Communities of Clarke County, Alabama*. Huntsville: Strode Publishers, 1977.

Clinton, Matthew W. *Matt Clinton's Scrapbook*. Tuscaloosa: Portals Press, 1976.

———. *Tuscaloosa, Alabama: Its Early Days, 1816–1865*. Tuscaloosa: Zonta Club, 1958.

Clinton, Thomas P. "Early History of Tuscaloosa." *Alabama Historical Quarterly* 1 (1930): 139–47, 169–78.

———. "The Military Operations of General John T. Croxton in West Alabama, 1865." Alabama Historical Society *Transactions* 4 (1899–1903): 449–63.

Coffee, John. *Surveyor's District: Northern Part*. Original Survey of Tuscaloosa County. 49 maps. 1820. In possession of E. L. Hendrix, Tuscaloosa, Alabama.

"Colbert County: Its Names and Some of Their Significance: A Compilation of Written History." *Arrow Points* 7 (1923): 58–60.

Colton, G. W. *Colton's Atlas of the World*. Map of Alabama, 1855. New York, 1856.

Colton, G. W., and C. B. Colton. *Colton's Alabama*. Map. New York, 1878.

Colton, J. H. *Alabama*. Map. New York, c. 1853, 1854, 1873, 1878.

———. *Colton's Alabama*. Map. New York: Johnson and Browning, 1859. Photocopy.

Comminge, L. J. Newcomb, and Martha Albers. *A Brief History of Baldwin County*. Mobile: Gill Printing Co., 1928.

Conecuh County Historical Society. *People and Places of Conecuh County, Alabama*. Privately printed, c. 1976.

Conrad, Timothy. *The First Geological Map of Alabama*. Washington, D.C.: Williams and Heinz, c. 1835. Geological Survey of Alabama Library, Tuscaloosa.

Craighead, Erwin. *Craighead's Mobile*. Ed. Caldwell DeLaney. Mobile: Haunted Bookshop, 1968.

———. *From Mobile's Past: Sketches of Memorable People and Events*. Mobile: Powers Printing Co., 1925.

———. *Mobile: Fact and Tradition: Noteworthy People and Events*. Mobile: Powers Printing Co., 1930.

Cram's Railroad and Township Map of Alabama. Chicago: George F. Cram Co., 1879, 1889, 1892.

Cresap, Bernarr. "The Muscle Shoals Frontier: Early Society and Culture in Lauderdale County." *Alabama Review* 9 (1956): 188–215.

Crow, Mattie T. *History of St. Clair County, Alabama*. Huntsville: Strode Publishers, 1973.

Cruikshank, George M. *A History of Birmingham and Its Environs*. 2 vols. Chicago: Lewis Publishing Co., 1920.

Cruikshank, M. H. *"Irona," Its Location and Surroundings*. Map. 1895. Birmingham Public Library.

Cumming, William P. *The Southeast in Early Maps: With an Annotated Check List of Printed and Manuscript Regional and Local Maps of Southeastern North America During the Colonial Period*. Chapel Hill: University of North Carolina Press, 1962.

Curry, J. L. M. "Reminiscences of Talladega." *Alabama Historical Quarterly* 8 (1946): 349–68.

Cushing, Marshall. *The Story of Our Post Office*. Boston: A. M. Thayer and Co., 1893.

Daniel, Adrian C. *The Formative Period of TVA: The Muscle Shoals Project, 1783–1916*. New York: Carlton Press, 1973.

———. "Navigational Development of Muscle Shoals, 1807–1890." *Alabama Review* 14 (1961): 251–58.

D'Anville. "Map of Louisiana." 1732. In *D'Anville's Atlas*. London, 1788.

Darby, William. *A Map of the State of Louisiana with Parts of the State of Mississippi and Territory of Alabama from Actual Survey*. New York: James Olmstead, 1816.

De Crenay, Baron. *The Territory Between the Chattahoochee and Mississippi Rivers*. Map. 1733. Reprinted in Swanton 1922. Pl. 5.

Deland, T. A., and A. David Smith, eds. *Northern Alabama: Historical and Biographical*. Birmingham: Smith and DeLand, 1888.

Delaney, Caldwell. *Remember Mobile*. Mobile, 1948.

———. *The Story of Mobile*. Mobile: Gill Printing Co., 1953.

Dodd, Donald B. *Historical Atlas of Alabama*. Cartography by Borden D. Dent. University: University of Alabama Press, 1974.

Dombhart, John M. *History of Walker County: Its Towns and Its people*. Thornton, Ark.: Cayce Publishing Co., 1937.

Doster, James F. "Early Settlements on the Tombigbee and Tensaw Rivers." *Alabama Review* 12 (1959): 83–94.

———. "People *vs.* Railroad at Ashville: A Community Squabble of 1881." *Alabama Review* 9 (1956): 46–53.

———. *Railroads in Alabama Politics, 1875–1914*. University: University of Alabama Press, 1957.

Dowling, H. G. *Tuscaloosa, Alabama: The Druid City: A Brief Sketch of the History Back of This Thriving City*. Tuscaloosa: Chamber of Commerce, 1939.

DuBose, Joel C. *Alabama History*. Atlanta: B. F. Johnson Publishing Co., 1915.

———. *Notable Men of Alabama*. Atlanta: Southern Historical Association, 1904.

DuBose, John W. *Alabama's Tragic Decade: Ten Years of Alabama, 1865–1874*. Birmingham, 1940.

———. "Chronicles of the Canebrake." *Alabama Historical Quarterly* 9 (1947): 475–613.

———. *Jefferson County and Birmingham, Alabama: Historical and Biographical*. Birmingham: Teeple and Smith, 1887.

Dugas, Tomie D. "Place Name Origins [Butler Co.]." *Alabama Life* 1 (Sept.–Oct. 1978): 78–80.

———. "Place Name Origins [Chambers Co.]." *Alabama Life* 1 (June–July 1978): 56–58.

———. "Place Name Origins [Monroe Co.]." *Alabama Life* 2 (Spring 1980): 94–98.

———. "Place Name Origins [Tallapoosa Co.]." *Alabama Life* 1 (Fall 1979): 86–88.

———. "A Recreation Guide for Marshall County." *Alabama Life* 1 (Nov.–Dec. 1978): 34–37.

———. "A Recreation Guide for Monroe County." *Alabama Life* 2 (Spring 1980): 84–88.

Duncan, Katherine M., and Larry J. Smith. *The History of Marshall County, Alabama.* Albertville: Thompson Printers, 1969.

Early Courthouses of Alabama Prior to 1860. Comp. National Society Colonial Dames of America. Mobile: Jordan Printing Co., 1966.

Early Days in Birmingham. Comp. Pioneers Club. Birmingham: Birmingham Publishing Co., 1937.

Early's Map of Georgia. N.p., c. 1818.

Edwards, Chris, and Faye Axford. *The Lure and Lore of Limestone County.* Tuscaloosa: Portals Press, 1978.

Edwards, Thomas H. "Lee County Present Day Place Names Showing Aboriginal Influence." *Arrow Points* 2 (1921): 112–14.

Elliott, Carl, ed. *Annals of Northwest Alabama.* 4 vols. Tuscaloosa: Privately printed, 1958, 1959, 1965.

Ellison, Rhoda C. *Bibb County, Alabama: The First Hundred Years, 1818–1918.* University: University of Alabama Press, 1984.

Farmer, Margaret P. *History of Pike County, Alabama.* Troy: Privately printed, 1952.

———. *One Hundred Fifty Years in Pike County, Alabama, 1821–1971.* Anniston: Higginbotham, 1973.

Fayette County Historical Society. *Fayette County Historical Society Collections.* 3 vols. Fayette, 1969–74.

Finley, A. *Alabama.* Map. Philadelphia, 1825, 1826, 1830.

Fleming, Mary L. "Dale County and its People During the Civil War." *Alabama Historical Quarterly* 19 (1957): 61–110.

Fleming, Walter L. *Civil War and Reconstruction in Alabama.* New York: Columbia University Press, 1905.

Flynt, J. Wayne. *Montgomery: An Illustrated History.* Woodland Hills, Calif.: Windsor Publications, 1980.

Foscue, Virginia O. *The Place Names of Sumter County, Alabama.* Publication of the American Dialect Society, no. 65 (1978).

Frazer, Mell A. *Early History of Steamboats in Alabama.* Alabama Polytechnic Institute Historical Studies. 3d ser. Auburn, 1907.

Fry, Anna M. *Memories of Old Cahaba.* Nashville: Publishing House of the Methodist Episcopal Church, South, 1908.

Gaines, George S. "Gaines' Reminiscences." *Alabama Historical Quarterly* 26 (1964): 133–230.

Gannett, Henry. "Origin of Certain Names in the State of Mississippi." *Publications of the Mississippi Historical Society* 6 (1902): 415–39.

———. *The Origin of Certain Place-Names in the United States.* 2d ed. U.S. Geological Survey. Bull. 258. Washington, D.C., 1905.

Gardiner, John. *Map of the Late Surveys in the Northern District of the Alabama Territory: Drawn from the Returns of the Surveyors by Peel and Sannoner.* Philadelphia: Tanner, Vallance, Kearney and Co., c. 1817.

Garner, William H., and Rubye M. Garner. *Collections and Recollections of Bullock County History.* Privately printed, 1980.

Garret, Mitchell B. *Horse and Buggy Days on Hatchet Creek.* University: University of Alabama Press, 1957.

Garrett, Jill K. *History of Florence, Alabama, with 1850 Census of Lauderdale County.* Columbia, Tenn., 1968.

———. *A History of Lauderdale County, Alabama.* Columbia, Tenn., 1964.

Garrett, William. *Reminiscences of Public Men in Alabama, for Thirty Years.* Atlanta: Plantation Publishing Company's Press, 1872.

Gatschet, Albert S. *A Migration Legend of the Creek Indians.* Part 1 in Brinton's *Library of Aboriginal American Literature,* no. 4 (1884). Part 2 in *Transactions of the Academic Sciences* [of St. Louis], (1888), vol. 5, nos. 1–2.

———. "Towns and Villages of the Creek Confederacy in the XVIII and XIX Centuries." Alabama Historical Society *Miscellaneous Collections* 1 (1901): 386–415.

Gentry, Dorothy. *Life and Legend of Lawrence County, Alabama.* Tuscaloosa: Privately printed, 1962.

Glass, Mary M., ed. *A Goodly Heritage: Memories of Greene County.* Eutaw: Greene County Historical Society, 1977.

Godfrey, Marie H. *Early Settlers of Barbour County, Alabama.* 2 vols. Privately printed, 1979.

Graves, John T. II. *The Book of Alabama and the South Commemorating the Silver Anni-*

versary of the Protective Life Insurance Company. Birmingham, 1933.

Gray, Daniel S. *Autauga County: The First Hundred Years, 1818–1918*. Prattville: Autauga County Public Library, 1977.

Gray, Frank A. *Gray's New Map of Alabama*. Philadelphia: O. W. Gray and Son, 1878. Geological Survey of Alabama Library, Tuscaloosa.

Greene County Commission. *Historic Greene County*. Eutaw, 1977.

Greenleaf, J. *Map of the State of Alabama*. Brattleboro, Vt.: G. R. French, 1842.

Griffith, Lucille B. *Alabama: A Documentary History to 1900*. Rev. ed. University: University of Alabama Press, 1972.

Guinn, J. M. K. *History of Randolph County*. Alabama Historical Quarterly 4 (Fall 1942).

Hahn, Marilyn D. *Butler County in the Nineteenth Century*. Birmingham: Privately published, 1978.

Halbert, H. S. "Choctaw Indian Names in Alabama and Mississippi." Alabama Historical Society *Transactions* 3 (1898–99): 64–77.

Halbert, H. S., and T. H. Ball. *The Creek War of 1813 and 1814*. Chicago: Donahue and Henneberg, 1895.

Hall, Benjamin W. *Preliminary Report on a Part of the Water Power of Alabama*. Geological Survey of Alabama. Bull. 7. Montgomery, 1903.

———. *Water Powers of Alabama*. U.S. Geological Survey. Water Supply and Irrigation Papers, no. 107. Washington, D.C., 1904.

———. *Water Supplies of Alabama*. Report 2. Geological Survey of Alabama. Tuscaloosa, 1916.

Hamilton, Peter J. *Colonial Mobile: An Historical Study*. Rev. ed. Boston: Houghton Mifflin Co., 1910.

———. "Early Roads of Alabama." Alabama Historical Society *Transactions* 2 (1897–98): 39–56.

———. *The Founding of Mobile*. Mobile: Commercial Printing Co., 1911.

Hamilton, Virginia V. *Alabama: A Bicentennial History*. New York: W. W. Norton and Co., 1977.

Hammond, Ralph. *Ante-Bellum Mansions of Alabama*. New York: Architectural Book Co., 1951.

Harder, Kelsie B. *Illustrated Dictionary of Place Names: United States and Canada*.

New York: Van Nostrand Reinhold Co., 1976.

Hardy, John. "History of Autauga County." *Alabama Historical Quarterly* 3 (1941): 96–116.

———. *Selma: Her Institutions and Her Men*. Selma: *Selma Times*, 1879.

Harris, W. Stuart. *Alabama Place-Names*. Huntsville: Strode Publishers, 1982.

———. *Dead Towns of Alabama*. University: University of Alabama Press, 1977.

———. "Rowdyism, Public Drunkenness, and Bloody Encounters in Early Perry County." *Alabama Review* 33 (1980): 15–24.

Hawkins, Benjamin. "Letters of Benjamin Hawkins, 1796–1806." *Georgia Historical Society Collections* 9 (1916).

———. "A Sketch of the Creek Country in the Years 1798 and 1799." *Georgia Historical Society Collections* 3 (1848). Reprint. Americus: Americus Book Co., 1938.

Haynes, Robert V. "Early Washington County, Alabama." *Alabama Review* 18 (1965): 183–200.

Henley, John C. *This Is Birmingham*. Birmingham: Southern University Press, 1960.

Higgenbotham, Jay. *Mobile: City by the Bay*. Ed. Cathy Patrick. Mobile: Azalea City Printers, 1968.

Historic Homes of Alabama. Comp. National League of American Pen Women. Birmingham, 1935.

"Historic Sites in Alabama." *Alabama Historical Quarterly* 15 (1953): 25–55, 340–75.

Hodge, Frederick W. *Handbook of American Indians North of Mexico*. U.S. Bureau of American Ethnology. Bull. 30. 2 vols. Washington, D.C.: GPO, 1907–10. Reprint. New York: Rowman and Littlefield, 1971.

Holcombe, Hosea. *History of the Rise and Progress of the Baptists in Alabama*. Philadelphia: King and Baird Printers, 1840.

Hollifield, Mollie. *Auburn: Loveliest Village of the Plains*. Auburn: Bulletin Publishing Co., 1955.

Holmes, Jack D. L. "Alabama's Forgotten Settlers: Notes on the Spanish Mobile District, 1780–1813." *Alabama Historical Quarterly* 33 (1971): 87–97.

Hood, Jack B., and E. L. Klein. *Rivers of Alabama*. Huntsville: Strode Publishers, 1968.

Hoppen, Harry E. "Randolph County Present Day Place Names Showing Aboriginal Influence." *Arrow Points* 3 (1921): 83–84.

Howard, Elizabeth S., ed. *The Dekalb Legend*. Official Publication of Landmarks of DeKalb County, Inc. 4 vols. Fort Payne: Fort Payne Printing Co., 1972–76.

Hudgins, Charles D. *Fact and Fiction of the Free State of Winston*. Double Springs: Privately printed, 1950.

Hunnicutt, John L. *Reconstruction in West Alabama*. Ed. William S. Hoole. Tuscaloosa: Confederate Publishing Co., 1959.

Ingram, William P. *A History of Tallapoosa County*. Birmingham: Privately printed, 1951.

Irons, George V. "River Ferries in Alabama Before 1861." *Alabama Review* 4 (1951): 22–37.

Ivey, Betty D. "From River to Rail in Pickens County." *Alabama Review* 7 (1954): 53–65.

Jackson, Andrew. *Correspondence of Andrew Jackson*. Ed. John S. Bassett. Washington, D.C.: Carnegie Institution, 1926–33.

Jackson, Walter M. *The Story of Selma*. Birmingham: Privately printed, 1954.

James, R. L. "Colbertians." *Alabama Historical Quarterly* 7 (1945): 159–222, 369–400, 500–536.

———. *Distinguished Men, Women, and Families of Franklin County, Alabama*. Russellville: Privately printed, 1928.

Jemison, E. Grace. *Historic Tales of Talladega, Prior to the Twentieth Century*. Montgomery: Paragon Press, 1957.

Jenkins, Nelle M. *Pioneer Families of Sumter County, Alabama*. Tuscaloosa: Willo Publishing Co., 1961.

Jenkins, William H. "Alabama Forts." *Alabama Review* 12 (1959): 163–79.

———. "Notes and Documents: Some Alabama 'Dead' Towns." *Alabama Review* 12 (1959): 281–85.

Jenkins, William H., and John Knox. *The Story of Decatur, Alabama*. Decatur: Decatur Printing, 1970.

Johnson's Georgia and Alabama. Map. Philadelphia: Johnson and Ward, 1861, 1863, 1872.

Jones, Margaret J. *Combing Cullman County*. Cullman: Modernistic Printers, 1972.

———. *Cullman County Across the Years*. Cullman: Modernistic Printers, 1975.

Kennamer, John R. *History of Jackson County, Alabama*. Winchester, Tenn.: Southern Printing and Publishing Co., 1935.

King, H. M. "Historical Sketches of Macon County." *Alabama Historical Quarterly* 18 (1956): 187–217.

Knox, John. *A History of Morgan County, Alabama*. Decatur: Morgan County Board of Revenue and Control, 1966.

Krakow, Kenneth K. *Georgia Place Names*. Macon: Winship Press, 1975.

Lambert, Alton. *History of Tuscaloosa County, Alabama*. 2 vols. Centre: Stewart University Press, 1977.

Landmarks of DeKalb County, Inc. *Landmarks: A Pictorial History of DeKalb County, Alabama*. Fort Payne: Fort Payne Printing Co., 1971.

La Tourette, John. *An Accurate Map of the State of Alabama and West Florida*. New York: Colton and Co., 1838.

———. *A Map of the Creek Territory in Alabama*. New York: S. Stiles and Co., 1833.

———. *Map of Mississippi by Counties, with a Large Portion of Louisiana and Alabama*. Mobile, 1839.

———. *Map of the State of Alabama*. Mobile, 1844.

———. *Map of the State of Alabama and West Florida*. Montgomery, 1856. Geological Survey of Alabama Library, Tuscaloosa.

Lawler, James C. *First Land Settlers of Marion County, 1820–1850*. N.p., 1981.

Lazenby, Marion E. *History of Methodism in Alabama and West Florida*. Nashville: North Alabama Conference and Alabama–West Florida Conference of the Methodist Church, 1960.

Lee County Historical Association. *Trails in History*. 12 vols. Opelika, 1969–80.

Lewis, S. *Mississippi Territory*. Map. Boston, 1805.

Lineback, Neal G., and Charles T. Traylor. *Atlas of Alabama*. University: University of Alabama Press, 1973.

Lipscomb, Oscar Hugh. "Bayou La Batre: A Sketch." *Alabama Review* 19 (1966): 20–27.

A List of Nineteenth-Century Maps of the State of Alabama. Birmingham: Birmingham Public Library, 1973.

Little, George. *Memoirs of George Little*.

Tuscaloosa: Weatherford Printing Co., 1924.

Little, John B. *The History of Butler County, Alabama, from 1815 to 1885.* Cincinnati: Elm St. Printing Co., 1885.

Lucas, Fielding. *Geographical, Statistical, and Historical Map of Alabama.* N.p., 1822.

McCall, H. G. *A Sketch, Historical and Statistical, of the City of Montgomery.* Montgomery: W. D. Brown and Co., 1885.

McCalley, Henry. *The Valley Regions of Alabama.* Montgomery: Geological Survey of Alabama, 1897.

McClellan, R. A. *Early History of Limestone County, Alabama. Athens Limestone Democrat,* 1927.

McCorvey, Thomas C. *Alabama Historical Sketches.* Charlottesville: University of Virginia Press, 1960.

———. "The Highland Scotch Element in the Early Settlement of Alabama." *Alabama Historical Quarterly* 1 (1930): 41–49.

———. *Introduction to the History of Tuscaloosa, Alabama.* Tuscaloosa: Weatherford Printing Co., 1925.

McEachin, Archibald B. *The History of Tuscaloosa, 1816–1880.* Ed. William S. Hoole and Addie S. Hoole. Tuscaloosa: Confederate Publishing Co.

McNeel, F. J. "Local History of Autaugaville." *Alabama Historical Quarterly* 8 (1946): 269–75.

Malone, Thomas S. "Scraps." *Alabama Historical Quarterly* 18 (1956): 309–80.

Marks, Henry S., ed. *Who Was Who in Alabama.* Huntsville: Strode Publishers, 1972.

Marlin, Lloyd G. *The History of Cherokee County.* Atlanta: Walter W. Brown Publishing Co., 1932.

Marshall, James W. *The Presbyterian Church in Alabama.* Ed. Robert Strong. Montgomery: Presbyterian Historical Society of Alabama, 1977.

Martin, Thomas A. *The Story of Electricity in Alabama Since the Turn of the Century, 1900–1952.* Birmingham: Alabama Power Co., 1952.

Martin, Thomas W. *French Military Adventures in Alabama, 1818–1828.* Birmingham: Birmingham Publishing Co., 1940.

Martin, Will I. *If Memory Serves.* Comp. Frances L. Underwood. Gadsden: *Gadsden Times,* 1953.

Matte, Jacqueline A. *The History of Washington County: First County in Alabama.* Chatom: Washington County Historical Society, 1982.

Melish, John. *Map of Alabama Prior to 1818.* Philadelphia, 1819.

———. *Map of the Southern Section of the United States.* Philadelphia, 1813, 1814, 1816. Reprinted in Swanton 1922.

Memorial Record of Alabama. 2 vols. Madison, Wis.: Brant and Fuller, 1893.

Mims, Shadrack. "History of Autauga County." *Alabama Historical Quarterly* 8 (1946): 241–68.

Mitchell, John. *The Southeastern Part of the Present United States.* Map. 1755. Reprinted in Swanton 1922.

Mitchell, S. Augustus. *County Map of the States of Georgia and Alabama.* [Philadelphia], 1860, 1870.

———. *Map of the States of Louisiana, Mississippi, and Alabama.* Philadelphia, 1836.

———. *Mitchell's New Universal Atlas of the World.* Philadelphia: T. Cowperthwait and Co., 1853.

———. *A New Map of Alabama with Its Roads and Distances.* Philadelphia, 1847.

———. *Traveller's Guide Through the United States: A Map of the Roads, Distances, Steamboats, and Canal Routes.* Philadelphia, 1834.

Moore, Albert B. *History of Alabama.* University: University of Alabama Press, 1951.

Morse, Sidney E., and Samuel Breese. *Map of Alabama.* N.p., 1842.

Murray, William M. *Thomas W. Martin.* Birmingham: Southern Research Institute, 1978.

Nelms, Jack N. "Adventures of an Amateur Historian." *Alabama Review* 15 (1962): 163–74.

Nelson, Mildred M. "Folk Etymology of Alabama Place-Names." *Southern Folklore Quarterly* 4 (1950): 193–214.

Nesbitt, C. H. *Annual Report of Coal Mines: State of Alabama.* Birmingham: Alabama Mineral Map Co., 1912.

Neville, Bert. *Directory of River Packets in the Mobile-Alabama-Warrior-Tombigbee Trades, 1818–1932.* Selma: Coffee Printing Co., 1962.

———. *Directory of Steam—Some Motor— Towboats and U.S. Engineer Department Vessels in the Mobile-Alabama-Tom-*

bigbee-Warrior Rivers, 1881–1947. Selma: Coffee Printing Co., 1964.

Newell, Herbert M., Jr., and Mrs. Herbert M. Newell, Jr. *History of Fayette County, Alabama*. Fayette: Newell Offset Printing, 1960.

Nunn, Alexander, ed. *Lee County and Her Forebears*. Opelika: Probate Judge and Commissioners of Lee County, 1983.

Nuzum, Kay. *A History of Baldwin County*. Bay Minette: *Baldwin Times*, 1971.

Owen, Marie B. *The Story of Alabama: A History of the State*. 6 vols. New York: Lewis Historical Publishing Co., 1949.

Owen, Thomas M. *History of Alabama and Dictionary of Alabama Biography*. 4 vols. Chicago: S. J. Clarke, 1921.

Peale, A. C. *Mineral Springs of the United States*. U.S. Geological Survey. Bull. 32. Washington, D.C.: GPO, 1886.

Phillips, William B. *Iron Making in Alabama*. Tuscaloosa: Geological Survey of Alabama, 1896, 1898, 1912.

Pickett, Albert J. *History of Alabama and Incidentally of Georgia and Mississippi, from the Earliest Period*. Charleston: Walker and James, 1851.

Porter, Elizabeth. *A History of Wetumpka*. Wetumpka: Chamber of Commerce, 1957.

Powell, E. A. "Fifty-five Years in West Alabama." *Alabama Historical Quarterly* 4 (1942): 459–641.

Powell, George. "A Description and History of Blount County." *Alabama Historical Quarterly* 27 (1965): 95–133.

Prouty, William F. *Preliminary Report on the Crystalline and other Marbles of Alabama*. Geological Survey of Alabama. Bull. 18. Tuscaloosa, 1916. Map, 1915.

Purcell Map. c. 1770. Reprinted in Swanton 1922.

Purcell, Joseph. *A Map of the States of Virginia, North Carolina, South Carolina, and Georgia: Comprehending the Spanish Provinces of East and West Florida*. c. 1792.

Rand McNally Commercial Atlas and Marketing Guide. Chicago, 1976.

Rand McNally. *Map of Alabama*. Chicago, 1910, 1930, 1934, 1972, c. 1980.

Rand McNally. *New Business Map of Alabama*. Chicago, 1893, 1894, 1895, 1899, 1903, 1904.

Rand McNally Road Atlas: United States,

Canada, Mexico. Chicago, 1976.

Read, William A. *Indian Place Names in Alabama*. Louisiana State University Studies, no. 29. Baton Rouge, 1937. Rev. ed. with a Foreword, Appendix, and Index by James B. McMillan. University: University of Alabama Press, 1984.

Record, James. *A Dream Come True: The Story of Madison County and Incidentally of Alabama and the United States*. 3 vols. Huntsville: Privately printed, 1970.

Reid, Avery H. *Baptists in Alabama: Their Organization and Witness*. Montgomery: Alabama Baptist State Convention, 1967.

Reid, John. *Georgia from the Latest Authorities*. Map. New York, 1796.

Renfro, J. P., Jr. *The Beginning of Railroads in Alabama*. Alabama Polytechnic Institute Historical Studies. 4th ser. Auburn, 1910.

Rennick, R. M. *Kentucky Place Names*. Lexington: University of Kentucky Press, 1985.

Reynolds, Hughes. *The Coosa River Valley from DeSoto to Hydroelectric River*. Cynthiana, Ky.: Hobson Book Press, 1944.

Richards, E. G. "Reminiscences of the Early Days in Chambers County." *Alabama Historical Quarterly* 4 (1942): 417–45.

Richardson, Jesse M. *Alabama Encyclopedia and Book of Facts*. Northport: American Southern Publishing Co., 1965.

Riley, Benjamin F. *Alabama as It Is, or the Immigrant's and Capitalist's Guidebook to Alabama*. Atlanta: Constitution Publishing Co., 1888.

———. *History of the Baptists in Alabama from 1808 until 1894*. Birmingham: Roberts and Sons, 1896. Index by William R. Small, 1962.

———. *History of Conecuh County, Alabama*. Columbus, Ga.: Thomas Gilbert, 1881.

Robertson, W. G. *Recollections of the Early Settlers of Montgomery County and Their Families*. Montgomery: Excelsior Printing Co., 1892.

Roden, Jerry, Jr. "Place Name Origins [Marshall Co.]." *Alabama Life* 1 (Nov.–Dec. 1978): 52–53.

Romans, Bernard. *Romans Map*. 1772. Reprinted in Read 1937. Frontispiece.

Royall, Anne N. *Letters from Alabama, 1817–1822*. Southern Historical Publication

14 (1830). Reprint. University: University of Alabama Press, 1969.

Rumph, Catherine E. "Reminiscences of Perote in Bullock." *Alabama Historical Quarterly* 20 (1958): 481–521.

Russell County Historical Commission. *The History of Russell County, Alabama.* Dallas: National Share Graphics, 1982.

Russell, John. *Map of the Southern Provinces of the United States.* N.p., 1800.

Russell, Mildred B. *Lowndes Courthouse: A Chronicle of Hayneville, an Alabama Black Belt Village, 1820–1900.* Montgomery: Paragon Press, 1951.

Russell, Robert A. "Gold Mining in Alabama Before 1860." *Alabama Review* 10 (1957): 5–14.

Sanders, Irwin T. *Alabama Rural Communities: A Study of Chilton County.* Montevallo: Montevallo University Press, 1940.

Satz, Ronald N. *Tennessee's Indian Peoples: From White Contact to Removal, 1540–1840.* Knoxville: University of Tennessee Press, 1979.

Saunders, James E. *Early Settlers of Alabama.* New Orleans: L. Grahan and Sons, 1899.

Schoolcraft, Henry R. *Historical and Statistical Information Reflecting the History, Condition, and Prospects of the Indian Tribes of the United States.* Philadelphia: Lippincott, 1851–57.

Scott, E. C. S. (Mrs. Marvin). *History of Henry County, Alabama.* Abbeville: Henry County Historical Society, 1961.

Scott, Robert H. *Scott's Map of Mobile Bay and Parts of Mobile and Baldwin Counties, Alabama.* New Orleans, 1926.

Scruggs, J. H., Jr. *Alabama Postal History, 1811–1859.* Birmingham: N.p., 1950.

———. *Alabama Postal Roads with Maps, 1818–1845.* Birmingham: N.p., 1950.

Sealock, Richard B., Margaret M. Sealock, and Margaret S. Powell. *Bibliography of Place Name Literature: United States and Canada.* 3d ed. Chicago: American Library Association, 1982.

Searcy, Harvey B. *We Used What We Had.* Birmingham: Colonial Press, 1961.

Sellers, James B. *Slavery in Alabama.* University: University of Alabama Press, 1950.

Semmes, Douglas. *Oil and Gas in Alabama.* Alabama Geological Survey. Special Report 15. University: University of Alabama

Press, 1929. Map by M. M. Valerius Co.

Seventeenth-Eighteenth-Century Maps of America by French Cartographers: An Exhibit of Maps and Atlases from the Rucker Agee Collection, Birmingham Public Library, March–April, 1973. Birmingham: Birmingham Public Library, 1973.

Shelby County Historical Society. *Shelby County Historical Quarterly.* 8 vols., 1970–81.

Sketches of Alabama Towns and Counties: A Collection. Comp. Works Progress Administration. Birmingham, 1937.

Smith, Eugene A. *Report of Progress for 1874.* Geological Survey of Alabama. Montgomery, 1875.

———. *Report of Progress for 1875.* Geological Survey of Alabama. Montgomery, 1876.

———. *Report of Progress for 1880.* Geological Survey of Alabama. Montgomery, 1881.

———. *Statistics of the Mineral Production of Alabama for 1916.* Geological Survey of Alabama. Bull. 20. Tuscaloosa, 1916.

Smith, Maud W. "History of the Methodist Episcopal Church of Autaugaville." *Alabama Historical Quarterly* 8 (1946): 276–78.

Smith, Nelson F. *History of Pickens County, Alabama, from Its First Settlement.* Carrollton: *Carrollton Republican,* 1856.

Smith, Warren I. "Land Patterns in Ante-Bellum Montgomery County, Alabama." *Alabama Review* 8 (1955): 196–208.

Smith, Winston. *Days of Exile.* Demopolis: Marengo County Historical Society, 1967.

———. "Early History of Demopolis." *Alabama Review* 18 (1965): 83–91.

Snedecor, Victoria Gayle. *Map of Greene County.* N.p., 1856.

Some Early Alabama Churches (Established Before 1870). Comp. Mabel P. Wilson for The Alabama Society, Daughters of the American Revolution. Birmingham: Parchment Press, 1973.

Stewart, George R. *American Place Names.* New York: Oxford University Press, 1970.

———. *Names on the Land: A Historical Account of Place-Naming in the United States.* 2d ed. Boston: Houghton-Mifflin Co., 1958.

Stewart, Margaret T. (Mrs. Frank R.). *Alabama's Calhoun County.* 2 vols. Centre:

Stewart University Press, 1976.

——. *Alabama's Pike County.* Centre: Stewart University Press, 1976.

——. *Cherokee County History, 1836–1956.* 2 vols. Birmingham: Birmingham Printing Co., 1958.

Stone, James H. "Surveying the Gaines Trace, 1807–1808." *Alabama Historical Quarterly* 33 (1971): 135–52.

Street, Oliver D. "Houston County in the Great Bend of the Tennessee." *Alabama Historical Quarterly* 6 (1944): 50–59.

Sulzby, James F., Jr. *Historic Alabama Hotels and Resorts.* University: University of Alabama Press, 1960.

Summersell, Charles G. *Mobile: History of a Seaport Town.* University: University of Alabama Press, 1949.

Swanton, John R. *Early History of the Creek Indians and Their Neighbors.* U.S. Bureau of American Ethnology. Bull. 73. Washington, D.C.: GPO, 1922.

——. Review of *Indian Place Names in Alabama,* by William A. Read. *American Speech* 12 (1937): 212–15.

Taitt, David. "Journal of David Taitt." In Newton D. Mereness, *Travels in the American Colonies.* New York: Macmillan Publishing Co., 1916.

Tanner, B. *Georgia from the Latest Authorities.* Plate 19 in William Winterbotham's *The American Atlas.* New York: John Reid, 1796.

Tanner, H. S. *Georgia and Alabama.* Map. Philadelphia, 1823, 1825, 1836, 1839.

——. *A New Map of Alabama with Its Roads and Distances.* Philadelphia, 1836, 1841, 1845.

——. *The Traveler's Pocket Map of Alabama with Its Roads and Distances from Place to Place, Along the Stage and Steamboat Routes.* Philadelphia, 1830.

Tap Roots: A Historical Account of Southern Union State Junior College and Areas in Randolph County. Comp. Iota Iota Chapter, Phi Theta Kappa. Roanoke: *Roanoke Leader,* 1976.

Taylor, Elberta. *Stories of Alabama.* Richmond, Va.: Johnson, 1924.

Taylor, Thomas J. "Early History of Madison County." *Alabama Historical Quarterly* 1 (1930): 101–11.

——. *A History of Madison County and Incidentally of North Alabama, 1732–1840.*

Tuscaloosa: Confederate Publishing Co., 1976.

The Territory of Alabama, 1817–1819. Vol. 15 of *The Territorial Papers of the United States.* Comp. Clarence E. Carter. Washington, D.C.: GPO, 1952.

The Territory of Mississippi, 1798–1817; 1809–1817. Vol. 5–6 of *The Territorial Papers of the United States.* Comp. Clarence E. Carter. Washington, D.C.: GPO, 1952.

Thompson High School Local History Class. *Good Morning, Yesterday.* Alabaster, 1977.

Thompson, Mattie T. *History of Barbour County, Alabama.* Eufaula: Privately printed, 1940.

Thompson, Wesley S. *"The Free State of Winston": A History of Winston County, Alabama.* Winfield: Pareil Press, 1968.

Thomson, John. *Southern Provinces of the United States.* In *A New General Atlas.* Edinburgh: John Thomson and Co., 1817.

Timetables of Alabama Railroads. Roland Harper Papers.

Trorer, Ellen L. *Chronology and Documentary Handbook of the State of Alabama.* Dobbs Ferry, N.Y.: Oceana Publications, 1972.

Tuomey, Michael. *First Biennial Report on the Geology of Alabama.* Montgomery: Geological Survey of Alabama, 1850.

——. *Geological Map of Alabama.* 1849. Geological Survey of Alabama Library, Tuscaloosa.

——. *Second Biennial Report on the Geology of Alabama.* Montgomery: Geological Survey of Alabama, 1858.

Turner, Sue. *Bouquets, Brambles, and Buena Vista or "Down Home."* Huntsville: Strode Publishers, 1976.

U.S. Army Corps of Engineers. *Alabama Rivers.* Mobile: U.S. Engineer Office, 1943.

U.S. Board on Geographic Names. *Sixth Report, 1890 to 1932.* Washington, D.C.: GPO, 1933.

U.S. Board on Geographic Names. *Cumulative Decision List.* Washington, D.C.: GPO, various dates.

U.S. Bureau of American Ethnology. *Forty-Second Annual Report of the Bureau of American Ethnology to the Secretary of the Smithsonian Institution, 1924–1925.* Washington, D.C.: GPO, 1928.

U.S. Bureau of the Census. *Alabama Cen-*

sus: County Systems. Washington, D.C.: GPO, 1961.

U.S. Civil Service Commission. *Official Register of the United States*. Washington, D.C.: GPO, 1821–1959. Before 1861, published by the Department of State; 1907–32, published by the Bureau of the Census; 1933–59, published by the Civil Service Commission.

U.S. Coast Survey. *Southern Alabama and Georgia*. Map. Washington: U.S. Coast Survey Office, 1865.

U.S. Department of Agriculture. Soil Maps of Alabama Counties. Washington, D.C., various dates.

U.S. Department of Commerce. *Alabama: Minor Civil Divisions*. Washington, D.C.: GPO, 1934.

U.S. General Land Office. *Map of Alabama*. Washington, 1805, 1833, 1837, 1878, 1889, 1891, 1915.

U.S. Geological Survey. *Alabama Geographic Names: Alphabetical Finding List*. 2 vols. Reston, Va.: Office of Geographic and Cartographic Research, 1982.

U.S. Geological Survey. State of Alabama: Base Maps. Washington, D.C., 1966.

U.S. Geological Survey. Topographic Maps of Alabama. Washington, D.C., various dates.

U.S. Post Office Department. *Directory of Post Offices*. Washington, D.C.: GPO, 1956–.

U.S. Post Office Department. *Post Route Map of the States of Alabama and Mississippi*. Washington, D.C., 1891, 1951.

U.S. Post Office Department. *United States Official Postal Guide*. Washington, D.C.: GPO, 1876, 1879, 1887–1956.

U.S. Statutes at Large. Washington, D.C.: GPO, various dates.

Vandiver, Wellington. "Pioneer Talladega: Its Minutes and Memories." *Alabama Historical Quarterly* 16 (1954): 9–297.

Walker, Anne K. *Backtracking in Barbour County: A Narrative of the Last Alabama Frontier*. Richmond, Va.: Dietz Press, 1941.

———. *Russell County in Retrospect*. Richmond, Va.: Dietz Press, 1950.

Walker, James H. *Roupes Valley: A History of Pioneer Settlement of Roupes Valley*. McCalla: Privately printed, 1972.

Walker, Robert H., Jr. *History of Limestone County, Alabama*. Athens: Limestone County Commission, 1973.

Wallace, Katherine T. "Notes and Documents: Elk County, Alabama." *Alabama Review* 19 (1966): 227–33.

Ward, William C. *The Building of the State*. Montgomery: Alabama Historical Society, 1904.

Ward, Wyley D. *Early History of Covington County, Alabama, 1821–1871*. Huntsville: Privately printed, 1976.

Warren, Hoyt M. *Chattahoochee Trails*. Abbeville: Henry County Historical Society, 1981.

———. *Henry's Heritage: A History of Henry County, Alabama*. Abbeville: Henry County Historical Society, 1978.

———. *Henry—the Mother Country, 1816–1903*. 2d printing. Abbeville: Henry County Historical Society, 1978.

Waters, Annie C. *History of Escambia County, Alabama*. Huntsville: Strode Publishers, 1983.

Watson, Elbert L. *A History of Etowah County, Alabama*. Birmingham: Roberts and Sons, 1968.

Watson, Fred S. *Coffee Grounds: A History of Coffee County, Alabama, 1841–1970*. Anniston: Higginbotham Co., 1970.

———. *Forgotten Trails: A History of Dale County, Alabama, 1824–1966*. Birmingham: Banner Press, 1968.

———. *Hub of the Wiregrass: A History of Houston County, Alabama, 1903–1972*. Anniston: Higginbotham Co., 1972.

———. *Piney Wood Echoes: A History of Dale and Coffee Counties, Alabama*. Elba: Elba Clipper, 1949.

West, Anson. *History of Methodism in Alabama*. Nashville: Publishing House of the Methodist Episcopal Church, South, 1893.

West, William B. *America's Greatest Dam: Muscle Shoals, Alabama*. 2d ed. New York: Fred E. Cooper, 1925.

Whitaker, Walter C. *History of the Protestant Episcopal Church in Alabama, 1763–1891*. Birmingham: Roberts and Sons, 1898.

Who's Who in Alabama. Birmingham: Dubose Publishers, 1952–.

Williams, Abner. "Talladega in 1833." *Alabama Historical Quarterly* 8 (1846): 400–406.

Williams, Clanton W. *The Early History of Montgomery and Incidentally of the State of Alabama*. Ed. William S. Hoole and Addie S. Hoole. Tuscaloosa: Confederate Publishing Co., c. 1979.

Woodward, Thomas S. *Woodward's Reminiscences of the Creek, or Muscogee Indians, Contained in Letters to Friends in Georgia and Alabama*. Montgomery: Berret and Wimbish, 1859.

Wyatt, Thomas E. *Chilton County and Her People: A Brief History*. Clanton: *Clanton Union-Banner*, 1940.

Wyman, W. S. "Early Times in the Vicinity of the Present City of Montgomery." Alabama Historical Society *Transactions* 2 (1897–98): 28–33.

Yerby, William E. W. *History of Greensboro, Alabama, from Its Earliest Settlement*. Montgomery: Paragon Press, 1908.

Young and Company's Business and Professional Directory of the Cities and Towns Throughout the State of Alabama. Atlanta: Young and Co., 1905, 1910.

Young, J. H. *Geographical, Statistical and Historical Map of Alabama*. N.p., c. 1827.

II. Unpublished Works

Ackley, Alice L. "A Place-Name Study. of Morgan County, Alabama." Research paper, University of Alabama, 1973.

Akens, David S. "Clarke County to 1860." Master's thesis, University of Alabama, 1956.

Akens, Helen M. "Clarke County, 1860–1865." Master's thesis, University of Alabama, 1956.

Avant, Gladys B. "History of Washington County, Alabama, to 1860." Master's thesis, University of Alabama, 1929.

"Baldwin County Private Land Grants." 1835–39. Baldwin County Courthouse, Bay Minette, Alabama.

Bell, Robert K. "Reconstruction in Tuscaloosa County." Master's thesis, University of Alabama, 1933.

Biggs, Martha. "A Place-Name Study of Autauga County, Alabama." Research paper, University of Alabama, 1973.

Boozer, Jack D. "Jacksonville, Alabama, 1833–1846." Master's thesis, University of Alabama, 1951.

Boucher, Morris R. "Factors in the History of Tuscaloosa, Alabama, 1816–1846." Master's thesis, University of Alabama, 1947.

Brown, Marie L. "A Social History of Tuscaloosa from 1816 to 1850." Master's thesis, University of Alabama, 1930.

Brown, Nancy F. "The Place Names of Pickens County, Alabama." Research paper, University of Alabama, 1977.

Browning, Mary T. "Place-Names of South-central Etowah County: A Tentative Study." Research paper, University of Alabama, 1973.

Bush, Robert J. "A Survey of the Place-Names of Baldwin County, Alabama." Research paper, University of Alabama, 1974. Published as "An Initial Survey of the Place-Names of Baldwin County, Alabama." Baldwin County Historical Society *Quarterly* 6 (Jan. 1979): 29–46.

Clinton, Matthew W. "Economic Conditions in Tuscaloosa City and County, 1865–1880." Master's thesis, University of Alabama, 1942.

"Copies of the Field Notes of the Original Government Surveys: Greene County." Montgomery, Alabama, 1889.

Covington, Elizabeth. "A Place-Name Study of Chilton County, Alabama." Research paper, University of Alabama, 1977.

Dorsey, John T. "The Community and Government of Tuscaloosa, Alabama." Master's thesis, University of Alabama, 1950.

Dubose, Euba E. "The History of Mount Sterling." Master's thesis, University of Alabama, 1931.

Elliot, James E. "A History of Methodism in Western Alabama, 1818–1870." Master's thesis, University of Alabama, 1948.

Ellis, Patricia M. "The Place Names in Barbour County, Alabama." Research paper, University of Alabama, 1973.

"Field Notes of the Original Government Surveyor, Thomas H. Reynolds." 1832. Tax Assessor's Office, Talladega County Courthouse, Talladega, Alabama.

Freeman, WyNora. "Montgomery County, Alabama, Place-Names: An Investigation." Research paper, University of Alabama, 1983.

Gant, Paula F. "A Tentative Place-Name Study of Walker County, Alabama." Research paper, University of Alabama, 1973.

Graves, Fannie L. M. "History of Elmore County Through 1876." Typescript.

Hagood, Thomas N. "Place Name Patterns in Jefferson County, Alabama." Master's thesis, Birmingham-Southern College, 1960.

Hartsook, Richard. "A Study of the Personal Interview Method for Determining the Locally-Accepted Educated Pronunciation of Alabama Place-Names." Master's thesis, University of Alabama, 1955.

"History of DeKalb County." Typescript, n.d.

Holliman, Margie P. "Place Name Study of Hale County." Research paper, University of Alabama, 1977.

Hopkins, Byron. "The Place-Names of Coosa County, Alabama: A Tentative Study." Research paper, University of Alabama, 1973.

Huston, Claudia M. "A History of Early Baptist Churches in Alabama." Master's thesis, University of Alabama, 1960.

Jackson, Sarah E. "Alabama County Names." Typescript of paper read at annual meeting of American Name Society, Los Angeles, 1982.

Johnson, David, and Carleen Alexander. "Marengo County, Alabama: A Place-Name Study." Research paper, University of Alabama, 1973.

Johnson, Dewey M. "History of Coffee County, Alabama, 1840–1871." Master's thesis, University of Alabama, 1947.

Jolly, James L., Jr. "A Place-Name Study of the Western Half of Etowah County, Alabama." Research paper, University of Alabama, 1973.

Knight, Joan. "The Place-Names of Franklin County, Alabama." Research paper, University of Alabama, 1973.

Lamb, Osie K. "A Study of the Social Development and Social Structure of the Community of Leighton, Alabama." Master's thesis, University of Alabama, 1931.

League of Municipalities. "Incorporated Municipalities in Alabama." Montgomery, 1984. Mimeographed copy.

Lindsey, Bertha D. "A Study of Some Place Names in Calhoun County, Alabama." Master's thesis, Auburn University, 1962.

Lowe, Willa. "Place Names of Coffee County, Alabama." Research paper, University of Alabama, 1983.

McMillan, James B. "Dictionary of Place Names in Talladega County, Alabama." Typescript, 1985.

McNair, C.E. "Reconstruction in Bullock County." Master's thesis, University of Alabama, 1931.

"Map for General Jackson's Campaign Against the Creek Indians." 1813–14. Photocopy.

Mason, Mary G. "The Antebellum History of Limestone County." Master's thesis, University of Alabama, 1949.

Melancon, Richard. "Place Names of Jackson County." Research paper, University of Alabama, 1984.

Neighbors, Rubye G. "Plantation Life in Hale County." Master's thesis, University of Alabama, 1927.

Peoples, Rosalind. "Introductory Place Name Study of Fayette County." Research paper, University of Alabama, 1977.

Raughton, Linda G. "The Place-Names of Dekalb County, Alabama." Research paper, University of Alabama, 1977.

Reynolds, Marylee. "A Social and Economic History of Sumter County, Alabama, in the Antebellum Period." Master's thesis, University of Alabama, 1953.

Rich, John Stanley. "The Place Names of Greene and Tuscaloosa Counties, Alabama." Ph.D. diss., University of Alabama, 1979.

———. "The Place Names of St. Clair County, Alabama: A Preliminary Survey." Research paper, University of Alabama, 1973.

Roberts, Frances C. "Background and Formative Period in the Great Bend and Madison County." Ph.D. diss., University of Alabama, 1956.

Scribner, Robert L. "A Short History of Brewton, Alabama." Master's thesis, University of Alabama, 1935.

Sockwell, Sandra M. "The Place-Names of Colbert and Lauderdale Counties, Alabama." Ph.D. diss., University of Alabama, 1985.

Stewart, Clarence H. "The Historic Towns of Dallas County, Alabama." Master's thesis, University of Alabama, 1930.

Story, John N. "History of Marshall County, Alabama, prior to 1960." Master's thesis, University of Alabama, 1930.

Tamarin, Patricia A. "Some Place-names of Shelby County, Alabama." Research paper, University of Alabama, 1983.

Taylor, Sarah M. "Preliminary Survey of Folklore in Alabama." Master's thesis, University of Alabama, 1925.

Taylor, Thomas Jones. "The History of Madison County, Alabama, with an Autobiographical Sketch." Xeroxed copy.

Huntsville Public Library, Huntsville, 1940.

Thomas, Daniel H. "Fort Toulouse and Its Subsequent History." Master's thesis, University of Alabama, 1929.

U.S. Bureau of the Census. "1832 Census of Creek Indians." Washington: National Archives Microfilm T-275.

U.S. Bureau of the Census. "Enumeration of Population." Alabama Counties. 1830–1910. Microfilms.

U.S. Post Office Department. "Record of Appointment of Postmasters, 1789–1832." Washington: National Archives Microfilm M1131.

U.S. Post Office Department. "Record of Appointment of Postmasters, 1832–September 30, 1971." Washington: National Archives Microfilm M841.

U.S. Post Office Department. "Reports of Site Locations, 1837–1950." Washington: National Archives Microfilm M1126.

Vinson, Donald. "A Preliminary Check-List of the Place-Names of Eastern Etowah County, Alabama." Research paper, University of Alabama, 1973.

Whitehead, John. "Place Names of Cullman County." Research paper, University of Alabama, 1977.

Young, Hugh. "A Social and Economic History of Montgomery, Alabama, 1846–1860." Master's thesis, University of Alabama, 1948.

III. Informants Who Provided Information in Interviews or Letters

W. L. Blackmon, Opelika
Doris J. Brown, Chatom
Nancy F. Brown, Tuscaloosa
Ann Chambless, Scottsboro
Hal Cottingham, Centreville
Ruth Crump, Lanett
Bobby Day, Decatur
Dorothy DeVaughn, Prattville
Flora D. England, Marion
Billy C. Ford, Double Springs
WyNora Freeman, Tuscaloosa
Paula F. Gant, Tuscaloosa
Ann F. Gay, Butler
Myrtle Green, Huntsville
Wiley J. Hickman, Gadsden
Margie P. Holliman, Moundville
Byron Hopkins, Tuscaloosa
Guy W. Hubbs, Tuscaloosa
Jewel E. Hudgins, Tuscaloosa
Fred L. Huggins, Grove Hill
Nelle M. Jenkins, Emelle
James L. Jolly, Jr., Tuscaloosa
Joan Knight, Russellville
James C. Lawler, Hamilton
Willa Lowe, Tuscaloosa
James B. McMillan, Tuscaloosa
Frances D. Maddox, Phenix City
Richard Melancon, Tuscaloosa
Jack N. Nelms, Selma
Caroline Nigg, Cullman
W. W. Nordan, Abbeville
Alice A. Parker, Tuscaloosa
Samuel W. Pipes III, Mobile
Mack Price, Clayton
John Stanley Rich, Aiken, S.C.
Benjamin D. Roberts, Clanton
Nan P. (Mrs. Zack) Rogers, Butler
Alexander Sartwell, Tuscaloosa
Winston Smith, Demopolis
Sandra M. Sockwell, Florence
Elizabeth B. Stegall, Emelle
Doug Stewart, Jr., Anniston
Patricia A. Tamarin, Tuscaloosa
Judy Taylor, Greenville
Doris Thomas, Luverne
Dot Waldrop, Ashland
Winston E. Walker III, Montgomery
Annie C. Waters, Brewton
John F. Watkins, Montgomery
Warren Weaver, Oneonta
Eulalia Wellden, Athens
Marvin Y. Whiting, Birmingham
Lona Mae Wilson, Moundville

Appendix
Maps of Alabama,
1820–1903

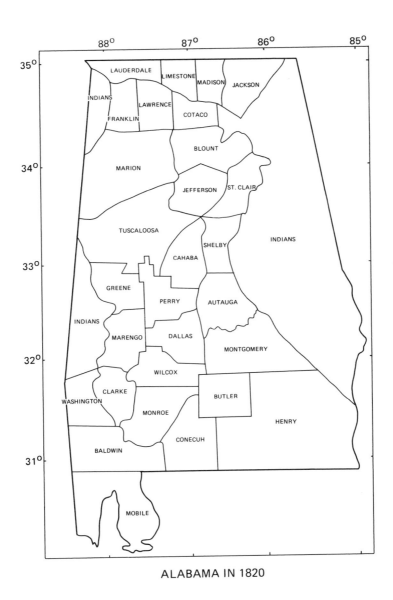

ALABAMA IN 1820

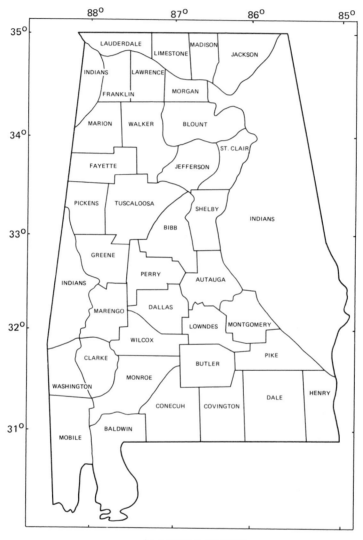

ALABAMA IN 1830

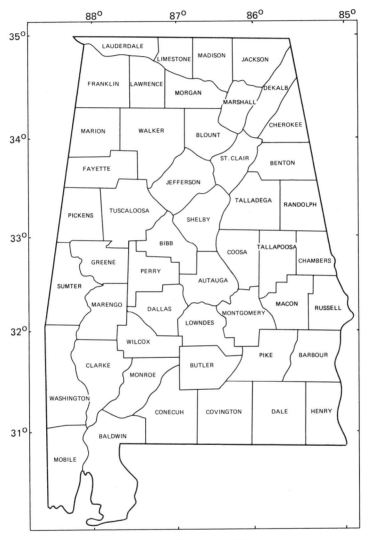

ALABAMA IN 1840

171

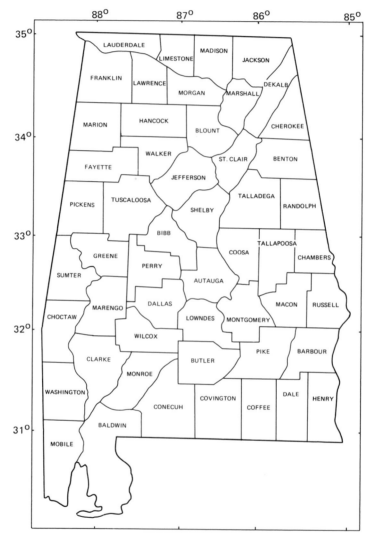

ALABAMA IN 1850 AND 1860

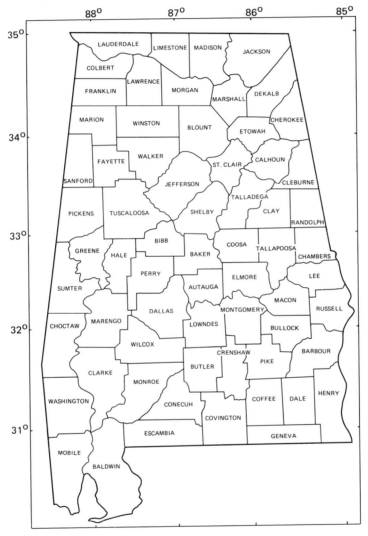

ALABAMA IN 1870

ALABAMA SINCE 1903

About the Author

Virginia O. Foscue is a Professor of English,
The University of Alabama.